WITHDRAWN
UTSA LIBRARIES

The Taxation of
Income from Capital

Studies of Government Finance
TITLES PUBLISHED

Federal Fiscal Policy in the Postwar Recessions, by Wilfred Lewis, Jr.
Federal Tax Treatment of State and Local Securities, by David J. Ott and Allan H. Meltzer.
Federal Tax Treatment of Income from Oil and Gas, by Stephen L. McDonald.
Federal Tax Treatment of the Family, by Harold M. Groves.
The Role of Direct and Indirect Taxes in the Federal Revenue System, John F. Due, Editor. A Report of the National Bureau of Economic Research and the Brookings Institution (Princeton University Press).
The Individual Income Tax, by Richard Goode.
Federal Tax Treatment of Foreign Income, by Lawrence B. Krause and Kenneth W. Dam.
Measuring Benefits of Government Investments, Robert Dorfman, Editor.
Federal Budget Policy, by David J. Ott and Attiat F. Ott. (Revised 1969.)
Financing State and Local Governments, by James A. Maxwell. (Revised 1969.)
Essays in Fiscal Federalism, Richard A. Musgrave, Editor.
Economics of the Property Tax, by Dick Netzer.
A Capital Budget Statement for the U.S. Government, by Maynard S. Comiez.
Foreign Tax Policies and Economic Growth, E. Gordon Keith, Editor. A Report of the National Bureau of Economic Research and the Brookings Institution (Columbia University Press).
Defense Purchases and Regional Growth, by Roger E. Bolton.
Federal Budget Projections, by Gerhard Colm and Peter Wagner. A Report of the National Planning Association and the Brookings Institution.
Corporate Dividend Policy, by John A. Brittain.
Federal Estate and Gift Taxes, by Carl S. Shoup.
Federal Tax Policy, by Joseph A. Pechman.
Economic Behavior of the Affluent, by Robin Barlow, Harvey E. Brazer, and James N. Morgan.
Intergovernmental Fiscal Relations in the United States, by George F. Break.
Studies in the Economics of Income Maintenance, Otto Eckstein, Editor.
Trusts and Estate Taxation, by Gerald R. Jantscher.
Negative Taxes and the Poverty Problem, by Christopher Green.
Economic Evaluation of Urban Renewal, by Jerome Rothenberg.
Problems in Public Expenditure Analysis, Samuel B. Chase, Jr., Editor.
Budget Concepts for Economic Analysis, Wilfred Lewis, Jr., Editor.
Studies in Economic Stabilization, edited by Albert Ando, E. Cary Brown, and Ann F. Friedlaender.
Consumer Response to Income Increases, by George Katona and Eva Mueller.
Alternative Approaches to Capital Gains Taxation, by Martin David.
The Taxation of Income from Capital, Arnold C. Harberger and Martin J. Bailey, Editors.

The Taxation of Income from Capital

ARNOLD C. HARBERGER
and MARTIN J. BAILEY
Editors

Studies of Government Finance

THE BROOKINGS INSTITUTION

WASHINGTON, D.C.

© 1969 by

THE BROOKINGS INSTITUTION
1775 Massachusetts Avenue, N.W., Washington, D.C.

ISBN 0-8157-3457-7 *(paper)*
ISBN 0-8157-3456-5 *(cloth)*

Library of Congress Catalog Card Number 68–31834
98765432

THE BROOKINGS INSTITUTION is an independent organization devoted to nonpartisan research, education, and publication in economics, government, foreign policy, and the social sciences generally. Its principal purposes are to aid in the development of sound public policies and to promote public understanding of issues of national importance.

The Institution was founded December 8, 1927, to merge the activities of the Institute for Government Research, founded in 1916, the Institute of Economics, founded in 1922, and the Robert Brookings Graduate School of Economics and Government, founded in 1924.

The general administration of the Institution is the responsibility of a self-perpetuating Board of Trustees. The trustees are likewise charged with maintaining the independence of the staff and fostering the most favorable conditions for creative research and education. The immediate direction of the policies, program, and staff of the Institution is vested in the President, assisted by an advisory council chosen from the staff of the Institution.

In publishing a study, the Institution presents it as a competent treatment of a subject worthy of public consideration. The interpretations and conclusions in such publications are those of the author or authors and do not purport to represent the views of the other staff members, officers, or trustees of the Brookings Institution.

BOARD OF TRUSTEES

DOUGLAS DILLON, *Chairman*
SYDNEY STEIN, JR., *Vice Chairman*
WILLIAM R. BIGGS, *Chairman, Executive Committee*

Dillon Anderson
Vincent M. Barnett, Jr.
Louis W. Cabot
Robert D. Calkins
Edward W. Carter
John Fischer
Kermit Gordon
Gordon Gray
Huntington Harris
Luther G. Holbrook
John E. Lockwood
Robert S. McNamara
Arjay Miller
Herbert P. Patterson
Peter G. Peterson
J. Woodward Redmond

H. Chapman Rose
Robert Brookings Smith
J. Harvie Wilkinson, Jr.
Donald B. Woodward

Honorary Trustees

Arthur Stanton Adams
Daniel W. Bell
Eugene R. Black
Leonard Carmichael
Colgate W. Darden, Jr.
Marion B. Folsom
Raymond B. Fosdick
Huntington Gilchrist
John Lee Pratt

Foreword

THE STUDIES in this volume are intended to provide a factual and analytical basis for improved understanding of the economic effects of one of the most controversial parts of the tax system–the part that deals with taxes on the returns to capital.

The broad scope of the subject is evident from the variety of the papers. All seek to quantify some aspect of the effect of current tax law on the allocation of resources and economic efficiency. Martin Bailey discusses the special tax treatment of capital gains, estimating the effective rate of the tax by comparing data on capital gains realized and declared with estimates of capital gains accrued. David Laidler investigates the distortion in the demand for housing arising from the exemption from taxation of imputed rent on owner-occupied dwellings. The special incentives offered the mineral industries by percentage depletion, expensing, and capital gains provisions of the tax law are analyzed by Susan R. Agria. Leonard Rosenberg's paper measures the aggregate burden of corporate income and property taxes by industry group and the variation among industries in the ratios of such taxes to income from capital. Luigi Tambini looks into the long-term pattern of financing of U.S. corporations to determine the effects of taxation on the choice between equity and debt capital. The econometric studies of Robert E. Lucas, Colin Wright, and Marvin Kosters inquire into some basic economic relationships affected by tax laws: Lucas focuses on the elasticity of substitution between labor and capital in manufacturing; Wright analyzes the responsiveness of savings to changes in the rate of interest; and Kosters estimates the effects of income taxation on the supply of labor.

The studies were carried out by the Research Group in Public Finance at the University of Chicago under a grant from the Brookings Institution's program of Studies of Government Finance, a special program of research and education in taxation and government expenditures supervised by the National Committee on Government Finance. The committee was established in 1960 by the trustees of the Brookings Institution; its program is supported with funds provided by the Ford Foundation. Susan R. Agria and Robert E. Lucas also received financial assistance from the Woodrow Wilson National Fellowship Foundation, and David Laidler received financial assistance from the Earhart Foundation.

The studies were directed by Martin J. Bailey and Arnold C. Harberger, to whom the authors are indebted for their valuable and continuous guidance. In addition, David Laidler wishes to acknowledge with gratitude the contributions of Margaret Reid and Richard F. Muth; Luigi Tambini, those of Lawrence Fisher and Richard W. Parks; Robert Lucas, those of H. Gregg Lewis, Dale W. Jorgenson, Zvi Griliches, and members of the econometrics and public finance workshops at the University of Chicago; and Marvin Kosters, those of H. Gregg Lewis.

The authors received constructive comments from a reading committee consisting of Albert Ando, George F. Break, O. H. Brownlee, and Albert Hart. They are grateful to Muriel A. Porter, who served as secretary to the research group and who typed the great bulk of the work produced by the group, both in early and final drafts. They also thank Alyce Monroe and Jeannette Graham, who assisted in the preparation of the final manuscript. The volume was edited by Verrick O. French and Mary E. Baker; Evelyn P. Fisher reviewed the statistical material for consistency and accuracy; and Florence Robinson prepared the index.

The views expressed in this volume are those of the authors and are not presented as the views of the Ford Foundation, the National Committee on Government Finance, or the staff members, officers, or trustees of the Brookings Institution.

KERMIT GORDON
President

May 1969
Washington, D.C.

Studies of Government Finance

Studies of Government Finance is a special program of research and education in taxation and government expenditures at the federal, state, and local levels. This program, which is supported by a special grant from the Ford Foundation, was undertaken and supervised by the National Committee on Government Finance, appointed by the trustees of the Brookings Institution.

MEMBERS OF THE NATIONAL COMMITTEE ON GOVERNMENT FINANCE

HOWARD R. BOWEN
    Professor of Economics, Claremont Graduate School

ROBERT D. CALKINS (Chairman)
    Vice Chancellor, University of California, Santa Cruz, and President Emeritus, The Brookings Institution

MARION B. FOLSOM
    Director and Management Advisor, Eastman Kodak Company

ERWIN NATHANIEL GRISWOLD
    Solicitor General of the United States, formerly Dean, Law School of Harvard University

ALVIN H. HANSEN
    Emeritus Professor of Political Economy, Harvard University

GEORGE W. MITCHELL
    Board of Governors, Federal Reserve System

DON K. PRICE
    Dean, John Fitzgerald Kennedy School of Government, Harvard University

JACOB VINER
    Emeritus Professor of Economics, Princeton University

WILLIAM C. WARREN
    Dean, Columbia University Law School

HERMAN B WELLS
    Chancellor, Indiana University

JOSEPH A. PECHMAN, Executive Director

MEMBERS OF THE ADVISORY COMMITTEE

ROBERT ANTHOINE
Attorney, Winthrop, Stimson, Putnam and Roberts

WALTER J. BLUM
Professor of Law, University of Chicago Law School

E. CARY BROWN
Professor of Economics, Massachusetts Institute of Technology

JAMES M. BUCHANAN
Professor of Economics, University of California at Los Angeles

JESSE BURKHEAD
Professor of Economics, Maxwell School, Syracuse University

GERHARD COLM*
Chief Economist, National Planning Association

L. LASZLO ECKER-RACZ
Formerly Assistant Director, Advisory Commission on Intergovernmental Relations

OTTO ECKSTEIN
Professor of Economics, Harvard University

LYLE C. FITCH
President, Institute of Public Administration

RICHARD GOODE
Director, Fiscal Affairs Department, International Monetary Fund

HAROLD M. GROVES
Emeritus Professor of Economics, University of Wisconsin

WALTER W. HELLER
Professor of Economics, University of Minnesota

NEIL H. JACOBY
Dean, School of Business, University of California at Los Angeles

RICHARD A. MUSGRAVE
Professor of Economics, Harvard University

RICHARD RUGGLES
Professor of Economics, Yale University

LOUIS SHERE
Professor of Economics, Indiana University

CARL S. SHOUP
Professor of Economics, Columbia University

DAN THROOP SMITH
Professor of Finance, Graduate School of Business, Stanford University

STANLEY S. SURREY
Professor of Law, Harvard University

GEORGE TERBORGH
Director of Research, Machinery and Allied Products Institute

NORMAN B. TURE
Principal, Economics Department, Planning Research Corporation

* Deceased.

Contents

Foreword	vii
Introduction *Arnold C. Harberger*	1
Capital Gains and Income Taxation	
Martin J. Bailey	11
Announcement Effects of the Income Tax Base	12
Accruals, Realizations, and Effective Capital Gains Tax Rates	15
Effect of Taxes on Corporate Rate of Return	26
Net Rates of Return and Incentive Effects of the Corporation Income Tax	30
Note on the Progressivity of the Personal Income Tax	33
Conclusion	38
Appendix A. Predictable Income in Capital Gains	40
Appendix B. The Realizations Ratio and the Effective Capital Gains Tax Rate	46
Income Tax Incentives for Owner-Occupied Housing	
David Laidler	50
Normative Analysis	51
Empirical Tests	64
Special Tax Treatment of Mineral Industries	
Susan R. Agria	77
Development of the Depletion Allowance	79
Percentage Depletion	92
Severance Taxes	101
Capital Gains	104
Lease Costs	107
Effects of Changes in Tax Law	110

Special Tax Treatment of Mineral Industries *continued*

Conclusion	114
Appendix A. Equations Underlying Tables	117
Appendix B. Treasury Survey Tables	121

Taxation of Income from Capital, by Industry Group
Leonard Gerson Rosenberg — 123

Income from Capital, by Industry Group	124
Taxes on Income from Capital, by Industry Group	153
Cost of Distortions	173
Conclusion	179

Financial Policy and the Corporation Income Tax
Luigi Tambini — 185

The Puzzle of Corporate Financial Structure	186
Debt, Equity, and Corporate Financial Structure	188
Plan of the Work	194
Theory of the Firm, Cost Functions, and Risk Premiums	195
The Work of Fisher and Kolin	199
Some Empirical Results	201
The Equilibrium Path	208
Conclusions	215
Appendix A. Definition and Measurement of the Variables	216
Appendix B. The Effect of a Change in Leverage on the Coefficient of Variation of Earnings	219
Appendix C. Fisher's Cost Functions of Debt and Kolin's Cost Functions of Equity	221

Labor-Capital Substitution in U.S. Manufacturing
Robert E. Lucas, Jr. — 223

Theoretical Background	225
Review of Empirical Work	232
Time Series Estimates of Elasticities of Substitution	245
Time Series Estimates	247
Conclusions	265
Appendix. Time Series Data	268

Saving and the Rate of Interest
Colin Wright — 275

Theory of the Relationship Between Consumption and the Rate of Interest	276
General Relationship Between Consumption and Rate of Interest	279
Measuring the Response of Consumption to Changes in the Rate of Interest	284

Table 7.	Incentive Ratios for Exploration and Development of Coal Industry with Capital Gains Tax on Sale of Coal, by Straight Line and Sum-of-Years Digits Depreciation Methods, 1958–60	107
Table 8.	Percentage Depletion Incentive Ratios for Exploration and Development of Oil and Gas Industries, Adjusted for Lease Costs, 1958–60	109
Table 9.	Effect of Changing Corporation Income Tax Rate on Percentage Depletion and Capital Gains Incentives for Exploration and Development, Oil and Gas, Coal, and Iron Industries, 1960	111
Table 10.	Effect on Percentage Depletion Incentives, with Partial Severance Taxes Included, of Lowering the Ratios of Percentage Depletion to Net Income and of Lowering Corporation Income Tax Rates, Oil and Gas, Coal, and Iron Industries, 1960	112
Table 11.	Effect on Percentage Depletion Incentives, Partial Severance Taxes Included, of Eliminating Expensing and Deductions for Depreciation, Abandonment Losses, and Deferrals, for Oil and Gas, Coal, and Iron Industries, 1960	113
Table B-1.	Income, Deductions, and Depletion Claimed, Coal and Iron Industries, Domestic United States, 1958	121
Table B-2.	Tax Treatment of Expenditures on Exploration, for Oil and Gas, Iron, and Coal Industries, United States, 1958	122
Table B-3.	Tax Treatment of Expenditures on Development and Acquisition Costs for Oil and Gas, Iron, and Coal Industries, United States, 1958	122

Rosenberg

Table 1.	Total Income from Capital (Excluding Property Tax Payments) by Non-Financial Industry Group, 1953–59 Average	126
Table 2.	Allocation of Return to Capital and Labor in Agriculture, 1953–59	138
Table 3.	Income of Non-Farm Unincorporated Enterprises, 1953–59 Average	139
Table 4.	Return to Equity Capital when Labor Return to Entrepreneurs Is Based on Average Employee Compensation, Selected Unincorporated Industries, 1953–59 Average	144
Table 5.	Employee Compensation and Wages and Salaries per Full-Time Equivalent Employee Compared with Income of Unincorporated Enterprises per Partner or Proprietor, Selected Industry Groups, 1953–59 Average	145
Table 6.	Estimated Return to Equity Capital, Assuming Equal Rate of Return after Tax on Corporate and Unincorporated Net Physical Assets, Selected Non-Farm Unincorporated Industries, 1953–59 Average	146

Table 7.	Alternative Estimate of Return to Equity Capital for Hotel, Motel, and Tourist Court Industry, 1953–59	149
Table 8.	Rental Income of Persons by Type of Property, 1953–59	150
Table 9.	Corporate Profits Tax Liability, by Non-Financial Industry Group, 1953–59 Average	155
Table 10.	Special Property Tax Payments That Are Excluded from This Study, 1953–59 Average	158
Table 11.	Estimate of Property Taxes Paid by Non-Financial Industry Group, 1953–59 Average	160
Table 12.	Estimate of Property Tax Rates for Manufacturing Industries, and Ratio of Internal Revenue Service to Bureau of the Census Partial Net Physical Assets, 1957	165
Table 13.	Alternative Estimate of Property Taxes Paid by Hotel, Motel, and Tourist Court Industry, Based on Fair Value of Property, 1953–58	172
Table 14.	Effect on the Use of Capital of Taxes on Corporate Profits and Property, Non-Financial Industry Group, 1953–59 Average	174
Table 15.	Effect on the Use of Capital of Taxes on Corporate Profits and Property, Non-Financial Industry Group, 1959	180

Tambini

Table 1.	Measures of Average and Marginal Cost of Debt and of Equity Financing by Stock Issues, Corporate Manufacturing, Benchmark Years, 1927–65	203
Table 2.	Marginal Tax Rates on Dividends and Capital Gains, Four Benchmark Years, 1949–65	206
Table 3.	Measures of Average and Marginal Cost of Debt and of Equity Financing by Retained Earnings, Corporate Manufacturing, Four Benchmark Years, 1949–65	207
Table 4.	Measures of Average and Marginal Cost of Debt and of Equity Financing by Both Stock Issues and Retained Earnings, Corporate Manufacturing, Four Benchmark Years, 1949–65	209
Table 5.	Ratios of Changes in Debt to Changes in Equity, Corporate Manufacturing, Selected Periods, 1946–63	210
Table 6.	Equilibrium Path of Debt Using Yearly Changes in Debt, Corporate Manufacturing, 1946–60 and 1946–63	213
Table 7.	Equilibrium Path of Equity Using Yearly Changes in Equity, Corporate Manufacturing, 1946–60 and 1946–63	214
Chart 1.	Corporate Tax Payments in Manufacturing as Percentage of Income from Capital and as Percentage of Profits, 1927–63	187

Contents xvii

Chart 2.	Cost of Debt, Cost of Equity, and Rate of Return to Assets, Corporate Manufacturing, 1927–63	188
Chart 3.	Financial Structure, Corporate Manufacturing, 1927–63	192

Lucas

Table 1.	Elasticities of Substitution Between Labor and Capital by Arrow, Chenery, Minhas, and Solow, Varying Countries and Industries, Mid-1950's	234
Table 2.	Elasticities of Substitution Between Labor and Capital by Minasian, 1957, and Solow, 1956, Selected U.S. Industries	235
Table 3.	Elasticities of Substitution Between Labor and Capital, Using Cross-Sectional Tests and Time Series Data, Chemical and Allied Products Industry, Twenty-five States, 1947, 1954, and 1958	243
Table 4.	Cross-Sectional Tests and Time Series of Elasticities of Substitution Between Labor and Capital, Tobacco Industry, Eleven States, 1947, 1954, and 1958 Pooled	244
Table 5.	Elasticities of Substitution Between Labor and Capital by McKinnon, Using Time Series Data, Eighteen U.S. Industries, 1947–58	246
Table 6.	Trends in Factor Quantities and Prices, Fourteen U.S. Industries, 1929–57	248
Table 7.	Elasticities of Substitution Using Wages and Prices, Current and Past, Fourteen U.S. Industries, 1931–58	250
Table 8.	Test of Use of Lagged and Other Wage and Price Restrictions in Elasticity of Substitution Regressions, Fourteen U.S. Industries, 1932–58	254
Table 9.	Test of Use of Lagged and Other Wage and Price Restrictions in Elasticity of Substitution Regressions, Three U.S. Industries, 1932–58	255
Table 10.	Test of Elasticities of Substitution Using Wage-Price Adjustment Patterns, Fourteen U.S. Industries, 1931–58	257
Table 11.	Runs Test for Serial Correlation, on Regression Equations (24) and (25), 13 U.S. Industries, 1931–58	262
Table 12.	Summary of Elasticities of Substitution Between Labor and Capital, U.S. Manufacturing Industries, 1931–58	265

Wright

Table 1.	Effect of Interest Rates on Consumption: Regression Results Using Gross and Net-of-Tax Bond Rates with Goldsmith Data, 1905–49, and Modigliani, Brown, and Ando Data, 1929–58	293

Table B-1.	Average Marginal Dividend and Interest Income Tax Rates, 1913–58	300
Chart 1.	Relation Between Consumption and Rate of Interest	277

Kosters

Table 1.	Effects of Wage Rate and Income on Hours of Work of Husbands Aged 50–64, Selected Regression Results, 1960	312
Table 2.	Wage Rate and Income Coefficients for Labor Force Participation Rates of Males Aged 25–54, 1960 and 1950	317
Table 3.	Wage Rate and Income Coefficients and Compensated Elasticities for Labor Force Participation Rates of Married Women with Husbands Present, Selected Areas, 1950 and 1960	319

ARNOLD C. HARBERGER

Introduction

OF THE 1967 U.S. net national product (NNP) of $720 billion, it is estimated that approximately $180 billion represented returns to capital in its various forms. Against these returns to capital can be allocated some $36 billion of corporation income taxes (federal and state), some $27 billion of property taxes, some $11 billion of indirect business taxes (representing capital's share in NNP times the total of indirect business taxes other than property taxes), plus probably $18 billion or more of personal income taxes on dividends, on the return to capital generated on farms and in unincorporated enterprises, and on capital gains. In all, more than half of the net national product generated by capital reached the fiscal till in one way or another, and accounted for about 40 percent of all government revenues (federal, state, and local) collected, and for over 50 percent of all taxes other than social security contributions.

The sheer weight of the taxes falling on the returns to capital, whether measured relative to those returns themselves or to total tax revenues, is itself an ample justification for studies such as those in this volume, which are aimed at improving our understanding of the economic effects of this large part of our tax system. But even apart from the dollar magnitude involved, the analysis of the taxation of income from capital commands interest because of the scope and variety of the problems it embraces. We may begin with the corporation income tax itself; here there is not only the puzzle of the ultimate incidence of the tax, but also serious problems of discrimination. The corporation income tax discriminates against the corporate sector of the economy and in favor of the non-corporate sector. Within the corporate sector it discriminates against capital-intensive activities. Among uses of corporate capital, it discriminates against those with capital structures weighted heavily toward equity as distinct from those uses which can readily finance a large proportion of their capital requirements by debt. Finally, within each company, incentives are created by the corporation income tax to shift the capital structure toward debt and away from equity financing.

The corporation income tax does not, however, stand alone as a discriminatory tax in a tax structure that is otherwise neutral. Alongside it stands the property tax, which also weighs differentially on the income generated by capital in distinct lines of activity. The variation here occurs because not all physical capital is covered by property taxation, and because of variations—both geographical and by type of capital—in property tax rates and in the ratios of assessed value to true value. Also present in the tax system is a profound discrimination in favor of owner-occupied housing, which stems from the failure to include the imputed rent on such housing in the personal income tax base. Finally, there is the personal taxation of dividends at income tax rates and of capital gains at preferential rates, with the preferential treatment of the latter tending somewhat to offset the discrimination against the corporate form implicit in the corporation income tax.

Apart from these major components of the structure of taxation of income from capital, there are a variety of special provisions that merit attention. In recent years, an investment credit has been introduced on most business investments, which operates as an investment incentive but also leads to discrimination between assets of different useful lives. Also, certain lines of activity (such as cattle-raising and timber-growing) have privileged access to capital gains treatment, and thus receive in effect an implicit subsidy as compared with most lines of economic activity. Finally, the mineral industries, most particularly oil and gas, are the beneficiaries of expensing and percentage depletion privileges which give a very substantial "artificial" stimulus to exploration for and production of the affected products.

In the present volume, a number of the problems raised in the analysis of this many-faceted pattern of taxation are explored.[1] The chapters by Martin J. Bailey, David Laidler, and Susan R. Agria deal with specific tax provisions. Bailey considers the effects of the special tax treatment of capital gains. By analyzing data on capital gains actually realized and declared on tax returns in a given period, and comparing them with estimates of the amounts of capital gains accruing in the same period, Bailey finds that a strikingly high proportion of all accrued capital gains are either held for very long periods before being realized and taxed, or else escape the capital gains tax altogether via transfer by inheritance or charitable gift. Bailey concludes that if past relationships between realizations and accruals continue to hold in the future, and if the tax rates and other provisions relating to capital gains remain the same, a typical dollar of capital gains accruing today will ultimately generate tax payments whose present value is no greater than 8 cents. Thus the *effective* rate of taxation on capital gains is less than 8 percent. Bailey then analyzes the relationship between the tax burdens on capital invested in corporate enterprise on the one hand and in unincorporated business on the other. Making the assumption that corporate savings by a company are normally reflected in a corresponding rise in the market value of that company's outstanding shares, he finds that for individuals with marginal tax rates above approximately 70 percent, the total tax burden on income from investments in corporate shares—stemming from the corporation income tax on the company's earnings, plus the personal income tax on dividends, plus the capital gains tax ultimately generated on

---

[1] Other problems studied by the Chicago Research Group during the period of Brookings sponsorship extended considerably beyond the studies in this volume. Published works by members of the group, dating from this period, include: Giorgio Basevi, "The United States Tariff Structure: Estimates of Effective Rates of Protection of United States Industries and Industrial Labor," *Review of Economics and Statistics*, Vol. 48 (May 1966); Eitan Berglas, "Investment and Technological Change," *Journal of Political Economy*, Vol. 73 (April 1965); and John G. Cragg, Arnold C. Harberger, and Peter Mieszkowski, "Empirical Evidence on the Incidence of the Corporation Income Tax," *Journal of Political Economy*, Vol. 75 (December 1967).

Four additional studies by Harberger were also by-products of the Research Group: "Taxation, Resource Allocation, and Welfare," in National Bureau of Economic Research and Brookings Institution, *The Role of Direct and Indirect Taxes in the Federal Revenue System* (Princeton University Press, 1964); "The Measurement of Waste," *American Economic Review*, Vol. 54 (May 1964); "Efficiency Effects of Taxes on Income from Capital," in M. Krzyzaniak (ed.), *Effects of Corporation Income Tax* (Wayne State University Press, 1966); and "The Corporation Income Tax," in *International Encyclopedia of the Social Sciences* (Macmillan and Free Press, 1968).

the basis of corporate savings—is less than the personal income tax to which the taxpayer would be liable, if instead of corporate shares he bought an interest in an unincorporated enterprise in which capital had the same gross-of-tax yield as corporate equity capital. Then, analyzing the data from tax returns for 1954–60, Bailey inquires whether the actual behavior of investors in different income brackets, in their allocation of investments between corporate shares and unincorporated enterprises, reflects the tax incentives thus calculated. He finds a rough correspondence between actual investor behavior and that predicted by his theoretical analysis, thus suggesting that investors do in fact perceive and act upon the tax incentives he analyzes.

David Laidler is concerned with the effects of the exemption from personal income tax of imputed rent on owner-occupied dwellings. This tax incentive operates to stimulate artificially the demand for owner-occupied housing. Laidler points out that this incentive is doubly regressive in its effect, first because the basic demand for housing has an income elasticity greater than unity—so that a flat-rate tax offset on this base would represent a higher fraction of the income of upper-income groups than of lower-income groups—and second because the stimulus itself is measured by the marginal tax rate of the individual concerned, and hence increases rapidly as one moves from lower- to higher-income brackets. Laidler next measures the cost to the economy stemming from the inefficient allocation of resources provoked by the exemption of imputed rent, and finds it to be in excess of $500 million per year. Finally, he undertakes to test whether consumers do in fact respond to the tax incentives to owner-occupation in the fashion that theoretical analysis would lead us to believe. He does this by an ingenious comparison of cross-sectional income elasticities of demand for housing by owners and by renters. On the assumption that the basic demand for housing has the same characteristics for owners and for renters, the measured income elasticity for owners should exceed that for renters, because as incomes rise renters acquire better housing facilities only as a response to the rise in income, while owners should respond both to the rise in income and to the increased tax incentive. In seven separate samples of census tracts, carefully controlled to eliminate confounding influences from variables like family size, age distribution, racial composition, and the like, Laidler finds the measured income elasticity of demand for housing by owners to exceed that of renters. Moreover, recognizing that the measured cross-sectional income elasticity for owners is the sum of the true income elasticity and a price effect which stems from the tax incentive, he calculates the price elasticity of response implied by the excess of the cross-sectional income elasticity measured for owners over that measured for renters. He finds that the average value of the implicit price elasticities calculated in this way for his seven samples is close to the values of the price elasticity of housing demand obtained by direct estimation, thus providing additional confirmation that the differential response of owners is indeed due to the tax incentive.

Susan Agria's chapter deals with the special tax treatment of mineral industries, particularly the special incentives given by the percentage depletion, expensing, and capital gains provisions of the U.S. tax law. After an extended review of the legislative history of these provisions, she uses data from a special tabulation of tax returns made by the U.S. Treasury Department for the 1958–60 period to estimate the magnitudes of the incentives favoring exploration for and production of minerals. Her analysis of the incentives for exploration represents a further refinement of the theoretical framework which I developed in 1955 and which was elaborated by Peter Steiner in 1959. An illustrative conclusion from her analysis is that, in 1960, a company could invest as much as $1.36 million in oil and gas exploration in order to produce the same expected contribution to the future national income as would be produced by corporate investments of only $1 million in other lines. Because of the special tax provisions governing minerals, the oil or gas company in the above example would nonetheless be able to earn the same after-tax rate of return as that applying to other corporate investments. The excess of 36 percent in the investment cost of producing a given stream of future product is simply the measure, at the margin, of the economic inefficiency caused by the special tax treatment of oil and gas. Agria's entire analysis is based on the assumption—frequently asserted to be true by representatives of the mineral industries—that these industries do not enjoy higher after-tax rates of return on capital than the rest of the corporate sector of the U.S. economy. She shows that if this assumption is correct, the principal consequences of the special tax treatment of mineral industries are serious misallocations of resources which impose a heavy real cost on the economy as a whole.

The next two studies in this volume—those by Leonard Rosenberg and by Luigi Tambini—relate to aspects of the corporation income tax. Rosenberg's paper is concerned with measuring the aggregate weight of corporate income taxation and property taxation by industry group, and with the ratios which these two forms of taxation bear to the total income from capital in the different industries in the economy. Drawing upon his substantial practical experience in the construction of national income accounts, Rosenberg undertakes three main tasks: (a) the estimation of the income from capital in unincorporated enterprise, by type of industry; (b) the estimation of property tax payments, by type of industry; and (c) the reclassification of some corporate profits which are carried in the national income accounts under the real estate industry as rents and royalties on business property, allocating these profits to the industry in which the capital was in fact employed. Rosenberg's estimates of the effective rates of corporation-income-cum-property tax show wide variations from industry to industry, ranging from 17 percent in agriculture to over 60 percent in water transportation. Obviously, variations across industries in the rate of effective tax on the income from capital induce distortions in the allocation of capital which entail real costs to the economy. Rosenberg estimates what these real costs would be if the distortions reflected in his figures on effective tax rates were the only relevant ones in the economy. His estimates of this cost are $587 million per year, based on average 1953–59 data, and $622 million per year, based on the 1959 data alone.

In his chapter, Luigi Tambini confronts the "puzzle" of why a tax system like the U.S. corporation income tax, which makes the cost to a firm of equity capital roughly twice the cost of debt capital, does not drive firms to shift their pattern of financing strongly in favor of debt capital. Tambini first distinguishes between the average cost of debt or equity capital (which is measured in the form of bond and stock yields) and their respective marginal costs, which are the relevant criteria for choice regarding changes in the pattern of financing. Tambini then shows how the relevant marginal cost of equity capital lies below the earnings yield on stocks, while the marginal cost of debt capital lies above the yield on bonds. He also obtains direct measures of the differences between marginal costs of debt and equity and the corresponding bond or earnings yields, basing his work in part on earlier studies by Lawrence Fisher and Marshall Kolin. On this basis he constructs estimates of the marginal cost of debt capital and of the

Arnold C. Harberger

marginal cost of equity capital for a series of benchmark years beginning in 1927 and ending with 1965. He finds that for the prewar years the relationship between the marginal cost of equity and the marginal cost of debt was quite close, indicating that corporations had approached an equilibrium financial structure. In the immediate postwar period, he finds that the financial structure of the corporate sector was substantially out of equilibrium, with the marginal cost of equity capital substantially higher than that of debt capital. This disequilibrium was probably due in part to the high productivity of physical capital equipment (owing to its war-induced scarcity) in the immediate postwar years, and in part to a depression-induced fear on the part of the investing public to bid up stock prices to levels where their yield after taxes was comparable to that on bonds. Be that as it may, Tambini shows that the disequilibrium between the marginal cost of equity and that of debt capital gradually narrowed through the 1950's, though it was not completely eliminated by the last benchmark year covered in his study. He also shows that during the 1950's corporations were indeed adapting their financial structures in the direction of reducing the disequilibrium. Subsequent to the last benchmark year analyzed by Tambini, the earnings yield on equities continued to fall, relative to the yield on bonds; this suggests that the corporate sector of the economy may once again, in recent years, have come quite close to financial equilibrium. If this is the case, there is no longer any "puzzle" to solve in connection with corporate financial structure, as the approximate equality of the marginal costs of debt and equity (which, of course, are defined taking tax considerations into account) would reflect that the tax incentives toward change in financial structure had already elicited a full adaptation of that structure.

The last three chapters in this volume—those by Robert Lucas, Colin Wright, and Marvin Kosters—are basic econometric studies inquiring into the magnitudes of certain parameters which play important roles in the analysis of the effects of taxation. Lucas focuses on the elasticity of substitution between labor and capital in manufacturing industries, a key parameter in analyzing both the incidence and the allocation effects of special taxes (such as the corporation income tax) on income from capital. Existing studies of this parameter have drawn predominantly on cross-section data. Lucas points out that reliance on cross-section data of the types that have been used builds into the estimation process strong biases in the direction of an estimated elasticity of unity. Relying on time series analysis for industries, Lucas obtains estimates of the elasticity of substitution which are consistently lower than those obtained from cross-section analysis of the same industries. Lucas then investigates a number of possible sources of bias in his time series estimates, and concludes that while some bias may exist, its magnitude could not plausibly be so great that adjusting for it would bring the time series estimates into rough correspondence with the estimates obtained from cross-sectional work. On the other hand, the implicit bias in the cross-sectional estimates can quite plausibly be of such magnitude that adjusting for the bias would bring the cross-sectional estimates—for at least some industries—to correspond roughly with the time series estimates obtained by Lucas. Lucas' conclusion is that rather than ranging around unity, as the cross-section studies suggest, the elasticities of substitution between labor and capital in most manufacturing industries are probably well below unity, with 0.4 or 0.5 as a reasonable measure of their central tendency.

Wright's study concerns the responsiveness of savings to changes in the rate of interest. Starting from a general model of consumer maximizing behavior over numerous time periods, Wright derives the result that changes in consumption can be expressed as a function of (a) changes in the current wealth position of consumers, (b) changes in the present value of their entire expected stream of present and future income from both labor and property, and (c) changes in the rate of interest. In this function, he shows that the income effects of changes in the rate of interest are captured in (b), so that the coefficient of (c) reflects the substitution effect of changes in the rate of interest, which should (with consumption as the dependent variable) be negative. Wright then applies his model to two sets of data, one developed by Goldsmith and the other by Modigliani, Brown, and Ando. He uses an exponentially weighted average of past incomes as a proxy variable for (b). In all cases the application of his model produces superior coefficients of determination (R^2) to alternative formulations. In addition, for what may be the first time in the history of work on consumption functions, Wright obtains uniformly negative (and in most cases statistically significant) estimates for the effect on consumption of increases in the rate of interest. His estimates of the elasticity of saving with respect to the rate of interest range about +0.2, suggesting that a rise from 4 percent to 6 percent in the rate of interest will, through the substitution effect, provoke an increase in savings of 10 percent or more. I say 10 percent "or more" because, although the theoretical analysis underlying Wright's work indicates that the income effects of changes in the rate of interest will be captured in (b), there is no guarantee that the proxy which was actually used for (b) fully captures these effects. To the extent that the proxy captures less than the full income effects of changes in the rate of interest, the estimated elasticity of saving with respect to the rate of interest, reflecting the substitution effect only, would be greater than 0.2.

The study by Kosters concerns the effects of income taxation on the supply of labor. While his study thus does not directly concern the taxation of income from capital, it is relevant in the sense that studies of the welfare cost of taxes, and of the incidence of the corporation income tax as well, have frequently been based on the convenient assumption that the aggregate supply of labor has zero elasticity. Kosters' work is therefore a test of the degree of validity of this simplifying assumption. Obviously, an appreciation of the elasticity of response of labor supply with respect to the wage rate is also relevant for many other issues of tax analysis.

Kosters studies principally the behavior of males in the age group from 50 to 64, on the assumption that this group would be more ready than other age groups to alter its labor market behavior in response to changes in wage rates and in income other than wages. Kosters finds, in spite of this presumption, that the average number of hours worked by those in the labor force shows no perceptible variation, via the substitution effect, in response to these changes. On the other hand, he does perceive a small elasticity of response of labor force participation with respect to the wage rate, but the elasticity is so small (about 0.06) as to be of minor importance.

All of Kosters' work is carried out within the framework of a theoretical model of family labor supply which he develops. In this model, the labor supplied by both husband and wife depends on the wage rates obtainable in the market by each of them, and on the income they have from non-labor sources. Within the framework of this model, Kosters reinterprets the results obtained by Mincer and by Cain in their studies of the labor supply of married women. He finds that the elasticities of labor supply of married women are probably somewhat lower than those inferred by Mincer and Cain from their studies, but are nonetheless substantial (of the order of 1.0) in size. Kosters, therefore, concludes that, while plausible tax changes would have no perceptible substitution effect on the male labor supply, they could have a significant influence on the amount of labor supplied by married women.

Kosters also presents estimates of the total elasticity of response of labor supply to wage changes—estimates including an income effect—which are relevant to certain types of income tax changes. He finds these elasticities to be negative for males, reflecting the familiar backward-bending supply curve of labor, but again small in absolute magnitude. For women, however, the elasticity of labor supply is substantial and positive even when the income effect is involved.

MARTIN J. BAILEY

Capital Gains and Income Taxation

THE TAX TREATMENT of capital gains, one of the most controversial facets of the tax structure, involves several closely related issues. The ultimate issue is the question of how capital gains should be treated for purposes of income taxation. Related to this issue are several distinct and unsettled questions about the facts of capital gains, their relevance for analysis of policy issues, and what the objectives of policy should be: How in fact have accrued capital gains been taxed; that is, what proportion of actual accruals have had constructive realization for tax purposes? To what extent are capital gains predictable income, such that their expected tax treatment affects investment decisions and resource allocation? To what extent does the special tax treatment of capital gains serve to offset the corporation income tax, and in the light of this treatment, what is the overall rate of tax on income from corporate equity? Specifically, how does the attractiveness of holding equity in corporations relative to holding equity in unincorporated businesses vary with the marginal personal income tax rate of taxpayers, when account is taken of the anticipated treatment of future capital gains? How has the special treatment of capital gains affected the degree of progressivity of the personal income tax and of the overall tax structure?

The purpose of this chapter is to establish from the available data factual information which will help to answer some of these questions, and to develop analytically some implications of these facts. Direct discussion of the more controversial issues of public policy will generally be avoided, since the main objective is to set forth as adequately as possible a factual and analytical basis for the use of those who wish to consider such issues. The procedure will be to glean as much pertinent information as possible from the data published in *Statistics of Income*,[1] after first considering analytically what data are needed for the determination of incentive effects, expected and actual tax burdens, and so forth. Special attention will be paid to the role of capital gains taxation in the expected tax incidence on the income from corporate equity, because of the great importance of corporate equity both in general economic terms and in terms of accrued and realized capital gains.

Announcement Effects of the Income Tax Base

Discussion of the appropriate base for the income tax most usefully proceeds under two principal headings, namely, the announcement or incentive effects of the chosen base and its distributional equity. A change from one base to another will generally involve changes under both these headings, although it is possible in principle to devise tax changes that change incentives without changing the after-tax income distribution, and vice versa. In the section which begins on p. 33, below, some evidence of how the tax treatment of capital gains affects the after-tax income distribution by income size is considered. This section and the remaining ones are primarily devoted to a consideration of announcement effects.

Announcement[2] or incentive effects occur when the relationship between expected taxes and expected income depends on factors such as the variability of income, the industry or activity in which the income is earned, and other factors which the recipient of income can control or influence by deliberate choice. If a given income before tax can be

[1] U.S. Treasury Department, Internal Revenue Service, *Statistics of Income, Individual Income Tax Returns*; *Statistics of Income, Corporation Income Tax Returns*; and *Statistics of Income, Fiduciary, Gift, and Estate Tax Returns*, annual issues.

[2] I use the term "announcement effects" as equivalent to incentive effects, following a usage first introduced by Arthur C. Pigou, which is widely accepted. *A Study in Public Finance* (Macmillan, 1928), Chap. 4.

earned in either of two activities but will be taxed differently in one activity than in the other, any owner of capital or other resource who can transfer it from the more highly taxed activity to the lower-taxed one has an incentive to do so, until such transfers equalize expected incomes after taxes.

Announcement effects depend on the relationship of expected taxes to expected income, and therefore will be affected by the tax treatment of pure windfalls or unexpected income only to the extent that such tax treatment has a positive or negative effect on total expected taxes. A well-known way in which such an effect occurs is through the differential impact of a progressive income tax on a risky or variable income compared to a steady income of equal expected size. A positive windfall in a fluctuating income stream puts the income of that year into a higher-than-normal income tax bracket and so pays a higher-than-normal marginal tax; a negative windfall puts the income of that year into a lower-than-normal income tax bracket and so reduces the year's tax bill at the correspondingly lower-than-normal marginal tax rate. Since the extra tax in the year of positive windfall is greater than the tax saving in a year of equal but negative windfall, a net expected additional tax arises because of variability alone. If it were not for this effect, however, the tax treatment of windfalls would be immaterial for the analysis of announcement effects (provided that the concept of "windfalls" is defined in such a way that the average expectation of them is zero). Having noted this effect, therefore, we can concentrate our main attention on expected or predictable income.

It should be clear also that the announcement effects of the capital gains tax depend on the relationship of expected taxes to expected capital accruals, regardless of how the accruals occur. Other things being equal, a growth of his wealth conveys the same benefit to a taxpayer whether it occurs through a diversion of ordinary income (for tax purposes) to the purchase of assets, through the sale of an asset at a profit and the purchase of a new one to replace it, or through the growth in value of an asset that is not sold at all. However, expected taxes differ according to the three cases, being zero for all accrued capital gains as long as they remain unrealized, and being lower for realized capital gains than for ordinary income. Therefore the special tax treatment of capital gains has announcement effects whenever the employment of capital in a given activity can be expected to result partly or wholly in capital gains accruals, rather than in what the tax laws define as ordinary income, and whenever the taxpayer can exercise control over his realizations. (Also, whenever such announcement effects are present, the frequently stated rule of equity that equals should be treated equally is violated.)

A conspicuous example of a tax provision giving rise to this type of announcement effect is that governing profits from the sale of livestock, all of which may be reported as capital gains for tax purposes. The income from capital employed in livestock enterprises thus is subject only to the capital gains tax rates rather than the higher tax rates on ordinary income; there is an incentive to move capital into such enterprises from those having similar risk but subject to normal tax treatment, until the after-tax rates of return are equal. Timber-growing and many mineral-producing enterprises also enjoy the privileged capital gains treatment.

Perhaps the single most important type of predictable income which is treated in part as capital gain for tax purposes is the accrual of real value in corporate shares. Over long periods corporate shares have continued to increase in real value (after due adjustment for changes in capital structure), though at a notoriously variable rate, and their owners talk and act as though such increases are expected to continue. These increases cannot be supposed to materialize out of thin air, but must be associated in some way with predictable increases in the earnings potential per share. The most obvious and measurable positive influence on earnings potential is the book value, or invested capital per share, which rises fairly steadily for most corporations through the retention of earnings for capitalization to surplus. If the productivity of the new investment financed by retention is typically the same as the discount factor applicable to the firm's prospective earnings, a dollar-per-share retention will necessarily add a dollar to the price of a share.

That retained earnings have, in practice, a productivity equal to the appropriate discount factor is sometimes disputed, on the grounds that corporate managements may typically make mistakes or may deliberately compromise the interests of the shareholders in their retention policies. Certainly any evidence to that effect would be worth considering, although I have none to offer here, and know of none that anyone else has produced. On the contrary, the data on accruals of real value in corporate shares over the longest period for which they are available, from 1871 to 1960, show a correspondence to real retentions that is close enough to be within the range of plausible error in the data; details of this calculation are given in Appendix A.

In any case, it should be borne in mind that what is at issue is not the real value of retentions per se but the real value of all investment by corporations. The corporate management that can compromise the interests of shareholders by its retention policies can compromise those interests by its policies regarding all investment, whether financed by new issues of bonds, by new issues of shares, or by retentions. Such behavior would best be discovered by a comparison of the movement of the market value with the movement of the book value of the entire capital of the corporate sector, with allowances for changes in the price level and possible errors in depreciation accounting. Making this comparison would go beyond the scope of the present study, and has not been attempted here.

Further, even though one may doubt the wisdom of the investment policies of typical corporate managements, or, more pertinently, may suspect that the typical price-setting trader in shares has such doubts, in the absence of better information the procedure of treating retentions as equal to expected capital gains is a good first approximation. It resembles the procedure of valuing the elements of private-sector gross national product (GNP) at market prices, and the government contribution to GNP at factor cost; I am not wholly convinced of the accuracy of this procedure at many points, but have employed it as the best available first approximation. Accordingly, in the later sections dealing with the announcement effects of the overall tax treatment of corporate equity, it is assumed that expected capital gains are equal to retained earnings.

Accruals, Realizations, and Effective Capital Gains Tax Rates

Any predictable income that is treated as capital gains receives privileged tax treatment for several related reasons. First, the tax rate is lower. Second, taxes are levied as of the time the income is received in cash, rather than at the time it is accrued; for capital gains, this distinction is particularly important. Third, capital gains escape income tax altogether when they are transferred by inheritance. These latter two considerations lower the effective rate of tax, so far as its announcement effects are concerned, below even the nominal rate.

To get an idea of the importance of the effects of deferral and of avoidance through gift and succession (and evasion), let us examine what existing data seem to show about the extent to which accrued capital gains on corporate shares are realized for tax purposes. Table 1 shows the estimated value of all corporate shares from 1925 through 1961, the Standard and Poor's index of share prices for the same years, and estimated capital gains accrued on corporate shares for the period 1926–61. Annual data on the net consolidated value of shares were obtained by interpolating between and extrapolating from Goldsmith's benchmark estimates using the value of all shares listed on the New York Stock Exchange.[3] Each year's accrued capital gain was then estimated by applying to the previous year's value of the market the appropriate Standard and Poor's price relative minus one. In addition, Table 1 shows total capital gains realized on all assets by individuals and fiduciaries from 1926 through 1960, estimated from data in the U.S. Treasury Department's *Statistics of Income*, in dollar terms. These figures set a plausible upper limit on capital gains realized by individuals and fiduciaries in the stock market, except for the deep depression years in which total realized capital gains were negative or small. For the one year of the years covered in this study—1959—for which useful data estimating the proportions of capital gains originating from various sources exist, the proportion due to corporate shares was 48.4 percent.[4]

[3] Data published by the U.S. Securities and Exchange Commission (SEC), in *Volume and Composition of Individuals' Saving* (September 1962 and April 1963), Table 2, suggest that these figures may be too high for recent years. However, even if so, the results of this section are only slightly affected, as indicated below. SEC data for year-end value of investment company shares and preferred and common shares (in billions of dollars) are:

1954	229.7	1959	393.0
1955	283.5	1960	375.5
1956	294.4	1961	466.6
1957	259.1	1962	409.1
1958	358.1		

Data for 1959–62 are revised as of April 1963.

[4] See Table A-1. In addition to the 1959 Treasury study of capital gains, used for that table, the only other such study was a 1936 breakdown for three large states (New York, Pennsylvania, Illinois) reported by Lawrence H. Seltzer in *The Nature and Tax Treatment of Capital Gains and Losses* (National Bureau of Economic Research, 1951), pp. 502–03. Unfortunately, capital gains in 1936 were just barely positive, and were substantial and negative for real estate. The ratio of net capital gains on corporate shares to total net capital gains for the three states was 0.836, but this figure is of little value as a guide to average conditions.

From 1926 through 1961 the unweighted mean annual rate of accrual of capital gains in corporate shares, obtained by averaging the Standard and Poor's year-end share price relatives, was 7.60 percent. For the same period the average of capital gains realizations as a percentage of the beginning of the year nominal value of the market was 1.28 percent. The ratio of the latter to the former is 0.168. A second measure of the ratio of realizations to accruals is obtained by taking the ratio of cumulated realizations over the whole period to cumulated accruals, as estimated in Table 1. This latter procedure places relatively greater weight on the later years, because of the growth over the period of the total value of the market. The resulting ratio, 0.268 (1926–60), is not markedly different from the first, but is probably less appropriate because of greater sensitivity of the latter procedure to recent fluctuations in the market, especially to the stock market boom of the mid-1950's. However, not all realized capital gains originate from corporate shares; if the 1959 proportions of total realized capital gains of corporate shares are used to adjust realizations, the ratio of realizations to accruals becomes 0.0813. (The SEC data, presented in footnote 3, do not cover enough years to provide an independent estimate of accruals. In the years 1954–61 the SEC figures, adjusted for their exclusion of fiduciaries, averaged only about 70 percent of the figures in column 1 of Table 1 for the same years. If this same average were applied to the entire column, accruals would be 70 percent of the estimates in column 3, and the ratio of realizations to accruals would be 0.116.)

Consideration must be given to whether this very low ratio of realizations to accruals could be the result of the deferral effect alone. For this purpose, dispersion among different stocks in rates of accrual, and variation from case to case in the length of time for which a stock is held, may be safely ignored. The deferral effect in a portfolio with a constant accrual rate and a steady first-in-first-out rollover of shares, each sold after it has been held a given constant period of time, is sufficient to illustrate the point.

If the entire portfolio were sold and reconstituted at least once every year, then all capital gains accrued during the year prior to such sale would be realized; the ratio of realization to accrual would be 1.0 at the time of sale. For small deviations from once-a-year sale, the ratio would continue to be approximately 1.0. For example, if complete turnover occurred every two years, with half being sold

TABLE 1. Estimated Value of All Corporate Shares, Accrued and Realized Capital Gains, and Corporate Retained Earnings, 1925–61
(Figures other than price index in billions of dollars)

Year	Aggregate value of shares, year-end[a] (1)	Composite price index, year-end[b] (1941–43 = 10) (2)	Accrued capital gains on shares[c] (3)	Total realized capital gains[d] (4)	True retained earnings in corporations[e] (5)
1925	102.8	12.76	—	—	—
1926	114.4	13.49	5.88	1.87	—
1927	148.2	17.66	35.36	2.36	—
1928	201.1	24.35	56.14	4.56	—
1929	192.8	21.45	−23.95	2.93	2.08
1930	146.1	15.34	−54.92	−1.38	−3.37
1931	79.5	8.12	−68.76	−2.75	−5.70
1932	67.9	6.89	−12.04	−2.71	−5.94
1933	98.6	10.10	31.64	−1.42	−2.27
1934	94.0	9.50	−5.86	−0.64	−1.60
1935	121.1	13.43	38.89	−0.09	−0.84
1936	147.3	17.18	33.81	0.60	−0.23
1937	90.2	10.55	−56.85	−0.11	−0.02
1938	104.0	13.21	22.74	−0.35	−0.88
1939	97.1	12.49	−5.67	−0.27	1.18
1940	87.6	10.58	−14.85	−0.44	2.49
1941	74.8	8.69	−15.65	−0.91	4.93
1942	81.1	9.77	9.30	−0.38	4.98
1943	99.5	11.67	15.77	1.07	5.67
1944	116.0	13.28	13.73	1.62	5.48
1945	154.2	17.36	35.64	4.37	3.31
1946	143.4	15.30	−18.30	6.67	9.09
1947	142.8	15.30	0	4.44	12.86
1948	140.1	15.20	−0.93	4.45	14.40
1949	159.4	16.76	14.38	3.19	9.90
1950	196.1	20.41	34.71	6.19	14.48
1951	228.9	23.77	32.28	6.40	11.22
1952	251.8	26.57	26.96	5.29	8.98
1953	245.2	24.81	−16.68	4.34	9.16
1954	353.4	35.98	110.39	7.48	8.64
1955	434.1	45.48	93.31	10.56	13.45
1956	458.1	46.67	11.36	10.14	12.55
1957	408.8	39.99	−65.57	7.77	10.57
1958	578.3	55.21	155.59	9.64	6.89
1959	643.1	59.89	49.02	13.91	11.74
1960	641.6	58.11	−19.11	11.71	8.86
1961	810.5	71.55	148.39	—	8.86

each year, the accrual on each half at the time of sale would be almost double what it would have been if the previous sale of that half had been only one year earlier instead of two. Thus the almost doubled capital gain per unit of portfolio sold nearly offsets the halved annual volume of sale, keeping realizations close to the unchanged annual accrual. As the holding period is increased and the annual turnover reduced, however, this approximation becomes less accurate and the ratio of realizations to accruals falls. If the rate of accrual per year is r and if (for example) the holding period is lengthened to $(1 + r)/r$,

---

NOTES TO TABLE 1

[a] The value of all stocks listed on the New York Stock Exchange, as reported by Standard and Poor's Corporation (*Standard and Poor's Trade and Securities Statistics, Banking and Finance*, Vol. 31, No. 9, Sec. 2 [September 1965], p. 28), multiplied by factors obtained for the years 1929, 1933, 1939, 1945, and 1949, using Raymond W. Goldsmith, *A Study of Saving in the United States*, Vol. 3 (Princeton University Press, 1956), Table W–18, p. 60. The ratios of the Goldsmith figures for common and preferred stocks to the Standard and Poor's figures were almost the same for 1929 and 1933, and again for 1939, 1945, and 1949. For the first two dates the ratios averaged 2.98; this was the factor used for 1925–33. For the latter three dates the ratios averaged 2.09, which was the factor used for 1939–61. For the years 1934–38 the factors used were 2.77, 2.58, 2.46, 2.35, and 2.19, respectively. These factors were obtained by using the liabilities of business failures as reported in U.S. Department of Commerce, Office of Business Economics, *Business Statistics*, various issues, to interpolate between 2.98 and 2.09. In this interpolation, for a year in which business failures were large, the factor was reduced by a correspondingly large amount (the yearly cumulated liabilities between 1934 and 1939 were divided by total liabilities for that period; the resulting ratios were used to distribute the difference between 2.98 and 2.09 among the years).

[b] Standard and Poor's Corporation, *Standard and Poor's Trade and Securities Statistics, Security Price Index Record* (1966), p. 4.

[c] Previous year-end aggregate value of shares (column 1), multiplied by the difference between the current year-end stock price index and the previous year-end stock price index (column 2), and divided by the previous year-end stock price index. That is,

$$C_t = V_{t-1}\left(\frac{p_t}{p_{t-1}} - 1\right)$$

where C_t is accrued capital gains on shares in the current year, V_{t-1} is aggregate value of shares at the end of the previous year, p_t is stock price index at the end of the current year, and p_{t-1} is stock price index at the end of the previous year. This procedure understates capital gains slightly because it omits gains on new issues during the current year.

Although gains, if perfectly measured, would be algebraically less than the change in column 1 by the amount of new issues, the incomplete coverage of the Standard and Poor's price index (column 2) means that the correspondence will be less than perfect. For example, the 1947 value in column 1 is less than the 1946 value, but the index from 1946 to 1947 held steady; and in other years the implied new issues are implausible. However, these errors may be assumed to cancel each other over the whole period.

[d] Basic data for this series are from U.S. Treasury Department, Internal Revenue Service, *Statistics of Income, Individual Income Tax Returns* and *Fiduciary Income Tax Returns*, or equivalent combined volumes for the respective years. Lawrence H. Seltzer, in *The Nature and Tax Treatment of Capital Gains and Losses* (National Bureau of Economic Research, 1951), p. 367, presents a combined table of the official data for 1917–46, with details about changes in tax regulations and reporting concepts. Data for all returns, including those with statutory net deficits, begin only in 1928. Corresponding 1926–27 totals were estimated by the regression method, using 1928–46 values for returns with statutory net deficits as the dependent variable, and the values for the returns with statutory net incomes as the independent variable. "Excess of gain" was the pertinent concept throughout.

Seltzer's data, and the later data through 1951, include only taxable fiduciaries. Reports on all fiduciaries appear for 1952, 1954, 1956, and 1958, but there are no reports for other years since 1951. On the basis of information on non-taxable fiduciaries contained in these recent even-year reports, approximately 1 percent was added to the grand totals for all years prior to 1952 to adjust for the exclusion of non-taxable fiduciaries in those years. Fiduciary capital gains for the years in which they are missing were estimated by the regression method from individual capital gains for 1945–58, using trend as an additional independent variable. Although these estimating methods are bound to involve errors, the magnitudes involved are small. Incomparabilities over time due to changes in concept, explained by Seltzer, pp. 321–56, are a more serious and intractable problem.

[e] Estimated from data on retained earnings and on depreciation allowances of corporations as reported in U.S. Department of Commerce, Office of Business Economics, *Survey of Current Business*, Vol. 45 (August 1965), Table 11, pp. 40–41. The former were adjusted by the assumed error in the latter by 17.6 percent, based on the estimate from George Terborgh that depreciation allowance in 1953 should have been 18.3 percent higher. See Appendix A.

the total proceeds of sale each year equals the annual accrual. Since the cost basis (that is, value at previous time of purchase) of the sold assets is greater than zero, the realized capital gain is evidently less than the year's accrual. For example, at an annual rate of accrual of 5 percent (compounded annually), the cost basis of an asset held twenty-one years is 0.36 of its sale price, and the ratio of realized to accrued capital gain is 0.64, as can be verified by applying equation (1) below.

For a general formulation of this ratio, let T be the holding period and hence $1/T$ the fraction of the portfolio sold each year. The cost basis per unit sold is $1/(1 + r)^T$, and the annual accrual per unit of portfolio is $1 - 1/(1 + r) = r/(1 + r)$. The ratio R of realized capital gains to accruals is therefore

$$(1) \qquad R = \frac{1 - 1/(1 + r)^T}{rT/(1 + r)} = \frac{1 + r - (1 + r)^{1-T}}{rT}.$$

One can readily verify that $R = 1$ when $T = 1$. Values of R given by equation (1) for holding periods T ranging from one to 100 years and for rates of accrual r of 2 percent, 5 percent, and 8 percent appear in Chart 1.

It is apparent at once that the deferral effect, illustrated in Chart 1, cannot by itself explain the very low estimated ratio of realizations to accruals in corporate shares. None of the curves, not even the lowest one, falls below 0.12 within the range shown on the chart. If the deferral effect alone is relied upon, the estimate of the average time corporate shares are held between sales would have to be well over 100 years! This result is clearly unacceptable; therefore it must be concluded that gift and succession (and possibly evasion) account for a considerable part of the difference between realizations and accruals.

Although there is no way to determine exactly the relative roles of deferral and avoidance in reducing the ratio of realizations to accruals, it is possible to set plausible limits on the importance of avoidance. To do that two alternative models of behavior are considered, each involving a succession effect but differing in the extent to which there is also a deferral effect. In the first model there is no deferral effect at all, so that all the explaining is done by the succession effect. In the second model there is a maximum deferral effect, so that the role of avoidance through succession is minimal. In both models it is assumed that succession occurs every forty years on the average,

CHART 1. Ratio of Capital Gains Realizations to Accruals as a Function of Interest Rate and Holding Period

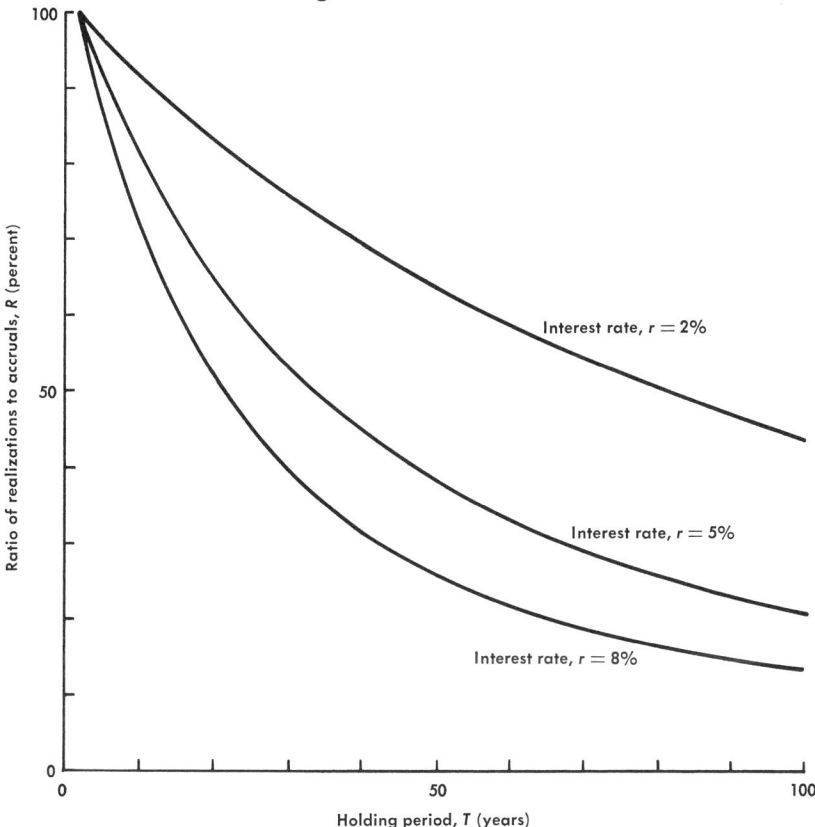

Source: Equation (1) in text, p. 20. See also Appendix Table B-1.

and that the typical portfolio adds new shares at a rate of 3 percent a year by saving from dividends and other income; that is, that the rate of new issues is 3 percent annually of the value of the market.

In the first model it is assumed simply that no one sells any share held for more than one year, but that in the aggregate, 10 percent of all previously existing shares are sold each year. Because the total value of shares is increased 3 percent each year through newly purchased new issues, 13 percent by value of all shares in a typical portfolio have been purchased the previous year. Of these, some ten-thirteenths are sold again the next year, and again 3 percent is added to the total portfolio through new issues. All other shares are held until succession. Because the shares that are resold have been held only one year before resale, on these shares realizations equal one year's accruals exactly. The accruals on these shares are precisely 10 percent of total accruals, assuming they gain value at the same average rate as the portfolio as a whole. The accruals on the other 90 percent of all shares that are not resold before succession go permanently unrealized for capital gains tax purposes.

In the second model an opposite extreme is assumed: that everyone sells his entire previously inherited estate just before he dies, and bequests without resale the shares purchased during his lifetime. This behavior implies a very low turnover of shares, compared to the previous model which implied a 10 percent turnover annually. With a forty-year period between successions, 2.5 percent of the wealth passes by succession each year. With the assumed rate of accumulation through savings of 3 percent per year, wealth at succession is $(1.03)^{40}$ times, or about three times, the current value of the previous inheritance, and turnover is therefore one-third of 2.5 percent, or about 0.8 percent.[5] With this behavior the ratio of realizations to accruals is just one-third what it would be if *all* shares had constructive realization for tax purposes after forty years; that is, the ratio is one-third the value given by equation (1) and shown in Chart 1. For the 7.60 percent annual accrual rate observed in the period 1926–61, the ratio of realizations to accruals given by this model would be one-third of 0.33, or some 11 percent. This is approximately the ratio observed in that period. Thus with this extreme model, which maximizes the deferral effect because all shares sold are held for forty years, two-thirds of all shares pass from one generation to the next without constructive realization. This fraction is about the minimum that can be reconciled with the observed low ratio of realizations to accruals. If within reason the assumed period between successions is shortened, the fraction can be lowered only a little.

The true behavior of the community must be between these two extremes, because not all shares sold have been held for as long as forty years or for as short a period as one year. As shown in Table A–1, long-term capital gains on corporate shares sold in 1959 were

---

[5] Turnover reported on the New York Stock Exchange (NYSE) has run at a rate of some 15 percent per year since World War II. On other exchanges it is probably considerably lower, and could well be lower on the NYSE if it were weighted by value. Some of the turnover is undoubtedly multiple turnover within a single year. Probably the relevant figure would come out between the two figures given by our extreme models.

some $5 billion, which was about 30 percent of the gross sales value of those shares of $17 billion.[6] This fraction of gain implies an average holding period before sale of about four years at most, not forty. Consequently it may fairly be inferred that the proportion of shares whose gains avoid tax through succession is well above two-thirds, and less than nine-tenths.

An alternative behavior model specifies that inheritors reshuffle their portfolios immediately at the time of inheritance to whatever extent they desire (because they can do so without incurring capital gains taxes); thereafter they turn over their portfolios and add to them out of savings at constant annual rates, with their sales distributed randomly—that is, without regard to the length of time the individual shares have been held. If the average time span between legal successions is forty years, the annual turnover of shares 2 percent of the total, and the annual rate of new issues 3 percent, nearly 60 percent of all shares inherited or purchased from savings are held (except for possible sales, as mentioned, at the time of inheritance) for the entire lifetime of the purchaser. The ratio of realizations to accruals, *apart* from the deferral effect, is about 20 percent, and the deferral effect reduces it to about 14 percent, at the rate of accrual observed in Table 1. (The arithmetic leading to these results is tiresome, and need not be set down here.) This figure of 14 percent is still high compared to the estimate of a 10 percent ratio of realizations to accruals, but is close enough for purposes of illustration. The turnover rate, including new issues, rollover, and sales at the time of inheritance lies between 5 and 7 percent, depending on the third of these items; this figure is reasonable, though perhaps low.

Although for the period 1926–61 the rate of accruals ran over 7 percent, as noted above, for a much longer period the accrual rate has been lower. In Appendix A it is shown that the real rate of accruals since 1871 has been under 3 percent, and the real rate of retentions just over 2 percent, of market value. These values are probably closer to what can be expected in the future. If so, and if the behavior pattern suggested in the preceding paragraph is the relevant

---

[6] Since this table was prepared, the 1962 data have been released. The corresponding figure was less than 35 percent. It was low that year because of the stock market decline. U.S. Treasury Department, Internal Revenue Service, *Statistics of Income—1962, Supplemental Report, Sales of Capital Assets Reported on Individual Income Tax Returns* (1966), pp. 61 and 87.

one, the ratio of realizations to accruals will rise to nearly 20 percent on the average.

Regardless of the behavior pattern that results in the observed low ratio of realizations to accruals, it is evident that the expected rate of capital gains tax at the time of a purchase of shares—the rate appropriate for evaluating announcement effects—is lower than the capital gains tax rate at the time it is collected. This is so, first, because the prospective rate is reduced in the proportion of the typical portfolio which is expected at acquisition time to be held for the lifetime of its holder. Second, even the part that will be sold enjoys a reduction in effective tax rate due to a deferral effect similar in nature to that discussed above in connection with the ratio of realizations to accruals.

For evaluating the deferral effect on the effective capital gains tax rate (that is, the rate appropriate for evaluation of announcement effects), the proportion by which the tax reduces the expected annual accrual rate must be determined. That is, the implied annual rate of accrual net of ultimate tax must be compared with the rate of accrual before tax; the proportion by which the former rate of accrual is less than the latter is the effective capital gains tax rate, g. The capital on realization after T years per unit of initial investment is $(1 + r)^T$, and the net capital after tax, say C_T, is

$$C_T = [(1 + r)^T - 1][1 - t_g] + 1 = (1 - t_g)(1 + r)^T + t_g,$$

where r is the expected accrual rate and t_g is the capital gains tax rate at the time of realization. The annual net or tax-free rate of accrual, s, that would generate this value of C_T is

$$s = \sqrt[T]{C_T} - 1.$$

Finally,

(2) $$g = \frac{r - s}{r} = 1 - \frac{s}{r}.$$

That g depends on both r and T is illustrated in Chart 2, which plots g against T for various values of r, for the case $t_g = 0.25$. The scale on the right measures g. The scale on the left measures g/t_g; that is, it measures the proportion by which delaying realization reduces the effective (discounted) burden of the capital gains tax. Using the left-hand scale, this proportionate reduction may be com-

CHART 2. Effective Rate of Capital Gains Tax for a Realization Rate of 25 Percent as a Function of Interest Rate and Holding Period

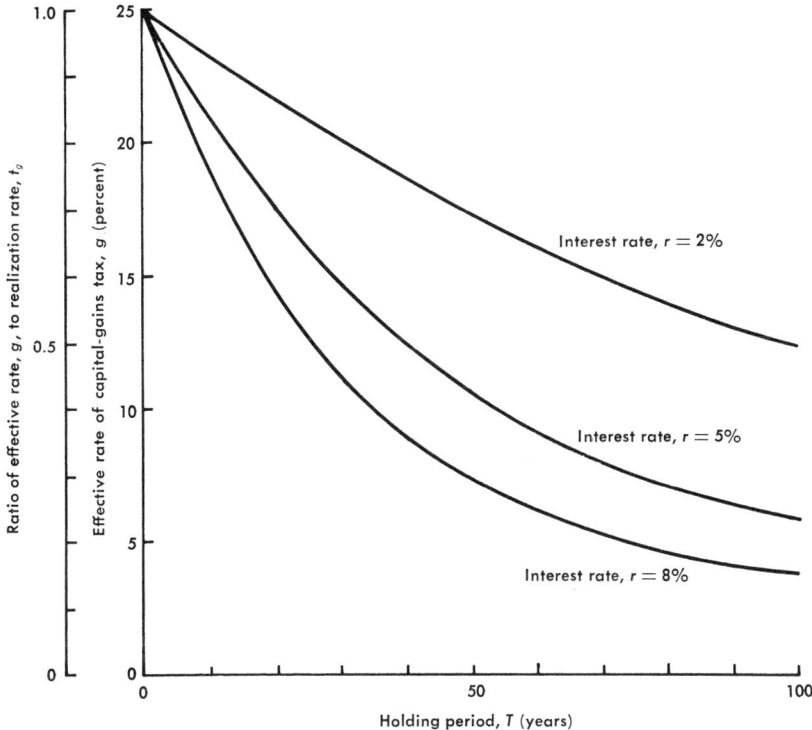

pared with the corresponding reduction in realizations relative to accruals for the same r and T, shown in Chart 1. The reduction in g/t_g, shown in Chart 2, is about the same as that for the ratio of realizations to accruals, because both reflect the effects of compound interest in a similar way.

This correspondence between g and Rt_g is a considerable convenience, because for many problems R is much easier to calculate than is g. It can be shown that such variations as reduction in realizations due to gift and succession and variation in holding periods among different shares affect R and g proportionately the same to a first approximation.[7] Consequently Rt_g is a good rule-of-thumb estimator for g.

In the case under consideration, these results indicate that the value of g implied by the 1926–61 ratio of realizations to accruals

[7] See Appendix B.

would be of the order of 0.05 for persons using the alternative tax—that is, those for whom t_g is 0.25. Under the more likely condition that a real rate of capital gains accruals in the range from 2 to 3 percent is expected, g is of the order of 0.08 or 0.09.

For the purposes of analyzing announcement effects, then, the prospective capital gains tax rate can be taken to be well under 10 percent, unless there is some reason to expect realizations to rise to almost four times their 1926-60 ratio to accruals. (From 1951 to 1960, the ratio averaged about 23 percent, or some 30 percent for 1954-60 if the SEC data are used instead of those in column 1 of Table 1.) In any case, this tax rate is readily and reliably estimated from the prospective ratio of realizations to accruals, multiplied by the tax rate at realization time. Further, it is difficult, if not impossible, to reconcile the observed low ratios of realizations to accruals with a behavior pattern involving less than about half of all purchased and/or inherited shares being held until gift or subsequent succession, except for possible unreported transactions.

Effect of Taxes on Corporate Rate of Return

Next to be considered is the combined impact of all taxes on income from corporate equity, as distinguished from other equity.[8] The investor who operates a sole proprietorship or who participates in a partnership pays (only the) personal income tax on all net income of the business, whether it is reinvested in the business or not. The investor who owns corporate shares has deducted from his portion of the corporation's net income before taxes its corporation income tax liability; he then pays personal income tax on any dividends paid out to him by the corporation, and expects to pay capital gains tax on the increase in value, if any, which accrues between the purchase and the resale of any of the shares. The proportion of earnings taken by these combined taxes varies according to the marginal personal income tax rate of the taxpayer, the proportion of earnings paid out by the corporation, and the extent to which the taxpayer realizes his accrued capital gains, among other things. If the proportion of earnings taken exceeds the taxpayer's marginal personal income tax rate, the combination of tax provisions for his corporate earnings involves to that extent an extra tax relative to his income from other sources.

---

[8] The calculations in this and subsequent sections were based on individual and corporation income tax rates applying to the years 1954 through 1963.

The combined tax rate on a taxpayer's share of corporate earnings is the sum of the corporation income tax rate, his marginal personal income tax rate times the fraction of the corporation's earnings paid out in dividends, and his effective (discounted) capital gains tax rate times the fraction of earnings retained. More precisely, if this combined effective rate is expressed symbolically using the following notation,

t^* = the effective marginal tax rate on corporate earnings
t = the taxpayer's marginal personal income tax rate
p = the expected (average) ratio of corporate dividends to corporate earnings, or the payout ratio
c = the corporation income tax rate
g = the effective marginal tax rate on capital gains, discounted on account of deferred liability and avoidance

(3) $$t^* = c + tp(1 - c) + g(1 - p)(1 - c).$$

This rate will vary from one taxpayer to the next, because t and g differ according to the taxpayer's taxable income. Also the taxpayer may choose among traded shares of corporations on the basis of expected payout ratios, which are known to differ from one corporation to the next. Specifically, the derivative of t^* with respect to the payout ratio is

(4) $$\frac{dt^*}{dp} = (t - g)(1 - c).$$

Because for practical purposes c is the same for all taxpayers, and because t exceeds g under present tax laws, this result implies not only that the higher the payout ratio the higher is t^*, but also that the effect of p on t^* is greater the greater is the excess of t over g. Under present tax laws the excess of t over g is uniformly greater when t is greater. Thus all taxpayers have a tax incentive to hold shares in corporations with relatively low expected payout ratios, and this incentive is greater the higher the marginal personal income tax rate of the taxpayer, other things being equal.

Parallel to possible differences in the payout ratio associated with differences in individual taxpayers' marginal personal income tax rates, there may be differences among taxpayers in their expected holding periods. Under existing income tax laws the tax rate on realized long-term capital gains is half the marginal personal income tax rate when the latter is less than 50 percent, and is otherwise 25 percent.[9] That is, the tax rate on realized long-term capital gains increases with the personal income tax rate up to a point; accordingly a greater tax incentive for deferral of realization exists when t is high than when it is low.

If it were not for uncertainty about the relationship between t and p and about the relationship between t and the holding period, a simple relationship between t^* and t could be obtained from equation (3). In particular, if p and the holding period were constant for taxpayers in all personal income tax brackets, as c is assumed to be, then t would be the only variable on the right-hand side of equation (3). The uncertainty involved is in a known direction, however, because the direction of the incentives to alter p and the holding period are known. As a first approximation these effects can usefully be disregarded, and it can then duly be noted how they would modify the results if exact data on them existed.

Estimation of the value for t^* follows. Assumed are a payout ratio, p, of 0.5, which reflects the recent practice of the corporate sector, and the observed values of the realization ratio R given in the preceding section. For these assumed representative values of p and R, Chart 3 shows the relationship between t^* and t for all marginal personal income tax rates, t, from 0.18 to 0.90. At a marginal rate of about 0.70 the taxpayer expects to retain net of tax as high a percentage of his share of corporate earnings as he does from unincorporated business; at lower marginal rates the corporate income tax imposes a net additional tax, and at higher marginal rates unincorporated business suffers the higher rate of tax. At no positive marginal tax rate is the excess of t^* over t as high as 0.52 (the excess being the vertical distance between the curve and the 45° line); at a t of zero, t^* would be precisely 0.52. In fact even this additional tax as a proportion of income *after* personal income tax—that is, $(t^* - t)/(1 - t)$, is also less than 0.52. Hence the additional tax rate imposed by the corporation income tax, either as a proportion of income before any tax or as a proportion of income that would remain after simply a

---

[9] Several colleagues have pointed out to me that this statement, and statements elsewhere, that the maximum marginal tax rate on long-term capital gains is 25 percent, is inaccurate when capital gains are a sufficiently large fraction of a taxpayer's income to straddle and exceed the 50 percent bracket. Because of the all-or-nothing character of the alternative tax on long-term capital gains, such a taxpayer will elect it only after his marginal rate exceeds 50 percent.

CHART 3. Effective Combined Tax Rate on Income from Corporate Equity and Effective Marginal Tax Rate on Capital Gains as a Function of Marginal Personal Income Tax Rates

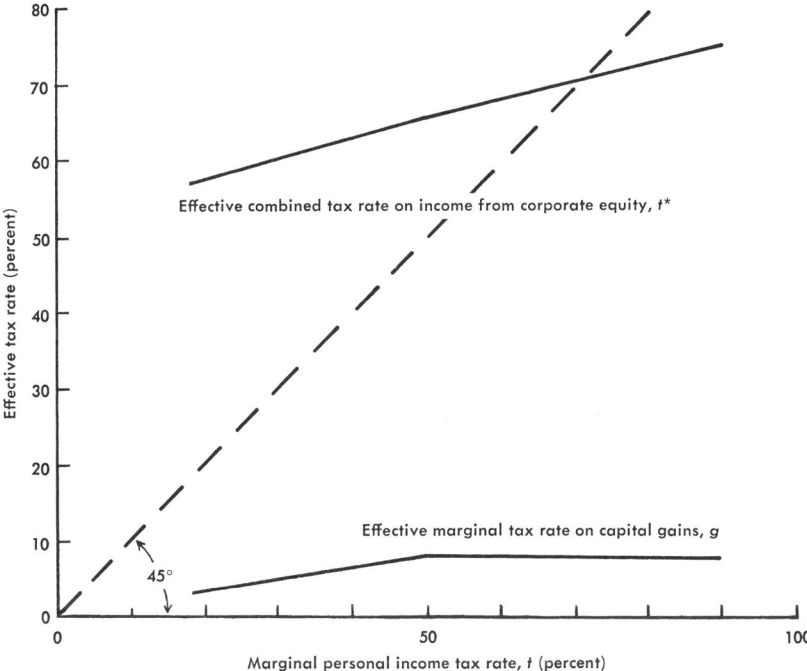

personal income tax, is less than the nominal rate of corporation income tax when the personal income tax is not zero. The additional tax is still substantial, however, at the more moderate rates of personal income tax applying to the majority of taxpayers.

How is the curve in Chart 3 modified by a tendency for taxpayers to respond to the tax incentives to lengthen holding periods and to favor low payout ratios? We noted that both these incentives are stronger for the taxpayer with a high t than for one with a low t. Hence a response to these incentives will mean that taxpayers with higher incomes will have a lower R and lower p than will taxpayers with lower incomes; that is, taxpayers with higher incomes will have a lower R and lower p than average, whereas taxpayers with lower incomes will have a higher R and higher p than average. These tendencies lower t^* along the upper part of the scale and raise it along the lower part (although they have no effect on the taxpayer who expects to pay no personal income tax).

Net Rates of Return and Incentive Effects of the Corporation Income Tax

If there were no special economic advantages to incorporation or to remaining unincorporated in any industry or line of business, the choice would be determined by tax considerations. An absence of economic advantage either way amounts to saying that the production function is the same for both. Furthermore, it is to be presumed that both incorporated and unincorporated businesses would pay the same price for a given input and would receive the same price for a given product. Consequently the rate of return before taxes would be the same for both types of business producing the same product. Rates of return might differ among industries because of considerations of risk or for related economic reasons, but not because of any tendency for taxpayers in any given tax bracket to concentrate their holdings in any one industry. If an industry did have a higher rate of return than other industries with similar risk and related characteristics, low-income and high-income taxpayers alike with holdings in such other industries would be attracted to the high-return industry until its rate of return fell into line with the others.

In such a world, rates of return before taxes would be the same in all industries, except for risk considerations and the like, and rates of return before taxes would be the same for incorporated and unincorporated businesses. The same would be true if there were deviations from competition—for example, if there were formal or tacit cartel arrangements in some industries. In that case the rate of return might be higher than otherwise, but the firms in the cartel could be either incorporated or unincorporated. Consequently incorporation would exist solely as a device for lowering the tax rate, t^*, on the highest-income taxpayers. If the parameters used in the preceding section for deriving the values of t^* for different t's are the appropriate ones, it would be observed that all corporate shares were held exclusively by taxpayers with anticipated marginal income tax rates of 70 percent or over, and that such taxpayers would hold no interest in unincorporated business.

In any calendar year the above conclusion would have to be qualified because of year-to-year fluctuations in income. Income from business enterprise fluctuates from year to year; taxpayers who expect to be under but near the 70 percent bracket in a typical year will earn enough to exceed that level in exceptionally good years, and taxpayers who expect to be just over the 70 percent bracket in a typical year will sometimes fall below that level. Measured incomes as reported on personal income tax forms will be misleading to that extent regarding the taxpayers' long-run expectations and adjustments thereto. Some taxpayers who report incomes over the 70 percent bracket in any given year will have had an exceptionally good year, and some who report incomes below that level will have had an exceptionally poor year. Consequently it is reasonable to expect to find some income from unincorporated enterprises reported among incomes over the 70 percent tax bracket, and some income from the ownership of corporate shares among incomes below that level. The latter tendency should be slight, however, because dividend income has little variability and because capital losses may be set off against other income only to a maximum of $1,000 per taxpayer.

The data support these expectations only in a rough and partial fashion. Chart 4 shows the percentage of adjusted gross incomes from

CHART 4. Percentages of Total Adjusted Gross Income from Unincorporated and Incorporated Enterprises, by Adjusted Gross Income Classes, 1959

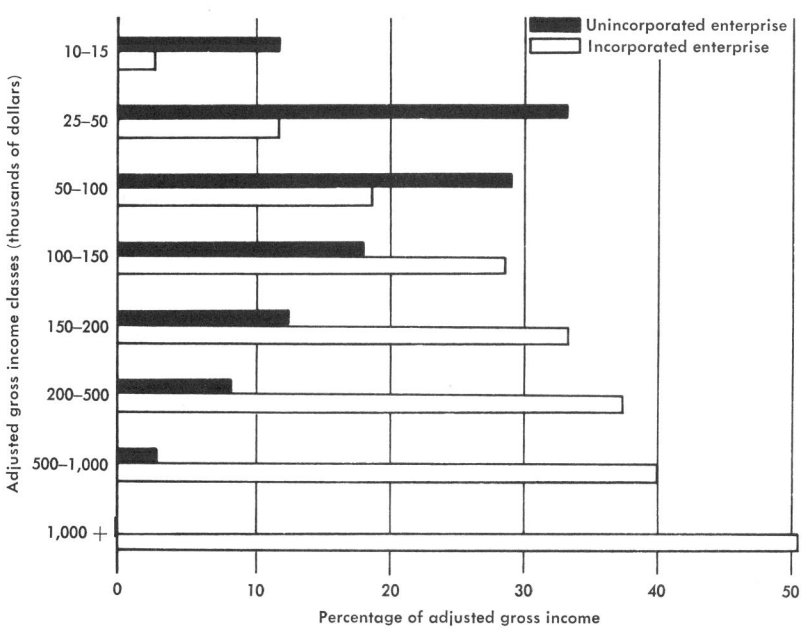

the two sources just discussed, by adjusted gross income classes, for 1959. The 70 percent marginal income tax rate becomes applicable at adjusted gross incomes roughly in the range from $50,000 to $60,000, depending on circumstances specific to each taxpayer. Just about as the analysis of t^* suggested, the importance of income from unincorporated enterprise drops sharply, and that from dividends jumps sharply, for incomes above the $50,000 level. For adjusted gross incomes over $100,000, dividends exceed proprietary income in relative importance; and if capital gains were included, income from corporate shares would exceed proprietary income for adjusted gross incomes in the $50,000 to $100,000 group. The failure of proprietary income to fall off more rapidly as incomes rise over the $50,000 level might be rationalized in terms of the variability of business incomes. However, variability alone cannot be relied upon to rationalize the substantial importance of dividend income (and, as noted below, of capital gains) in the income range from $10,000 to $50,000. In that range dividends provide income equal to about one-fourth the amount coming from proprietary sources; and the detailed data of the *Statistics of Income* show that some 25 percent of all dividends reported by individuals in past years were reported by those with adjusted gross incomes less than $15,000.

This phenomenon is not difficult to rationalize. It is very likely true that diseconomies of scale in the partnership form of business combined with a large minimum efficient size of firm in some industries effectively restrict those industries to the corporate form of business. Similarly, in some industries the minimum efficient size of firm may be small enough to permit the operation of partnerships, but only very wealthy ones (whose owners, say, were just below the 70 percent bracket). These would then suffer no competition from partnerships and proprietorships headed by taxpayers in the lower-income tax brackets, and could thus maintain higher rates of return to capital than those attainable in industries where very small firms can operate. Hence it could be true that taxpayers in the lower-income levels would have opportunities for investment in unincorporated business only at rates of return lower than those attained by higher-income taxpayers and by corporations (before taxes). Because of this lower rate of return they would be willing also to hold corporate shares.

(For example, casual observation suggests that most salaried persons with incomes in the range from $5,000 to $50,000 have virtually no opportunities worth considering to enter into proprietary business, except in the ownership of their homes. If so, it is understandable that such salaried persons should hold substantial amounts of corporate shares even when the mortgages on their homes are not paid off, and especially when their capital exceeds the value of their homes.)

If after-tax yields to the individual taxpayer on capital employed in corporate and unincorporated enterprise are the same, it must be concluded from the evidence that the before-tax yield on capital employed in unincorporated enterprise rises with the marginal personal income tax rate of the taxpayer. The proportionate difference between this yield and the yield before taxes on corporate capital measures the tax inducement for capital to move into unincorporated enterprise instead of corporate enterprise. This inducement is thus not a simple number but a schedule dependent on the income level of the owner of the capital. In particular, if r_u is the return before tax to capital in unincorporated enterprise and r_c is the return before tax to capital in corporate enterprise, $r_u(1 - t) = r_c(1 - t^*)$, or

(5) $$\frac{r_u}{r_c} = \frac{1 - t^*}{1 - t}.$$

Equation (5) is shown graphically in Chart 5. The curve terminates in the neighborhood of $r_u/r_c = 1$; that is, where $t^* = t$, because beyond this point it pays the unincorporated enterprise to incorporate (apart from legal costs and the like in so doing).

The upshot of this analysis is that the resource allocation effects of the corporation income tax, combined with the special treatment of capital gains, differ according to the income levels of the holders of corporate equity. The overall effect is accordingly more complex than would be the case if the tax impact created a uniform difference between the rates of return to unincorporated and corporate enterprise.

Note on the Progressivity of the Personal Income Tax

In a recent study Musgrave found that the tendency to progressivity in the personal income tax, when he counted all long-term capital gains as income, is remarkably moderate.[10] His earlier finding

[10] Richard A. Musgrave, "How Progressive Is the Income Tax?" in *Tax Revision Compendium*, House Committee on Ways and Means, 86 Cong. 1 sess. (1959), Vol. 3, pp. 2223–33.

CHART 5. Ratio of Before-Tax Rate of Return to Capital in Unincorporated Enterprise to Before-Tax Rate of Return to Capital in Corporate Enterprise, as a Function of Marginal Personal Income Tax Rate

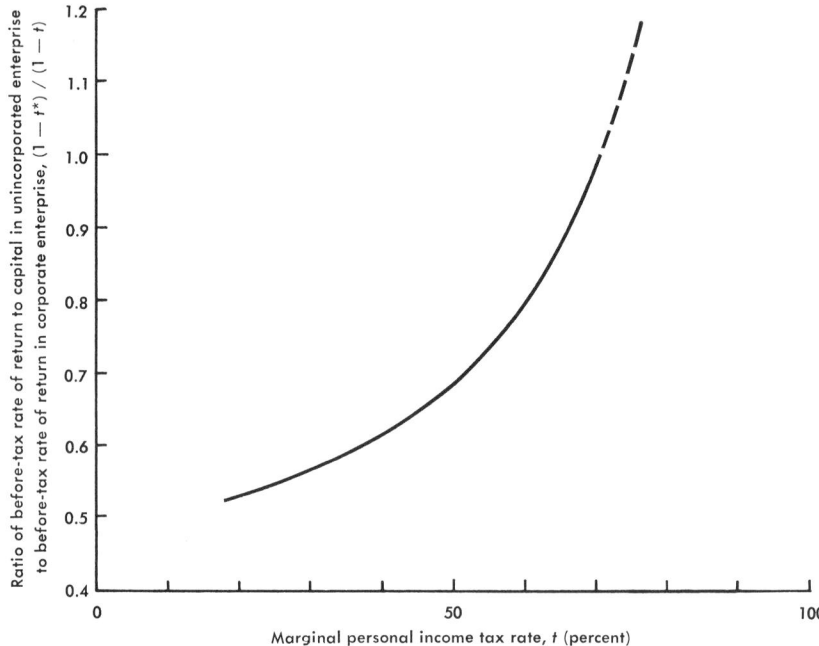

had been that the impact of the remainder of the tax structure in this country is predominantly regressive.[11] Consequently a question arises whether the overall tax structure is or is not progressive. Furthermore, the analysis of this study raises further doubt about the degree of progressivity of the personal income tax. Musgrave's calculation included only realized capital gains in income, which, as noted above, are less than accruals. It would therefore be logical to consider how Musgrave's calculation would differ if all accruals of capital gains were included in income for the purpose of determining the ratio of taxes to income.

In Musgrave's calculation, the maximum percentage of adjusted gross income taken by the personal income tax was below 50 percent when averages were computed for each adjusted gross income class; the maximum occurs in the income range over $500,000. When the

---

[11] Richard A. Musgrave, "The Incidence of the Tax Structure and Its Effects on Consumption," in *Federal Tax Policy for Economic Growth and Stability*, Joint Committee on the Economic Report, 84 Cong. 1 sess. (1955), pp. 96–113.

tax-excluded 50 percent of long-term capital gains is added to adjusted gross income, the maximum average tax rate falls to around 36 percent.[12] In view of our finding, above, that realizations run less than 10 percent of accruals, the effect, on the calculated average tax rate on these high incomes, of including all accruals (instead of realizations alone) in the base income would evidently be spectacular.

Because a thorough analysis of the progressivity of the tax structure is outside the scope of this study, the indicated calculation has not been made, nor have the other possible calculations and adjustments that would be necessary for such analysis. However, I shall note some of the ways in which the remarks above should be qualified. First, it must be supposed that at least some of the incidence of the corporation income tax falls on capital; Harberger concluded that most of it does.[13] If so, its impact is progressive because the share of income from capital rises with total income. Second, some capital gains accruals have been nominal rather than real, and thus are not income in any pertinent sense. Income from unincorporated enterprise could also include a nominal element, but for the middle- and lower-income groups as a whole any such nominal element is bound to be of minor importance. Third, a true measure of tax incidence should take into account reductions in income before taxes that the taxpayer willingly accepts in order to maximize his income after taxes. For example, upper-income taxpayers sometimes hold tax-exempt municipal bonds, whose yields are lower than those of other bonds of comparable quality and term. Any such reduction in before-tax income is the same in effect to the taxpayer as a tax; a true calculation of tax incidence would compare the taxpayer's after-tax income with what his before-tax income would be if he maximized it (holding risk and the like constant).

The considerations just mentioned qualify our proposition that the income tax is much less progressive than it seems. However, there are also considerations that tend to strengthen it. It was noted in the discussion of t^*—the combined tax taken from income earned in corporate enterprise—that higher-income taxpayers have an incentive

---

[12] Musgrave, "How Progressive Is the Income Tax?" p. 2226, Table 2, columns 1 and 2. Column 2 also reflects the inclusion of some interest and dividends assumed to escape tax at present; however, the numerical magnitude involved is small.

[13] Arnold C. Harberger, "The Incidence of the Corporation Income Tax," *Journal of Political Economy*, Vol. 70 (June 1962), pp. 215–40.

to buy shares in corporations with low payout ratios ("growth" stocks) and to have low ratios of realizations to accruals. To the extent that their response increases with these incentives, taxpayers reduce the progressivity of the income tax.

Chart 6 shows the average ratio of total long-term capital gains to total dividends reported in the years 1954–60, by adjusted gross income classes. This ratio tends to fall with rising incomes up to the neighborhood of $100,000 and then to rise sharply for the still higher incomes. That is, relative to dividend receipts, a disproportionately large share of realized long-term capital gains is concentrated among the lowest and the highest incomes. This curve is readily interpreted in the light of the different incentives faced by taxpayers in the different adjusted gross income classes. (The sources of the long-term capital gains are immaterial to the analysis of these data.)

Three main factors have a bearing on what sort of tendency one would expect to find in the data shown in Chart 6. First, capital gains realizations are more volatile than dividend receipts. Therefore a regression phenomenon should result in a greater concentration of capital gains realizations than of dividends in the upper levels of adjusted gross income (which, as calculated, include half of realized long-term capital gains). Second, the greater incentive for the higher-income groups to accrue as much income as possible in the form of

CHART 6. Average Ratio of Total Long-Term Capital Gains Reported to Total Dividends Reported, by Adjusted Gross Income Classes, 1954–60

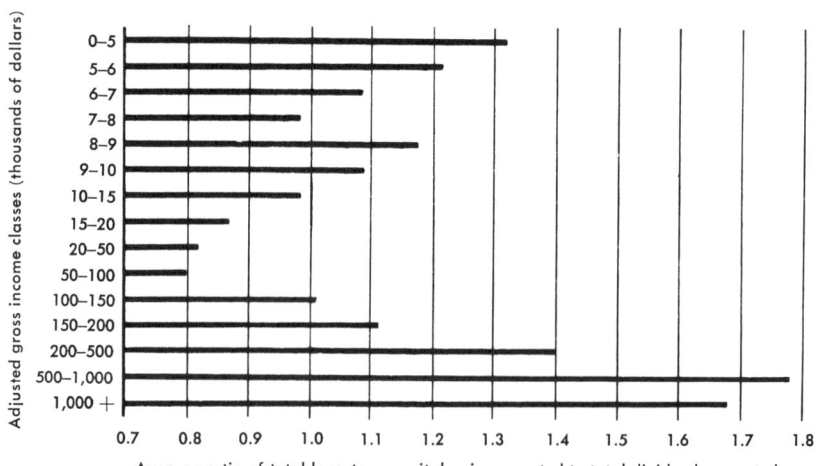

long-term capital gains (for example, through holding "growth" stocks rather than "income" stocks) implies a lower ratio of dividends to long-term capital gains for the higher-income groups than for the lower-income groups. Both these factors imply a rising trend for the curve shown in Chart 6. Third, however, it was noted that the upper-income groups have a greater incentive to minimize realizations than the lower-income groups, although this incentive is the same for everyone above the 50 percent tax bracket. This factor implies a falling trend for the curve shown in Chart 6, up to something over $50,000 adjusted gross income, where the 50 percent rate is reached, and implies a horizontal line thereafter.

It appears from the data for these years that the third factor, the rising incentive to minimize realizations, is the dominant one over that range on which it varies. Over the higher range on which it is constant, however, the other two factors show themselves—the regression phenomenon and the rising incentive to convert income to capital gains. This latter incentive rises most sharply after incomes rise above the 50 percent bracket, of course, because at that point the long-term capital gains tax rate stops rising.

The data shown in Chart 6 thus tend to reinforce the conjecture that taxpayer behavior has acted to reduce the progressivity of the income tax. Furthermore, the tax burden on the upper-income groups is overstated by Musgrave's method of taking the ratio of tax payments to income, even as modified by the considerations just discussed, because of the element of deferral in the capital gains tax. It was noted in finding values for g—the prospective burden of the tax—that g is less than t_g (the tax rate at realization). The value of g suggested by the data on the ratio of realizations to accruals, and used above in the analysis of the tax burden on the income from corporate equity, was only 0.07 for the higher-income taxpayers, a little more than one-fourth of their apparent capital gains tax rate of 0.25. For these taxpayers, long-term capital gains represent a large fraction of their adjusted gross incomes; the fraction becomes very high indeed for recent decades if unrealized accruals are included in the income base for the calculation. Their effective tax rate accordingly appears to be very low, if the qualifying factors mentioned earlier are disregarded.

Therefore, although a precise statement of the effect of the qualifying factors is not possible, I would not be greatly surprised if it were ultimately shown that the present tax structure in this country is on balance only mildly progressive. The key element in the tax structure that makes this conjecture plausible is the special treatment of capital gains.

Conclusion

The preceding discussion has established the following points:

(1) The announcement effect of the corporation income tax on corporate equity versus other types of equity is partly offset by an opposite announcement effect of the tax treatment of capital gains, because anticipated capital gains make up part of the expected income from corporate equity. The degree of the offset varies with the marginal personal income tax bracket of the taxpayer, and is a complete offset at a marginal rate of about 70 percent.

(2) Given the finding that, for all except the wealthiest taxpayers, income from corporate equity incurs a net additional tax over that paid on income from unincorporated business, the equilibrium rate of return to capital before tax will be less in unincorporated business than in incorporated business. The equilibrium rate of return in unincorporated business may vary from industry to industry according to the amount of wealth required to participate in a workable partnership in each industry; if so, it will tend to rise with the wealth of the typical partner or proprietor.

(3) Capital gains realized from all sources for tax purposes are a small fraction of total accrued capital gains estimated for corporate shares alone. The limited data available suggest that the accrued capital gains on more than half of corporate shares go permanently unrealized because of the regulations governing their treatment on gift or bequest, and that those assets that are sold are held for periods of several years on the average. The mere lapse of time between sales reduces the ratio of realizations to accruals, and similarly reduces the expected value of the capital gains tax.

(4) The aggregate data loosely suggest that taxpayers respond to tax incentives in the management of their portfolios. Very wealthy taxpayers realize a large share of their incomes in the form of long-term capital gains, and both wealthy and moderately wealthy taxpayers evidently limit realizations relative to accruals even more than do other taxpayers. Consequently the income tax and the tax structure

as a whole are much less progressive than they would otherwise appear.

These points are clearly important both in connection with the announcement and resource-allocation effects of tax policy, and in connection with equity and distributional effects of tax policy. The analysis which established them also indicates substantial gaps in our knowledge of capital gains and the taxation of income from capital.

APPENDIX A

Predictable Income in Capital Gains

THE PROCEDURE OF THE SECTION of the text beginning on page 15 enables us to learn something about the average holding period for corporate shares, but not about the division of accrued capital gains into predictable income, fortuitous gains, and changes in the general price level. For that purpose, one can consider first the 1959 breakdown of long-term capital gains by source, shown in dollar amounts and percentages in Table A–1. (Short-term gains and all losses are of minor importance in most years.) The most important items other than corporate shares are livestock, natural resources (timber, minerals), real estate, and assets used in trade or business. Well-known and transparent cases of privileged treatment comprise the first two items, which can be considered to consist wholly of ordinary income converted to capital gains for tax purposes. The case of real estate is less clear. On the one hand, there has almost certainly been a rise in the price level of real property, much of the rise being connected with inflation in the general price level. On the other hand, if the frequent allegation that real estate depreciation allowances have exceeded true economic depreciation under the tax regulations of recent years is true, some part of the capital gains on real estate is due to this excess depreciation and is ordinary, predictable income. However that may be, it is clear that a considerable amount of the long-term capital gains in 1959 on assets other than corporate shares can be classified as ordinary income.

For corporate shares it has already been observed that there was a considerable accrual of value over the period 1926–61, averaging a rate of 7.6 percent per year. How much of this was predictable income? As a first

TABLE A-1. Realized Long-Term Capital Gains, by Type of Asset, 1959

Type of asset	Net long-term gain or loss (millions of dollars)	Percentage of total, excluding share of partnerships and fiduciaries[a]
Corporation stocks, including rights	5,116.3 }	48.4
Distributions from regulated investment companies	360.4 }	
U.S. obligations	−22.2	−0.2
Other bonds, notes, and certificates of indebtedness	211.7	1.9
Livestock	701.1	6.2
Natural resources (timber, oil, and minerals)	262.6	2.3
Assets used in trade or business	537.6	4.7
Real estate not used in trade or business, and farm land	2,217.4	19.6
Sales of other type assets	1,936.8	17.1
Subtotal	11,321.7	100.0
Share of gain or loss from partnerships and fiduciaries	1,010.2	(8.9)
Total	12,331.9	—

Source: U.S. Treasury Department, Internal Revenue Service, *Statistics of Income, Supplemental Report, Sales of Capital Assets Reported on Individual Income Tax Returns for 1959* (1962), Table 2, p. 10.

[a] The procedure followed for combining distributions from regulated investment companies with corporation stocks overstates the importance of the latter to whatever extent such companies hold other assets, but the amount involved is relatively small. The exclusion of the item, share of gain or loss from partnerships and fiduciaries, is equivalent to assuming that their capital gains have the same composition as those reported specifically by individuals. Unfortunately no information is available on this point.

approximation, we may assume the predictable element in share capital gains is that part which corresponds to earnings retained by corporations. If corporation managements invest their capital resources wisely, the investment will add to the earning power and dividend-paying power of their corporations; in particular, a dollar per share of retained earnings so invested will add to the potential dividend-paying power per share sufficiently to add a dollar to the value of the share. Since the evidence for recent decades suggests that corporate investment on the whole has been sucessful, the hypothesis that retained earnings give rise to predictable capital gains is well supported.

However, care must be taken to allow for any gross errors in depreciation practices when using retained earnings data. If total earnings are misstated because of erroneous depreciation, retained earnings are equally misstated. For help in this matter I have relied on Terborgh's study.[1]

[1] George Terborgh, *Realistic Depreciation Policy* (Chicago: Machinery and Allied Products Institute, 1954), Chaps. 4–11.

Terborgh sets out three major causes of error in depreciation allowances: (1) Straight line depreciation accounting makes insufficient allowance for the relatively rapid decline in economic value of a piece of equipment in the early years of its life; (2) group rather than item accounting leads to a substantial understatement of depreciation when there is considerable dispersion in the useful lives of different pieces of equipment of a given type; and (3) there has been considerable inflation. Terborgh's first point is well supported both by his own data and by independent research.[2] His second point, though difficult to document, is plausible and agrees with prevailing opinion among tax analysts; I accept it at face value.

Terborgh's third point is more debatable, even though it is widely accepted. To consider it, the war and peacetime years should be treated separately. In peacetime since the mid-twenties and exclusive of 1946-48, the officially measured rise in the general price level has averaged just over 1 percent per year, with a moderately higher rate of rise for capital goods. However, such individual studies of durable and capital goods as exist have indicated that adjustment for quality change overlooked in the official indexes lowers the rate of rise in the prices of these goods by from 1 to 2 percent per year.[3] Thus in peacetime the apparent rise in the price level may have been entirely spurious. In wartime and in the postwar inflation of 1946-48 this has surely not been the case; however, wartime practices of accelerated depreciation and expensing of some capital goods had an obvious and large effect on the amount of depreciation taken. At the same time, maintenance expenditures rose sharply during wartime, slowing down the rate of true economic depreciation of the affected equipment.[4] Consequently it is more likely that depreciation was overstated rather than understated during war periods since the twenties. As a result of these considerations, I discount the inflation argument entirely, and make no allowance for it.

There is probably also an error which is larger than negligible in the average lives of depreciable assets used for tax purposes compared to true

[2] *Ibid.*, pp. 28-47 and 173. See also Zvi Griliches, "The Demand for a Durable Input: Farm Tractors in the United States, 1921-57," and Gregory Chow, "Statistical Demand Functions for Automobiles," both in Arnold C. Harberger (ed.), *The Demand for Durable Goods* (University of Chicago Press, 1960), pp. 199 and 167, respectively.

[3] Compare with the corresponding official price indexes those obtained by M. L. Burstein, "The Demand for Household Refrigeration in the United States," in Harberger (ed.), *The Demand for Durable Goods*, p. 133; Zvi Griliches, "Hedonic Price Indexes for Automobiles: An Econometric Analysis of Quality Change," Price Statistics Review Committee of the National Bureau of Economic Research, Staff Paper 3 (processed; Bureau of the Budget), printed in *Government Price Statistics*, Hearings before the Joint Economic Committee, 87 Cong. 1 sess. (1961), pp. 173-96.

[4] See Yehuda Grunfeld, "The Determinants of Corporate Investment," in Harberger (ed.), *The Demand for Durable Goods*, pp. 212-18.

economic lives. No estimate of this error is possible, however, and I have disregarded it.

Terborgh's estimates imply that, for 1958, depreciation allowances should have been 17.6 percent higher on account of the first two factors mentioned above.[5] To correct the figures for corporate earnings, we used data on corporate depreciation for the years 1929–61 published in the August 1965 issue of *Survey of Current Business*. The percentage depreciation error derived from Terborgh was then applied to corporate depreciation for these years to obtain an annual correction factor for retained earnings. Retained earnings corrected by this estimate of depreciation error, then, are taken as the estimate of predictable capital gains accruing to corporate shares. These results appear in Table 1 in the last column.

It is instructive to consider in this same light the period 1871–1937, analyzed by Cowles.[6] He found that each dollar of retained earnings during that period added an average of 72 cents to the value of corporate shares; in estimating this effect on value he made no adjustment for depreciation error or for changes in the price level.[7] As already noted, a change in the value of corporate shares due to a change in the price level (which in effect enhances the nominal market value of the undepreciated part of the corporations' capital) is a purely nominal rather than real capital gain; it should therefore be disregarded in determining whether events bore out what we say the shareholder could reasonably expect. Now for the period 1929–60 the adjustment for depreciation error resulted in a reduction in estimated true retained earnings below their reported figure by some 23 percent. If the same reduction is appropriate for 1871–1937 (and no better guess is now available), a dollar of reported retained earnings for that period represented only 77 cents of true retained earnings, which is very close to the realized rise in value estimated by Cowles. However, the price level was not strictly free of trend in that period. The wholesale price index was 89.1 in 1871 and 86.3 in 1937 (1926 = 100); the consumer price index, pre-1913 estimates of which appeared in recent National Bureau of Economic Research studies,[8] is set by those estimates at 53.7 in 1871 and 61.4 in 1937, on the basis 1947–49 = 100. That is, the wholesale price index fell by a total of 3.2 percent, or 0.05 percent per year, while the consumer price index rose by a total of 14.3 percent, or 0.2 percent per year. Cowles' estimate of

[5] *Realistic Depreciation Policy*, p. 107.
[6] Alfred Cowles III and Associates, *Common-Stock Indexes, 1871–1937* (Bloomington, Ind., Principia, 1938).
[7] *Ibid.*, pp. 42–43.
[8] Clarence D. Long, *Wages and Earnings in the United States, 1860–1890* (Princeton University Press for National Bureau of Economic Research, 1960), p. 60, Table 17. Albert Rees, *Real Wages in Manufacturing, 1890–1914* (Princeton University Press, 1961), p. 117.

the rise in price of corporate shares for the period 1871–1937 was 1.8 percent per year. If this figure is converted to its equivalent real rise by adding the fall in the wholesale price index, the estimated annual rise in the price of shares is thereby increased to 1.85 percent per year. The corresponding correction using the consumer price index reduces the estimated annual rise in the price of shares by 0.2 percent. True retentions work out at an annual average of 1.92 percent of the market value of shares. Hence the rate of change of the real value of shares corrected using the wholesale price index agrees closely with the estimated true rate of retentions, but not when corrected using the consumer price index. In either case the correspondence is better than it was made to appear by Cowles, who used the nominal figures at face value. In his style of putting it, it can be said that a dollar of true retentions apparently resulted in a rise in the real value of shares of from $0.83 to $0.96 in the period 1871–1937.

For the period 1938–60, the rise in the nominal value of corporate shares was by contrast considerably greater than could have been expected from my estimate of true retentions. This estimate averaged 3.9 percent of the market value of the stock, compared with an average annual rate of rise in the stock price index (Standard and Poor's) of some 9.0 percent (see Table 1). However, the average annual rise in the general price level must be deducted from the annual nominal rise in the price of shares in order to obtain the rate of rise in the real value of shares. During the period 1938–60 the consumer price index rose at an average rate of 3.3 percent per year; the wholesale price index rose at an average rate of 3.9 percent per year. Thus the annual rate of rise of the real value of shares was 5.7 percent or 5.1 percent, depending on which deflator is used. Even after this adjustment, the real rate of rise clearly was greater than the estimated true rate of retention of earnings; in this period a dollar retained appeared to be associated with $1.31 to $1.46 of real capital gain. If, as is frequently argued, the two price indexes used here have a considerable upward trend bias, this impression is further strengthened. In any case, the result for this period contrasts sharply with that for the earlier period, 1871–1937.

Many reasons could be adduced for the disparate behavior of the real value of shares relative to retentions in the earlier and later periods; detailed analysis of which lies outside the scope of this study. Both periods may have been characterized by trend bias in the price indexes, but such trend bias could scarcely account for the difference between the two periods. Other pertinent factors are changes in the appropriate interest rate for discounting expected future earnings or dividends, and the shifting fortunes of the corporate sector itself, including the effects of the quality of its management, relative to what was expected previously. Probably the single most important reason is that 1937 was in the middle of the Great Depression. Stock prices were therefore probably low compared to long-run prospects in that year, making the rate of accrual of capital gains lower in the earlier period and higher in the later period than they would otherwise be.

If the two periods are consolidated, the average retention rate over the entire period 1871–1960 was of the order of 2.4 percent and the average rate of accrual of real value in shares was on the order of 2.8 percent, implying that about $1.17 of capital gains was produced for each dollar of retentions. The excess of capital gains over retentions seems well within the range of probable error in the adjusted data. For comparison with these numbers, it should be noted that the average rate of retentions at face value was about 3 percent over the whole period, compared to a nominal rate of accruals of 3.5 percent. Thus from 1871 to 1960 the nominal retention rate was reasonably close both to the real accrual rate and to the nominal accrual rate.

APPENDIX B

The Realizations Ratio and the Effective Capital Gains Tax Rate

As noted earlier, the effective capital gains tax rate, g, is approximately equal to the realizations ratio (the ratio of realizations to accruals), R, times the capital gains tax rate at realization, t_g; this apparent coincidence occurs because compounding of interest or discount rates acts on g and R in a similar way. It is helpful to consider first how these numbers appear when compounding is disregarded—that is, when we treat interest as simple or linear.

As a first approximation (for example, using a Taylor's expansion and disregarding all terms of second and higher orders), the capital built up by holding a unit of initial investment that increases in value annually for T years is

$$G_T = (1 + r)^T \cong 1 + rT,$$

before taxes, where G_T is total capital.

The tax on the gain is then approximately

$$rTt_g,$$

and the (linear) rate of accrual that produces the net capital remaining,

$$C_T \cong 1 + rT(1 - t_g),$$

is approximately

$$s \cong r(1 - t_g).$$

This results in

$$g = 1 - \frac{s}{r} = 1 - \frac{r(1 - t_g)}{r} = t_g.$$

Thus, as a first approximation (that is, with simple interest) the effective capital gains tax rate is the same as the rate at realization time.

If the portfolio consists of T shares, acquired one per year, each being sold after it has been held for T years, and if share prices increase (at simple interest) at r per year, then the total capital of the portfolio will increase by rT each year. The gain realized by the sale of the one share is

$$1 + rT - 1 = rT,$$

so that the ratio of realization to accrual is

$$R \cong \frac{rT}{rT} = 1.$$

Thus, trivially,

$$g = Rt_g = t_g.$$

Compounding of accruals tends both to reduce R and to make $s > r(1 - t_g)$; that is, to make $g < t_g$. It has been noted already that these two effects are almost equiproportional over the relevant range of values. Table B-1 shows a sample of comparisons of g and Rt_g for the case already considered of a steady rollover of a fixed proportion of the portfolio on a first-in-first-out basis.

Throughout Table B-1, g is about 1 percentage point above Rt_g. (When both numbers drop to and below about 0.05 the excess of g over Rt_g also falls to and below half a percentage point.)

When the behavior model is changed to include avoidance through gift and succession, both R and g are affected similarly. For example, if all

TABLE B-1. Comparison of Effective Capital Gains Tax Rate and Product of Realizations Ratio and Capital Gains Tax Rate, Assuming Selected Accrual Rates, by Portfolio Holding Periods[a]

Portfolio holding period T (years)	Accrual rate $r = 2$ percent		Accrual rate $r = 5$ percent		Accrual rate $r = 8$ percent	
	Effective capital gains tax rate g	Realizations ratio × capital gains tax rate Rt_g	Effective capital gains tax rate g	Realizations ratio × capital gains tax rate Rt_g	Effective capital gains tax rate g	Realizations ratio × capital gains tax rate Rt_g
10	0.234	0.229	0.212	0.203	0.193	0.181
20	0.217	0.208	0.177	0.163	0.147	0.133
30	0.201	0.190	0.149	0.135	0.114	0.101
40	0.187	0.176	0.126	0.113	0.092	0.081
50	0.174	0.160	0.109	0.096	0.076	0.066

[a] Capital gains tax rate at realization, $t_g = 25$ percent.

shares of each portfolio are sold exactly halfway through the lifetime of their holder and then are not sold again until succession, and if for the sake of simplicity it is assumed that additions to the portfolio through savings (other than capital gains accruals) can be disregarded, the effect of this behavior on realizations is the same as if half of all shares avoided the capital gains tax: a constant fraction of all outstanding shares will be sold each year and reported for capital gains tax purposes, and the same fraction will pass unreported for this tax through succession each year. Realizations and consequently R will be half what they would be if constructive realization occurred at succession.

The effect on g is less easily obtained. At the mid-point, say twenty-five years after inheritance, the holder realizes and pays capital gains tax on his accruals up to that point. Then he pays no more and passes on subsequent accruals intact, so far as the capital gains tax is concerned. His final capital, per unit of initial inheritance, is

(6) $$C_{50} = [(1 + r)^{25}(1 - t_g) + t_g](1 + r)^{25}$$
$$= (1 + r)^{50} - t_g[(1 + r)^{50} - (1 + r)^{25}],$$

and the presumptive accrual rate that produces it, as before, is

$$s = \sqrt[50]{C_{50}} - 1.$$

If the gross accrual rate, r, is 3 percent, the net of tax rate, s, works out at 2.71 percent, for a g of 0.097, or almost exactly half the g for a twenty-five-year first-in-first-out rollover, which is 0.192. The value of Rt_g for the present example is 0.090, so that the relationship between Rt_g and g remains reassuringly close to that shown in Table B–1.

The intuitive plausibility of this result is strengthened by the following argument. Let N be the typical number of years between successions and M be the number of years after succession that a holder of shares waits, after a possibly costless initial portfolio shuffle, to turn over his entire portfolio. Then the expression (6) becomes

$$C_N = [(1 + r)^M(1 - t_g) + t_g](1 + r)^{N-M}$$
$$= C_M(1 + r)^{N-M}.$$

The presumptive net accrual rate that produces C_N is

(7) $$s_N = \sqrt[N]{C_M(1 + r)^{N-M}} - 1$$
$$= (1 + s_M)^{M/N}(1 + r)^{1-M/N} - 1.$$

Because both the exponents in (7) are fractions, it is a good approximation to write

$$s_N \cong \left(1 + \frac{M}{N}s_M\right)\left(1 + \frac{N-M}{N}r\right) - 1$$
$$\cong \frac{1}{N}[Ms_M + (N - M)r].$$

Then

$$g_N = 1 - \frac{s_N}{r} \cong 1 - \frac{M}{N}\frac{s_M}{r} - \frac{N-M}{N}$$

$$= 1 - \frac{M}{N}(1 - g_M) - \frac{N-M}{N}$$

$$= \frac{M}{N} g_M.$$

That is, to a first approximation, g is affected in the same proportion as R by the change from a full realization first-in-first-out rollover model (the one first considered) to fractional realization due to succession. The effects of multiple compounding are already reflected in g_M; then finding g_N by the above method involves merely linear (instead of geometric) interpolation between s_M and r, for which the error is tolerably small.

Broadly, if one starts from a point on one of the g-curves in Chart 2 and makes local approximations by linear methods the results will approximate two significant digits, in the range of accrual rates and behavior patterns under consideration. Making the addition to Rt_g indicated by the relationship in Table B-1 and the accompanying discussion gives the same degree of approximation.

The behavior model in the text, in which the portfolio holder sells a randomly selected constant fraction of this portfolio each year, is an extension of the behavior model just considered, and so has the same general consequences. The time between initial purchase or inheritance and sale (if any) varies from share to share, but the analysis just given essentially applies to the wealth contained in each share and in the reinvestment of its sale proceeds. Consequently the Table B-1 relationship between g and Rt_g has a similar reliability for this case, and for others that are extensions or modifications of it.

Thus, to obtain the effective rate of capital gains tax, g (for analysis of announcement effects), we can safely use the approximation

$$g = Rt_g + \Delta$$

where $\Delta \backsim 0.01$, when

$$Rt_g \geq 0.05$$

and where $\Delta \backsim 0.005$, when

$$Rt_g \leq 0.05.$$

Inasmuch as the actual R is easy to obtain from data, and alternative values are easy to estimate from realization models like those given here, this approximation can save the reader the difficult direct calculations of g.

DAVID LAIDLER

Income Tax Incentives for Owner-Occupied Housing

THE FEDERAL PERSONAL INCOME tax does not cover all income, and the most important income which escapes taxation is that which accrues from the ownership of durable goods. The flow of service income from these goods is completely tax free; and, according to the conventional economic theory that consumers tend to equalize after-tax rates of return on capital, this exclusion provides a considerable incentive for ownership of such goods. Of these goods the most important is the owner-occupied house, because it is by far the most valuable durable asset owned by most households. This study is concerned with some of the economic consequences of the failure to tax the service income provided by owner-occupied housing.

The problems dealt with are both normative and positive. First is presented an estimate of the degree to which the progressiveness of the personal income tax is lessened by excluding housing income from it; this is followed by a measure of the loss in economic welfare arising from this anomaly. These estimates are based on certain assumptions about the price and income elasticities of demand for housing, and the positive problem dealt with in this chapter is that of checking to see whether these assumptions are in fact justifiable in view of the empirical evidence.

David Laidler 51

In brief, the conclusions reached are these: Home ownership makes a noticeable difference in effective tax rates. The welfare loss exceeds $500 million per year. Finally, though the evidence is not conclusive, empirical tests strongly suggest that the assumptions upon which these normative conclusions are based are reasonable descriptions of reality.

Normative Analysis

It is necessary to have some knowledge of the relationship between income and housing expenditure in order to assess the amount of income tax avoided by home ownership. At the same time, the calculation of the economic welfare measure used in this study—Marshallian consumer surplus—requires a knowledge of the price elasticity of demand for housing. The two main sources of information on the demand for housing in the United States are Margaret Reid's *Housing and Income* and Richard F. Muth's "The Demand for Non-Farm Housing." Fortunately, these two independent sources provide estimates of the necessary parameters that are, to all intents and purposes, the same.[1]

Reid, after analyzing an enormous body of evidence, concludes that the income elasticity of demand for housing lies between 1.5 and 2.0; Muth's estimates (1.68–1.87) also fall within this range. In addition, all the estimates which I have computed in the course of this study (save one) are greater than unity, and all those for owner-occupiers are in the region of 1.5.[2] As to the price elasticity of demand for housing, Reid offers no direct measure, but on the basis of indirect evidence suggests that it is probably close to unity, and perhaps a little greater.[3] Muth gives two direct estimates of this parameter; his results suggest that the price elasticity of demand for owner-occupied housing is −1.59 and that for rental housing is −1.47. My own

---

[1] Margaret Reid, *Housing and Income* (University of Chicago Press, 1962); Richard F. Muth, "The Demand for Non-Farm Housing," in Arnold C. Harberger (ed.), *The Demand for Durable Goods* (University of Chicago Press, 1960).

[2] See Reid, *Housing and Income*, p. 6, where she summarizes her results, and Muth, "The Demand for Non-Farm Housing," Table 4. Note that some of the results given by Muth are for the demand for the structure of a dwelling only. The ones cited here, however, include the demand for the site, as they should for our purposes. For my results, see Table 4 of this chapter.

[3] "Greater" is here used as equivalent to "more elastic." It is so used throughout this chapter.

results, though certainly less reliable than Muth's, do not contradict his conclusions. In the analysis that follows, the income elasticity of demand for housing is assumed to be 1.427, an estimate taken from one of my own regressions. This is a slightly conservative estimate compared to those of Reid and Muth that would tend to understate, if anything, the effects it is being used to measure. The price elasticity estimate employed is -1.5, a figure that is consistent with Muth's results and my own, though perhaps it is a little larger than Reid's indirect evidence would suggest.

Subsidy Effects of Not Taxing Income from Owner-Occupied Housing

The failure to tax the income arising from owner-occupied housing, a good for which the income elasticity of demand appears to be well in excess of unity, must obviously lessen the degree of progression in the income tax structure. Table 1 presents some estimates of the magnitude of this effect at different levels of income on what I would regard as a not atypical family. The family in question is assumed to consist of four persons, to have a 50 percent equity in its home, and to be paying an interest rate of 6 percent per year on its mortgage. The relationship between its demand for housing and its income, adjusted for taxes and the implicit return on its equity in its home, is assumed to be given by the relationship

$$\ln V = -1.291 + 1.427 \ln Y,$$

where V equals the value of the house and Y equals household income. This equation is the result of work reported in more detail below, and is based on data for thirty-three Chicago census tracts having an average family size of about four. The tax rates used in Table 1 are based on the same assumptions as is the income elasticity estimate used to obtain the value-of-house data employed.[4]

The table should be virtually self-explanatory. Its last two columns present data for taxes actually paid as a proportion of income including that accruing to equity in the house, and also data for those that would be paid at the same tax rates if this latter component of household income were subject to income tax. The dollar amounts involved are given in columns 3 and 4. Whether the differences involved here are regarded as "large" or "important" is, of course, a matter of opinion, but to this writer they do not seem trivial, par-

[4] Additional detailed assumptions are set out in the notes to Table 1.

ticularly in the upper-income brackets. Table 1 suggests that families having annual incomes of between $10,000 and $15,000 receive annual tax advantages of between $400 and $1,000 from home ownership. Estimates for higher levels of income would not be accurate since the top of the income range over which the regression was fitted was just over $13,000 before taxes.

There is no question but that a case can be made for subsidizing housing on the ground of the existence of external economies. Moreover, a case for subsidizing owner-occupied housing in particular can be built on propositions that widespread property ownership leads to social stability. It is not my purpose here to assess any of these arguments in any way, but merely to note their existence and then to raise the question as to whether the particular type of subsidy cur-

TABLE 1. Effect of Including Imputed Income of Owner-Occupied Housing in Tax Base, Selected Income Levels, 1962[a]

Annual income (dollars) (1)	Value of house[b] (dollars) (2)	Actual tax[c] (dollars) (3)	Tax if value of owner-occupied housing were taxed[d] (dollars) (4)	Income if value of owner-occupied housing were included[e] (dollars) (5)	Tax as percentage of income if imputed income of owner-occupied housing were included	
					Actual[f] (6)	Including value of owner-occupied housing[g] (7)
5,000	9,700	332	478	5,291	6.3	9.0
10,000	26,100	1,114	1,544	10,783	10.3	14.3
15,000	46,500	2,072	3,018	16,395	12.6	18.4

[a] Assumes a family of four people with a 50 percent equity in its home and paying an interest rate of 6 percen a year on its mortgage. The reasons for various other assumptions in the table are given on page 55.
[b] Calculated on the basis of the income elasticity computed for 33 Chicago census tracts using the equation on p. 52. Census tract data are from U.S. Bureau of the Census, U.S. Censuses of Population and Housing: 1960, Census Tracts, PHC(1)–26 (1962).
[c] Calculated on the basis of 1962 income tax rates, assuming four exemptions, a deduction of 10 percent of income up to $1,000, and further deductions of 6 percent of one-half of the value of the house for mortgage interest and 1.5 percent of the value of the house for state and local taxes.
[d] Calculated by adding the gross return on the house to the initial figure for income, and deducting, in excess of those items already mentioned, 2.25 percent of value for depreciation and 1.25 percent for maintenance. The gross rate of return is thus 11 percent (the sum of the rates for interest, state and local taxes, depreciation, and maintenance).
[e] Column 1 plus the net return on owner's equity in the house. Equity is taken to be 50 percent of the value of the house, and is assumed to yield a rate of return of 6 percent. Thus column 5 equals column 1 plus 3 percent of column 2.
[f] Column 3 as percentage of column 5.
[g] Column 4 as percentage of column 5.

rently given to owner-occupied housing is compatible with the arguments. The answer that must be given, it seems to me, is a largely negative one.

Even in the absence of a subsidy, the income elasticity of demand for housing appears to be high, so that one would expect high-income families to provide themselves with high-quality housing without extra encouragement. Moreover, richer families tend in any case to be owner-occupiers. If subsidies are being given with the aim of encouraging owner-occupation, they would be most effective, one would expect, if they were concentrated among lower-income groups. The subsidy under consideration here, however, is weighted in precisely the opposite direction. The higher the family's income, the more valuable is the house that it will own, and the higher will be its marginal rate of income tax. These two factors combine to make the effective subsidy on owner-occupied housing, whether considered as an absolute figure or as a proportion of income, increase with income—as Table 1 shows. Thus, whether the objective is to capture the social economies that arise from the existence of high-quality housing in general, or to encourage owner-occupation per se, it is doubtful that the income tax subsidy currently given is very effective in achieving either of these ends.

The subsidy in question does, however, have one strong effect—it lowers the degree of progression implicit in the income tax structure. Whether this is to be regarded as a "good" thing or not depends on some judgment about what is a "just" income distribution, and this is a matter not under consideration here. However, regardless of this aspect, if the desire is to cut the tax burden of the rich, it is clear that the method of subsidizing a particular good is not the best way available. If this subsidy were replaced by a general lowering of tax rates, leaving disposable income unchanged, its recipients could still (if they wished) consume just the same goods as under present arrangements; if they chose to substitute on the margin some other goods for housing, they would presumably be moving to a preferred consumption pattern. Thus such a change could not make any group worse off than it is at present, and would in all likelihood enable it to improve its position at no extra resource cost to the community. I will now turn to a closer analysis of this matter, and will present a quantitative measure of the amount by which such a change might be expected to increase economic welfare.

Analysis of Welfare Costs of Tax Subsidy

The simple propositions about economic welfare contained in the preceding discussion are of a qualitative nature and, as the reader will understand, rest only on the premise that consumers are endowed with an ordinal utility function. In order to produce any quantitative statements, rather stronger (and perhaps less generally acceptable) premises are needed. What is involved in the way of a theoretical basis for the results that I shall present, then, should be quite clear at the outset. First, a cardinal utility function is assumed. Second, it is posited that, over the relevant range for the changes to be considered, the marginal utility of income may be treated as constant. Third, it is assumed that the marginal utility of income is the same for all consumers. These are really not premises that can be attacked or defended, since if one wishes to do the kind of piecemeal applied welfare economics that is involved here, one is forced to make such assumptions.

Of the three assumptions involved, acceptance of the first is largely a matter of taste, and acceptance of the second probably depends mainly on the magnitude of the changes being analyzed. In the present context the reader need not worry unduly, since (relative to the total levels of income involved) the changes are small. The third is a different matter, however. In the present context, any serious doubts about its validity imply that, in dealing with the matter at hand, any concrete policy proposals would have to be based on careful consideration of questions concerning the income distribution, in addition to questions concerning the allocation of resources. It is usual to separate these issues in welfare economics; in this study I am dealing only with resource allocation problems. The reader should therefore be warned that he must make up his own mind about income distribution questions before deciding how much importance he should attach to the measures of economic welfare I shall present, and before deciding what concrete policy proposals might be based on these measures.

The type of analysis employed will be familiar. In Chart 1, the curve DD represents the demand curve for some good, in this case housing services per year. It is, of course, a marginal utility curve, and the assumption that the marginal utility of income is constant enables us to interpret the area under it as a measure in money terms

CHART 1. Welfare Loss from Omitting Imputed Income of Owner-Occupied Housing from Tax Base

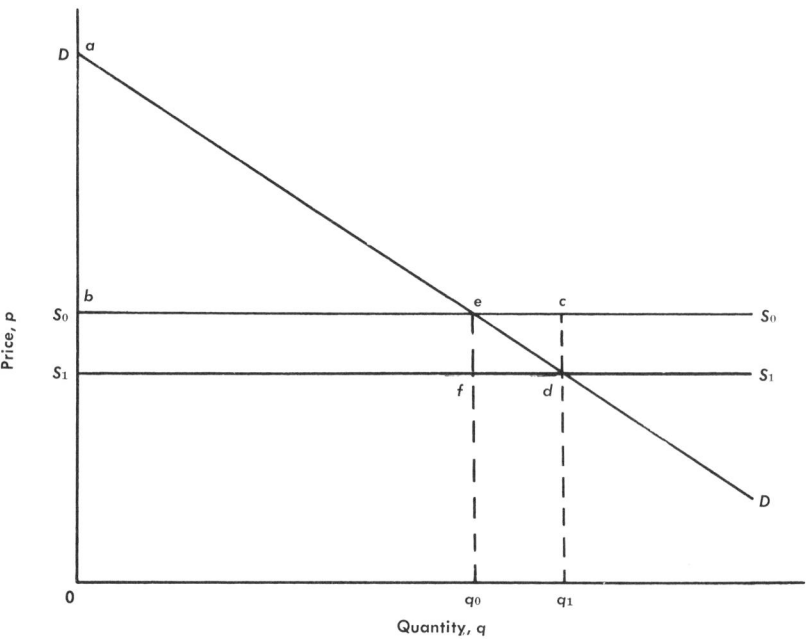

of the total utility derived from consuming housing. The curve S_0S_0 represents a supply curve and, in the absence of externalities or distortions in the rest of the economy, the area under it may be interpreted as measuring in money terms the utility forgone elsewhere by devoting resource services to the provision of housing. The difference between the area under the demand curve and that under the supply curve, the triangle *abe*, then measures the net gain from consuming Oq_0 of housing as against none at all.

The introduction of a subsidy to the good in question will, from the consumers' point of view, lower the supply curve to S_1S_1, so that it no longer measures the marginal social cost of providing housing, which is still given by S_0S_0. Demand will now be at Oq_1, and between Oq_0 and Oq_1 more is added to the cost of housing in terms of utility forgone elsewhere than is added to the utility derived from housing itself, the net loss being measured by the area of the triangle *cde*. Provided we permit interpersonal comparisons of utility, this type of analysis, usually confined to the individual consumer, may be extended to deal with the entire community. This is what is done here; an attempt is made to measure a triangle similar to this one for the owner-occupied housing market in the United States.

In order to do so, it is evident that the following information is needed: One must know the marginal social and private costs of producing housing services over the relevant range and the size of the subsidy given, and must also have a measure of the amount by which the quantity of housing consumed would fall if the subsidy were withdrawn. One must also assume that the resources withdrawn from housing remain in the hands of consumers so that they may be devoted to producing other goods. Analysis is made of the effects of a policy change in which the tax subsidies given to housing are withdrawn simultaneously with a reduction in tax rates sufficient to leave the government with no more command over resources than before, *or* the government withdraws the subsidies and uses the extra resources it gains to provide services to the consumer sector in an optimal fashion.

The data needed for this exercise are not hard to find, with the exception of data on the marginal cost of production of housing services. What is needed here is a figure for the rate of return on capital, plus information on depreciation rates and maintenance expenses for housing. These figures were roughly estimated at the following amounts.

The rate of return on capital in housing was assumed to be 6 percent per year, a figure close enough to private mortgage rates to be reasonable. To this were added state and local tax rates, assumed to run at 1.5 percent per year of the value of housing. A depreciation rate of 2.25 percent per year was taken, based on the federal government's allowable useful life of forty-five years for rented dwellings, and maintenance costs were assumed to run at 1.25 percent per year. The sum of these (11 percent) times the value of the house is the marginal private cost of providing the housing services that flow in any year from a house of any given value. It is not, however, necessarily the marginal social cost, and it is precisely when these two concepts are not measured by the same figure that so-called "second best" problems arise. Depreciation and maintenance costs create little problem since they represent real costs of the consumption of housing services. However, whether the rest of the components, that total

7.5 percent per year, measure the before-tax net rate of return on capital elsewhere in the economy is a moot point.

In this case, I would argue that they represent an understatement of the true figure; 6 percent is hardly a high guess for the after-tax (but before personal income tax) rate of return on capital in the United States, and as Rosenberg has shown, state and local taxes on housing are levied at a rate considerably below those imposed upon income from capital in other forms.[5] Nevertheless, in the analysis that follows it will be assumed that a figure of 11 percent of value per year also measures the marginal social cost of providing housing. The effect of this will be to influence downward the welfare cost measure I shall calculate.

Consider Chart 2, which is similar to Chart 1 except that S_0S_0 represents the marginal social cost of housing, S_1S_1 the marginal private cost, and S_2S_2 the marginal private cost in the presence of a subsidy. The removal of the subsidy will still not achieve an optimal situation, but will increase welfare by the area given by *abcde*. Clearly the triangle *cde* understates this amount, but that is what I shall measure in the analysis that follows. The analysis will also assume that the marginal cost of providing housing is constant over the relevant range. This is in accordance with Muth's findings that the flow of resources into housing in the long run is virtually perfectly elastic with respect to the price of housing.[6]

The responsiveness of the demand for housing to the withdrawal of the subsidy was measured by assuming a price elasticity of demand for housing of -1.5, a figure firmly grounded in empirical evidence, and by applying this figure to data for the total housing stock in the United States in order to get at a dollar figure for the change in quantity demanded.

The housing stock figures were calculated from data given in the Metropolitan Housing series of the 1960 Census,[7] and this choice again reflects a conscious effort to give a downward bias to the welfare measure being calculated. The dwellings covered are single

---

[5] See Leonard G. Rosenberg, "Taxation of Income from Capital, by Industry Group," this volume, p. 125.

[6] See Muth, "The Demand for Non-Farm Housing," p. 46.

[7] U.S. Bureau of the Census, *U.S. Census of Housing: 1960*, Vol. 2, *Metropolitan Housing, United States and Divisions* (1963).

David Laidler

CHART 2. Gain in Welfare from Including Imputed Income of Owner-Occupied Housing in Tax Base

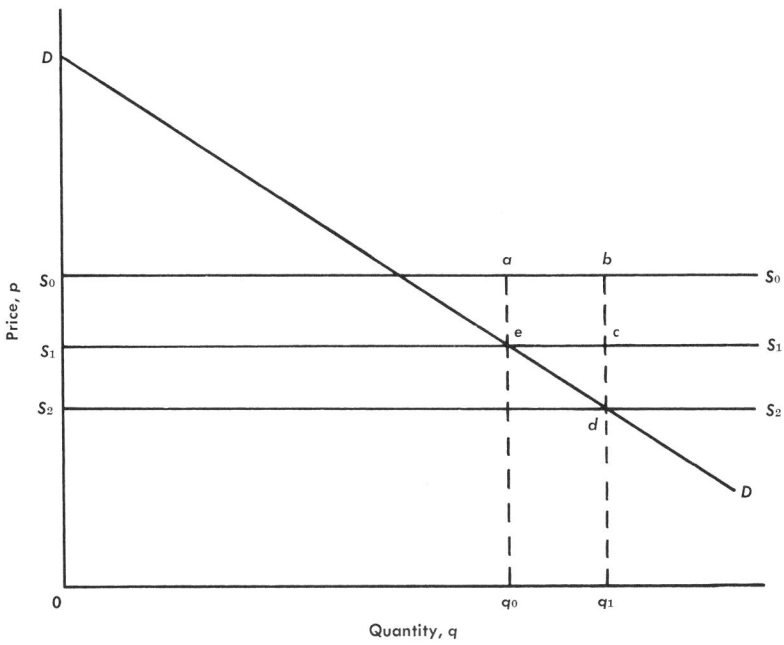

family units only. Thus, all structures of which the owner inhabits part and rents out the rest, all dwellings that are also used as places of business, and all co-operative apartment dwellings are excluded from the series used. All in all about 6.5 million housing units are left out in this way.

The subsidy rate is the last datum needed, and this was imputed in the following way. If income from housing were taxed like other income, the owner would have to declare as income the gross rate of return, here assumed to be 11 percent, times the value of his house; from this he would be permitted to deduct maintenance and depreciation expenses, state and local taxes, and mortgage interest payments, and would be taxed on the net income accruing from his equity in the house. In present circumstances, state and local taxes and mortgage interest payments are deductible against *other* income, and the imputed income to equity is not declared or taxed. Thus, only depreciation (2.25 percent) and maintenance (1.25 percent) fail to obtain

TABLE 2. Welfare Cost of Omitting Imputed Income of Owner-Occupied Housing from Tax Base, by Income Class, United States, 1960

Income class of owner (dollars) (1)	Value of owner-occupied housing stock[a] (millions of dollars) (2)	Marginal income tax rate[b] (percent) (3)	Implied rate of subsidy[c] (percent) (4)	Percent overinvested in housing[d] (5)	Percent overinvested in housing as proportion of existing stock[e] (6)	Amount overinvested[f] (millions of dollars) (7)	Welfare loss per year[g] (millions of dollars) (8)
Less than 2,000	29,432	0	0.0	0.0	0.0	0	0
2,000– 3,000	14,723	0	0.0	0.0	0.0	0	0
3,000– 4,000	17,759	20	13.6	20.4	16.9	3,001	22
4,000– 5,000	24,757	20	13.6	20.4	16.9	4,184	31
5,000– 6,000	35,537	20	13.6	20.4	16.9	6,006	45
6,000– 7,000	37,201	20	13.6	20.4	16.9	6,287	47
7,000– 8,000	34,031	22	15.0	22.5	18.4	6,262	52
8,000–10,000	51,963	22	15.0	22.5	18.4	9,561	79
10,000–15,000	61,956	26	17.7	26.6	21.0	13,011	127
15,000 and over	48,010	34	23.2	34.8	25.8	12,387	158
Total	355,369					60,699	561

Source: U.S. Bureau of the Census, *U.S. Census of Housing: 1960*, Vol. 2, *Metropolitan Housing, United States and Divisions* (1963), Table A–3.
[a] The total values appearing for each income class were obtained by multiplying the central value for each value-of-house class by the number of houses in the class, and summing these values over the entire distribution. For the open-ended top value class, a mean was attributed for each income class by use of a Pareto distribution. See Table 3, footnote a.
[b] Based on the midpoint of each income class, except for the top of the distribution, which is based upon a mean for this class attributed by an application of Pareto's law. The calculations for the marginal tax rates assume exemptions for a family of four and the 10 percent standard deduction as set forth in the Internal Revenue Code.
[c] Column 3 $\times$ 7.5/11. (The value of housing services is estimated as 11 percent of the house value, of which all but 3.5/11 is either deductible without being reflected in declared gross income, or is undeclared income to owner's equity.)
[d] Column 4 $\times$ 1.5.
[e] Column 5 $\div$ (100 + column 5).
[f] Column 6 $\times$ column 2.
[g] (Column 7 $\times$ column 4 $\times$ 0.11) $\div$ 2.

special tax treatment under present U.S. law. Of the estimated value of housing services (11 percent of house value), all but an estimated 3.5/11 is either deductible without being reflected in declared gross income, or is undeclared income to owner's equity. The implicit subsidy involved is therefore estimated to be the owner's marginal tax rate times 7.5/11.[8]

Marginal tax rates vary with income. Therefore, it is desirable to compute the effects of the tax subsidy separately for consumers at different levels of income, imputing an appropriate tax rate at each level. Moreover, the tax rate that is relevant for the present problem is not that applying to a family in any particular year, when a host of factors might cause its income to deviate from its long-run level, but rather the tax rate which applies on the average over the long run. Steps have been taken to deal with both of these matters. In Table 2, the calculations of the welfare costs of the income tax subsidy to housing are carried out separately for families in different income brackets. The calculations are also carried out in Table 2 for data given by the census in terms of housing-value distributions by income class and in Table 3 for data given for income distributions by value-of-house class. As is well known, the latter classification leads to a more accurate picture of the relationship between housing expenditure and the kind of long-run income concept which is really needed here.[9] Thus one can place greater reliance on the results emerging from Table 3.

Tables 2 and 3 should be virtually self-explanatory, though two points might be noted. First, since the marginal cost (both social and private) of providing housing services was assumed to be a constant fraction of the value of the housing stock, it was possible (and computationally convenient) to measure initially the decrease in the demand for housing that would take place if the subsidy were to be lifted in terms of a decline in the value of the housing stock (see Table 2, column 7, and Table 3, column 8). The conversion of this figure to flow terms was accomplished in the course of calculating the final column of the tables which shows the annual welfare loss arising from the subsidy.

[8] Note that the assumption that the mortgage interest rate is equal to the net of tax rate of return on capital of 6 percent makes the proportion of equity an owner has in his home an irrelevant statistic.

[9] The question of the correct income concept to apply to the demand for housing is taken up below.

TABLE 3. Welfare Cost of Omitting Imputed Income of Owner-Occupied Housing from Tax Base, by Value-of-House Class, United States, 1960

Value-of-house class (dollars) (1)	Median annual income of owner (dollars) (2)	Value of owner-occupied housing stock[a] (millions of dollars) (3)	Marginal income tax rate[b] (percent) (4)	Implied rate of subsidy[c] (percent) (5)	Percent overinvested in housing[d] (6)	Percent overinvested in housing as proportion of existing stock[e] (7)	Amount overinvested[f] (millions of dollars) (8)	Welfare loss per year[g] (millions of dollars) (9)
Less than 5,000	2,800	7,954	0	0.0	0.0	0.0	0	0
5,000– 7,500	4,500	20,006	20	13.6	20.4	16.9	3,381	25
7,500–10,000	5,400	31,024	20	13.6	20.4	16.9	5,243	39
10,000–12,500	6,100	46,065	20	13.6	20.4	16.9	7,785	58
12,500–15,000	6,800	48,641	20	13.6	20.4	16.9	8,220	61
15,000–20,000	7,700	82,654	22	15.0	22.5	18.4	15,208	125
20,000–25,000	9,200	42,741	22	15.0	22.5	18.4	7,864	65
25,000 and over	12,700	67,020	26	17.7	26.6	21.0	14,074	137
Total		346,105					61,775	510

Source: U.S. Bureau of the Census, U.S. Census of Housing: 1960, Vol. 2, Metropolitan Housing, United States and Divisions (1963), Table A–3.
[a] The midpoint of each class is assumed to represent the mean value-of-house class, except for the top class, where a Pareto distribution was applied. The discrepancy between Tables 2 and 3 for the total value-of-housing stock is due to the Pareto distribution being applied only to the total housing stock distribution in Table 3 rather than to separate distributions for each income class as in Table 2.
[b] Based upon a median family income for each value-of-house class (for the top class, at least, it represents an understatement of the true rate, thus biasing downward the true effects of not taxing the value of owner-occupied housing even more than would the use of mean income in Table 2). The calculations for the marginal tax rates assume exemptions for a family of four and the 10 percent standard deduction as set forth in the Internal Revenue Code.
[c] Column 4 × 7.5/11. See Table 2, footnote c.
[d] Column 5 × 1.5.
[e] Column 6 ÷ (100 + column 6).
[f] Column 3 × column 7.
[g] (Column 8 × column 5 × 0.11) ÷ 2.

Second, though the actual computation of the welfare loss is straightforward, it is probably worth explaining. Associated with the "overinvestment in housing" (given in the next to last column of Tables 2 and 3) is a flow of resource services going to provide housing which, in other uses, could be yielding utility equal in value to 11 percent of this stock figure per year. Because housing is subsidized, however, this flow is instead providing utility equal on the margin to 11 percent less the subsidy rate per year. Were the subsidy to be removed, resources would be devoted to other uses until in housing they provided utility on the margin equal to that in other uses. The subsidy expressed in terms of dollars per year is obviously equal to 11 percent of the value of housing times the relevant subsidy rate given in column 4 of Table 2 and column 5 of Table 3. Taking the figure for "quantity over-invested" as the relevant stock figure, the computation of this subsidy gives us the area of a rectangle such as *ecdf* in Chart 1. Dividing this area by 2 gives us the area of a triangle similar to *cde* in the same chart; this is the welfare measure required, and is given in the final column of Tables 2 and 3.

Relative Welfare Cost of the Tax Subsidy

The figures given in the final columns of Tables 2 and 3 are conscious underestimates of the welfare cost of the failure to levy income tax on the service accruing to owner-occupiers. For reasons noted above, the welfare costs given in Table 3 are slightly to be preferred, and these are the lower of the two sets of estimates. Even so, we have a figure of more than $500 million per year as a minimum estimate of this welfare cost. The question naturally arises as to whether this is a large figure or not; the answer depends, of course, on what one compares it with.

Relative to some of the other welfare measures contained in this volume, it is large. Rosenberg, for example, gives a figure of $587 million per year as the welfare cost of all the distortions involved in the structure of corporation and property taxes.[10] My figure is the result of one anomaly in the taxation of income from one capital good, while Rosenberg's measures the total effect of many anomalies. Thus, relative to other distortions arising from the structure of taxes on income from capital, the one dealt with in this study would appear to be important.

[10] See Rosenberg, "Taxation of Income from Capital."

On the other hand, if one expresses the figure of $500 million as a measure of welfare per capita, the result is only a little over $2.50 per year, not a very impressive amount. However, this is perhaps not the right way to view it, for since it measures the welfare that would be gained by abolishing the tax subsidy to housing and leaving the public with no less command over productive resources than they have at present, it may also be interpreted as giving the dollar value of extra resources the government *could* take away from the public if it were to abolish the subsidy and seek to leave consumers at the same level of economic welfare that they enjoy at present. Relative to government expenditure on foreign economic aid, for example, or on urban renewal, $500 million per year no longer appears as a trivial figure. I will leave it to the reader to pick his own pet government spending project, and to work out how significant to its progress would be an extra $500 million per year, obtained with no loss in welfare to the community.

Empirical Tests

Quite apart from the inherently untestable propositions about utility functions that underlie the preceding analysis, the analysis is also based on certain testable assumptions. Values of the price and income elasticities of demand for housing were employed and it was assumed without question that the consumer sector would react to a subsidy hidden in the income tax structure in exactly the same way it reacts to a change in the market price of housing service. Economic theory predicts this, of course, but that does not mean it is true.

The reader who is satisfied that these positive assumptions are acceptable can safely stop reading at this point, but the skeptic might continue, for I shall now describe some tests devised to check on their validity. The results, however, are by no means conclusive on all matters, and it is doubtful that all his suspicions will be allayed. The really critical issue is that of the responsiveness of consumers to the hidden subsidy; and the tests performed to deal with this matter yield, as by-products, estimates of price and income elasticities of demand for housing. Thus my analysis will center on the problem of consumer responsiveness to the tax subsidy.

Testing Consumer Response to the Tax Subsidy

The conventional way of testing for the existence of a relationship between more than two variables in applied economics is multiple regression analysis. Such a straightforward procedure is impossible to apply in this case, however, for evidence on the responsiveness of consumer demand for housing to the tax subsidy is being sought. An income variable in some shape or form is also an important determinant of the demand for housing; and unfortunately, since the tax subsidy is progressive with income, the two variables are virtually perfectly correlated.

As income rises the demand for housing rises for two reasons—first because income is increasing, and second because, as a result of the progressiveness of the income tax subsidy, the relative price of housing is falling. If one had a measure of the relationship between housing expenditures and income under these circumstances, and one of what it would be if the progressive subsidy were absent, the difference between the two relationships would be attributable to the subsidy. The latter is hard to obtain, for there is no such owner-occupied housing market in the United States. There is, however, a rental housing market which does not have a subsidy that increases with income. In the analysis that follows, the relationship between income and the demand for rental housing is used as a proxy for what the relationship between income and expenditure on owner-occupied housing would be in the absence of a tax subsidy. This is not a completely happy choice, since owners and renters typically differ in many more respects than that of the markets in which they buy their housing, but the reader may judge how well the difficulties inherent in the choice have been dealt with in the analysis that follows.

If this proxy relationship is assumed to be a good one, two predictions can be made at once. A measured income elasticity of demand for owner-occupied housing will contain an income effect and an effect resulting from the falling relative price of housing, while a similar measure of the demand for rental housing will pick up only the first of these, and should therefore be smaller. Furthermore, since the rate at which the tax rates progress is easily measured, it should be possible to calculate the price elasticity of demand for owner-occupied housing implied by the difference in question. Both these tests were carried out, and the evidence is fairly firm that the income elasticity of demand for owner-occupied housing is greater than that for rental housing, so that the first prediction is confirmed. As to the second prediction, the results are perhaps less decisive. However, the implied price elasticities are close enough to those independently calculated by Muth to suggest that, if anything, the balance of the evidence is in favor of the latter hypothesis. Thus, the positive assumptions that underlie the preceding welfare analysis are on the whole strengthened by the results I shall now describe.

The empirical tests were all carried out on cross-section data for census tracts taken from the 1960 Census of Housing.[11] In the selection of data, two problems in particular were borne in mind. First, the role of rental housing in this study is as a proxy for owner-occupied housing, and renters are notoriously a more heterogeneous group than owner-occupiers. They include inhabitants of subsidized public housing, a disproportionate number of minority group members whose rents are distorted by racial discrimination, and a large number of unrelated individuals living in rooming houses and the like who are counted as renters of separate accommodation by the census so long as the room has cooking facilities within it, as well as a high proportion of young people whose housing expenditure relative to income can hardly be expected to be at a long-run equilibrium level.

Second, as Reid and Muth have both argued, the demand for housing is not related so much to measured income as to permanent income, a concept which takes in the roles that used to be attributed to wealth and income separately in the theory of demand.[12] This is not a measurable concept per se, and in any case the census gives only data for measured income in 1959. The usual way of getting

---

[11] U.S. Bureau of the Census, *U.S. Censuses of Population and Housing: 1960, Census Tracts*, PHC (1) (1962), various volumes. Data on income come from Table P-1, and those for rent and value of house from Table H-2.

[12] In theory, at least, permanent income is the return, at a constant rate of interest, on the value of all capital both human and non-human. The conventional two variables, "wealth" (that is, non-human wealth) and "income," used often as separate determinants of demand, are thus subsumed into one variable. For a detailed discussion of this matter, see Milton Friedman, *A Theory of the Consumption Function* (Princeton University Press for the National Bureau of Economic Research, 1957), and also his "Windfalls, the 'Horizon,' and Related Concepts in the Permanent-Income Hypothesis," in Carl F. Christ and others, *Measurement in Economics: Studies in Mathematical Economics and Econometrics in Memory of Yehuda Grunfeld* (Stanford University Press, 1963).

David Laidler 67

around such problems is to classify one's observations in some other way than by income class, and to try to make the families entering the observations as homogeneous a group as possible. Classifying observations by census tract deals with the first point, but the second requires some care to be taken in the selection of the tracts themselves. In particular, position in the life cycle is probably an important variable here, as is family size which might, a priori, be expected to influence the demand for housing.

CONTROL CRITERIA. Rather than try to find appropriate proxy variables for all the factors involved and then to perform multiple regression analysis, observations were selected according to what seemed appropriate criteria, and then simple regression analysis was used.[13] A census tract observation was admitted to a sample if

1. The modal age of the adult male population lay between 45 and 50 (40–45 and 50–55, in two cases),
2. The median age of the population lay between 30 and 40 (25–40 and 30–45, in two cases),
3. Less than 10 percent of the population were those aged 65 and over,
4. Less than 5 percent of the population were unrelated individuals,
5. Population per household lay between 3 and 4, and
6. Less than 5 percent of the population were classified as nonwhite.

The first three criteria on age characteristics were meant to ensure similarity of household type between tracts, and also to try to cancel out the effects of the life cycle on the relationship between housing and income. In particular, high proportions of young people among renters and large numbers of people living on retirement incomes are likely to be excluded by these criteria. The restriction on family size helps ensure similarity of households again and should cancel out the effect of family size on housing expenditure from the relationships measured. The exclusion of nonwhites rids the data of the influences of racial prejudice on housing prices and also makes it unlikely that

[13] Information on the criteria in question were all taken from Tables P-1 and P-2 of the *Census Tracts*, various volumes.

subsidized public housing enters to distort the rental data. The restriction on unrelated individuals has already been explained.

The reader must judge the adequacy of these control criteria: had they been any stricter no tests could have been performed, so tightly did they limit the available observations. From Chicago, thirty-three tracts satisfied the criteria; from Philadelphia, fifty-six, fifteen, and fifteen (the latter two being those for which age distribution criteria differ in the manner noted above); from Los Angeles, twenty-two; and from San Francisco, only twelve. New York was omitted altogether because of its rent control regulations, and other metropolitan areas simply did not yield enough observations to be worth studying.[14]

RELEVANT DATA. The data that are relevant to the relationship between housing and income, that are available for census tracts, and that were used in the tests, are as follows: Median value of owner-occupied house for the tract, median gross rent for the tract, and median income for the tract. It is particularly unfortunate that separate data on incomes are not available for owners and renters, since there is a real possibility that tract income is more representative of owners than it is of renters; the former make up about 80 percent on the average of the populations of the tracts included.[15] However, this is not the only difficulty with the raw data, for though the value-of-house data are immediately usable on the basis of the assumption that the price of a flow of housing services is a constant proportion of the value of the house, and that this price per unit of services is invariant with respect to quantity supplied, the other data are not.[16]

The *income series* is for before-tax money income, and what is needed is a disposable income figure, adjusted in the case of owner-occupiers for the income flow coming from owner's equity in housing.

[14] In addition to the selection criteria, lack of data caused some observations to be dropped.

[15] Results reported below, however, suggest that this factor does not introduce any systematic bias into the income elasticity estimates.

[16] If houses of lower value are also older, their cost of maintenance and depreciation will be higher than that of newer and more expensive structures. The ratio of their market rental to their value will be higher than that for more expensive property, and my assumption of proportionality will not hold. Unfortunately the census does not give enough data for this possibility to be checked, and it must hence be noted as a possible source of bias in the results presented here—bias moreover in favor of the hypothesis tested. I am grateful to Professor Jacques Dreze of the University of Louvain, Belgium, for drawing my attention to this point.

Such a figure was obtained for renters by taking tract income and deducting income tax imputed at the rate appropriate for a family of four who take a standard deduction of 10 percent of income (up to $1,000). For owner-occupiers the same procedure was followed, except that mortgage interest payments, calculated on the assumption of a 50 percent mortgage carrying a 6 percent interest rate, were deducted *in addition to* the standard deduction, before tax was computed. Furthermore, to after-tax income was added the return on the owner's 50 percent equity in his house, also at a rate of 6 percent.[17]

Gross rent is a series that includes expenditures on fuel, light, and refrigeration, and the series needed here is one for housing expenditures per se. This was obtained by measuring the relationship between the utilities expenditure and income, with due allowances being made for intercity and climatic differences, and by using this relationship to impute utilities expenditures to each observation. The latter figure was then subtracted from gross rent, to arrive at the net rent figure used in the regressions.

The data were adjusted in accordance with the following regression for fuel, light, and refrigeration expenditures, where F is expenditure, Y is income, O is the owner-occupier proportion in the observation, D is mean degree-days in the city from which observations are taken, and C, P, and SF are dummy variables for Chicago, Philadelphia, and San Francisco.

$$F = a + 0.009(Y) + 1.635(O) + 0.014(D) + 21.910(C) +$$
$$ (0.001) \quad\ \ (0.185) \quad\ \ (0.006) \quad\ (20.577)$$

$$40.399(P) - 3.464(SF) \ldots$$
$$(16.160) \quad\ (13.827)$$

Los Angeles was the city permitted to determine the value of a, and data for eighteen other metropolitan areas were also used. These

---

[17] These adjustments are, of course, arbitrary, and before settling on them a good deal of preliminary work was done using other, and equally reasonable, assumptions. The results obtained proved not to be sensitive to changes in these assumptions, since the attribution of some taxes and some return to owner's equity, at any reasonable rate, proved to make a change in the income figure that was very large relative to the difference made by changing the assumptions on which the actual attribution was made. Thus the results given below are not heavily dependent upon the particular assumptions listed here.

It might also be noted that in dealing with data for Los Angeles and San Francisco, account was taken of the California state income tax.

expenditure data[18] are for cash outlays, and hence do not include renter purchases that are included in contract rent; nor do the data distinguish between owner-occupiers and renters. However, a figure is given for the proportion of owner-occupiers making up the sample yielding the observation, and since it may be presumed that their cash outlays are the equivalent of total expenditure, and since this variable entered with a significantly positive sign as expected, the value of its coefficient was multiplied by 100 and added to the intercept in extrapolating the total utilities expenditure included in gross rent. Mean degree-days is a figure based on the number of days on which the temperature falls below 65° and on how far below 65° it falls, and hence is a good one for picking up intercity variations in the need for heating.

It should be noted that the data used were for 1950 expenditures at 1950 prices. No adjustment was made here because, although prices could have been adjusted upward, no allowance could have been made for the considerable improvements in the efficiency of appliances (both heating and other types) that took place between 1950 and 1959. These two influences would work in opposite directions on the expenditures in question and there can be no a priori assumption that the failure to adjust for price changes has resulted in a worse estimate than was possible otherwise.

It should be noted also that the data used were for expenditure by income class. Inasmuch as permanent rather than measured income determines the demand for utilities, the marginal propensity to consume as measured here will be biased downward. In terms of adjusting the gross rent data, this involves subtracting too much at low levels of income and too little at high levels, so that the procedure biases the measured income elasticity of demand for rental housing upward—i.e., against the hypothesis under test.

ESTIMATING THE INCOME ELASTICITY OF DEMAND. Log linear regressions were then fitted separately to the data for each city, both for renters and owner-occupiers, and the resulting income elasticities of demand are given in Table 4. These results obviously confirm the hypothesis under test. In every one of the six cases, the income elasticity of

[18] The data used came from University of Pennsylvania Wharton School of Finance and Commerce, *Study of Consumer Expenditures, Incomes and Savings; Statistical Tables: Urban United States, 1950*, Vol 4 (1956); the income variable is from column 2 of Table 3–4, and the expenditure variable is from column 14 of the same table.

TABLE 4. Income Elasticity of Demand for Owner-Occupied and Rental Housing Based upon Intra-City Samples of Census Tract Data for 1960

City	Owners		Renters	
	Income elasticity	Coefficient of determination R^2	Income elasticity	Coefficient of determination R^2
Chicago	1.427 (0.090)	0.890	1.338 (0.184)	0.631
Philadelphia Sample 1	1.948 (0.276)	0.793	1.774 (0.254)	0.790
Sample 2	1.753 (0.222)	0.827	1.120 (0.221)	0.663
Sample 3	1.515 (0.087)	0.850	1.172 (0.136)	0.580
Los Angeles	1.486 (0.154)	0.823	1.295 (0.226)	0.543
San Francisco	1.559 (0.133)	0.932	0.732 (0.300)	0.374

Source: U.S. Bureau of the Census, *U.S. Censuses of Population and Housing: 1960*, Census Tracts, PHC(1)–26, 82, 116, 137 (1962), Table P-1 (for income data) and Table H-2 (for rent and value of house data). See also footnote 18 above and explanation in text. Figures in parentheses are standard errors of the regression coefficients

demand for owner-occupied housing is greater than that for rental housing. Though none of the differences is statistically significant when taken by itself, if combined they are significant. Were the obtained results a chance happening, one would expect the probability of obtaining a higher income elasticity for owner-occupied housing to be 0.5. Thus the chance of getting six such results in six independent tries is 0.5^6 or 0.016. Hence it is extremely unlikely that the results presented in Table 4 are the results of chance.

A further test was performed in order to make sure that the selection and correction procedures used for the data in the above experiments were not inadvertently responsible for the results obtained. Census tract data taken from Chicago were again used, but this time selected according to very loose criteria. Tracts were rejected only if they contained more than 10 percent unrelated individuals or nonwhite inhabitants, or if some necessary data happened to be missing. This yielded a sample of 247 observations, and rather than go through the laborious task of adjusting all these data along the lines outlined earlier, it was decided to perform the test first and to adjust the results after the event by means of a method which is described below.

This decision also permitted economy of calculation. If tract income is used for both owners and renters, the difference in income elasticity between them can be estimated by performing the regression of (log value of house − log rent) on the logarithm of tract income.[19] This was done. Also included as independent variables were the proportion of adults 65 and over in the tract, the proportion of adult males between 45 and 55, and the proportion of owner-occupiers.

The estimate of the difference in the income elasticities of demand for owner-occupied and rented housing was corrected in the following way for the bias introduced by not adjusting the income data for taxes and such, and the rental data for utility expenditures. Regressions were performed on the data for the thirty-three Chicago tracts used in an earlier test but using raw census data. The difference in the regression coefficients for owners and renters was calculated. It proved to be considerably greater in this case than in the case of the calculations presented in Table 4; the resulting difference was subtracted from the coefficient of income in the large sample regression in order to make it into an estimate of the "true" difference in the income elasticities of demand for owner-occupied and rental housing. This calculation is shown in Table 5 and, as will be seen, the difference remains positive after correction and hence provides some further confirmation of the hypothesis under test—though, again, once corrected the coefficient in question is not statistically significant.

Three points emerge from all this. First, it appears that the correction procedures used in dealing with the data which generated the results given in Table 4 tend to bias those results *against* the hypothesis under test. The difference in income elasticities is considerably smaller when obtained from these corrected data. This is all to the

[19] If $\log V = a_0 + b_0 (\log Y)$ and $\log R = a_1 + b_1(\log Y)$ then it follows that $\log V - \log R = a_0 - a_1 + (b_0 - b_1)(\log Y)$.

TABLE 5. Difference in Income Elasticity of Demand for Owner-Occupied and Rental Housing with Adjusted Regression Coefficient, 1960[a]

Calculation of Adjustment Factor

Test data	Income elasticities		
	Owners	Renters	Difference
33 Chicago census tracts, 1960			
Raw data	1.332	1.020	0.312
Corrected data	1.427	1.338	0.089
Adjustment factor[b]			0.223
Adjustment of Income Coefficient			
Original Coefficient	Adjustment Factor	Adjusted Coefficient	
0.337	0.223	0.114	

Source: See Table 4.
[a] The results of the regression from which the income is taken are: log value − log rent = 0.928 + 0.337 (0.117) log income; proportion of household heads aged 45–55 = +0.551 (0.302); proportion of population over age 65 = +0.054 (0.144); proportion of owner-occupied dwellings = −9.807 (3.617), R^2 = 0.064. Data are for 247 observations in Chicago census tracts. Figures in parentheses are standard errors of the regression coefficients.
[b] Line 1 minus line 2.

good; one's confidence in the results obtained must to some extent be strengthened if they cannot be attributed to this correction. Second, the proportion of owner-occupiers in a tract is included in the large sample test, and as a glance at the note to Table 5 will show, it is statistically significant. However, even in its presence there still emerges a positive coefficient for the income variable. This suggests that the earlier good results given in Table 4 cannot be explained away by considering that variations in the owner-occupier proportion in the tracts were systematically biasing the results in favor of the hypothesis tested. Though all qualms about the representativeness of tract income as a proxy for renter income cannot be settled by this result, they should at least be somewhat diminished. Finally, it should be clear that the selection procedures used previously cannot be held responsible for the results obtained, since a similar result emerges here where they are not followed.

ESTIMATING THE PRICE ELASTICITY OF DEMAND. One step now remains to be taken, and that is to discover the value of the price elasticity of demand for housing implied by the differences in the income elasticity estimates given in Table 4. This is not a difficult task. It is posited that the demand function for housing may be reasonably approximated by

$$H = aP^{b_0}Y^{b_1}.$$

This function may be rewritten as

$$\log H - b_1 \log Y = \log a + b_0 \log P.$$

A function of the latter form was used to estimate the price elasticity of demand for owner-occupied housing. The logarithm of expenditure on housing is a perfect proxy for the logarithm of quantity bought, provided the market price per unit is invariant with respect to the quantity supplied; also throughout this study a constant ratio has been assumed between annual expenditure on housing services and the value of the house owned. Clearly these two assumptions permit the substitution of data for value-of-house for H. All differences of units and dimension involved will affect only the intercept of the regression and will not bias the estimate of b_0. Obviously, Y must be represented by owner-occupier income, while b_1, the income elasticity of demand for housing, may be taken as equal to an income elasticity computed for *rental* housing as given in Table 4. The assumption all through this study has been that this parameter is a good estimate for the income elasticity of demand for owner-occupied housing in the absence of the tax subsidy.

The relevant price variable is as easily defined. As noted earlier in this chapter, the tax subsidy falls on only a portion of the supply price of owner-occupied housing—7.5/11 or 1/1.47 of it, to be precise. Now consider the quantity of housing demanded as defined in units priced at $1.47 each. For each unit bought, $1.00 of the expenditure is subsidized at the buyer's marginal tax rate so that, if he is in the 20 percent marginal tax bracket, the units cost him $1.27 each, and if he is in the 22 percent bracket, $1.25 each, and so on. For each observation in the data, it is possible to attribute the marginal tax bracket—call it T—and hence it is possible to define the price of our standard unit of housing as $[\$1.47 - (T \times \$1.00)]$.[20]

Again, the only effect of defining units in such an arbitrary way is on the intercept of the regression. Thus, where V is value of house,

---

[20] The income range of the data available for all the tests reported here was such as to make marginal federal tax rates vary only between 20 and 26 percent. This quite small variability in the independent variable should be borne in mind when the results are assessed.

Y is owner-occupier income, b_1 is the income elasticity of demand for rental housing for the city from which the observation is taken (as given in Table 4), and T is the marginal tax rate appropriate to the income observation, the regression actually performed was

$$(\log V - b_1 \log Y) = a + b_0 \log [\$1.47 - (T \times \$1.00)].$$

The data from all samples were pooled into one regression, and dummy variables were attached to the cities whence they came in order to pick up intercity differences in average value-to-rent ratios. The experiment was performed both including and excluding the San Francisco sample, for the reader will have noted that the income elasticity of demand for rental housing there was not estimated with any high degree of statistical significance, nor was it of the same order of magnitude as the estimates for other cities (see Table 4).

The resulting estimates of b_0 may be interpreted as price elasticities and are given in the first two rows of Table 6. As will be seen, the exclusion of the San Francisco data lowers the estimated value of this parameter and brings it somewhat closer to the estimates of Muth, which were in the region of -1.5. Both estimates are of the right sign and are significantly different from zero; they do not significantly differ from a value of -1.5, the value used in the welfare analysis, but they are greater than this figure. This evidence, then, is in favor (though not strongly so) of the hypothesis that the differences between owner-occupier and renter income elasticities of demand for housing may be explained in terms of a response to relative price differences arising from the income tax subsidy to the former. Certainly there is no reason to doubt the hypothesis in the light of this evidence.

The last two rows of Table 6 present price elasticity estimates obtained by using the large Chicago sample which also generated the results in Table 5. Here, the logarithm of the ratio of value-of-house to average monthly gross rent for each census tract was regressed on the logarithm of a price variable exactly similar to that just described—first with this as the only independent variable, and then with the other variables (including income) that appeared in the regression whose result is given in Table 5. As has already been shown, the failure to correct the data used here for tax payments, utilities expenditures, and the like influences upward the rate at which the ratio of value to rent increases with income, so that the price elasticity

Income Tax Incentives for Housing

TABLE 6. Price Elasticity of Demand for Owner-Occupied Housing, 1960

Data on which estimate is based	Price elasticity	Coefficient of determination R^2
Pooled census tract data[a]		
Including San Francisco	−3.057	0.996
	(0.802)	
Excluding San Francisco	−2.451	0.994
	(0.847)	
Sample of 247 observations on Chicago census tracts		
Price variable only	−3.568	0.021
	(1.543)	
Including other variables	−4.212	0.078
	(2.253)	

Source: See Table 4. Figures in parentheses are standard errors of the regression coefficients.
[a] The cities in the pooled regression are those shown in Table 4.

estimates given in the last two rows of Table 6 are overestimates of this parameter. The resulting estimates are indeed on the high side, as one would expect; again, though they are not highly significant, they do not refute the hypothesis under test.[21]

These then are the results of the empirical tests. They are not as decisive as one might have liked, but as far as they go, they tend rather to confirm than to refute the positive hypotheses underlying the preceding welfare analysis. To this extent, the analysis is put on a more solid basis by the test results. I will, however, leave it to the reader to decide how much extra faith he wishes to put in the welfare analysis as a result of this evidence.

[21] Demand elasticities were also computed by a different but related technique. Where d is the difference in income elasticities, y is some arbitrarily chosen income range, Y is the value of income at the bottom of that range, T the marginal tax rate at Y, and t its change over the range y, an estimate of the price elasticity of demand is given by the formula $\left(d\frac{y}{Y}\right)\left(\frac{1.47 - T}{t}\right)$. Such estimates were calculated for a value of y of $500 over the total income range entering each sample and averaged within each sample. Four of the seven sets of data used here gave estimates of between -1.5 and -2.1, including the large Chicago sample where the corrected difference in income elasticities was used. The San Francisco sample and the last two Philadelphia samples yielded estimates of between -6.0 and -11.5. These results are not, of course, independent of those given in Table 6, but they do show that, for four of the seven sets of data used in this study, the implied price elasticity of demand falls roughly in the range predicted, though with an uncertain degree of statistical significance.

SUSAN R. AGRIA

Special Tax Treatment
of Mineral Industries

THE PRESENT U.S. INCOME TAX LAW imposes vastly different rates of taxation on income from different sources. The best known example is the heavy taxation of income from corporate equity capital through the corporation income tax, as compared with the lighter taxation of other income from capital. Another important instance is the especially light taxation of income from mineral extraction industries. As a result of the percentage depletion and capital gains provisions, with the related expensing privileges, income from corporate equity capital is taxed at a considerably lower rate in mineral industries than it is in other corporate enterprises.

The depletion allowance was intended to provide capital recovery for mineral properties in a fashion similar to the depreciation allowance. Unlike the depreciation allowance, however, percentage depletion is based not on cost but on gross income, so that there is no strict relation between the amount of capital invested in a particular project and the total amount of depletion allowed on that property. A certain percentage of gross income is deducted from net income in calculating the tax base, with the restriction that the amount of depletion allowed may not exceed 50 percent of net income before depletion. In addition to the depletion allowance, depreciation is allowed on tangible property, certain exploration and development costs may be currently expensed, and losses on abandonment may be deducted. The concurrent deduction of both the depletion allowance and these items in effect constitutes a double deduction for a large percentage of exploration and development costs.

The capital gains provisions provide an alternative form of tax saving in the mineral industries. Producers in natural resources have opportunities to take advantage of capital gains which the manufacturer does not ordinarily have. A natural resource firm may take a lease on a promising area, develop it to the point of production, and then sell its interest and opt for capital gains treatment on the net revenue. Since the firm currently may deduct a large proportion of exploration and development costs from ordinary income, 48 percent of most of its costs is offset while its revenue is taxed at only 25 percent, excluding the 10 percent surtax enacted, effective July 1, 1968. With both percentage depletion and capital gains, the expensing privilege provides a strong incentive for the creation of integrated or diversified firms capable of generating sufficient ordinary income from which these deductions can be subtracted.

These tax advantages provide a powerful incentive for investment in the mineral extractive industries. To the extent that more exploration and development of mineral properties take place than would have under a system of neutral taxation, real resources are misallocated and the total product of the economy is smaller than it needs to be.

To the extent that mineral land values are bid up, it is possible that little extra exploration and development take place and few real resources are misallocated. Here the argument against percentage depletion is one of equity, on the ground that the owners of mineral interests gain at the expense of the general taxpayer.

The major concern of this study is with measuring the incentive to overinvest capital in mineral industries. An attempt will be made to estimate to what extent the nominal incentive to invest in mineral industries represents only a transfer payment from the general taxpayer to the holder of mineral interests and to what extent real resources are represented. These questions are dealt with in detail in the main body of the study, following a summary of the historical development of the provisions of federal income tax law concerning the depletion allowance.

Susan R. Agria

Development of the Depletion Allowance

The law regarding depletion provisions for natural resources is quite complex and has been altered many times by Treasury rulings, court decisions, and statutes. The somewhat haphazard development of the law has had the effect, in general, of liberalizing the depletion allowance and related provisions. The general form of this portion of the study will be to indicate the important sections of the *Internal Revenue Code, 1954* and then to present the evolution of law leading up to the particular sections, and the changes which have been made since 1954 in each section. Some economic implications of the various sections will be noted.

Section 611: Allowance of Deduction for Depletion

GENERAL RULE.

"In case of mines, oil and gas wells, other natural deposits, and timber, there shall be allowed as a deduction in computing taxable income a reasonable allowance for depletion. . . ."

The concept of "reasonable allowance" has changed considerably over the years and differs markedly for the various minerals. Almost without exception the "reasonable allowance" has been increased and has been extended to more minerals.

The first provision, in the 1913 revenue statute, did not call the allowance "depletion" and was rather small. The statute gave as a deduction "a reasonable allowance for the exhaustion, wear and tear of property arising out of its use or employment in the business, not to exceed, in the case of mines, 5 per centum of the gross value at the mine of the output for the year . . ." (38 Stat. 167). Here can be seen the beginnings of the concepts later applied in the depletion allowances. A percentage of gross income is given and this gross income is calculated on the value of the product at the mine.

The 1916 statute allowed deduction for depletion, not to exceed the market value of the product which has been mined and sold for the year, and in the aggregate not to exceed capital originally invested or the March 1, 1913 fair market value (39 Stat. 768). This latter provision was made because Congress did not want to tax any appreciation of capital value which took place before 1913, the year the tax was first imposed. However, it soon seemed unfair to Congress to tax differently according to when the taxpayer began operations. So in 1918, largely on the ground that new discoveries which contributed to the war effort were less favorably treated than pre-1913 discoveries, discovery depletion was first enacted. For properties discovered on or after March 1, 1913, a taxpayer was allowed to use as the basis for depletion the value of the well or mine at discovery or within thirty days thereafter, if his cost was materially disproportionate to fair market value (40 Stat. 1078–79). The basis for depletion no longer was the amount originally invested, and the depletion allowance lost some of its similarity to the depreciation allowance.

Congress soon became concerned with the size of the depletion allowances and, in 1921, limited the annual allowance to 100 percent of net income computed without depletion allowance (42 Stat. 256) and, in 1924, to 50 percent of net income from the property on which the discovery was made (43 Stat. 260).

Many difficulties arose in the administration of discovery depletion. A Senate Select Committee on the Investigation of the Bureau of Internal Revenue (the Couzens Committee) made an extensive study of the problem and published a report in 1926.[1] The committee found that the bureau administered the law poorly, making gross discriminations among individual taxpayers and among different minerals. The depletion allowances were generally excessive and often were arrived at by bargaining with the taxpayer. Rulings were not published and taxpayers often hired away employees of the Bureau of Internal Revenue in order to gain knowledge of the regulations and precedents. The bureau was far behind in its work of evaluating discoveries; in 1926, for example, it was evaluating 1919 discoveries.

Another objection which the committee made was that the law was not doing what was intended by Congress. Depletion allowances were not limited to new discoveries, and large companies rather than the small wildcatters were primarily benefiting from the deduction.

The major problem cited by the committee was the method of evaluating the deposits discovered in order to determine the size of the depletion allowance. The analytic method of evaluating discoveries provided estimates which depended too heavily on the individual judgment of the engineer. Discount rates were set too low and in some cases were disregarded. Mr. S. M. Greenidge, head of the

[1] *Partial Report*, Senate Select Committee on the Investigation of the Bureau of Internal Revenue, 69 Cong. 1 sess. (1926).

engineering division of the Income Tax Unit, testified that he believed the discount factor was of negligible importance and that he would not discount at all.[2] Evaluations of deposits were often based on the highest possible prices. In addition, since the bureau was so far behind in evaluating discoveries, prices in effect long after the discovery was made were used, even though the evaluation was supposed to be as of discovery or thirty days thereafter. All these factors combined to make evaluations and therefore depletion allowances excessively high.

The committee recommended another method for evaluation whereby actual annual profits would be discounted back to the basic date to determine annual depletion allowances. Congress did not accept this recommendation, but instead, in the 1926 statute, introduced percentage depletion. For oil and gas, depletion allowances were computed as 27.5 percent of gross income from the property during the taxable year, not to exceed 50 percent of net income of the taxpayer, and never to be smaller than the depletion allowance computed on cost (44 Stat. 16).

In 1932, percentage depletion was extended to other minerals. Coal was allowed 5 percent of gross income from the property during the taxable year, metal mines 15 percent, and sulphur 23 percent (47 Stat. 203). The percentages granted were supposed to approximate the amount of depletion granted under discovery depletion. However, since one of the major objections to discovery depletion was that the allowances granted under it were excessive, the substitution of percentage depletion was no improvement in this sense. The aggregate amount of percentage depletion depends on demand and cost conditions and is not limited to a determinate amount but continues as long as the mine or well yields a net income. The computation of percentage depletion is probably simpler than discovery depletion, although the tremendous amount of litigation over percentage depletion allowances may cast doubt on this conclusion. But simplicity of computation is no argument for preferring percentage depletion over cost depletion, particularly since both must be computed under present law.

The Supreme Court decision in *Anderson* v. *Helvering* (310 U.S. 404, 1940) attempted to clarify the status of percentage depletion. The

[2] *Ibid.*, p. 71.

deduction was found to be an act of grace of Congress and compensation for capital assets consumed in the production of income, similar to the depreciation deduction. The court emphasized that being an arbitrary percentage of gross income did not detract from the fact that the deduction was a tax-free return of capital consumed.

The 1942 revenue statute extended percentage depletion (at 15 percent) to ball and sagger clay, rock asphalt, and fluorspar (56 Stat. 840). In 1944 several other minerals were given percentage depletion but the allowance was only to be extended until the end of the war.[3] It was during this period that the national defense argument for percentage depletion was pushed the farthest. Producers lobbied for every mineral which had any possible connection with the war effort. In 1947 the wartime limitation for these minerals was repealed and several other minerals received percentage depletion.[4] In lobbying for extension of the depletion privilege the producers argued that if it were not extended they would be the only taxpayers whose taxes would be increased after the war.

The Revenue Act of 1951 added many more minerals and raised the allowance for coal to 10 percent (65 Stat. 497–98).[5] In 1954 "all other minerals" with some stated exceptions (such as air) were given percentage depletion at 15 percent and discovery depletion was eliminated.[6]

[3] Added in 1944, at 15 percent: flake graphite, vermiculite, potash, beryl, feldspar, mica, talc, barite, lepidolite, spodumene (58 Stat. 44–45).

[4] Added in 1947, at 15 percent: bauxite, phosphate rock, trona, bentonite, gilsonite, thenardite (61 Stat. 919–20).

[5] Added in 1951, at 5 percent: sand, gravel, slate, stone (including pumice and scoria), brick and tile clay, shale, oyster shell, clam shell, granite, marble, sodium chloride, and if from brine wells, calcium chloride, magnesium chloride, bromine; at 10 percent: asbestos, brucite, dolomite, magnesite, perlite, wollastonite, calcium carbonates, magnesium carbonates; at 15 percent: aplite, garnet, china clay, borax, fuller's earth, tripoli, refractory and fire clay, quartzite, diatomaceous earth, metallurgical grade limestone, chemical grade limestone (65 Stat. 497).

[6] Added or raised in 1954, at 23 percent: uranium, and if from U.S. deposits, anorthosite, asbestos, bauxite, beryl, celestite, chromite, corundum, fluorspar, graphite, ilmenite, kyanite, mica, olivine, quartz crystals (radio grade), rutile, block steatite talc, zircon, and ores of the following metals: antimony, bismuth, cadmium, cobalt, columbium, lead, lithium, manganese, mercury, nickel, platinum and platinum group metals, tantalum, thorium, tin, titanium, tungsten, vanadium, and zinc; at 10 percent: lignite, sodium chloride; at 15 percent: all other minerals not specified at a different rate except when used as rip rap, ballast, road material, rubble, concrete aggregates, or for similar purposes—this last group receives percentage depletion at 5 percent. Minerals receiving percentage depletion do not include: soil, sod, dirt, turf, water or mosses or minerals from sea water, the air, or similar inexhaustible resources. (See U.S. Treasury Department, *Internal Revenue Code, 1954*, Sec. 613.)

The concept of a reasonable allowance has changed considerably since 1913. With percentage depletion first granted in 1926 for oil and gas, other minerals have been increasingly successful in gaining the privilege, particularly since the beginning of World War II. In most cases there has been little debate over the principle, most controversy having centered around the inclusion of different minerals and their respective rates. In some cases the rates have been established through bargaining among different congressional interests and industry representatives.

SPECIAL RULES.

(1) *Leases.* "In the case of a lease, the deduction under this section shall be equitably apportioned between the lessor and lessee."

The principle determining who can take percentage depletion is the concept of "economic interest" which resulted from judicial interpretation. In *Palmer* v. *Bender* (287 U.S. 551, 1933) the Supreme Court decided that nothing in the law confined the depletion allowance to those who are technically lessors. There are two requirements to be eligible for percentage depletion. The taxpayer must have acquired by investment the interest in oil in place and he must look solely to production for a return on his property. Oil in the ground is "a reservoir of capital investment of the several parties."

Treasury regulations issued under the 1939 statute (Bureau of Internal Revenue, Regulations 103, 19.23 (m)–1) incorporated this concept of the Supreme Court. Royalties, overriding royalties, participating interests, production payments in kind or cash, working interests, net profits interests, and receipt of property for services rendered all were held to constitute "economic interest."[7]

In *Commissioner* v. *Southwest Exploration Co.* (350 U.S. 308, 1956) the Supreme Court first allowed a person outside the legal chain of title to claim an economic interest. In this case the owners of land adjacent to offshore oil leases had an economic interest in the oil in place because the only access was through their land.

In *Parsons* v. *Smith* (359 U.S. 215, 1959) the court ruled that strip mining contractors who are paid by the ton do not have an economic interest in the mineral in place because they have made no investment.

With the exception of this last case the class of taxpayers who

---

[7] Kenneth G. Miller, *Oil and Gas Federal Income Taxation* (Chicago: Commerce Clearing House, 1957), pp. 18–25.

have economic interest in minerals in place and who, therefore, may take percentage depletion has been generally widened. One criticism of the depletion allowance has been that while it was created in part to aid the small wildcatter with high risk, it was extended to persons little involved with risk.

Section 612: Basis for Cost Depletion

The basis for cost depletion is the adjusted basis for purpose of determining gain upon sale of property. From 1932 to 1951 depletable cost was adjusted by the higher of allowed or allowable depletion of prior years. Beginning January 1, 1952, depletable cost had to be adjusted by the higher of (1) the amount of depletion allowed in computing taxable income, to the extent the deduction resulted in a reduction of the taxpayer's income taxes, or (2) the amount of depletion allowable in computing taxable income.[8]

Annual cost depletion allowances are figured on a per barrel or per ton basis: unrecovered depletable costs divided by estimated recoverable units times units sold. The basis for cost depletion includes capitalized (not expensed) drilling and development costs (CFR 1.612–1 (b)).

Section 613: Percentage Depletion

"(a) . . . the allowance for depletion under section 611 shall be the percentage, specified in subsection (b), of the gross income from property excluding from such gross income an amount equal to any rents or royalties paid or incurred by the taxpayer in respect of the property. Such allowance shall not exceed 50 per cent of the taxpayer's taxable income from the property (computed without allowance for depletion)."

The interpretations of the terms "gross income from property" and "taxable income from property" are of great economic interest.

GROSS INCOME. For oil and gas, gross income from property means the amount for which taxpayers sell the oil or gas in the immediate vicinity of the well. If not sold on the premises the gross income is assumed to be equivalent to market or field price of oil or gas before conversion or transportation (CFR 1.613–3).

[8] Arthur Andersen and Co., *Oil and Gas Federal Income Tax Manual* (Arthur Andersen and Co., 1960), pp. 147, 148.

In *Helvering* v. *Mountain Producers Corp.* (303 U.S. 376, 1938), a producing company entered into contract with a refining company whereby the refiner bought oil from the producer and also would drill and maintain the wells. The producer claimed that his gross income for depletion was the cash received for oil plus the value of the development and maintenance of the wells done by the refiner. If the producer had developed and maintained the wells himself, the oil would have been sold for an amount covering development and maintenance. However, the Supreme Court allowed only the cash payments made to the producer as his gross income.

In *Helvering* v. *Elbe Oil Land Development Co.* (303 U.S. 372, 1938), the court decided that the sales price of leases was not gross income from property because when the property was disposed of, no investment was retained. It was held that gross income from property as used to govern the allowance for depletion meant gross income received from the operation of oil and gas wells by one who had a capital investment therein—not income from the sale of oil and gas properties themselves.

In *Helvering* v. *Twin Bell Oil Syndicate* (293 U.S. 312, 1934), the court determined that the lessee's gross income is gross production less royalties paid and the lessor's gross income is royalty income. A single depletion allowance is apportioned among the interested parties. Overriding royalties, production shares, oil payments, net profits payments, and bonuses are on the same footing as royalties.[9]

"(c)(1) The term 'gross income from the property' means, in the case of a property other than an oil or gas well, the gross income from mining."

The definition of mining as to the cut-off point between mining and manufacturing has caused much litigation, since it is in the producers' interest to include as many processes as possible before gross income from sale is computed.

Under the Income Tax Act of 1913, Treasury Regulations 33 defined "gross value at the mine" to be the market value of ore, coal, crude oil, and gas at mine or well. Treasury Regulations 62 under the 1921 act provided that if mineral products were not sold as raw material but were manufactured or refined, gross income was assumed to be equal to market or field price of the raw material.

---

[9] Miller, *Oil and Gas . . . Taxation*, pp. 118–22.

Under the Revenue Act of 1932, Regulations 77 listed certain processes which could be applied before figuring gross income. Coal could be cleaned, broken, and so forth. In the Revenue Act of 1943 a definition of treatment processes allowed before figuring gross income was first put into law: "The term 'mining' as used herein, shall be considered to include not merely the extraction of the ores or minerals from the ground but also the ordinary treatment processes normally applied by mine owners or operators in order to obtain the commercially marketable mineral product or products" (58 Stat. 45). Following this, the statute lists eligible processes. The "commercially marketable" test has led to difficulties of interpretation. The Revenue Act of 1950 allowed costs of transportation of ores from point of extraction to plants for "ordinary treatment processes" up to 50 miles unless the secretary found further transportation necessary (64 Stat. 931).

The Treasury has adopted a "mining vs. manufacturing" test for determining what processes may be included in gross income for new minerals receiving percentage depletion privileges. The courts have been more liberal, however, in including processes under mining, and generally have applied the "marketability" test under which all processes are included until a commercially marketable product is reached.

In the *Black Mountain Corp.* case (21 T.C. 246, 1954), the court allowed dust allaying as a mining process although 90 percent of all coal is sold without this process having been applied. In *U.S. v. Cherokee Brick and Tile Co.* (218 Fed 2d 424, 1955), all processes up to the production of burnt brick and tile were allowed because these were the first marketable products in the production process. In *Dragon Cement Co. v. U.S.* (244 Fed 2d 513, 1957), the Supreme Court allowed depletion to be computed upon the sale of cement.[10]

In some cases the courts have applied a profitability test. In *California Portland Cement Co. v. Riddell* (S.D. Cal. 1958; 59–1 U.S.T.C. 9156), the company was allowed to compute gross income in different stages because it could sell only a certain amount at each stage. In *U.S. v. Cannelton Sewer Pipe Co.* (268 Fed 2d 334, 1959), the Circuit Court allowed the company to compute percentage deple-

---

[10] Lawrence P. Sherfy, "Recent Developments in Meaning of 'Gross Income from Mining' for Computation of Percentage Depletion," in Rocky Mountain Mineral Law Institute, *Papers* (1961), p. 155.

tion on the sales of sewer pipe although there was a market for fire clay and shale, because the company could not make a profit on that market.[11]

In 1959 the Treasury presented a proposal altering the definition of mining to the House Committee on Ways and Means. The draft bill had two major provisions. First, it eliminated the commercially marketable product test for determining what processes enter into mining. The draft bill specified which processes were to be considered mining and which were not. Generally, those processes necessary to separate waste materials from the mineral were to be considered a mining process while those which produce a chemical change were to be treated as a manufacturing process. Second, the draft bill specified a definite cut-off point, stating that any process following a process not considered as mining would also not be considered mining.[12]

The committee took no action on the proposal because the Supreme Court granted certiorari in the *Cannelton* case. The court held for the government and rejected the profitability test, holding that the depletion allowance was intended to be based on the value of raw materials. If the mineral was worthless when it came out of the ground, it was not entitled to depletion. The fact that the company was integrated made no difference. If allowed to figure depletion on the value of the finished product, the taxpayer would, in effect, be receiving a depletion allowance on his manufacturing plant.

One week before the *Cannelton* decision (364 U.S. 76, 1960) the Senate passed the Gore amendment embodying the 1959 Treasury proposal. Although changed somewhat in conference committee, this amendment to the *Internal Revenue Code*, passed in 1960 (74 Stat. 292–3), contained much of the language and substance of the Treasury proposal, but differed in two important respects. The amendment was more specific as to processes, and the general cut-off point was left out. Specific cut-off points for some minerals were stated. This left open the question as to whether processes which are considered mining by the act might not also be considered mining when employed in a later stage. The processes listed in the act were exclusive but the secretary could add others. Thus the 1960 amend-

[11] *Ibid.*, pp. 166–69.
[12] *Mineral Treatment Processes for Percentage Depletion Purposes*, Hearings before the House Committee on Ways and Means, 86 Cong. 1 sess. (1959), pp. 1b–2.

ment reversed the trend toward allowing an increasing number of processes to be applied before gross income is computed.

TAXABLE INCOME. The limitation on depletion of 50 percent of taxable income makes it necessary to compute taxable income separately for each property. Taxable income is defined as gross income from property less allowable deductions attributable to the property CFR 1.613-14). Depreciation, intangible drilling and development costs which are expensed, attorney fees, interest on borrowed money, geological and land development expenses, and overhead expenses must all be allocated to the different properties in arriving at taxable income. Not all of geological and land development expenses need be allocated to producing properties, however. Some may be attributed to non-producing properties.[13] It is in the taxpayers' interest to allocate as much as possible of expenses to non-producing properties in order to make taxable income for producing properties as high as possible, thus raising the ceiling of 50 percent of net income on the annual depletion allowance. In properties other than oil or gas, expenses involved in the allowed mineral processes must be deducted. The importance of determining what is a separate property, caused by the taxable income limitation, is discussed below under Section 614.

"(a) In no case shall the allowance for depletion under section 611 be less than it would be if computed without reference to this section."

If depletion is computed by the percentage depletion method, it must also be computed by cost depletion to determine which is larger. Percentage depletion may not be taken if cost depletion would be greater.

Section 614: Definition of Property

"(a) . . . the term 'property' means each separate interest owned by the taxpayer in each mineral deposit in each separate tract or parcel of land."

This was the definition used by the Treasury Department until 1954. Under this rule the allowance for depletion had to be computed upon income from separate properties and not upon combined income. "Separate tract or parcel of land" did not include non-contiguous properties even if they were obtained under the same lease.

[13] Miller, *Oil and Gas . . . Taxation*, pp. 141-46.

Even adjacent leases acquired in different transactions had to be treated as separate properties. On the other hand, each well could not be considered a separate property. This regulation led to much administrative difficulty and litigation.

In 1954 the above quoted passage was adopted by statute as the general rule but a special rule for operating mineral interests was also adopted. The special rule (*IRC* 614 (b)(1)) gave the taxpayer the option of aggregating two or more mineral interests within one operating unit. The interests did not have to be contiguous but merely part of one operating unit. The taxpayer was not allowed, however, to form more than one aggregation of mineral interests within any one operating unit.

In 1958 the code was further amended to allow in the case of mines (but not oil or gas wells) more than one aggregation of interest within one operating unit and to allow separate mines to be treated as separate properties even though they were part of one mineral interest.

The necessity for figuring income from separate properties stems from the limitation on the depletion allowance of 50 percent of net income. The special rule allowing aggregations of mineral interests into one property for tax purposes is advantageous to the taxpayer in many cases. If the limitation of 50 percent of the taxable income is operative upon any interest, the total percentage depletion allowance will always be larger if that interest is combined with one upon which the limitation is not operative. This situation may give incentive to drill doubtful wells in order not to "waste" some of the 50 percent limitation of a highly profitable well with which the new well might be aggregated. However, other considerations are involved in the aggregation of properties. The election to aggregate is binding for the life of the properties. If a marginal well with high leasehold cost is aggregated with others and then is abandoned, these costs cannot be recovered through cost depletion or loss on abandonment as would be the case if the abandoned well were a separate property. If the properties are aggregated, these costs may be recovered only through percentage depletion on the producing wells.

Section 263 (c): Capital Expenditures

Oil and gas producers are granted the option to deduct as expenses intangible drilling and development costs.

Although not incorporated into law until 1954, the option of expensing drilling and development costs was permitted under Treasury regulations beginning in 1917. Regulations 77 termed these "intangible drilling and development costs." In general only those costs relating to items which do not have salvage value may be expensed. Expenditures represented by physical goods must be recovered through depreciation.

The election to expense drilling and development costs is binding for all subsequent years and for all properties of the taxpayer. At first only the property owner or lessee doing his own drilling and development was given the expensing option. Later the provisions were liberalized until the expensing option was available under almost any type of contract.[14]

In 1942 the Treasury made a proposal to Congress to eliminate the expensing privilege through statute (even though the privilege was not yet statutory).[15] In 1950 the Treasury proposed to have gross income for computing percentage depletion reduced by the amount of intangible drilling and development costs expensed.[16] Both proposals were rejected, and in 1954 the privilege was made statutory.

Section 615: Exploration Expenditures

Up to $100,000 per year of exploration expenditures may be charged off by a taxpayer as expense in each of four tax years for mineral deposits other than oil and gas. These four years need not be consecutive (CFR 1.615–4, revised January 1968).

Before 1951 all outlays for exploration for mineral properties were recoverable through depletion. The Revenue Act of 1951 allowed $75,000 per year for four years to be charged off either against current income or on a deferred basis. In 1954 the limit was raised to $100,-000. The exploration stage is defined as that period before the disclosure of a commercial deposit (*IRC* 1954, Sec. 615).

Section 616: Development Expenditures

For minerals other than oil or gas, development expenditures may be charged off against current income from other sources or, if in

---

[14] U.S. Bureau of Mines, *Federal Mineral Taxation* (1952), p. 57.

[15] *Percentage Depletion and Option on Intangible Costs*, House Committee on Ways and Means, 77 Cong. 2 sess. (1942).

[16] *Revenue Revision of 1950*, Hearings before the House Committee on Ways and Means, 81 Cong. 2 sess. (1950), pp. 818–95.

excess of net receipts from ores or minerals, treated as deferred expenses and deducted from income as production proceeds. This privilege, granted first in 1951, allows an increase in total deductions over the pre-1951 allowance. Regulations 45 under the 1918 act required development expenditures in excess of net receipts from minerals to be charged to capital account. After the production stage was reached, all development expenditures could be deducted as current expenses or treated as deferred expenses to be written off per unit of production. Since development expenditures in excess of net income were treated more favorably in the production period than in the development period, there was an incentive to reach the production period as soon as possible. (The production period is reached when the principal activity of the mine is the production of ore.[17])

The Revenue Act of 1951 made the deductions for development expenditures statutory and gave the same treatment to development expenditures in excess of current income in the development period as to those in the production period.

As indicated earlier, a large proportion of expenditures receive a double deduction. In the mineral industries there are five ways in which the taxpayer may recover his investment tax free:[18] through (1) depreciation, (2) depletion, (3) charges against current income, (4) prepaid expense as production proceeds, and (5) losses upon abandonment. The taxpayer would prefer that outlays be recoverable in forms other than depletion since percentage depletion continues as long as there is net income, whether or not charges are made to other accounts. If a dollar of outlay can be changed from depletion to another account, the total deduction is increased by one dollar. There is one qualification, however; if the limitation of 50 percent of taxable income is operable, then one dollar changed from depletion to, say, depreciation will result in a 50 cent increase in total deductions. The reduction of taxable income by one dollar will reduce the percentage depletion allowance by 50 cents while depreciation will increase by one dollar.

Since 1951, the expensing privileges have, in general, been more favorable to the mining industries than to the oil and gas industry. In the exploration period, the taxpayer in mining is allowed to expense or to treat as deferred expenses $100,000 per year for four years, while in oil and gas he has no such privilege. However, in exploring

[17] U.S. Bureau of Mines, *Federal Mineral Taxation*, p. 9.
[18] *Ibid.*, p. 4.

for oil and gas, intangible drilling and development costs and dry hole costs for exploratory holes may be expensed.

In the development period the mining taxpayer has an annual option to charge development costs against current income or to recover them as prepaid expense, while the oil and gas taxpayer has a single binding election to capitalize or expense. In addition, mining development expenditures in excess of net income may be recovered as prepaid expense on a per unit of production basis. This option is not available in oil and gas. It is particularly valuable to the small operator who may have no other income against which to offset deductions.

The same distinction holds for development expenditures in the production period. The mining taxpayer has an annual option and may expense the costs or treat them as prepaid expenses. The oil and gas taxpayer has one election and may not opt to treat development outlays as prepaid expenses.

Since its inception in 1913 the depletion allowance has been broadened in several respects. The magnitude of a reasonable allowance has increased considerably and more minerals are eligible for the allowance. The definition of who has economic interest, and can therefore take depletion, has been widened. The definition of what constitutes mining has been widened, although there was a reversal of this trend in 1960. Taxpayers have been given the privilege of aggregating properties for tax purposes which work to their advantage. The expensing privilege for oil and gas has been made statutory and more generous expensing privileges have been extended to other minerals. Little has been accomplished in the way of reducing the depletion allowance and related privileges.

Percentage Depletion

The model used here is an elaboration of that used by Professors Arnold C. Harberger[19] and Peter O. Steiner[20] to demonstrate the

[19] Arnold C. Harberger, "The Taxation of Mineral Industries," in *Federal Tax Policy for Economic Growth and Stability*, Joint Committee on the Economic Report, 84 Cong. 1 sess. (1955), pp. 439–49; Arnold C. Harberger, "The Tax Treatment of Oil Exploration," *Proceedings of the Second Energy Institute* (American University, School of Business Administration, 1961).

[20] Peter O. Steiner, "Percentage Depletion and Resource Allocation," in *Tax Revision Compendium*, House Committee on Ways and Means, 86 Cong. 1 sess. (1959), Vol. 2, pp. 949–66.

special incentive given to investment in mineral industries, particularly petroleum. It is assumed here that competition and mobility of resources are such that the after-tax rates of return of favored and non-favored industries are the same. In addition, for the next three sections of the discussion it is assumed that all expenditures represent real resources. This assumption will be modified later.

The majority of the data comes from a depletion study made by the Treasury Department for the years 1958–60.[21] A similar unpublished study for the years 1950–52 was also consulted.[22] The Treasury study gives the amounts of depletion taken, expenditures (a) currently expensed, (b) deferred, and (c) expenses to be subsequently charged to depreciation, loss on abandonment, acquisition costs, net income, and the like, for a large sample of corporations.[23] Besides being grouped by the industrial classifications, the data are classified by "principal mineral product." Each mineral extraction interest of the taxpayer is grouped according to mineral product. This is quite important in an industry such as petroleum, where integration, diversification, and the large amounts of oil interests owned by other industries make classification by predominant business activity rather misleading.

Oil and gas, coal, and iron are the three minerals examined here. Oil and gas taxpayers took by far the largest amount of depletion claimed in 1958–60, but iron and coal taxpayers also took substantial amounts.[24]

Symbols used in computing investment incentives are listed below:

$Y =$ Present value of expected income stream from mineral deposit or machine, net of all costs but before depletion and depreciation

$C =$ Accumulated costs incurred in producing asset ($Cp =$ petroleum; $Cc =$ coal; $Ci =$ iron; $Cm =$ machine)

$a =$ Percentage of exploration and development costs currently expensed

---

[21] *President's 1963 Tax Message*, Hearings before the House Committee on Ways and Means, 88 Cong. 1 sess. (1963), Pt. 1, pp. 290–350.

[22] U.S. Treasury Department, Tax Analysis Staff, "Statistics of Corporation Mineral Depletion Deductions and Related Allowances, 1950, 1951 and 1952" (processed; March 10, 1955).

[23] Appendix B, below, consists of portions of the tables in the Treasury study which are used here.

[24] In 1950–52, iron and coal were the second and third largest mineral products in terms of depletion claimed. It was impossible to determine ranking from the 1958–60 study.

b = Percentage of exploration and development costs charged to depreciation

c_1 = Percentage of exploration and development costs ultimately written off as loss on abandonment

c_2 = Percentage of exploration and development costs deferred to be written off as production proceeds

$c = c_1 + c_2$

d = Discount factor depending on rate of return and life of asset

f = Discount factor depending on rate of return and time-path of write-off of expenditures charged to loss on abandonment

g = Discount factor depending on rate of return and life of depreciable equipment used in exploration and development

p = Percentage which depletion allowance bears to net income before depletion

r = Statutory rate of percentage depletion on gross income

s = Percentage which severance tax payments bear to net income before depletion

t = Corporation income tax rate

Consider two capital assets, a mineral deposit and a machine, which are similar in that the expected income streams gross of taxes and tax offsets have identical paths through time. The economic incentives for entrepreneurs to invest to acquire these assets should therefore in principle be the same. But percentage depletion and the expensing privileges give incentive to invest more capital to produce a given income stream from natural resources than from the machine.

The effective cost, net of tax offsets, of exploration for and development of the mineral asset is

(1) $\qquad [1 - .52(a + fc)] \, Cp,$

where it is assumed that there is sufficient other income (taxed at 52 percent)[25] against which to offset costs. Since there are no tax offsets associated with the acquisition of ordinary capital assets, the cost of acquiring a machine, for example, is Cm.

Revenue is derived as follows:

	For a natural resource,	For a machine,
(2)	$Y - 0.52(Y - pY - gbCp)$.	$Y - 0.52(Y - dCm)$.

[25] A 52 percent corporation income tax rate is used here and in the following sections because this was the rate in effect during 1958–60, the period for which the Treasury data are available. Effects of changing the corporation income tax rate are discussed beginning on p. 110.

Under competition, production will be carried to the point where cost net of tax offsets equals revenue net of taxes.

For a natural resource,
$$[1 - .52(a + fc)] \, Cp = Y - .52(Y - pY - gbCp)$$

(3)
$$Cp = \frac{Y(.48 + .52p)}{1 - .52(a + gb + fc)}.$$

For a machine,
$$Cm = Y - .52(Y - dCm)$$

(4)
$$Cm = \frac{.48Y}{1 - .52d}.$$

Comparing the two costs,

(5)
$$\frac{Cp}{Cm} = \frac{(.48 + .52p)(1 - .52d)}{[1 - .52(a + gb + fc)](.48)}.$$

Percentage depletion and expensing provisions give the producer in natural resources an incentive to incur costs which are up to $(.48 + .52p)(1 - .52d)/[1 - .52(a + gb + fc)](.48)$ times as high as those which would be incurred to produce the same income stream elsewhere in the corporate sector.

In order to measure this incentive for capital to flow into natural resource development, the values of several parameters must be estimated. The data on domestic properties only were considered, but fortunately, it is possible to estimate most of the parameters directly from the Treasury study.[26] The fraction of expenditures currently expensed, a, and the fraction charged to depreciation, b, were estimated directly. In group c the part deferred, c_2, was estimated directly. However, loss on abandonment, c_1, is included in the Treasury classification "charged to depletable asset account." Some part of the amount charged to depletable assets each year will subsequently be charged to loss on abandonment. The current year deductions for loss on abandonment average around 50 percent of the amount charged to depletable assets for oil and gas, 40 percent for coal, and 20 percent for iron. These percentages of amounts charged to the depletable asset account have been taken as estimates of amounts which will ultimately be charged to loss on abandonment to estimate parameter c_1.

[26] See Appendix B, Table B–2.

For the estimation of p, the net income given in the Treasury study had to be altered.[27] In formula (3) the income concept Y is net of all costs but before depreciation or depletion. Depreciation, expensed costs (which would be part of depreciation in a normal industry), deferrals, and loss on abandonment had to be added back into the net income given in the Treasury study, and p was estimated as the ratio of actual depletion allowances to income thus obtained.

Discount factors must be applied to some of the groups of expenditures because in a given year a deduction to be taken in some future year is not worth as much to the taxpayer as it would be in the current year. The discount factors all depend on the rate of return on capital and the life of the asset. A 10 percent rate of return was used in all cases. For oil and gas a life of ten years was assumed for the well and equipment.[28] For discount factor f, applied to group c, the time-path of write-off is needed for these deductions. This was not available in the Treasury study, but Steiner had this information for his sample for 1955–57.[29] His discount factor, 0.71, was used for this group.

For coal, a life of depreciable equipment of 20 years[30] and a life of mines of 30 years were used, and for iron a life of 20 years for equipment and 25 years for mines were used. For discount factor f, it was assumed that deductions in group c were spread evenly over the life of the mine.

These estimated lives of assets are probably rather conservative, but the shorter the life of the asset the smaller will be the incentive calculated. The discount factors were calculated using both the straight line and sum-of-the-years digits methods of write-off. Discount factors were not calculated for the double declining balance method because these would fall between those calculated under the other two methods. Table 1 shows the discount factors used.

The findings suggest that there is an incentive to invest about 1.5 times as much capital to produce a given income stream in oil exploration and development as in another industry not accorded the depletion and expensing privileges (Table 2). These estimates of Cp/Cm and the parameters agree closely with Steiner's estimates for

[27] See Appendix B, Table B–1.
[28] See U.S. Treasury Department, Bureau of Internal Revenue, *Bulletin F*, Revised (January 1942), p. 52.
[29] Steiner, in *Tax Revision Compendium*, p. 961.
[30] See U.S. Treasury, *Bulletin F*, pp. 50–51.

TABLE 1. Discount Factors by Straight Line and Sum-of-Years Digits Depreciation Methods, for Oil and Gas, Coal, and Iron Industries

	Discount factor based on 10 percent rate of return and:					
	Life of asset[a] d		Time-path of write-off of abandonment loss f		Life of exploration and development equipment g	
Mineral product	Straight line	Sum-of-years digits	Straight line	Sum-of-years digits	Straight line	Sum-of-years digits
Oil and gas	0.61	0.70	0.71	0.71	0.61	0.70
Coal	0.31	0.44	0.31	0.44	0.43	0.55
Iron	0.36	0.49	0.36	0.49	0.43	0.55

Source: Estimated by author. Further details and assumptions are given in the text.

[a] For oil and gas a life of 10 years was assumed for the well and equipment. For coal, a life of 30 years for mines and 20 years for equipment were assumed, and for iron, a life of 25 years for mines and 20 years for equipment.

TABLE 2. Oil and Gas, Coal, and Iron Industries: Percentage of Costs Expensed, Depreciated, and Written-Off; Ratio of Depletion Allowance to Income; and Percentage Depletion Investment Incentive Ratios, by Straight Line and Sum-of-Years Digits Depreciation Methods, 1958–60

Mineral product and year	Percentage of costs			Ratio of depletion allowance to income before depletion allowance p	Percentage depletion investment incentive ratios	
	Currently expensed a	Depreciated b	Deferred and lost on abandonment c		Straight line	Sum-of-years digits
Oil and gas					C_p/C_m	
1958	0.595	0.203	0.106	0.291	1.53	1.45
1959	0.560	0.189	0.130	0.299	1.51	1.42
1960	0.524	0.189	0.148	0.306	1.48	1.40
Coal					C_c/C_m	
1958	0.603	0.029	0.210	0.433	1.91	1.80
1959	0.567	0.022	0.240	0.466	1.91	1.80
1960	0.507	0.038	0.208	0.487	1.85	1.74
Iron					C_i/C_m	
1958	0.978	0.007	0.003	0.267	2.14	1.97
1959	0.973	0.002	0.004	0.272	2.14	1.96
1960	0.985	0.001	0.003	0.279	2.17	2.00

Source: Estimated by author. Further details and assumptions are given in the text.

1955–57.[31] The reason for the decline in parameter a (and consequently in Cp/Cm) over the three years was an increase in the fraction of total expenditures spent on lease acquisition. These expenditures must be charged to depletion $(1 - a - b - c)$ and are the only part which does not receive a double deduction.

For coal, there is incentive to invest around 1.8 times as much capital as in a normal industry. As in the case of oil, the decline in the value of a is due to an increase in acquisition expenditures. Taxpayers in the iron industry are able to expense around 98 percent of total exploration and development expenditures in the year they are incurred. This results in an incentive to spend around twice as much capital to produce a given income stream as in an industry without special privileges.

In all cases the incentives computed with sum-of-the-years digits discount factors are lower than those computed with the straight line method. The more rapid rate of write-off with the sum-of-the-years digits method is advantageous both to the mineral industry and to non-mineral industries, but since the mineral industry can write off a large part of capital costs in the year incurred and a non-mineral industry must depreciate them over the life of the asset, the new methods of write-off are relatively more advantageous to the non-mineral industry.

While percentage depletion and expensing privileges may have increased exploration for petroleum and natural gas, there has probably been little recent exploration for new coal or iron deposits.[32] However, the depletion and expensing privileges also give an incentive to overproduction. Considered below are two ways to increase production, P—by increasing facilities, S; and by increasing the rate of extraction with given facilities, Q:

(6) $$P = SQ$$
$$\frac{\partial P}{\partial D} = \frac{\partial Q}{\partial D} S + \frac{\partial S}{\partial D} Q,$$

where D is the rate of percentage depletion.

[31] Steiner, in *Tax Revision Compendium*, p. 964.

[32] The Treasury study (*President's 1963 Tax Message*, Hearings, Pt. 1, pp. 290–350) reported that in 1960 its sample group of oil and gas producers expended $919 million on exploration while the sample of coal producers expended only $805,000 and the sample of iron producers $762,000.

TABLE 3. Development Incentive Ratios under Percentage Depletion for Oil and Gas, Coal, and Iron Industries, by Straight Line and Sum-of-Years Digits Depreciation Methods, 1958–60

	Development incentive ratios					
	Oil and gas Cp/Cm		Coal Cc/Cm		Iron Ci/Cm	
Year	Straight line	Sum-of-years digits	Straight line	Sum-of-years digits	Straight line	Sum-of-years digits
1958	1.60	1.54	2.27	2.14	2.19	2.00
1959	1.63	1.56	2.27	2.14	2.20	2.00
1960	1.60	1.54	2.44	2.28	2.21	2.03

Source: Estimated by author. Further details are given in the text.

Depletion law is actually more favorable to enlarging facilities by drilling new holes in already proven areas or further developing old mines than to exploring for and developing new deposits, since exploration costs are not treated as favorably as development costs. In the case of the oil industry, geophysical, geological, and land acquisition costs may not be expensed but must be capitalized and charged to depletion. For coal and iron, only $100,000 per year in each of four years of exploration costs may be expensed. Thus tax treatment of enlarging facilities where no exploration is necessary is more favorable than that accorded to exploration and development of new deposits.

The Treasury study divided the categories of deductions into exploration, development, and land acquisition costs,[33] from which it was possible to calculate the incentive to develop oil wells and mines in known mineral areas. For this purpose, only the development cost figures were used. Income figures for all properties had to be used, since the income data were not broken down by type of property. This usage makes an implicit assumption that the relation of depletion taken to net income, p, is the same for development properties as for all properties (Table 3).

In all cases the incentives are higher for development than for exploration, although for iron the increase is slight. For oil and coal the elimination of acquisition costs which must be charged to deple-

[33] See Appendix B, Tables B-2 and B-3.

TABLE 4. Incentive Ratios for Additional Capital Equipment Investment under Percentage Depletion, for Oil and Gas, Coal, and Iron Industries, 1958–60

	Additional capital equipment incentive ratios		
Year	Oil and gas C_p/C_m	Coal C_c/C_m	Iron C_i/C_m
1958	1.31	1.47	1.29
1959	1.32	1.50	1.29
1960	1.33	1.53	1.30

Source: Estimated by author. Further details are given in the text and Appendix A.

tion caused the percentage of total costs expensed in the year incurred to be higher for development than for exploration, and hence resulted in an increase in the incentives. Acquisition costs were very small for iron, so their elimination made little difference.

Production may also be increased by installing additional capital equipment in already existing facilities (Table 4). Expenditures for this purpose are charged to depreciation.[34]

Percentage depletion also provides an incentive to increase the rate of extraction with given facilities. Under ordinary tax treatment, a producer will use resources up to the point where a dollar of incremental cost produces a dollar of incremental revenue from the sale of the additional output. By contrast, under percentage depletion, it pays the producer to spend up to $(1 + 0.52r)$ dollars of incremental costs to produce an additional dollar's worth of revenue from sales, where r is the statutory rate of percentage depletion and 0.52 is the assumed tax rate. The reason is that a dollar of additional revenue reduces the producer's tax bill by $0.52r$, for his depletion allowance will increase by r dollars, carrying with it the indicated reductions in tax liability. Given the current rates of percentage depletion for the corresponding minerals, the marginal cost of producing a dollar of additional revenue from existing facilities will tend to be $1.14 for oil and gas, $1.05 for coal, and $1.08 for iron.

Where the 50 percent of net income limitation is effective and depletion is based on net income rather than gross income, there will

[34] For the equation on which Table 4 is based, and its derivation, see Appendix A, equation (4) and the preceding discussion.

be no incentive to increase production by increasing variable costs, for a subsidy on net income will not increase production from given facilities.

Severance Taxes

In defending the depletion allowance, industry representatives often point out that the mineral extraction industries, particularly oil and gas, must pay severance taxes which other industries do not pay. In this section, severance taxes will be incorporated into the analysis.

Y is redefined as the present value of the expected net income stream before depletion, depreciation, income taxes, and severance taxes. Where s is the ratio of severance tax payments to net income, Y, revenue for the mineral industry is

(7) $$Y - sY - t(Y - pY - sY - gbCp),$$

while costs, as before, are

(8) $$[1 - t(a + fc)] Cp.$$

Setting cost equal to revenue,

(9) $$Cp = \frac{Y(1 - s - t + tp + ts)}{1 - t(a + gb + fc)}.$$

In the non-mineral industry it is assumed that no severance taxes are paid so that, as before,

(10) $$Cm = \frac{Y(1 - t)}{1 - td}$$

and

(11) $$\frac{Cp}{Cm} = \frac{(1 - s - t + tp + ts)(1 - td)}{[1 - t(a + gb + fc)](1 - t)}.$$

This equation is based on the assumption that severance taxation constitutes an extraordinary tax upon mineral industries, in no way a substitute for other taxes such as the property tax. Data on property taxation of mineral industries are extremely scarce, but in at least one state, Oklahoma, equipment, tools, material, or property which is used and actually necessary in the production of minerals, oil and gas, and upon which a gross production tax is paid, are exempt from the property tax.[35] To the extent that other taxes are reduced because

---

[35] Commerce Clearing House, *State Tax Guide* (Chicago: CCH, 1959), p. 2164.

TABLE 5. Incentive Ratios for Exploration and Development under Percentage Depletion, with and without Severance Taxes, for Oil and Gas and Iron Industries, by Straight Line and Sum-of-Years Digits Depreciation Methods, 1958–60

Mineral product and year	Incentive ratios without severance taxes			Incentive ratios with partial severance taxes			Incentive ratios with all severance taxes		
	Ratio of severance taxes to income	Mineral industry to other industries		Ratio of severance taxes to income	Mineral industry to other industries		Ratio of severance taxes to income	Mineral industry to other industries	
	s	Straight line	Sum-of-years digits	s	Straight line	Sum-of-years digits	s	Straight line	Sum-of-years digits
		C_p/C_m			C_p/C_m			C_p/C_m	
Oil and gas									
1958	0	1.53	1.45	0.047	1.45	1.38	0.059	1.44	1.36
1959	0	1.51	1.42	0.052	1.43	1.35	0.064	1.41	1.33
1960	0	1.48	1.40	0.053	1.40	1.33	0.066	1.39	1.31
		C_i/C_m			C_i/C_m			C_i/C_m	
Iron									
1958	0	2.14	1.97	0.124	1.88	1.73	0.154	1.81	1.67
1959	0	2.14	1.96	0.150	1.82	1.67	0.185	1.74	1.60
1960	0	2.17	2.00	0.045	2.07	1.91	0.057	2.05	1.89

Source: Estimated by author. Further details and assumptions are given in the text and Appendix A.

of the severance tax, the preceding formula will understate the incentives.

To compute s, the amount of severance tax paid by each mineral industry was needed. Available from the Census Bureau are severance tax collections by state and, for the most part, by mineral, although for some states collections are given only as "severance taxes."[36] A comparison of tax law and rates with mineral production from the *Minerals Yearbook*[37] was made and the tax collections were allocated to the various minerals.[38]

It was necessary to allocate some part of severance tax collections to the Treasury sample producers, but only a rough approximation was possible. It would have been preferable to calculate s on an industry basis, using net income figures from *Statistics of Income*,[39] but data from this source are given by industrial classification while the severance data are classed by mineral product. Particularly in the cases of oil and gas, the two methods are not comparable.

In the Treasury study are estimates of the fraction of total depletion taken by those firms included in the study, but these estimates are unfortunately by industrial classification, not by mineral product. About 80 percent of total depletion taken by the crude petroleum and natural gas industries is covered by the study. The fractions are 57 percent for coal and 78 percent for iron. On the rather shaky assumptions that the fraction of total depletion taken by producers of a particular mineral in the sample was the same as that taken by that industrial group, and that the sample of mineral producers paid the same fraction of total severance taxes as the fraction of total depletion they took, it was estimated that the sample producers bore 80 percent of total severance tax collections in oil and gas, 57 percent in coal, and 78 percent in iron.

To provide a lower bound, a second assumption was made that all of the severance taxes paid in each industry were borne by the companies in the sample. This clearly gives an overstatement of s and therefore an underestimate of the incentive (Table 5).

[36] U.S. Bureau of the Census, *Detail of State Tax Collections* (annually, 1958–61).
[37] U.S. Bureau of Mines, *Minerals Yearbook*, Vol. 3: *Area Reports* (annually, 1958–61).
[38] In one state, New Mexico, some severance tax is collected on a local basis. Amounts collected were not available and are not included here.
[39] U.S. Treasury Department, *Statistics of Income, Corporation Income Tax Returns* (annually, 1958–60).

Severance tax collections were so small for coal that the incentives were not affected by their inclusion. In Table 5 the incentives are estimated for oil and gas and iron under three assumptions: (1) severance taxes were not taken into account; (2) a fraction of total severance taxes collected (80 percent in oil and gas, 78 percent in iron) were assigned to the sample producers; and (3) all severance taxes collected were assigned to the sample producers.

The estimates in Table 5 may be regarded only as rough approximations and as a sort of industry average. Severance tax rates and bases vary from state to state. Louisiana levies the tax on a per barrel basis, Texas on a percentage of gross sale value, and Oklahoma on both bases. Minnesota's tax is levied as a percentage of the sale value of ore. Ideally, an incentive could be estimated for each state, but the Treasury data were not subdivided by states.

Among the mineral incentives, the incentive for iron ore was the most strongly affected by the inclusion of severance taxes. Much iron ore is mined in Minnesota, which has a very high severance tax rate.[40] The computed incentive for oil and gas falls by about 8 percentage points when severance taxes are included. While severance taxation is a slight offset to the depletion allowance, its inclusion in the formulas does not materially affect the incentives except in the case of iron ore, and even in that case the special incentive is by no means eliminated.

Capital Gains

One tax reform sometimes discussed would eliminate percentage depletion but allow mineral industries cost depletion, which is similar to depreciation for other industries. The capital gains provisions of the federal income tax law now offer an alternative form of tax savings to the mineral industries, however. Capital gains treatment is accorded to the sale of capital assets held for investment under Section 1231 of the Internal Revenue Code (assets used in taxpayer's trade or business and held for more than six months). Corporations can use either of two methods of computing tax for capital gains: (1) the regular method, under which net gains are included in computing taxable income and are taxed at the regular rate; or (2) the alterna-

[40] The drop in s for iron in 1960 is due to a drop in severance tax collections in Minnesota in that year.

tive method, under which net gains are excluded in computing taxable income and are taxed at 25 percent.

When a corporation has ordinary income the alternative method yields the smaller tax. However, when allowable deductions exceed ordinary income, the excess may not be applied against net capital gains if the alternative method is used.[41] The only way to get the full allowable deduction is to use the regular method under which capital gains are taxed at 52 percent. This is quite important in the oil industry. If there is not sufficient ordinary income to cover allowable deductions, a firm cannot take advantage of the expensing privilege. When there is no ordinary income, it becomes more advantageous for the taxpayer to capitalize all exploration and development expenditures, thereby increasing the basis of the property for purposes of capital gains when the property is sold. However, the taxpayer who is a producer of oil or gas[42] can make only a single election to expense or capitalize, which is binding for all subsequent years and for all properties. If he has elected to expense but for a given year has insufficient ordinary income to cover deductions, he must either lose part or all of his deductions or have his capital gains taxed at the ordinary rate. These provisions give an incentive for diversification in order that there always will be ordinary income.

As Table 6 shows, capital gains treatment in conjunction with the expensing privilege produces an incentive to invest in natural resources analogous to the one provided by percentage depletion.[43] In calculating these figures, it was assumed that a period of three years was used for exploration and development of a mineral deposit, which was then sold to a purchaser who subsequently elected cost depletion, an alternative often chosen in the case of purchased and developed mineral deposits.[44] It was also assumed that a purchaser would be willing to spend the same amount to obtain a mineral deposit or a machine yielding the same pattern of income stream. The incentive was then stated, as in the case of percentage depletion, as a ratio of the costs which would be incurred by the investor in a mineral deposit to those which would be incurred by the machine investor.

[41] Prentice-Hall, *Federal Tax Guide*, Editorial Volume (Prentice-Hall, 1961), p. 4922.

[42] The coal or iron producer has an annual option to expense or to capitalize.

[43] For the equations on which Tables 6 and 7 are based and their derivation, see Appendix A.

[44] See Harberger, "The Tax Treatment of Oil Exploration," p. 18.

106 Special Tax Treatment of Mineral Industries

TABLE 6. Capital Gains Tax Incentive Ratios for Exploration and Development of Oil and Gas, Coal, and Iron Industries, by Straight Line and Sum-of-Years Digits Depreciation Methods, 1958-60

	Incentive ratios, mineral industries to other industries					
	Oil and gas C_p/C_m		Coal C_c/C_m		Iron C_i/C_m	
Year	Straight line	Sum-of-years digits	Straight line	Sum-of-years digits	Straight line	Sum-of-years digits
1958	1.50	1.47	1.52	1.48	1.83	1.78
1959	1.48	1.45	1.48	1.46	1.82	1.77
1960	1.46	1.43	1.36	1.33	1.84	1.79

Source: Estimated by author. Further details and assumptions are given in the text and Appendix A.

The incentive to invest in exploration and development for oil and gas under capital gains provisions is almost exactly the same as the incentive under percentage depletion. In both cases the developer would be willing to spend about 1.5 times as much to obtain the same income stream in oil exploration and development as he would in machine production. For both coal and iron, the incentives are somewhat lower under capital gains than under percentage depletion but are still large. The elimination of percentage depletion would not eliminate special tax privileges for the mineral industries without the modification or elimination of the expensing provisions or the modification of capital gains law.

While the privilege of capital gains treatment is moderately important in the oil and gas industries, it is doubtful that very many coal mines are discovered, developed, and sold for capital gains. However, under some contractual arrangements, the coal producer may take capital gains treatment on the sale of coal, itself, while retaining the mine. Section 631 of the *Internal Revenue Code* allows any owner who disposes of coal held more than six months under a contract where he retains economic interest in the coal to treat the difference between the amount realized on disposal and the adjusted basis as a capital gain or loss. He may not take percentage depletion in addition. This privilege is not open to the actual operator but only to the owner, lessor, or sublessor who sells the right to mine coal to another party.

The difference between income and basis for cost depletion

TABLE 7. Incentive Ratios for Exploration and Development of Coal Industry with Capital Gains Tax on Sale of Coal, by Straight Line and Sum-of-Years Digits Depreciation Methods, 1958–60

	Incentive ratios, coal industry to other industries, C_c/C_m	
Year	Straight line	Sum-of-years digits
1958	2.19	2.07
1959	2.15	2.03
1960	2.01	1.90

Source: Estimated by author. Further details are given in the text and Appendix A.

(usually on a per ton basis) is considered a gain or loss under Section 1231. The basis for cost depletion consists of land costs plus capitalized and deferred exploration and development costs. It does not include depreciation which may be deducted from ordinary income, as may expensed exploration and development costs. When there is insufficient or no ordinary income, exploration and development costs in excess of ordinary income will be deferred and the basis per ton will be increased accordingly.

Capital gains treatment of the sale of coal gives an incentive to invest over twice as much capital to produce a given income stream in the development of coal as in industries without this privilege (see Table 7). This privilege is therefore even more valuable to the coal producer than percentage depletion.

Lease Costs

It has been assumed to this point that all costs incurred by the mineral producer for exploration and development have represented real resources. If this were true, then for a mineral such as petroleum, for which there is a strong demand, the tax-induced incentives calculated here should produce an excess of exploration and development over what would occur under neutral taxation. However, if because of an inelasticity of supply of mineral lands or for some other reason the price paid to landowners in the form of leases and royalties has been bid up above what would be paid under neutral taxation, percentage depletion may result in a transfer payment from the general taxpayer to the landowner and not in additional exploration.

108   Special Tax Treatment of Mineral Industries

In the case of petroleum, the producer typically takes a lease on promising land, pays a lease bonus which may run from 25 cents to over $10,000 per acre,[45] pays an annual delay rental which averages around $1.00 per acre until drilling begins, and after oil or gas is discovered, pays the owner about 15 percent of gross revenue from the wells. The leases usually run for a fixed period but if oil or gas is discovered, the lease runs as long as the well produces. After drilling is completed on oil lands, the surface area of the land may be used for other purposes, such as grazing.

These payments to the holders of mineral rights may be considered a real rent which serves to ration the crude oil in the ground over time. This rent would occur under neutral taxation. Considered in this light, lease bonuses, delay rentals, and royalties serve an economic function and the incentives calculated in earlier sections are not affected.

However, percentage depletion and related privileges may have caused these payments to mineral rights holders to be bid up above the rents which would otherwise exist. In this case, the incentives calculated earlier would not entirely represent real resources and would contain some element of a transfer payment. To take this factor into account, the extreme assumption was made that one-half of all payments to holders of mineral rights are the result of percentage depletion.

On the revenue side, no adjustment is required. The income which the oil producer expects is his share, net income less royalty payments. This was the concept used in deriving the formulas presented above. On the cost side, however, the lease bonuses and delay rentals are included in total costs in the formulas. An adjustment must be made here, which is perhaps best demonstrated by an illustration of the breakdown of costs of a typical oil producer. The proportions used are the proportions from the 1960 calculations for the incentive to exploration and development under percentage depletion.[46]

An oil producer expends $100 on exploration and development. Of this, $52 is expensed in the current year, $19 is charged to depreciation, and $29 is charged to the depletable asset account. Eighty

[45] Charles Jackson Grayson, Jr., *Decisions Under Uncertainty: Drilling Decisions by Oil and Gas Operators* (Harvard University, Division of Research, 1960), p. 86.
[46] See Table 2.

TABLE 8. Percentage Depletion Incentive Ratios for Exploration and Development of Oil and Gas Industries, Adjusted for Lease Costs, 1958–60

	Incentive ratios of oil and gas industry to other industries, Cp/Cm		
Year	Original	Adjusted	Adjusted, with partial severance taxes
1958	1.53	1.38	1.31
1959	1.51	1.31	1.25
1960	1.48	1.28	1.21

Source: Estimated by author. Further details and assumptions are given in the text and Appendix A.

percent of this latter amount represents lease bonuses.[47] Four percent of total expenditures on exploration and development is spent on delay rentals.[48] Total lease costs are then

(12)   (.80) ($29) + ($4) = $27.20.

Assuming that one-half of all lease costs are a result of percentage depletion, then $13.60 more was spent on lease bonuses and delay rentals than would have been spent under neutral taxation. This is approximately 14 percent of total expenditures on exploration and development.

If Cp/Cm is to be considered the incentive to invest *real* resources in exploration and development of oil, then the original incentives calculated must be reduced somewhat. The oil producer is willing to spend $1.48 to produce an income stream worth only $1.00, but only 86.4 percent of the $1.48, or $1.28, represents real resources. Therefore, Cp/Cm, if viewed as representing only real resources, should be 1.28. The rest represents a transfer payment. Table 8 shows the results of similar calculations performed for each of the three years included in this study.

The correction for lease costs reduces the estimated incentive for real resources to flow into oil exploration and development but it

[47] This is the percentage reported for 1960 in the Treasury study (*President's 1963 Tax Message*, Hearings, Pt. 1, pp. 290–350).
[48] *Joint Association Survey, Estimated Expenditures and Receipts of U.S. Oil and Gas Producing Industry, 1959*, Sec. 2, p. 8 (published jointly by the American Petroleum Institute, Independent Petroleum Association of America, and the Mid-Continent Oil and Gas Association, 1961).

by no means eliminates the incentive. Moreover, the assumption that half of lease costs are the result of percentage depletion is probably overly generous.

The incentives involved in drilling deeper, using new methods of recovery, and developing existing mineral deposits further[49] are not altered by consideration of lease bonuses and delay rentals, since no new leases need be taken if an area is already under lease and producing.

Lease acquisition costs are negligible for iron ore, so these incentives would not be affected. Since there are some lease acquisition costs in the coal industry, the incentives for coal will be affected somewhat but not as much as in the case of oil and gas.

Effects of Changes in Tax Law

This section investigates the effects of various changes in tax law on the incentive to invest in mineral exploration and development. All calculations were made with straight line method discount factors and without the lease cost correction. The corporation income tax rate is denoted by t.

First, it is interesting to note the changes expected in the incentives which occur when the corporation income tax rate is changed (see Table 9). The corporation income tax rate was 13.5 percent at the inception of percentage depletion, reached 52 percent in the 1950's and, as a result of the 1964 tax law, was reduced to 48 percent. Corporate capital gains were first accorded a special tax rate of 25 percent in 1942 when the highest corporation income tax rate was 40 percent. As a result of the increase in tax rates, the estimated incentive to invest in exploration and development of mineral deposits has increased by about 30 percentage points for oil and gas, over 50 points for coal, and over 80 points for iron since each mineral first received percentage depletion. The fairly modest incentive which Congress may have intended when percentage depletion was first granted has increased substantially simply because of higher tax rates.

One possible tax reform would be to reduce the statutory rate of percentage depletion, r. This would have the effect of lowering p, the ratio of percentage depletion to net income. Other proposals, such as tightening the rules governing the definition of "property"

[49] See Tables 3 and 4.

TABLE 9. Effect of Changing Corporation Income Tax Rate on Percentage Depletion and Capital Gains Incentives for Exploration and Development, Oil and Gas, Coal, and Iron Industries, 1960

		Exploration and development incentive ratios		
Mineral product	Corporation income tax rate t	Percentage depletion	Percentage depletion with partial severance taxes	Capital gains
Oil and gas	0.10	1.05	0.99	—
	0.20	1.11	1.05	—
	0.30	1.19	1.13	—
	0.40	1.30	1.23	1.23
	0.48	1.41	1.34	1.38
	0.50	1.45	1.37	1.42
	0.52	1.48	1.40	1.46
	0.60	1.67	1.58	1.70
	0.70	2.05	1.93	2.12
	0.80	2.81	2.65	2.93
Coal	0.10	1.09	—	—
	0.20	1.19	—	—
	0.30	1.33	—	—
	0.40	1.52	—	1.17
	0.48	1.72	—	1.29
	0.50	1.78	—	1.32
	0.52	1.85	—	1.36
	0.60	2.17	—	1.55
	0.70	2.85	—	1.88
	0.80	4.19	—	2.52
Iron	0.10	1.10	1.05	—
	0.20	1.24	1.18	—
	0.30	1.42	1.35	—
	0.40	1.68	1.60	1.39
	0.48	1.97	1.89	1.66
	0.50	2.08	1.98	1.74
	0.52	2.17	2.07	1.84
	0.60	2.73	2.61	2.33
	0.70	3.98	3.82	3.41
	0.80	7.17	6.86	6.00

Source: Estimated by author. The incentives were calculated with straight line method discount factors shown in Table 1, column 1, but without the lease cost correction.

TABLE 10. Effect on Percentage Depletion Incentives, with Partial Severance Taxes Included, of Lowering the Ratios of Percentage Depletion to Net Income and of Lowering Corporation Income Tax Rates, Oil and Gas, Coal, and Iron Industries, 1960

Mineral product	Ratio of percentage depletion to net income p	Incentive ratios, partial severance taxes included, with corporation income tax rate of	
		40 percent	48 percent
Oil and gas	0.25	1.20	1.30
	0.20	1.16	1.25
	0.10	1.09	1.14
Coal	0.30	1.37	1.51
	0.20	1.30	1.40
	0.10	1.22	1.29
Iron	0.25	1.59	1.86
	0.20	1.54	1.79
	0.10	1.45	1.65

Source: See Table 9.

for purposes of percentage depletion and tightening the net income limitation would also have the effect of reducing p. For oil and gas, p has been about 0.30, for coal, about 0.45, and for iron, about 0.27. In Table 10 incentives have been calculated with values for p of 0.25, 0.20, and 0.10 for oil and gas and iron, and 0.30, 0.20, and 0.10 for coal. Corporation income tax rates of 40 and 48 percent are used.

With a 48 percent tax rate, reducing p (within the limits noted here) is not a particularly effective way of reducing the incentives for any of the minerals examined here. Even if p were zero, with a 48 percent tax rate the incentives would be around 1.04 for oil and gas, 1.19 for coal, and 1.50 for iron because of the expensing privilege. With a lower tax rate this method is somewhat more effective.

Another possible tax reform would be to eliminate the present double deduction by doing away with the privilege of expensing and deducting for depreciation, loss on abandonment, and deferrals. This would leave percentage depletion as the only method of recovering capital tax free. Table 11 shows the incentives for percentage depletion taking into account severance taxes but excluding the double deduction.[50]

[50] See Appendix A.

TABLE 11. Effect on Percentage Depletion Incentives, Partial Severance Taxes Included, of Eliminating Expensing and Deductions for Depreciation, Abandonment Losses, and Deferrals, for Oil and Gas, Coal, and Iron Industries, 1960

Corporation income tax rate t	Incentive ratios, partial severance taxes included		
	Oil and gas C_p/C_m	Coal C_c/C_m	Iron C_i/C_m
0.10	0.92	1.02	0.95
0.20	0.90	1.05	0.95
0.30	0.88	1.10	0.95
0.40	0.86	1.16	0.97
0.48	0.86	1.26	0.99
0.50	0.86	1.26	1.00
0.52	0.86	1.28	1.01
0.60	0.88	1.41	1.06
0.70	0.93	1.67	1.12
0.80	1.08	2.22	1.44

Source: See Table 9.

Without the expensing and deduction privileges, the oil and gas producer would prefer cost depletion and the iron producer would be about indifferent at the 48 percent tax rate. For coal a positive though reduced incentive would still remain after elimination of the double deduction. The larger value of p for coal is largely responsible for this difference.

Eliminating the expensing privilege similarly would improve the situation for capital gains. Costs then would receive tax offsets at the same rate at which revenues are taxed, and the Treasury would share in costs and revenues in the same proportion.

Of the tax changes examined here, the first, reduction of the corporation income tax rate, would be dependent on many other considerations besides reducing the special incentive to mineral industries. Reducing r, the rate of percentage depletion, would reduce the special incentive moderately. At least for oil and gas, the elimination of the expensing privilege would be too effective, in a sense, since most producers would probably opt for cost depletion without the expensing privilege. If this were the desired result, the elimination of percentage depletion would be a neater method. However, the elimination of expensing would also reduce the incentive given by capital gains treatment.

If percentage depletion were eliminated without taking away the expensing privilege, the interest-free loan feature of expensing a large percentage of costs would remain. Of course, if the capital gains law were not also modified, a substantial incentive would remain through that channel.

Conclusion

Percentage depletion and capital gains provisions of federal income tax law provide a substantial incentive for investment in the mineral industries beyond that which would occur under neutral taxation. To the extent that these incentives are effective and added exploration, development, and production take place, a case may be made against percentage depletion on the grounds of resource allocation. Increased activity in one part of the economy occurs at the expense of other parts. Relative priorities should be established through the market mechanism by relative prices. These special tax incentives induce capital to flow to projects whose return (before tax) is lower than that of other comparable projects in the economy. Resources are misallocated and the total product of the economy is smaller than it could be.

To the extent that percentage depletion causes the value of mineral rights to be bid up, a case against percentage depletion may be made on equity grounds. Holders of mineral rights are enriched at the expense of the general taxpayer whose tax rates are higher because of the existence of percentage depletion. Moreover, general tax morality may be lowered because of provisions such as percentage depletion.

One of the major arguments employed for percentage depletion for petroleum and against its elimination has been made on the grounds of national defense.[51] It is argued that percentage depletion induces exploration and development of the petroleum deposits needed to provide a large domestic reserve in case of war. The elimination of percentage depletion would drastically reduce exploration and development and some other means would have to be employed to

[51] For a more exhaustive examination of the pros and cons of percentage depletion, see U.S. Library of Congress, Legislative Reference Service, *Depletion Allowances Under Federal Income Tax and Allowances for Exploration and Development Costs, Pro and Con Discussion* (1962); and *The Federal Revenue System: Facts and Problems*, Joint Economic Committee, 84 Cong. 1 sess. (1955), pp. 35–47.

ensure the necessary reserves. But if percentage depletion encourages more intensive development and production from existing fields, it also contributes to more rapid exhaustion of total domestic reserves. More intensive use of foreign oil during peacetime would be one way of conserving domestic supplies for national defense. However, there are restrictions on the import of foreign oil. Moreover, the enrichment of mineral rights holders is an undesirable byproduct of this method of inducing more exploration and development of oil deposits. If exploration and development of domestic deposits beyond what would occur with neutral taxation were deemed necessary, a system of direct subsidy to operators might be more desirable.

Another argument used for percentage depletion is that oil exploration is particularly risky and special incentives are necessary to ensure an adequate supply. But if oil exploration is truly risky and requires a higher rate of return than in other industries, the economy should be willing to pay higher prices directly, rather than indirectly through tax concessions, if it wants more oil. In fact, oil exploration is not as risky to the individual corporation as industry spokesmen would like it to appear. Exploring companies make use of several devices for pooling risk, such as selling part interest in wells they are drilling and buying part interest in exploratory wells of other companies. The large companies have better experience in drilling productive wells than do the small "wildcatters" and yet large companies can take much better advantage of the expensing provisions because of their larger other incomes.[52]

One argument for percentage depletion with some validity is that the tax advantage has been capitalized and present holders of mineral shares would suffer capital losses if the percentage depletion provisions were eliminated. Moreover, producers have made contractual agreements on royalties with lessors on the basis of the existence of percentage depletion. Its elimination would impose hardships on these producers. However, someone always gains or loses when tax laws are changed and this consideration should not be used to limit the tax structure to the status quo.

Arguments for other minerals are usually based on an alleged special need of the economy for the mineral, or a special circumstance

---

[52] For a discussion of the effect of risk on incentives in petroleum, see Arnold C. Harberger, *Notes on the Distinctive Tax Treatment of Petroleum Exploration* (mimeographed), University of Chicago, 1962.

of the industry, or on the grounds that because some minerals have percentage depletion, all should. But a tax policy which is as neutral as possible among industries and among taxpayers will go a long way toward achieving an economy where resources are allocated by the price mechanism to their most productive use, and where a high tax morality exists. Percentage depletion, which favors some taxpayers and asset holders over others, and which provides incentives for resources to flow into projects whose before-tax return is lower than others, materially diminishes the neutrality of the present tax system.

APPENDIX A

Equations Underlying Tables

SHOWN BELOW ARE text table numbers and the equations used to calculate data shown in the tables:

Table Number	Equation
2, 3, 9	$\dfrac{Cp}{Cm} = \dfrac{(.48 + .52p)(1 - .52d)}{[1 - .52(a + db + fc)](.48)}$
4	$\dfrac{Cp}{Cm} = \dfrac{(.48 + .52p)}{.48}$ (The same equation is used for $\dfrac{C_c}{C_m}$ and $\dfrac{C_i}{C_m}$.)
5, 9, 10	$\dfrac{Cp}{Cm} = \dfrac{(1 - s - t + tp + ts)(1 - td)}{[1 - t(a + gb + fc)](1 - t)}$
6, 9	$\dfrac{Cp}{Cm} = \dfrac{.75(1 - .52d^*)}{[1 - .52(a + fc_1) - .25d^*(b + c_2)](.48)}$
7	$\dfrac{Cc}{Cm} = \dfrac{.75(1 - .52d)}{[1 - .52(a + fc_1 + gb) - .25dc_2](.48)}$
11	$\dfrac{Cp}{Cm} = \dfrac{(1 - t + tp)(1 - td)}{(1 - t)}$

In the equations for Table 9, the values for the general corporation income tax rate, t, shown in the first column, were substituted for 52 percent. The equations underlying the incentives for installation of new capital equipment (Table 4) and for percentage depletion treatment with the elimination of all other deduction privileges (Table 11) are modifications of the original percentage depletion equation. The equations underlying the computed incentives to exploration and development given by capital gains treatment on the sale of an asset (Table 6) and by capital gains treatment on the sale of coal (Table 7) are similar in construction to that worked out for percentage depletion on pages 92–95 in the text.

Percentage Depletion and Added Equipment

The percentage depletion treatment of the installation of additional capital equipment is similar to the percentage depletion treatment of exploration and development, except that all deductions are charged to depreciation. In the case of the mineral deposit, capital equipment will be installed up to the point where the cost of such additional equipment is equal to the additional revenue, as follows:

$$Cp = Y - .52(Y - pY - gCp)$$

(1) $$Cp = \frac{Y(.48 + .52p)}{(1 - .52g)}.$$

This investment must be compared with investment in a machine with the same expected life and which produces the same expected income stream:

$$Cm = Y - .52(Y - dCm)$$

(2) $$Cm = \frac{.48Y}{(1 - .52d)}$$

and

(3) $$\frac{Cp}{Cm} = \frac{(.48 + .52p)(1 - .52d)}{(1 - .52g)(.48)}.$$

Since the capital equipment for the mineral deposit and the machine have the same life span and expected return, discount factors d and g will be identical, and the terms $(1 - .52d)$ in the numerator and $(1 - .52g)$ in the denominator are the same and will cancel each other out, reducing the expression to

(4) $$\frac{Cp}{Cm} = \frac{(.48 + .52p)}{.48}.$$

Capital Gains Treatment of the Sale of an Asset

Consider two capital assets, a natural resource deposit and a machine, each producing identical income streams and each requiring the same period of production. Assume a prospective purchaser chooses to take cost depletion on the deposit after purchase (an alternative often chosen when the already-developed deposit is purchased). The purchase price he pays for the asset will have the same present value, S, in both cases, evaluated as of the date when production of the asset begins. Therefore differences in the resources used to produce the income streams appear only on the cost side.

The machine producer, paying the ordinary income tax rate, will produce to the point where costs net-of-tax offsets equal net-of-tax revenue from the sale of the machine, as follows:

$$Cm - .52d^* Cm = S(1 - .52)$$

(5) $$Cm = \frac{.48S}{(1 - .52d^*)},$$

where d^* is discount factor depending on rate of return and period of holding asset before sale.

However, for the natural resource deposit for which capital gains treatment is available, some costs receive offsets at a higher rate than the rate at which the gains are taxed. When there is ordinary income, costs currently expensed, a, and costs ultimately written off as loss on abandonment, c_1, receive a 52 percent tax offset. Those charged to depreciation, b, and those deferred to be written off as production proceeds, c_2, form the basis on which the capital gain is calculated and hence in effect receive a 25 percent tax offset. As before, costs net-of-tax offsets are set equal to revenue net of taxes:

$$Cp - .52(a + fc_1) Cp = S - .25[S - d^* (b + c_2) Cp]$$

(6) $$Cp = \frac{.75S}{[1 - .52(a + fc_1) - .25d^* (b + c_2)]}$$

and

(7) $$\frac{Cp}{Cm} = \frac{.75(1 - .52d^*)}{[1 - .52(a + fc_1) - .25d^* (b + c_2)] (.48)}.$$

A three-year period of exploration and development for the mineral deposit and of production for the machine is assumed. The discount factor, d^*, based on a life of three years and a rate of return of 10 percent, is 0.83 for straight line method and 0.86 for sum-of-years digits method. The discount factor, f, is based on the same rate of return and on the time-path of write-off of group c_1 and is the same as in Table 1.

Capital Gains Treatment of the Sale of Coal

Here the case of the machine will be the same as worked out in the text for percentage depletion:

(8) $$Cm = \frac{.48Y}{(1 - .52d)}.$$

However, the developer of a coal mine will be willing to incur more costs to produce the same income stream, Y, because of the capital gains provisions. His revenues are taxed at 25 percent while a large part of his costs—those expensed, a, those charged to depreciation, b, and those ultimately written off as loss on abandonment, c_1—may be written off against ordinary income and thus receive a 52 percent offset. Only those deferred become part of the cost basis and thus receive a 25 percent offset:

(9)
$$Cc - .52(a + gb + fc_1)Cc + .25(Y - dc_2Cc) = Y$$
$$Cc = \frac{.75Y}{1 - .52(a + gb + fc_1) - .25dc_2}$$

and

(10)
$$\frac{Cc}{Cm} = \frac{.75(1 - .52d)}{[1 - .52(a + gb + fc_1) - .25dc_2](.48)}.$$

Discount factors used are the same as those used for the percentage depletion case in Table 1.

Percentage Depletion Treatment, All Other Deductions Eliminated

In this case it is assumed that percentage depletion is the only method of recovering capital tax free, and that expensing, depreciation, loss on abandonment, and deferrals are not allowed. In mineral exploration and development, production will be carried to the point where

(11)
$$Cp = Y - t(Y - pY)$$
$$Cp = Y(1 - t + tp).$$

For the machine the equation will be the same as in the case of percentage depletion on page 95 above (with t substituted for the specific tax rate of 52 percent):

(12)
$$Cm = \frac{Y(1 - t)}{1 - td}$$

and

$$\frac{Cp}{Cm} = \frac{(1 - t + tp)(1 - td)}{(1 - t)}.$$

Discount factor, d, is the same as for the percentage depletion case shown in Table 1.

APPENDIX B

Treasury Survey Tables

TABLE B-1. Income, Deductions, and Depletion Claimed, Coal and Iron Industries, Domestic United States, 1958[a]
(Millions of dollars)

Income, deductions, and depletion claimed	Coal		Iron
	Anthracite	Bituminous[b]	
Gross income from mineral production	125,787	860,123	390,360
Deductions for exploration, development, and abandonment losses on producing properties	4,145	8,031	38,766
Other deductions	108,459	729,458	205,172
Balance: net income before depletion	13,183	122,634	146,422
Total depletion claimed	7,064	57,598	54,591
Based on gross income rate	3,201	25,433	41,775
Based on net income	2,995	30,706	11,255
Adjusted basis	868	1,459	1,561
Deductions for exploration, development, and abandonment losses on nonproducing properties	40	1,389	4,194
Balance: net income	6,079	63,647	87,637

Source: From special tabulations by U.S. Treasury Department, Office of Tax Analysis, prepared for the author for this study. They differ slightly in classification of data from the tables published in the *President's 1963 Tax Message.*

[a] The sample consisted of four anthracite coal mining firms, forty-six bituminous coal mining firms, and twenty-five iron mining firms.

[b] Includes lignite.

121

TABLE B-2. Tax Treatment of Expenditures on Exploration, for Oil and Gas, Iron, and Coal Industries, United States, 1958
(Thousands of dollars)

Mineral product and type of producer	Total	Exploration expenditures			
		Deducted as current expense	Charged as deferred expense	Charged to depletable asset account	Charged to depreciable asset account
Oil and gas					
Domestic	891,749	741,374	25,212	94,951	30,212
Foreign	297,017	164,141	51,690	42,699	38,488
Iron					
Domestic	348	212	—	136	—
Foreign	67	45	—	22	—
Bituminous coal[a]					
Domestic	2,098	491	80	1,420	107
Foreign	—	—	—	—	—
Anthracite coal	—	—	—	—	—

Source: See source for Table B-1.
[a] Includes lignite.

TABLE B-3. Tax Treatment of Expenditures on Development and Acquisition Costs for Oil and Gas, Iron, and Coal Industries, United States, 1958
(Thousands of dollars)

Mineral product and type of producer	Total	Development expenditures				Other acquisition costs charged to depletable asset account
		Deducted as current expense	Charged as deferred expense	Charged to depletable asset account	Charged to depreciable asset account	
Oil and gas						
Domestic	1,513,815	937,704	445	33,129	542,539	418,704
Foreign	374,752	229,800	367	16,661	127,925	65,112
Iron						
Domestic	39,953	39,657	—	—	296	456
Foreign	15,032	15,032	—	—	—	—
Bituminous coal[a]						
Domestic	7,154	6,513	222	38	381	2,887
Foreign	—	—	—	—	—	—
Anthracite coal						
Domestic	4,520	3,078	1,442	—	—	50
Foreign	—	—	—	—	—	—

Source: See source for Table B-1. Figures are rounded and will not necessarily add to totals.
[a] Includes lignite.

LEONARD GERSON ROSENBERG

Taxation of Income from Capital, by Industry Group

THE MAJOR PURPOSE of this study is to estimate the taxation of total income from capital in the American economy by non-financial industry groups for the 1953–59 period. This effort involves obtaining useful estimates of income from capital and of the corporate profits tax liability and property taxes paid by the industry groups included in the study.

The general prototype for this study was the paper by Arnold C. Harberger, "The Corporation Income Tax: An Empirical Appraisal," which was submitted to the House Committee on Ways and Means during the program of public panel discussions on income tax reform beginning in November 1959, and was included in Volume I of *Tax Revision Compendium* (1959). That article, dealing with the 1953–55 period, provides a theoretical structure for measuring the cost of the distortions in capital use which are due to the non-neutrality of the tax system. One of the goals of this study is to provide better empirical estimates than those used by Harberger. Not only do the empirical estimates in this study have an intrinsic value of their own, but they may also be used with any other suitable welfare cost analysis.

The limitations of the various estimates of income and taxes are clearly outlined in the sections related to each item. There is no need to overemphasize the general paucity of our empirical knowledge of the workings of the economic system. This is well known by anyone who has dealt seriously with the applied side of economic analysis.

The postwar 1953–59 period was chosen because it both coincided with the only time period for which adequate information was available and avoided the major revenue effect of the corporate excess profits tax imposed during the Korean War period. Although a seven-year period may be considered a relatively short time period for this type of analysis, it is long enough to bring out (1) the characteristics of the taxation of income from capital for different industry groups and (2) the orders of magnitude of the welfare cost of a nonneutral tax system on investment and consumption decisions in the economy.

The first part of the study deals with the measurement of the income from capital. The second part provides the estimates of taxes paid by this income from capital. Government expenditures are considered neutral. The analysis is confined to the federal and state corporate profits tax liabilities and to property taxes paid. It is assumed that the personal income tax is neutral in its impact by nonfinancial industry group. The third part of the study sums up the cost of the distortions in capital use for the years 1953–59 and presents a comparative estimate for the year 1959 using the Harberger analysis of welfare costs.

Income from Capital, by Industry Group

The most meaningful measure of income would be "the maximum that could be consumed in a given period consistent with the maintenance of wealth or of income potential."[1] This concept of income includes both realized and unrealized net income; for example, the net cash income available after payment to all the factors of production used jointly with capital plus the increases (or decreases) in the value of wealth due to relative changes in market value. It would exclude increases (or decreases) in wealth due to general price level movements.

[1] Martin J. Bailey, *National Income and the Price Level* (McGraw-Hill, 1962), p. 270.

Definition of Income from Capital

The definition of income from capital for non-financial industry groups used in this chapter is only an approximation of this income concept. It includes the following items:
1. Corporate sector net income before corporate profits tax liability and property tax payments. This is the corporate sector return on equity capital.
2. For the unincorporated sector, the portion of the total income of the unincorporated enterprise that is a return on equity capital, plus property tax payments.
3. Net monetary interest paid by businesses on borrowed capital in the form of debt obligations.
4. Net rent paid by an industry to persons for the use of physical capital.
5. Net realized capital gains by the corporate sector that are considered as income to an industry.

The changes in unrealized real wealth gains for all sectors of the economy and net realized capital gains of the unincorporated sector are excluded. Tax depreciation is assumed to be approximately equivalent to true economic depreciation. The available information is inadequate to make estimates for any of these excluded items for the industry detail included in this study.

The capital for which income estimates are to be made is net physical capital, e.g., net depreciable and depletable assets, land, inventories, and other working capital. Income from financial assets, except insofar as it reduces net monetary interest paid, is excluded. Interest received on investments in debt obligations is netted out against monetary interest paid on borrowed capital, when calculating net monetary interest paid. Dividends received on investments in equities of other firms are excluded.

Table 1 provides estimates of total income from capital before property tax payments. The derivation of these estimates is explained in the remainder of this section.

Corporate Profits before Tax

The U.S. Department of Commerce publishes by industry group annual corporate profits, before tax, originating in the United States. These corporate profits estimates are after inventory valuation adjust-

TABLE 1. Total Income from Capital (Excluding Property Tax Payments) by Non-Financial Industry Group, 1953–59 Average
(Millions of dollars)

Industry group	Corporate return on equity capital			Net monetary interest paid			Return on unincorporated equity capital[g] (7)	Other returns assigned from real estate[h] (8)	Grand total[i] (9)
	Net profits before corporate profits tax[a] (1)	Net realized capital gains[b] (2)	Total[c] (3)	Direct industry payment[d] (4)	Assigned from real estate[e] (5)	Total[f] (6)			
Grand Total	35,604	1,309	36,913	8,909	1,083	9,992	18,144	2,983	68,032
Total, farms, agricultural services, forestry, and fisheries	—	43	43	6	9	15	6,164	21	6,243
Farms	—	—	—	—	—	—	6,138	—	6,138
Agricultural services, forestry, and fisheries	—	43	43	6	9	15	26	21	105
Total mining	1,093	102	1,195	85	8	93	14	173	1,475
Metal mining	290	5	295	5	1	6	(13)	1	289
Bituminous coal mining	89	24	113	7	1	8	(25)	3	99
Crude petroleum and natural gas	541	49	590	63	5	68	51	167	876
Non-metallic mining and quarrying; and anthracite mining	173	24	197	10	1	11	1	2	211
Contract construction	543	54	597	146	26	172	261	55	1,085

Total manufacturing	22,946	615	23,561	927	240	1,167	761	1,018	26,507
Food and kindred products	1,850	27	1,877	128	28	156	103	61	2,197
Tobacco manufactures	443	1	444	29	—	29	3	1	477
Textile mill products	569	1	570	54	9	63	30	18	681
Apparel and other finished fabric products	196	3	199	39	13	52	119	28	398
Lumber and wood products (except furniture and fixtures)	352	195	547	41	5	46	58	11	662
Furniture and fixtures	201	5	206	11	6	17	28	12	263
Paper and allied products	1,013	77	1,090	35	7	42	15	15	1,162
Printing and publishing	751	28	779	36	15	51	79	117	1,026
Chemicals and allied products	2,703	43	2,746	73	14	87	17	30	2,880
Petroleum and coal products	2,098	72	2,170	63	44	107	9	431	2,717
Rubber products	375	5	380	22	7	29	—	16	425
Leather and leather products	134	1	135	12	3	15	12	6	168
Stone, clay, and glass products	1,035	18	1,053	21	6	27	11	12	1,103
Primary metal industries	2,367	25	2,392	113	9	122	30	21	2,565
Fabricated metal products (including ordnance and accessories)	1,056	18	1,074	56	14	70	76	29	1,249
Instruments	488	5	493	18	6	24	8	12	537
Machinery (except electrical and transportation)	2,128	39	2,167	82	17	99	104	36	2,406
Electrical machinery	1,495	19	1,514	42	15	57	13	118	1,702
Motor vehicles and equipment	2,582	13	2,595	(22)	4	(18)	14	7	2,598
Transportation equipment (except motor vehicles)	780	7	787	40	10	50	2	21	860
Miscellaneous manufactures	330	13	343	34	8	42	30	16	431

Footnotes to table appear on p. 129.

TABLE 1—Continued

Industry group	Corporate return on equity capital			Net monetary interest paid			Return on unincorporated equity capital[g] (7)	Other returns assigned from real estate[h] (8)	Grand total[i] (9)
	Net profits before corporate profits tax[a] (1)	Net realized capital gains[b] (2)	Total[c] (3)	Direct industry payment[d] (4)	Assigned from real estate[e] (5)	Total[f] (6)			
Total trade	4,557	172	4,729	810	517	1,327	2,740	1,101	9,897
Wholesale trade	2,051	76	2,127	288	88	376	1,201	187	3,891
Retail trade and automobile services	2,506	96	2,602	522	429	951	1,539	914	6,006
Real estate—non-farm residential dwellings	421	100	521	5,250	—	5,250	7,736	—	13,507
Total transportation	1,207	113	1,320	485	119	604	35	253	2,212
Railroads	627	25	652	325	73	398	—	157	1,207
Local and highway passenger transportation	61	10	71	22	3	25	(8)	6	94
Highway freight transportation and warehousing	184	26	210	66	22	88	58	46	402
Water transportation	90	19	109	19	4	23	(7)	10	135
Air transportation (common carriers)	58	28	86	18	11	29	—	23	138
Pipeline transportation	126	1	127	23	1	24	(8)	1	152
Services allied to transportation	61	4	65	12	5	17	(8)	10	84

Total communications and public utilities	4,304	47	4,351	980	23	1,003	(17)	61	5,398
Telephone, telegraph, and related services	1,566	12	1,578	189	13	202	(4)	28	1,804
Radio broadcasting and television	153	8	161	8	3	11	(3)	7	176
Utilities: electric and gas	2,537	17	2,554	758	6	764	—	25	3,343
Local utilities and public services not elsewhere classified	48	10	58	25	1	26	(10)	1	75
Total services[j]	533	63	596	220	141	361	450	301	1,708
Hotels and lodging places	54	18	72	112	26	138	28	55	293
Personal services	81	5	86	23	39	62	78	83	309
Business services not elsewhere classified	266	15	281	27	23	50	332	49	712
Miscellaneous repair services and hand trades	16	1	17	7	26	33	9	56	115
Motion pictures	40	19	59	23	8	31	5	18	113
Amusements (except motion pictures)	76	5	81	28	19	47	(2)	40	166

[a] U.S. Department of Commerce, *Survey of Current Business*, various July issues.
[b] U.S. Treasury Department, *Statistics of Income, Corporation Income Tax Returns*, various annual issues.
[c] Column 1 plus column 2.
[d] Unpublished information obtained from the U.S. Department of Commerce, National Income Division. The figure in parentheses is a negative value.
[e] See Table 8 and discussion, p. 152.
[f] Column 4 plus column 5.
[g] U.S. Department of Commerce, *Survey of Current Business*, various July issues. Except for farms, agricultural services, forestry, and fisheries; contract construction; highway freight transportation and warehousing; hotels and other lodging places, and miscellaneous repair services and hand trades, the return on unincorporated sector equity capital was calculated as follows: For each industry group, corporate profits before corporate profits tax liability, net monetary interest paid, and the return to labor (including that of entrepreneurs) was deducted from income originating. The return to labor was measured by the product of the average employee compensation and the ratio of production workers engaged in each industry to full-time equivalent employees. The figures in parentheses are negative values.
The derivation of the estimate for farms is presented in Table 2. The estimates for the other industry groups mentioned above are presented in Table 6.
[h] See Table 8, column 6 and column 7 and discussion, pp. 151ff.
[i] The sum of columns 3, 6, 7, and 8.
[j] Engineering and other professional services are not included in this study.

ment and are based on the company tabulations of corporation income tax returns published annually by the Internal Revenue Service (IRS) of the U.S. Treasury Department, in *Statistics of Income, Corporation Income Tax Returns*.

Beginning with these Internal Revenue Service data, the U.S. Department of Commerce adjusts the corporate profits series to make them suitable for the conventions adopted in the national income accounts. Total depletion deductions taken for tax purposes are added back into the compiled net profit of the IRS.[2] Net realized capital gains are excluded except for part of one industry group. Domestic dividends received and income from equities in foreign corporations and branches are deducted from the compiled net profit. The exclusion of the total earnings from equity investments eliminates the return from these financial assets as an element of the income of the corporate firm.

Corporate profits plus net realized capital gains (Table 1, column 3) accounted for 54 percent of the income from capital excluding property tax payments. This $36.9 billion return to corporate equity capital out of the $68.0 billion total income from capital (column 9) can certainly be considered as the most reliable of the income estimates being utilized.

The major economic deficiency of the corporate profits series is the understatement of the depreciation of fixed assets as the current costs of using depreciable assets in production. Tax depreciation based on historical costs as reported in the corporation income tax returns understates this cost element and, thereby, overstates business profits. This overstatement of business profits was probably substantial in the period preceding the liberalization of tax depreciation in 1954. A subsequent easing of tax depreciation regulations has undoubtedly further narrowed the differential between original cost and replacement cost depreciation allowances. There are no overall estimates available of the magnitude of this overstatement of business

---

[2] A special survey for 1950–52 by the U.S. Treasury indicated that about 95 percent of tax depletion deductions taken for minerals by corporations were based on percentage depletion. The remainder, about $80 million, was based on cost depletion. If this past relationship was accurate for the 1953–59 period, then corporate profits before taxes are overstated for the non-financial sector by approximately $130 million. This is the approximate amount of cost depletion added back to corporate profits. See U.S. Treasury, Tax Analysis Staff, "Statistics of Corporation Mineral Depletion Deductions and Related Allowances, 1950, 1951 and 1952" (processed; March 10, 1955).

profits for 1953–59.³ The inclusion of this adjustment in the corporate profits series would require an industry-by-industry analysis of the amount of the differential and its effect on the profits of each individual industry.

The two other most apparent deficiencies of the corporate profits series for our purposes relate to the company nature of the industrial classification and the almost total exclusion of the net realized capital gains shown on the corporation income tax returns.

INDUSTRIAL CLASSIFICATION OF MAJOR NATIONAL INCOME SERIES. Since the corporate profits series is based on company tax returns, the only method of industrial classification must be on a company basis. This technique places the total profits of a firm in an industry group, according to the major activity of the company as measured by the receipts of the various activities. These total profits may be earned from different and unrelated activities, but the total profits are necessarily assigned to one industry.

Distortions in the corporate profits series for the manufacturing sector, although most evident for the integrated industries that contain substantial extractive activities (such as petroleum and coal products and primary metal industries), are also a normal occurrence in manufacturing.⁴ Although it seriously decreases the meaningfulness of interindustry comparisons, there is no ready alternative solution to this problem.

The company classification also affects the use of the other components of national income originating by industry sector in conjunction with corporate profits. "The establishment basis is used for the industrial classification of wages and salaries, supplements to wages and salaries, income of unincorporated enterprises and inventory

³ It has been suggested that in spite of the post-1954 liberalizations in depreciation allowance, the overstatement of business profits was still substantial in the period covered by this study. The limited evidence presented is not entirely convincing and does not permit any quantification of the extent of overstatement. An inference can be made from the discussion that an order of magnitude of $2–3 billion per annum for the corporate sector would fit the term "substantial." Edgar O. Edwards and Philip W. Bell, *The Theory and Measurement of Business Income* (University of California Press, 1961), pp. 165–67.

⁴ A recent study by Michael Gort, *Diversification and Integration in American Industry* (Princeton University Press for the National Bureau of Economic Research, 1962), presents an analysis of the product record of a sample group of 111 large manufacturing enterprises. Tables 13, pp. 38–39, and 33, pp. 94–95, illustrate the difficulties of comparing the profit records of two-digit industry groups in manufacturing.

valuation adjustment, and interest paid by non-corporate enterprises. But, because of statistical necessity, the company basis of industrial classification is used for corporate profits, the corporate inventory valuation adjustment, and interest paid and received by corporations."[5]

This difference in industrial classification among the major national income series are not likely to seriously affect the results of the allocation methods used below for non-farm unincorporated enterprises. The major areas of distortion will be in the manufacturing sector which is predominantly organized in corporate form.

NET REALIZED CAPITAL GAINS AS INCOME. The total amounts of net realized capital gains that were excluded by the National Income Division of the U.S. Department of Commerce from corporate profits averaged $2,055 million per annum for 1953–59. For the nonfinancial industry groups, the amount excluded was $1,309 million. Table 1 includes these net realized capital gains as income in column 2. No tax adjustments are made in the corporate profits tax series by the National Income Division for the excluded net realized capital gains.

The list below presents the average 1953–59 amounts of net realized capital gains (in millions of dollars) that were excluded by the National Income Division from the corporate profits series by the account item as published by the Internal Revenue Service in *Statistics of Income, Corporation Income Tax Returns;* item 5 is from material supplied to the author by the National Income Division:

1. Net short-term capital gain reduced by net long-term capital loss   56
2. Plus: Net long-term capital gain reduced by net short-term loss   2,257
3. Plus: Net gain, sales other than capital assets   1,097
4. Less: Net loss, sales other than capital assets   611
5. Less: Operating profits of speculative builders—net gain (less loss) from sales other than capital assets   744

Total excluded 2,055

The rationale put forth by the National Income Division for excluding net realized capital gains from the corporate profits series is the lack of any current production or output corresponding to these

---

[5] U.S. Department of Commerce, *National Income: 1954 Edition, A Supplement to the Survey of Current Business* (1954), p. 67.

income receipts. For our purposes, this limitation is not relevant. Insofar as a net capital gain is not generated by an increase in the general price level and is an income attributable to physical capital, it should be included as income. Although the available information is not conclusive, there is sufficient evidence to include the net realized capital gains of the non-financial industry groups in the corporate profits series. The remainder of this section is devoted to justifying this inclusion.

Section 1231 of the Internal Revenue Code of 1954. Under Section 1231 of the Internal Revenue Code of 1954, not only can the net profit from the sale of timber and coal property (if held more than six months) be treated as a long-term capital gain with a maximum 25 percent tax rate, but (1) the owner of the timber is entitled to a capital gains treatment on the increase in value from the time the timber was acquired until the first day of the year in which the timber was cut; (2) the owner of timber who disposes of it under a cutting contract receives capital gains treatment if the timber was held for six months prior to its disposal and if he retains an economic interest in the timber; and (3) an owner of a coal mine who disposes of the coal under a royalty contract treats his gain or loss as a capital gain or loss under the same conditions mentioned for (2) above. Of the approximate $1.3 billion shown in column 2 of Table 1, $300 million or about 20 percent of the total was assigned to the Section 1231 category. The net realized capital gains for bituminous coal mining ($24 million); lumber and wood products, except furniture and fixtures ($195 million); paper and allied products ($77 million); and a portion of printing and publishing ($28 million) would most likely fall into this capital gains category.

Sale of Mineral Property. The sale of mineral property held for six months or more is a convenient method of discounting a future income stream into a present value and benefiting from the preferential capital gains tax treatment afforded the profits from such a sale. There can be little doubt that net realized capital gains from the sale of this type of mineral property is income. The total net realized capital gains included in Table 1, column 2, for crude petroleum and natural gas and products of petroleum and coal was $121 million for 1953–59.

Real Estate. Net realized capital gains for the real estate industry for 1953–59 that are still excluded by the National Income Division from the corporate profits series are $191 million and may reflect in part increases in the general price level. But the professional occupation of the real estate industry is the buying and selling of property; changes in the value of property may be determined by the skill of the professional sellers in the opening up of better marketing opportunities.

A capital gain in real estate, therefore, reflects in part a change in relative prices favorable to the property seller either because of his superior marketing skills and/or because of the relative scarcity and increased demand for his product. In real estate particularly, it has also been noted that the tax allowance for depreciation often exceeds the true economic depreciation of the capital assets.[6] Other things being equal, this tax overdepreciation would of itself produce a situation in which market value would exceed book value by the amount of the overdepreciation. The amount of the overdepreciation would then be subject to the capital gains tax treatment.

The major portion of the net realized capital gains excluded by the National Income Division still remains to be explained. Capital gains can arise through the overdepreciation of used machinery and equipment sold by business firms. This would make the market value, without taking into account price level increases, substantially higher than the book value using tax depreciation deductions. Net income of the owners of such equipment in previous periods would have been reduced by the difference between the tax and the true economic depreciation. The only other major source of capital gains for business would be in the sale of financial assets. Since our study excludes the financial and insurance sectors, this source does not appear to merit serious consideration here.

Net Monetary Interest Paid by Non-Farm Sectors

Net monetary interest paid is the difference between monetary interest paid on borrowed capital and monetary interest received by business enterprises on loans of debt capital. It represents the net monetary return on borrowed capital.

Column 4 of Table 1 shows that the direct payment by industry group of net monetary interest, excluding the farm sector, averaged

[6] Louis Winnick, *Rental Housing: Opportunities for Private Investment* (McGraw-Hill, 1958), pp. 147–51.

$8.9 billion in 1953–59. The estimates are based on unpublished data made available by the National Income Division of the U.S. Department of Commerce.

In column 5 of Table 1, the net monetary interest payments assigned from the real estate sector are $1.1 billion. The rationale for this assignment and the methodology used are discussed below in the section devoted to the real estate industry.

Net monetary interest paid differs from the net interest paid used in the national income accounts. The national income imputation of a net interest received by the non-financial business sector from the banking sector is not acceptable for the purposes of this study. This imputation is primarily utilized in the national income accounts to avoid a negative value added estimate for banking. This would readily come about since the interest received by banks is substantially greater than interest payments and outweighs other factor payments included in the value added for the banking sector.

For all the financial intermediaries, except commercial banks, the flows of imputed interest paid are treated as going entirely to persons. A portion of the imputed interest paid by commercial banks is allocated among corporate industry sectors on the basis of the cash and deposits shown on the balance sheets filed with annual corporate tax returns. For the non-farm unincorporated sector, a more indirect method is used based on the ratio of cash and deposits to total receipts of small corporations in the respective industries.[7]

The national income imputation of interest received implicitly assumes that the deposits owned by a non-financial industry sector generated the property income. The responsibility of the financial intermediary in the income generation is, therefore, minimal. This implicit assumption understates the positive function of the banking system in converting the deposits of some firms into loans for other firms. It also neglects the liquidity function of these liquid assets in the working capital structure of the depositor.

Unpublished information from the National Income Division shows that net interest paid by the non-farm non-financial industry groups in the 1953–59 period averaged $8.1 billion or $1.9 billion less than net monetary interest paid. Manufacturing ($0.8 billion), total trade ($0.7 billion), and transportation and services ($0.1 billion each) were responsible for practically all of the difference.

[7] U.S. Department of Commerce, *National Income*, p. 102.

Return on Unincorporated Equity Capital

To compute the return on unincorporated equity capital, it was necessary to estimate the return to capital in agriculture and to capital in unincorporated businesses.

RETURN ON CAPITAL IN AGRICULTURE. Unlike corporate profits, any estimate of the return to capital in agriculture requires some method of allocating the total return between labor and capital. The total returns for both factors in this predominantly unincorporated sector are made up of the sum of the following accounts:
1. The net income of farm operators (including inventory changes), which is the total return to the unpaid labor of the entrepreneur and any family workers plus a return to the capital employed in the enterprise.
2. Cash wages and value of perquisites paid to hired labor.
3. Net rent paid non-farm landlords.
4. Interest paid on farm mortgage and non-real estate debt.

For the agricultural sector, because of the more adequate financial and statistical information, the distribution of the total return between labor and capital can be accomplished in several ways. A return can be imputed either to labor or capital and the residual assigned to the remaining factor of production. A return can be imputed to both factors of production and the residual distributed to both factors. Of primary importance in any imputation of a return to capital is the dominant position of farm real estate in the balance sheet of agriculture. According to annual comparative balance sheets of the U.S. Department of Agriculture, the market value of this physical asset accounted for almost 70 percent of the total market value of physical assets in 1953–59, for example, $106.2 million out of $154.6 million.

Scofield,[8] dealing with the 1940–59 period, initially imputed a return to total farm labor and non-real estate capital and allocated the residual to real estate capital.[9] In an alternative allocation, Scofield

[8] William H. Scofield, "Returns to Productive Capital in Agriculture," in U.S. Department of Agriculture, *Current Developments in the Farm Real Estate Market*, ARS–43–118 (CD–54) (February 1960), pp. 20–26.

[9] The imputation of the return to farm labor was based on the average cash wage rate paid hired labor multiplied by the total number of man-hours used in farm work. The return to non-real estate capital was the sum of (a) interest and service costs paid

varied his methodology by directly imputing a return to all factors of production[10] and assigned the "surplus" between labor and capital based on the preresidual distribution of returns to labor and capital. The average total income for all farm capital was $5.9 billion for the 1953-59 period when the residual was assigned to real estate capital; with the "surplus" distribution the total return to capital averaged $5.7 billion.

Johnson,[11] for the 1910-46 period, assigned a return to real estate capital by assuming that the net rent paid to landlords on rented farm land was the proper market indicator. The total return to farm land was determined by the ratio of the total market value of farm land to the market value of rented farm land, multiplied by the net rent paid to landlords. For non-real estate farm capital, Johnson imputed a return based on a specific interest rate for the various time periods.

Table 2 presents the results of estimating the returns to farm capital for the 1953-59 period by (a) imputing a net rent payment to all farm real estate based on the net rent paid to landlords; (b) assuming that the opportunity cost for non-real estate farm capital is the farm mortgage interest rate on outstanding loans; and (c) assigning the residual as the return to farm labor.

The net rents approach does reflect some market valuation of returns to farm real estate. The net rent series is deficient because in some areas very little is rented and because of the special characteristics of some of the rented land. In spite of this limitation, it still accounts for approximately 37 percent of the market value of farm real estate and is a better indication of the returns that are earned on this physical asset than the other alternatives.

The average 1953-59 return to farm capital was $6.1 billion as

---

on non-real estate debt and (b) the imputation of a return on owned non-real estate capital based on an interest rate derived by giving equal weights to the rates for government bonds, dividends on common stock, and farm mortgages. The annual interest rate used on owned non-real estate capital was as follows: 1953, 4.5 percent; 1954, 4.1 percent; 1955, 3.9 percent; 1956, 4.1 percent; 1957, 4.3 percent; 1958, 4.3 percent; and 1959, 4.2 percent.

[10] The opportunity cost for real estate capital was obtained by multiplying the annual market value of real estate capital by the annual interest rates shown in note 9, above.

[11] D. G. Johnson, "Allocation of Agricultural Income," *Journal of Farm Economics*, Vol. 30 (November 1948), p. 726.

TABLE 2. Allocation of Return to Capital and Labor in Agriculture, 1953–59

(Money amounts in millions of dollars)

Year	Net income from agriculture[a] (1)	Net rent paid to landlords[b] (2)	Share of farm real estate owned by landlords[c] (percent) (3)	Imputed net rent on all farm real estate[d] (4)	Return to non-real estate farm capital[e] (5)	Return to farm capital[f] (6)	Return to farm labor[g] (7)	Percentage distribution Return to farm capital[h] (8)	Return to farm labor[i] (9)
1953	17,979	1,744	37.09	4,702	1,663	6,365	11,614	35.4	64.6
1954	17,315	1,711	37.15	4,606	1,521	6,127	11,188	35.4	64.6
1955	16,375	1,608	37.21	4,321	1,508	5,829	10,546	35.6	64.4
1956	16,334	1,705	37.27	4,575	1,482	6,057	10,277	37.1	62.9
1957	16,576	1,604	37.33	4,297	1,525	5,822	10,754	35.1	64.9
1958	18,671	1,807	37.39	4,833	1,683	6,516	12,155	34.9	65.1
1959	16,534	1,593	37.44	4,255	1,993	6,248	10,286	37.8	62.2
Average	17,112			4,513	1,625	6,138	10,974	35.9	64.1

[a] U.S. Department of Agriculture, *Farm Income Situation*, FIS–187 (July 1962), Table 2H, p. 39 (government payments are included); Table 16H, p. 54; and Table 14H, p. 52 (government payments are included). The cost of borrowed capital for 1953–57 is from William H. Scofield, "Returns to Productive Capital in Agriculture," *Current Developments in the Farm Real Estate Market*, ARS 43–118 (CD–54) (February 1960), Table 8, column 7, p. 23. For the years 1958 and 1959, revised estimates obtained from Mr. Scofield were used.

Net income from agriculture is defined as the sum of the net income of farm operators including inventory changes (Table 2H); cash wages and value of perquisites furnished to hired labor (Table 16H); interest on farm mortgage and non-real estate debt (Scofield); and net rents paid on farmland to non-farm landlords (Table 14H).

[b] U.S. Department of Agriculture, *Agricultural Statistics, 1960* (1961), p. 492.

[c] David H. Boyne, "Changes in the Real Wealth Position of Owners of Agricultural Assets, 1940–1960" (Ph.D. thesis, University of Chicago, 1962), Table 12, column 2, p. 62. Column 2 divided by column 3.

[d] Column 1 divided by column 3.

[e] The annual market value of non-real estate farm capital was obtained from the U.S. Department of Agriculture. The market value of non-real estate farm capital includes livestock, machinery and equipment excluding 60 percent of farm vehicles; that portion of demand deposits used in farm production; and one-half the market value of stocks and feed grains and forage stored on farms excluding Commodity Credit Corporation loans. The annual estimate of non-real estate farm capital was then multiplied by the farm-mortgage interest rate on outstanding loans, *Agricultural Statistics, 1961* (1962), p. 500.

[f] Column 4 plus column 5. [g] Column 1 less column 6. [h] Column 6 divided by column 1. [i] Column 7 divided by column 1.

TABLE 3. Income of Non-Farm Unincorporated Enterprises, 1953–59 Average

Industry group	Income (millions of dollars) (1)	Percentage distribution (2)
Agricultural services, forestry, and fisheries	370	1.7
Mining	246	1.1
Contract construction	4,195	18.7
Manufacturing	1,593	7.1
Total trade	11,783	52.6
Transportation	779	3.5
Communications and public utilities	66	0.3
Total services[a]	3,360	15.0
Total	22,392	100.0

Source: U.S. Department of Commerce, Survey of Current Business, various July issues and unpublished information provided by the U.S. Department of Commerce, National Income Division. Column 2 was calculated by dividing the absolute amount for each major industry group in column 1 by the total for column 1.

[a] Engineering and other professional services are not included in this study.

shown in column 6 of Table 2.[12] This estimate is $0.2 billion more than Scofield's estimate with the residual assigned to farm real estate and is $0.4 billion more than Scofield's estimate with the "surplus" distribution. The various procedures used thus appear to produce quite similar estimates of the total return to capital.

RETURN ON EQUITY CAPITAL OF NON-FARM UNINCORPORATED ENTERPRISES EXCLUDING REAL ESTATE. The income of non-farm unincorporated enterprises in the national income accounts is the joint return to the labor of the entrepreneur and any unpaid family workers plus a return to the equity capital invested in the business enterprise.

The income of unincorporated non-farm enterprises (excluding real estate) averaged $22.4 billion for 1953–59. Table 3 presents the distribution of this total by major industry group. The three major industry groups that account for the bulk of the total are total trade (52.6 percent); contract construction (18.7 percent); and total services

[12] In addition to this realized return to capital in agriculture, Boyne estimated that in 1953–59, non-conventional income amounted to $2,520 million. This total amount was composed of a $3,096 million gain in the real value of farm real estate and a $576 million loss in the real value of non-real estate capital. Non-conventional income was defined as the increase (or decrease) in real wealth of agriculture measured by the market value of agricultural assets after deducting investment expenditures and adjusting changes in the general price level. David H. Boyne, "Changes in the Real Wealth Position of Owners of Agricultural Assets, 1940–1960" (Ph.D. thesis, University of Chicago, 1962), Table 9, pp. 48–49, and Table 10, pp. 53–54.

included in this study (15.0 percent). The unincorporated sectors for these industry groups are also significant portions of their industry group.

The estimates made for the income of unincorporated enterprises are undoubtedly the best that can be done by the Department of Commerce.[13] A partial reason for this deficiency is obvious from the general structure of the non-farm unincorporated sector. The small firm is typically operated as a family enterprise and the business accounts are normally intermingled with the accounts of the proprietor's household. Accounting records, even when kept, are unlikely to be accurate in distributing the joint expenses of the household and business sector, or in properly recording all income earned from the business enterprise. Balance sheet information is practically non-existent and in general our economic information on the small business sector is extremely limited.

The data for this series are based primarily on tax returns filed either by sole proprietorships with their personal income tax returns (Schedule C of Form 1040) or by partnerships (Form 1065). Net realized capital gains are excluded and depletion deductions are added back to net profits. The net profits estimates available from the tax returns are adjusted by estimators but the primary data are sorely deficient.[14] This lack of adequate basic information is readily acknowledged by the United States in the results of the Audit Control Study of the Internal Revenue Service of 1949.[15]

[13] "... Because of the general inadequacy of the entrepreneurial series on a '2-digit' industry basis, the series is not published in such detail.... Revisions were quite sizable, however, even for some of these broader categories, and serve to point up the extreme difficulty of estimating entrepreneurial income well, particularly on an industry basis." U.S. Department of Commerce, *U.S. Income and Output, A Supplement to the Survey of Current Business* (1959), p. 90.

[14] "For the immediate future, the most important single step that could be taken to improve the accuracy of the national accounts would be to improve the data for non-farm sole proprietorships and partnerships ... they can be regarded as little more than informed guesses for the small-business sector." National Bureau of Economic Research, *The National Economic Accounts of the United States: Review, Appraisal, and Recommendations*, A Report by the National Accounts Review Committee of the National Bureau of Economic Research (U.S. Government Printing Office, 1958), p. 125.

[15] The Audit Control Study of the Internal Revenue Service of 1949 estimated that non-farm unincorporated net profits were understated by an average of 20 percent. Marius Farioletti, "Some Income Adjustment Results from the 1949 Audit Control Program," in *An Appraisal of the 1950 Census Income Data*, Studies in Income and Wealth, Vol. 23, by the Conference on Research in Income and Wealth (Princeton University Press for National Bureau of Economic Research, 1958), p. 247.

GENERAL ALLOCATION STUDIES. Most of the studies[16] that have included the allocation of the income of unincorporated enterprises between the return to labor and the return to equity capital have been primarily concerned with the long-term functional distribution of income in the economy. The return to capital in the unincorporated sector was treated as one aggregate number or at the most two, farm and non-farm.

In order to analyze the movement in relative income shares over the 1900–57 period, Kravis used four methods to divide the total income of unincorporated enterprises into a labor share and a property share. His methods generally involved a comparison of the total corporate and the total unincorporated sector and, as he stated, they are susceptible to considerable refinement. The methods he used were as follows:

Asset basis. "One possible assumption is that the rate of return upon entrepreneurial property has been the same as that upon other property. The entrepreneurial property share in national income can then be calculated by applying to the share of other property (i.e., the combined share of interest, rent and corporate profits) the ratio of the value of entrepreneurial property to other property."[17]

Labor basis. This method assumed that the annual value of the labor of a proprietor was equal to the annual earnings of a hired worker. The proprietors' labor earnings were obtained by multiplying the wage and salary share by the ratio of proprietors to employees.

Proportional basis. Since the entrepreneurial commitment of labor and capital is a joint arrangement, it is argued that fluctuations in the proprietor's income should be shared equally by both factors of production. The risk of lower returns should not be confined to one

[16] D. Gale Johnson, "The Functional Distribution of Income in the United States, 1850–1952," *Review of Economics and Statistics*, Vol. 36 (May 1954), p. 175; Edward F. Denison, "Income Types and the Size Distribution," *American Economic Review, Papers and Proceedings* of the American Economic Association, Vol. 44 (May 1954), p. 254; Denison, *The Sources of Economic Growth in the United States and the Alternatives Before Us*, Supplementary Paper No. 13 (Committee for Economic Development, 1962), pp. 25–26; Irving B. Kravis, "Relative Income Shares in Fact and Theory," *American Economic Review*, Vol. 49 (December 1959), p. 917; and Stanley Lebergott, "Factor Shares in the Long Term: Some Theoretical and Statistical Aspects," *The Behavior of Income Shares: Selected Theoretical and Empirical Issues*, Studies in Income and Wealth, Vol. 27, by the Conference on Research in Income and Wealth (Princeton University Press for National Bureau of Economic Research, 1964), p. 53.

[17] Kravis, "Relative Income Shares," p. 924.

component, but shared by both. This suggests that entrepreneurial income should be divided into the labor and property components in constant proportions. Kravis adopted the Johnson estimate of 65 percent as labor and 35 percent as property income.

Economy-wide basis. ". . . to divide the income of non-corporate business for each period in accordance with the current relationship between labor and property income in the entire economy excluding the entrepreneurial sector."[18]

If one must allocate, Lebergott would favor allocating the entrepreneurs' income between capital and labor in accordance with the ratio of property to wage income in the corporate sector, changing when that ratio changes. Denison's choice of an allocation method would be that the ratio of property income (profits after inventory valuation plus net monetary interest paid) to national income originating in the corporate sector would be used as the ratio by which to distribute the total income originating in the unincorporated sector and not the income of unincorporated enterprises.

IMPUTING A LABOR RETURN TO THE ENTREPRENEUR. Harberger[19] endeavored to determine a return to capital for most of the non-farm unincorporated sectors by a residual estimating procedure roughly equivalent to the Kravis labor basis. His computation was made by subtracting from the income originating from an industry sector, a total labor return component, net monetary interest paid, and corporate profits before corporate profits tax liabilities. Labor return was in turn measured by the product of employee compensation[20] and the ratio of the number of workers engaged in production to full-time

[18] *Ibid.*, p. 925.

[19] Arnold C. Harberger, "The Corporation Income Tax: An Empirical Appraisal," in *Tax Revision Compendium*, House Committee on Ways and Means, 86 Cong. 1 sess. (1959), Vol. 1, p. 231.

[20] "*Compensation of employees* is the income accruing to persons in an employee status as remuneration for their work" and "is the sum of wages and salaries and supplements to wages and salaries. *Wages and salaries* consists of the monetary remuneration of employees commonly regarded as wages and salaries, inclusive of executives' compensation, commissions, tips, and bonuses, and of payments in kind which represent income to the recipients. *Supplements to wages and salaries* . . . consists of employer contributions for social insurance; employer contributions to private pension, health, and welfare funds; compensation for injuries; directors' fees; pay of the military reserve; and a few other minor items of labor income." U.S. Department of Commerce, *National Income*, p. 59.

equivalent employees.[21] The residual estimate of the return to capital includes a return to equity capital plus the net interest paid on borrowed capital as defined in the national income accounts.

This method assigns as the imputed labor return per proprietor or partner an amount equal to the average compensation of employees in the same industry. This labor imputation includes salaried employees in managerial positions. It does not impute any labor return to unpaid family workers since they are not included in number of workers engaged in production series.

For certain industry groups in the non-farm unincorporated sector, Harberger did not utilize this imputation of a return to labor since the results were large negative returns to capital. The major non-farm unincorporated sectors so excluded were agricultural services, forestry, and fisheries; contract construction; highway freight transportation and warehousing; and in services, hotels and other lodging places, miscellaneous repair services, and hand trades.

Table 4 presents the results of using the imputation of a return to labor based on employee compensation in the same industry for the non-farm unincorporated sectors excluded by Harberger. Negative returns to capital in any sector are not as such implausible but the magnitudes shown in Table 4 are much too large to be acceptable without further corroborating information. Such information is not available.

Table 5 presents for 1953–59 a comparison of the annual average employee compensation and wages and salaries per full-time equivalent employee with the income of unincorporated enterprises per partner or proprietor for the same industry groups presented in Table 4. The differences are substantial and explainable only in the most general qualitative terms.

Although the National Income Division presumably counts as self-employed only those active proprietors of enterprises who devote the major portion of their time to the business, it is difficult to correct

---

[21] *Full-time equivalent employment* measures man-years of full-time employment of wage and salary earners and its equivalent in work performed by part-time workers. *Full-time employment* is defined simply in terms of the number of hours which is customary at a particular time and place. *Number of workers engaged in production* includes full-time employment plus active proprietors of unincorporated enterprises devoting the major portion of their time to business, but does not include unpaid family workers. *Ibid.*, pp. 196 and 202.

TABLE 4. Return to Equity Capital when Labor Return to Entrepreneurs Is Based on Average Employee Compensation, Selected Unincorporated Industries, 1953–59 Average
(Millions of dollars)

Industry group	Income of unincorporated enterprises[a] (1)	Imputed labor return to entrepreneur[b] (2)	Return to equity capital[c] (3)
Agricultural services, forestry, and fisheries	370	525	−155
Contract construction	4,195	6,232	−2,037
Highway freight transportation and warehousing	596	764	−168
Services			
Hotels and other lodging places	251	514	−263
Miscellaneous repair services and hand trades	695	1,763	−1,068

[a] U.S. Department of Commerce, *Survey of Current Business*, various July issues and unpublished information provided by the U.S. Department of Commerce, National Income Division.

[b] *Ibid.* The labor return to the entrepreneur was measured by the product of the average employee compensation in each industry and the ratio of production workers over full-time equivalent employees in that industry.

[c] Column 1 less column 2.

the series for partners who are not active and be very specific as to the extent of the participation in any business by the active proprietors. Some deflation of the number of proprietors to a full-time equivalent series is certainly required. It is also evident, for example, in the construction industry, that many of the workers consider themselves self-employed, whereas they are, for a portion of their work year, legally employees.[22]

A more basic explanation may be the difference in the quality of the individuals classified as self-employed. Many of the proprietors of rooming houses in the hotel and other lodging place service industries may not only be part-time self-employed, but are also possibly not qualified to be hired as employees in the hotel industry. Many individuals probably prefer self-employment over an employee status; others do not have the choice.

On the income side, the national income accounts exclude imputations of non-money income because of the lack of primary data.

[22] President's Committee to Appraise Employment and Unemployment Statistics, *Measuring Employment and Unemployment* (U.S. Government Printing Office, 1962), p. 370.

TABLE 5. **Employee Compensation and Wages and Salaries per Full-Time Equivalent Employee Compared with Income of Unincorporated Enterprises per Partner or Proprietor, Selected Industry Groups, 1953–59 Average**
(Money amounts in dollars per year)

Industry group	Compensation per employee[a] (1)	Wages and salaries per employee[b] (2)	Income of unincorporated enterprises per partner or proprietor[c] (3)	Income of unincorporated enterprises per partner or proprietor as percentage of	
				Compensation per employee (4)	Wages and salaries per employee (5)
Agricultural services, forestry, and fisheries	3,448	3,350	2,467	72	74
Contract construction	4,958	4,696	3,427	69	73
Highway freight transportation and warehousing	5,320	5,090	4,139	78	81
Services					
Hotels and other lodging places	2,752	2,630	1,321	48	50
Miscellaneous repair services and hand trades	4,508	4,338	1,778	39	41

[a] U.S. Department of Commerce, *Survey of Current Business*, various July issues and unpublished information provided by the U.S. Department of Commerce, National Income Division. The total compensation of employees was divided by the number of full-time equivalent employees.
[b] *Ibid.* Total wages and salaries were divided by the number of full-time equivalent employees.
[c] *Ibid.* The income of unincorporated enterprises was divided by the difference between the number of production workers engaged and the number of full-time equivalent employees.

TABLE 6. Estimated Return to Equity Capital, Assuming Equal Rate of Return after Tax on Corporate and Unincorporated Net Physical Assets, Selected Non-Farm Unincorporated Industries, 1953-59 Average
(Money amounts in millions of dollars)

Industry group	Net physical assets, 1959		Unincorporated as percentage of corporate (3)	Corporate profits after tax plus net realized capital gains, 1953-59 average[c] (4)	Estimated return to unincorporated equity capital[d] (5)
	Corporate[a] (1)	Derived unincorporated[b] (2)			
Agricultural services, forestry, and fisheries	2,264	1,382	61.0	43	26
Contract construction	4,184	3,894	93.1	280	261
Highway freight transportation and warehousing[e]	2,283	1,265	55.4	105	58
Services					
Hotels and other lodging places	2,832	3,179	112.3	25	28
Miscellaneous repair services and hand trades	1,356	1,441	106.3	8	9

[a] U.S. Treasury Department, Statistics of Income—1959-60, Corporation Income Tax Returns (1962), Table 2. Net physical assets are the sum of the net depreciable and depletable assets, inventories, and land.
[b] Based on data in U.S. Treasury Department, Statistics of Income—1959-60, U.S. Business Tax Returns (1962), Tables 5 and 14.
[c] U.S. Department of Commerce, Survey of Current Business, various July issues and U.S. Treasury Department, Statistics of Income—Corporation Income Tax Returns, various annual issues.
[d] Column 3 multiplied by column 4.
[e] Statistics on highway freight transportation and warehousing were provided by the U.S. Department of Commerce, National Income Division (Source Book Information).

Income-in-kind is likely to be more prevalent in an unincorporated sector where the business and household accounts are almost completely commingled.[23] An obvious example is the owner-operators of motels who reside on the business premises for which no imputation of income is made.

Column 7 of Table 1 incorporates a return to equity capital based on the labor share imputation suggested by Harberger for those industries for which his method gave positive returns. Although far from ideal, it is a plausible method of allocation and the detailed information required for its calculation is available. The return to equity capital for the other non-farm unincorporated sectors is discussed next.

IMPUTATION BASED ON NET PHYSICAL ASSETS. Table 6 uses the net physical asset data available for only one year, 1959, to estimate the return to equity capital for those non-farm unincorporated sectors in which the imputation of the labor return resulted in large negative returns to equity capital.

The results of these computations are included in column 7 of Table 1 and are based on the following assumptions:

1. The ratio of net physical assets (defined as the sum of net depreciable and depletable assets, inventories, and land) to business receipts is the same for partners not filing balance sheets and for sole proprietorships as for partners filing balance sheets with their tax returns.

2. The net rate of return to equity capital for the unincorporated and corporate sectors of an industry is assumed to be equal[24] and is, therefore, proportional to the ratio of net physical assets for the two segments of an industry group.

3. The ratio of the unincorporated net physical assets to corporate net physical assets for 1959 is applicable to the average 1953–59 corporate profits after corporate profits tax liabilities plus net realized capital gains.

[23] John E. Bregger, "Self-Employment in the United States, 1948–62," *Monthly Labor Review*, Vol. 86 (January 1963), p. 37.

[24] "It is likely that entrepreneurs are able to earn larger returns on the average through direct investment in their business—or at least expect to do so—than they or others can earn in other ways, if only because direct investment dispenses with the need for the services of brokers, financial institutions and other intermediaries." Milton Friedman, *A Theory of the Consumption Function* (Princeton University Press for the National Bureau of Economic Research, 1957), p. 78.

148   Taxation of Income from Capital, by Industry

Assumption number 1 overstates the net physical assets of these unincorporated sectors and, therefore, the return on equity capital. The partners filing balance sheets with their tax returns are usually the larger firms with a higher ratio of business receipts per partner than is true of sole proprietorships and of partners not filing balance sheets. These large firms are presumed to be more capital intensive since their ratios of fixed capital assets to business receipts are likely to be higher than for the smaller firms.

On the other hand, the use of 1959 information would tend to understate the return to equity capital for the non-farm unincorporated sectors, since the ratio of unincorporated to corporate net physical assets has been declining over time. The extremely limited information does not allow any judgment as to the direction or extent of the bias involved in the estimation procedure.

ALTERNATIVE CALCULATION OF RETURN TO EQUITY CAPITAL FOR HOTELS, MOTELS, AND TOURIST COURTS. For the hotel, motel, and tourist court industry, the available financial and statistical information permits an alternative calculation of the return to equity capital. Table 7 presents the results of this alternative calculation. The information was obtained from reports prepared by specialized accounting firms employed by the industry, articles published in trade association journals, and data from U.S. Censuses of Business for 1954 and 1958. The total annual average return to equity for this more narrowly defined service industry in 1953–59 was $181 million. This result exceeds by $81 million the direct total return to equity capital of $100 million shown in Table 1 (sum of columns 3 and 7).

The reconciliation of these two widely divergent results, based on different estimating procedures and sources of data, is not possible. The methodology in which the results are determined by the relationships between rates of earnings and total gross receipts for a sample group would undoubtedly overstate the return to equity capital. The sample group of 400 hotels is probably made up of the larger and more successful operations in the hotel industry. Not enough information is available on the composition of the sample group of motels and tourist courts to justify an opinion as to direction of the bias. The interest on owners' equity (Table 7, column 6) for this group definitely appears to be high relative to that of hotels (Table 7, column 3).

Leonard Gerson Rosenberg

TABLE 7. Alternative Estimate of Return to Equity Capital for Hotel, Motel, and Tourist Court Industry, 1953-59
(Money amounts in millions of dollars)

Year	Hotels			Motels and tourist courts			Total return on equity capital[g] (7)
	Total gross receipts[a] (1)	Return on capital[b] (percent) (2)	Total net earnings[c] (3)	Total gross receipts[d] (4)	Interest on owners' equity[e] (percent) (5)	Total net earnings[f] (6)	
1953	2,551	4.0	102	384	11.92	46	148
1954	2,405	4.0	96	457	11.30	52	148
1955	2,646	4.3	114	509	11.00	56	170
1956	2,772	4.9	136	706	10.70	76	212
1957	2,836	4.5	128	748	10.15	76	204
1958	2,794	4.1	115	850	8.42	72	187
1959	2,911	4.1	119	1,030	7.35	76	195
Average			116			65	181

[a] U.S. Bureau of the Census, *U.S. Census of Business: 1958*, Vol. 5, *Selected Services—Summary Statistics* (1961), Table 5A, p. 5–2, and U.S. Bureau of the Census, *U.S. Census of Business: 1954*, Vol. 5, *Selected Service Trades—Summary Statistics* (1957), Table 5A, pp. 5–16, provided benchmark data on gross receipts for 1954 and 1958. Harris, Kerr, Forster and Company, *Trends in the Hotel Business 1961*, Twenty-Sixth Annual Review (New York, 1962), Fig. 16, p. 5, was used as an index (1958 = 100) to extrapolate the census benchmarks to obtain estimates for the other years.
[b] *Ibid.*, Fig. 16, p. 10.
[c] Column 1 multiplied by column 2.
[d] The same U.S. Bureau of the Census publications noted for column 1 provided benchmarks for 1954 and 1958. An index was constructed with 1958 = 100, based on unpublished information provided by H. D. Cochran, Editorial Director of the *Tourist Court Journal*, Temple, Texas.
[e] *Annual Motel Financial Report* (Temple, Texas: Tourist Court Journal Company, Inc., July 1962), middle page, published the estimated interest on owners' equity for 1957 through 1959. The *Tourist Court Journal*, July 1954, Fig. 5, published an estimate for 1953. For 1954 through 1956, it was assumed that the decline in the percentage was linear and equal for each year.
[f] Column 4 multiplied by column 5.
[g] Column 3 plus column 6.

Other Returns Assigned from Real Estate

Net monetary interest paid by an industry was defined as the net return on borrowed capital in the form of long- and short-term interest-bearing debt. Another form of borrowed capital for any industry can be physical property. Payments for the use of this borrowed capital are made as net rents or net royalty payments.

NET RENTS PAID AND THE REAL ESTATE INDUSTRY. Conceptually, net rents paid should be added back to the other returns to capital for an industry. This is not done in the present structure of the national income accounts. The only rent information now published is the rental income of persons not primarily engaged in the real estate business.

TABLE 8. Rental Income of Persons by Type of Property, 1953–59
(Millions of dollars)

Year	Total rental income of persons[a] (1)	Rental income of non-farm landlords from farmland[b] (2)	Imputed net rent on owner-occupied non-farm dwellings[c] (3)	Rental income from non-farm property[d]				Total rental income from non-farm dwellings[e] (8)
				Total (4)	Rented dwellings (5)	Royalty earnings (6)	Business and industrial (7)	
1953	10,528	1,214	4,435	4,879	2,191	678	2,010	6,626
1954	10,869	1,159	4,735	4,975	2,234	692	2,049	6,969
1955	10,698	1,057	5,035	4,606	2,068	640	1,898	7,103
1956	10,913	1,109	5,335	4,469	2,007	621	1,841	7,342
1957	11,891	1,029	5,635	5,227	2,347	727	2,153	7,982
1958	12,208	1,161	5,935	5,112	2,295	711	2,106	8,230
1959	11,902	1,011	6,220	4,671	2,097	649	1,925	8,317
Average	11,287	1,106	5,333	4,848	2,177	674	1,997	7,510

[a] U.S. Department of Commerce, *Survey of Current Business*, Vol. 42 (July 1962), p. 6.
[b] U.S. Department of Agriculture, *Farm Income Situation*, FIS–187 (July 1962), Table 14H, p. 52 (government payments are included).
[c] For the years 1953 and 1959, unpublished information provided by the U.S. Department of Commerce, National Income Division. The 1954 through 1958 estimates were made as a simple extrapolation of the beginning and end of period estimates.
[d] Based on U.S. Department of Commerce, *National Income: 1954 Edition*, a supplement to the *Survey of Current Business* (1954), p. 86. The 1950 percentage distribution was used to distribute the total in column 4 (column 1 less the sum of columns 2 and 3) among the items for each year.
[e] Column 3 plus column 5.

Net rents paid in the business sector are now included as a cost deduction for the renting firm and as part of the net income or corporate profits of the owners of the rented property. A net rent paid series by industry group would require information on non-farm interfirm transactions that would permit the reduction of the gross rental payment to a net rent concept. It is still possible, though, to make a rough approximation of the industrial sources of the net rents and royalty earnings presently included in the real estate industry as presented in the national income accounts.

RE-DEFINITION OF THE REAL ESTATE INDUSTRY. The real estate industry as defined in the national income accounts includes all types of property. Our re-definition would include only non-farm residential dwellings, rented and owner-occupied. The returns to capital for any other type of property would be assigned to the industry group which would pay for the use of the property.

The income originating in the real estate industry is made up of the sum of compensation of employees, corporate profits before tax, inventory valuation adjustment, net interest paid, income of unincorporated enterprises, and rental income of persons not primarily engaged in the real estate business.

RENTAL INCOME OF PERSONS. Rental income of persons represents the largest portion of the industry's value added and is composed of the following items:
1. Net rent paid to non-farm landlords.
2. Imputed net rent for owner-occupied non-farm dwellings.
3. Net rental income from non-farm property consisting of (a) dwellings, (b) business and industrial property, and (c) royalty earnings.

In Table 8, a distribution of the rental income of persons is presented for 1953–59. Rental income of persons in 1953–59 averaged $11,287 million (column 1). Of this total $7,510 million (column 8) remains in the real estate industry, the payments of net rents of non-farm residential dwelling property. Net rents paid of $1,106 million on farm land to non-farm landlords have been previously included (Table 2) as a part of the income from agriculture.

The remainder of $2,671 million requires allocation to other industry groups and consists of net royalty earnings ($674 million in column 6) and net rents from business and industrial property ($1,997 million in column 7).

NET MONETARY INTEREST PAID. An estimate of net interest paid on non-farm residential dwellings of $5,190 million for 1953–59 was obtained from the National Income Division of the U.S. Department of Commerce. The corresponding estimate of net monetary interest paid is $5,250 million. The total net monetary interest paid in 1953–59 for the real estate industry as defined in the national income accounts averaged $6,508 million, leaving $1,258 million to be allocated to other industry groups.

ASSIGNMENT TO OTHER INDUSTRIES OF NET RENTS AND NET MONETARY INTEREST PAID. The net rental income of business and industrial property ($1,997 million) and the non-real estate portion of net monetary interest paid ($1,258 million) were distributed to other industry sectors on the basis of the percentage distribution of the tax return deduction taken by businesses in 1959 for rent paid on business property.[25]

Royalty earnings ($674 million) were distributed as follows: 75 percent to oil and gas production; 12.5 percent to printing, publishing, and allied industries; and 12.5 percent to electrical machinery (mainly phonograph records). This approximate breakdown of royalty earnings was obtained from the National Income Division of the U.S. Department of Commerce.

The distribution of the royalty earnings assigned to oil and gas, $506 million, was allocated among crude petroleum and natural gas (mining), products of petroleum and coal (manufacturing), and electric and gas utilities, on the basis of the depletion deductions taken by each industry group for tax purposes in 1959.[26]

INCOME OF UNINCORPORATED ENTERPRISES. The portion of the income of unincorporated enterprises allocated as return to equity capital was determined by using the average employee compensation paid per full-time equivalent employee in the industry as the imputation of the entrepreneurial labor share. This procedure was discussed in

[25] U.S. Treasury Department, *Statistics of Income—1959–60, Corporation Income Tax Returns* (1962), Table 2, for the corporate sector. U.S. Treasury Department, *Statistics of Income—1959–60, U.S. Business Tax Returns* (*1962*), Tables 5 and 12, for the unincorporated sector.
[26] *Ibid.*

a preceding section. The resulting return to equity capital of $430 million was then distributed between non-farm residential dwellings and business and industrial property, on the basis of the relationship of the rental income of rented non-farm property and business and industrial property for 1953-59 (as shown in Table 8). Of the $430 million income of unincorporated enterprises, a return to equity capital of $225 million (52.3 percent) remained in the real estate industry. The balance of $205 million (47.7 percent) was allocated to other industry sectors using the tax return information for 1959 on rent paid on business property.

CORPORATE PROFITS BEFORE TAX PLUS NET REALIZED CAPITAL GAINS. Corporate profits before tax plus net realized capital gains were initially distributed between real estate and other industry groups on the basis of the distribution of the average rental income for 1953-59 between rented non-farm dwellings and business and industrial property. The amount assigned to other industry sectors ($475 million out of the total $998 million) was allocated to individual industry groups using the 1959 rent paid on business property series.

CONCLUSION. The sum of columns 5 and 8 in Table 1 is an estimate of the income from capital that has been shifted out of the real estate industry—as defined in the national income accounts—to other non-financial industry groups. The total returns assigned were $4,066 million. Manufacturing ($1,258 million) and total trade ($1,618 million) were responsible for 70 percent of the total returns to capital that were transferred. The total return to capital for the real estate industry—now defined as consisting solely of non-farm residential dwellings—is $13,507 million (column 9 of Table 1).

Taxes on Income from Capital, by Industry Group

Corporate Profits Tax Liability

For the entire corporate sector, the average 1953-59 federal and state corporate profits tax liability on income originating in the United States was $20,465 million. Of this total amount, state corporate profits tax liability was $965 million or about 4.7 percent of the total *Survey of Current Business* data. These state corporate profits tax liabilities are distributed in the national income accounts among industry groups in proportion to their federal corporate profits tax liabilities.

Non-financial industry groups accounted for $18,306 million or about 90 percent of the total corporate profits tax liabilities during this period. Table 9 presents these tax liabilities and their percentage distribution by industry group. Manufacturing, $11,560 million (63 percent); total trade, $2,493 million (14 percent); and total communications and public utilities, $2,199 million (12 percent) were the prime contributors to the total revenue from the corporate profits tax.

The only adjustment made in this national income series was to redistribute a portion of the $418 million corporate profits tax liability of the real estate industry, in line with the re-definition of the real estate industry discussed above. The total real estate tax liability was initially allocated between non-farm residential dwellings and other types of rental property on the basis of the distribution presented in Table 8 of the total net rent from rented non-farm dwellings (52.2 percent) and business and industrial property (47.8 percent). The $200 million of corporate profits tax liability that required transfer was then assigned to other industry groups on the basis of the distribution of the 1959 rent paid on business property series (see Table 9, footnote b).

Property Tax Payments

Property tax revenues increased from $9.4 billion in 1953 to $15.0 billion in 1959. By 1961, they had further increased to $18.0 billion, or almost twice the 1953 total. In 1953–59, the average annual property tax revenues were $12.0 billion or approximately 60 percent of corporate profits tax liabilities for the same period. Unless otherwise stated, the statistics on property taxes that are used in this section are from U.S. Bureau of the Census, *Summary of Governmental Finances in 1955* (1956), and subsequent annual issues, and *Governmental Finances in 1961* (1962).

Property taxes are predominantly collected by local governments. A minor amount, averaging less than $500 million per annum during the 1953–59 period, is collected by state governments. The Bureau of the Census defines the property tax as "taxes conditioned on ownership of property and measured by its value, and applicable either to all property, to all tangible property, or to all real property, not

TABLE 9. Corporate Profits Tax Liability, by Non-Financial Industry Group, 1953–59 Average

(Money amounts in millions of dollars)

	Corporate profits tax liability			
Industry group	Direct[a] (1)	Assigned from real estate[b] (2)	Total[c] (3)	Percentage distribution[d] (4)
Total corporate profits tax liability	18,334	172	18,306	100.0
Total, farms, agricultural services, forestry, and fisheries	62	2	64	0.3
Farms	60	—	60	0.3
Agricultural services, forestry, and fisheries	2	2	4	[e]
Total mining	320	1	321	1.8
Metal mining	117	—	117	0.6
Bituminous coal mining	32	—	32	0.2
Crude petroleum and natural gas	104	1	105	0.6
Non-metallic mining and quarrying; and anthracite mining	67	—	67	0.4
Contract construction	321	3	325	1.8
Total manufacturing	11,522	38	11,560	63.1
Food and kindred products	977	5	982	5.4
Tobacco manufactures	231	—	231	1.3
Textile mill products	301	2	302	1.6
Apparel and other finished fabric products	113	3	115	0.6
Lumber and wood products (except furniture and fixtures)	149	1	150	0.8
Furniture and fixtures	112	1	113	0.6
Paper and allied products	542	2	543	3.0
Printing and publishing	396	3	398	2.2
Chemicals and allied products	1,422	3	1,424	7.8
Petroleum and coal products	452	11	459	2.5
Rubber products	206	2	207	1.1
Leather and leather products	72	1	73	0.4
Stone, clay, and glass products	494	1	495	2.7
Primary metal industries	1,190	1	1,191	6.5
Fabricated metal products (including ordnance and accessories)	572	3	574	3.1

Footnotes to table appear on p. 157.

TABLE 9—Continued

	Corporate profits tax liability			
Industry group	Direct[a] (1)	Assigned from real estate[b] (2)	Total[c] (3)	Percentage distribution[d] (4)
Total manufacturing (continued)				
Instruments	264	1	265	1.4
Machinery (except electrical and transportation)	1,166	4	1,167	6.4
Electrical machinery	820	3	823	4.5
Motor vehicles and equipment	1,418	1	1,420	7.8
Transportation equipment (except motor vehicles)	436	2	438	2.4
Miscellaneous manufactures	189	2	190	1.0
Total trade	2,411	82	2,493	13.6
Wholesale trade	1,056	14	1,070	5.8
Retail trade and automobile services	1,355	62	1,423	7.8
Real estate	418	—	218	1.2
Non-farm residential dwellings	218	—	218	1.2
Other	200	—	—	—
Total transportation	740	26	759	4.1
Railroads	377	12	389	2.1
Local and highway passenger transportation	40	—	40	0.2
Highway freight transportation and warehousing	105	3	108	0.6
Water transportation	71	1	72	0.4
Air transportation (common carriers)	50	2	52	0.3
Pipeline transportation	63	—	63	0.3
Services allied to transportation	34	1	35	0.2
Total communications and public utilities	2,195	4	2,199	12.0
Telephone, telegraph, and related services	814	2	816	4.5
Radio broadcasting and television	86	1	87	0.5
Utilities: electric and gas	1,269	1	1,270	6.9
Local utilities and public services not elsewhere classified	26	—	26	0.1

TABLE 9—Continued

	Corporate profits tax liability			
Industry group	Direct[a] (1)	Assigned from real estate[b] (2)	Total[c] (3)	Percentage distribution[d] (4)
Total services[f]	345	14	367	2.1
Hotels and other lodging places	47	2	51	0.3
Personal services	40	3	46	0.3
Business services not elsewhere classified	147	3	151	0.8
Miscellaneous repair services and hand trades	10	2	14	0.1
Motion pictures	55	2	56	0.3
Amusements (except motion pictures)	46	2	49	0.3

[a] U.S. Department of Commerce, Office of Business Economics, *U.S. Income and Output, A Supplement to the Survey of Current Business* (1959), Table VI-6, and *Survey of Current Business*, various July issues.

[b] U.S. Treasury Department, *Statistics of Income—1959-60, Corporation Income Tax Returns* (1962), Table 2. The amount shown in column 1 for Real estate, Other, was assigned to other industry groups on the basis of the percentage distribution of the rent paid on business property by all industry groups for the year 1959. The amount assigned from Real estate, Other ($172 million) in column 2 is less than the $200 million in column 1 because a portion of the corporate profits tax liability was assigned to industry groups not included in this study.

[c] Column 1 plus column 2, except for Total corporate profits tax liability, Real estate, and Real estate, Other, which reflect the redistribution of real estate corporate profits tax liability in column 1 (see footnote b).

[d] Column 3 for each industry group divided by the total of column 3. Calculations are based on unrounded data.

[e] Less than 0.05.

[f] Engineering and other professional services are not included in this study.

specifically excepted, whether at a single rate or at classified effective rates."[27] The definition of a property tax base may differ between states; personal property in one state may be classified as real property in another state. Property tax rates on identical classes of property may differ from jurisdiction to jurisdiction, not only between counties but among the various local jurisdictions that may be included within the geographical confines of a county.

The 1957 and 1962 Census of Governments reports published assessed valuations by different types of property subject to the general property tax, as well as information on special property taxes. In order to make use of these assessed valuations to compute the general property tax revenues by types of property, one must assume that a state-wide average general property tax rate exists that is applicable to all types of property. This is an assumption that has many obvious limitations. In the section below on non-farm residential dwellings, this matter is briefly mentioned.

[27] U.S. Bureau of the Census, *U.S. Census of Governments: 1957*, Vol. 5, *Taxable Property Values in the United States* (1959), p. 1.

158   Taxation of Income from Capital, by Industry

The classification of the types of property in the Census of Governments is very broad and quite different from the industrial classification adopted in this study. Comparisons between the census estimates and our estimates of property taxes paid therefore are not useful for most of the industry groups. In two instances, the real property of non-farm residential dwellings and of railroads, estimates based on the Census of Governments have been used. These two industry groups accounted for 45.8 percent of the total property tax revenues included in this study.

Table 10 presents the estimates of property tax revenues for 1953–59 that have been excluded from this study. The notes to this table are self-explanatory as to the estimation procedure and sources of data. For the 1953–59 period, these exclusions averaged $661 million per annum.

TABLE 10. Special Property Tax Payments That Are Excluded from This Study, 1953–59 Average
(Millions of dollars)

Tax base	Amount
Motor vehicles[a]	269
Intangible personal property[b]	235
Corporate sector (financial)[c]	106
Unincorporated services[d]	51
Total	661

[a] The Advisory Commission on Intergovernmental Relations, *Measures of State and Local Fiscal Capacity and Tax Effort* (1962), n. 1, Table 37, p. 126, estimated that in 1960 motor vehicle property taxes were $542 million. The 1960 ratio of motor vehicle property taxes to total property tax revenue was assumed to be applicable to the 1953–59 period. Total property tax revenue is from U.S. Bureau of the Census, *Summary of Governmental Finances in 1955* (1956), and subsequent annual issues. Based on information obtained for the states of Illinois and California for the year 1959, it was estimated that 70 percent of the motor vehicle property tax was collected from personal autos, which are excluded from industry groups covered by this study. Illinois and California accounted for 34 percent of the motor vehicle property tax revenue in 1959. Motor vehicle property taxes paid on farm motor vehicles used in farm production are excluded since these property taxes are included in farm personal property taxes.

[b] Dick Netzer, in "Property Tax Revenues by Property-Use Classes, 1957," typewritten draft, April 9, 1963, summarized the results of a special tabulation done by the Bureau of the Census using data from the *Census of Governments, 1957* and estimated that personal property taxes on intangibles were $254 million in 1957. The ratio of the 1957 estimate to total property tax revenues for 1957 was assumed applicable to the entire 1953–59 period.

[c] U.S. Treasury Department, Internal Revenue Service, *Statistics of Income, Corporation Income Tax Returns*, various issues, and Table 12, column 1. The property taxes paid by corporate finance, insurance, and other services were estimated by multiplying their net physical assets by 1.79 percent, the property tax rate derived for total manufacturing (see Table 12).

[d] It was estimated that the property tax payments of those service industry sectors excluded from this study were 19 percent of the amount shown in Table 11, column 1, for the total services included. This percentage was determined on the basis of the relationship of the depreciation charges of the excluded service industries to the included service industries. For the unincorporated services, the relevant information was obtained from U.S. Treasury Department, *Statistics of Income, 1959–60, U.S. Business Tax Returns* (1962), Tables 5 and 12. The 1959–60 relationship was assumed to be applicable for the entire 1953–59 period. For the corporate services, the annual depreciation charges are published by the U.S. Department of Commerce, *Survey of Current Business*, in various July issues.

The total property tax revenues shown at the beginning of Table 11 were obtained by subtracting the amounts shown in Table 10 from the total property tax revenues reported by the Bureau of the Census. The remainder of this section will be devoted to explaining the derivation or source of the property tax estimates shown in Table 11.

It is not feasible to use the results of this study as a measure of the changing annual property tax payments by industry group. This can be done where industry sources and the U.S. Department of Agriculture provided annual property tax estimates for most of the period, but these instances consist of only about 20 percent of the total property tax revenues. For the majority of the property tax estimates, it has been assumed that the average property tax rate for 1957 was applicable to either the 1953–57 or the 1953–59 period, or else that the simple adjustment of a 1961 estimate was relevant for the years 1958 and 1959.

FARMS, AGRICULTURAL SERVICES, FORESTRY, FISHERIES (ITEM A)

Farms. Taxes on farm property are estimates of the U.S. Department of Agriculture. Taxes levied on farm property were obtained from *Farm Real Estate Taxes, Recent Trends and Developments* (October 1962), Table 1, page 2. Taxes levied on farm personalty were obtained from *Agricultural Finance Review* (April 1962), Table 29, page 102.

Taxes levied on farm personalty have been adjusted to eliminate 60 percent of the estimated taxes on farm automobiles and trucks. This is the family living share for motor vehicles based on a 1955 expenditure survey by the U.S. Department of Agriculture.

A study by the U.S. Department of Agriculture for the year 1949 indicated that automobiles and trucks represented 10.9 percent of the total taxes levied on farm personalty.[28] This percentage was used to estimate the motor vehicle portion of the taxes levied on farm personalty.

Agricultural Services, Forestry, and Fisheries. The annual total of net physical assets for the industry was multiplied by a property tax rate of 1.30 percent. Net physical assets are defined as the sum of net depreciable and depletable assets, land, and one-half of the inven-

---

[28] Ronald Bird, "Taxation of Personal Property Owned by Farmers in the United States," *Agricultural Finance Review*, Vol. 15 (November 1952), p. 41.

TABLE 11. Estimate of Property Taxes Paid by Non-Financial Industry Group, 1953–59 Average

(Money amounts in millions of dollars)

Industry group	Direct (1)	Assigned from real estate (2)	Total (3)	Percentage distribution (4)
Total property tax revenue	11,299	404^a	11,240^a	100.0
A. Total, farms, agricultural services, forestry, and fisheries	1,235	3	1,238	11.0
Farms	1,202	—	1,202	10.7
Agricultural services, forestry, and fisheries	33	3	36	0.3
B. Total mining	178	3	181	1.6
Metal mining	37	—	37	0.3
Bituminous coal mining	26	—	26	0.2
Crude petroleum and natural gas	90	2	92	0.8
Non-metallic mining and quarrying; and anthracite mining	25	1	26	0.2
C. Contract construction	100	10	110	1.0
D. Total manufacturing	1,811	93	1,904	17.0
Food and kindred products	181	10	191	1.7
Tobacco manufactures	15	—	15	0.1
Textile mill products	44	3	47	0.4
Apparel and other finished fabric products	25	5	30	0.3
Lumber and wood products (except furniture and fixtures)	54	2	56	0.5
Furniture and fixtures	27	2	29	0.3
Paper and allied products	69	3	72	0.6
Printing and publishing	48	6	54	0.5
Chemicals and allied products	137	5	142	1.3
Petroleum and coal products	295	16	311	2.8
Rubber products	31	3	34	0.3
Leather and leather products	11	1	12	0.1
Stone, clay, and glass products	51	2	53	0.5
Primary metal industries	188	3	191	1.7
Fabricated metal products (including ordnance and accessories)	126	5	131	1.2
Instruments	22	2	24	0.2

Footnotes to table appear on p. 162.

TABLE 11—Continued

Industry group	Direct (1)	Property taxes Assigned from real estate (2)	Total (3)	Percentage distribution (4)
Total manufacturing (continued)				
Machinery, (except electrical and transportation)	161	6	167	1.5
Electrical machinery	67	6	73	0.6
Motor vehicles and equipment	152	6	158	1.4
Transportation equipment (except motor vehicles)	80	4	84	0.7
Miscellaneous manufactures	28	3	31	0.3
E. Total trade	809	191	1,000	8.9
Wholesale trade	272	33	305	2.7
Retail trade	537	158	695	6.2
F. Real estate and household effects	5,385	—	4,922[a]	43.8
Non-farm residential dwellings	4,922	—	4,922	43.8
Real property	4,823	—	4,823	42.9
Personal property (household effects)	99	—	99	0.9
Other	463[a]	—	[b]	—
G. Total transportation	427	44	471	4.1
Railroads	304	27	331	2.9
Local and highway passenger transportation	14	1	15	0.1
Highway freight transportation and warehousing	46	8	54	0.5
Water transportation	24	2	26	0.2
Air transportation (common carriers)	4	4	8	0.1
Pipeline transportation	21	—	21	0.2
Services allied to transportation	14	2	16	0.1
H. Total communications and public utilities	1,083	8	1,091	9.7
Telephone, telegraph, and related services	303	5	308	2.7
Radio broadcasting and television	8	1	9	0.1
Utilities: electric and gas	749	2	751	6.7
Local utilities and public services not elsewhere classified	23	—	23	0.2

TABLE 11—Continued

Industry group	Property taxes			
	Direct (1)	Assigned from real estate (2)	Total (3)	Percentage distribution (4)
I. Total services[c]	271	52	323	2.9
Hotels and other lodging places	122	10	132	1.2
Personal services	41	14	55	0.5
Business services not elsewhere classified	29	8	37	0.3
Miscellaneous repair services and hand trades	30	10	40	0.4
Motion pictures and other amusements	49	10	59	0.5

Source: Estimated by author on basis of U.S. Bureau of the Census data. See pp. 159–73 for sources and derivation. Figures are rounded and will not necessarily add to totals.

[a] The difference between the $463 million shown in column 1 for Real estate, Other, and the $404 million assigned from Real estate, Other, to other industry groups in column 2 is due to the amounts transferred to the finance, insurance, and service industries that are excluded from this study. The difference is also excluded in the $11,240 million shown for Total property tax revenue in column 3, and the $4,922 million for Real estate and household effects.

[b] Real estate, Other, property taxes in column 1 were redistributed. See footnote a.

[c] Engineering and other professional services are not included in this study.

tories. The property tax rate used is an unweighted average of the ratio of farm property taxes to market value of physical assets in agriculture (0.80 percent) for 1953–59 and the property tax rate computed for the manufacturing sector (1.79 percent) for 1957.

The annual net physical assets for the corporate sector of the industry were obtained directly from U.S. Treasury Department, *Statistics of Income, Corporation Income Tax Returns*. For the unincorporated sector, partial estimates of net physical assets are available for only 1959 in U.S. Treasury Department, *Statistics of Income— 1959–60, U.S. Business Tax Returns*. These estimates are only for partners filing balance sheets with their tax returns. The basic assumptions underlying the calculation of net physical assets for the unincorporated sector are as follows:

1. The ratio of net physical assets to business receipts is the same for partners not filing balance sheets and for sole proprietorships as for partners filing balance sheets with their personal income tax returns.
2. The ratio of the 1959 net physical assets for unincorporated to the corporate sector is applicable to the entire 1953–59 period.

TOTAL MINING (ITEM B)

The estimate of property taxes paid by corporate mining was obtained by multiplying the annual corporate net physical assets by the property tax rate computed for the manufacturing sector (1.79 percent).

For unincorporated mining, it was initially assumed that the depreciation charged in the national income accounts for the individual subsectors was distributed in accordance with the distribution published for the corporate subsectors. This assumption permitted the allocation of the total unincorporated mining depreciation charges to specific subsectors. The ratio of the allocated unincorporated depreciation charges to the corporate depreciation charges by subsector was then multiplied by the property tax payments for the corporate subsectors.

CONTRACT CONSTRUCTION (ITEM C)

Property taxes paid by corporate contract construction were estimated by multiplying the net physical assets by the manufacturing property tax rate (1.79 percent). Corporate net physical assets were obtained directly from various annual issues of U.S. Treasury Department, *Statistics of Income, Corporation Income Tax Returns.*

For the unincorporated contract construction, it was assumed that the ratio of the unincorporated depreciation charge to the corporate depreciation charge multiplied by the property taxes paid by the corporate sector produced a reasonable approximation.

MANUFACTURING (ITEM D)

Property taxes paid by the manufacturing sector were published for the year 1957 by the U.S. Bureau of the Census.[29] The 1957 census property tax estimate for manufacturing of $1,450.4 million was on an establishment basis. The 1953–59 average of property taxes paid shown in Table 11 was $1,811 million or 16.0 percent of the property tax revenues.

In order to convert the census information to the company industrial classification consistent with most of the income and tax data being utilized, it was initially assumed that net physical assets were an adequate measure of the property tax base. Net physical assets

[29] U.S. Bureau of the Census, *U.S. Census of Manufactures: 1958*, Vol. 1, *Summary Statistics* (1961), pp. 9–8 and 9–9.

164   Taxation of Income from Capital, by Industry

for this purpose were defined as the sum of net depreciable and depletable assets, land, and one-half the inventories.[30] The following procedure was then used:

1. Partial net physical assets (net physical assets, excluding land) at the end of 1957 for manufacturing published by the Bureau of the Census in *U.S. Census of Manufactures: 1958*, Volume 1, were compared with the partial net physical assets published by the IRS in *Statistics of Income, Corporation Income Tax Returns* for the tax accounting period from July 1957 to June 1958. The value of land was excluded since it was not available in the census data.

2. When the census partial net physical assets exceeded the IRS partial net physical assets, the census property tax estimates were *accepted*. When the IRS partial net physical assets exceeded the census partial net physical assets, the ratio of the IRS to census partial net physical assets was applied to the census property tax payments to obtain an adjusted property tax estimate.

3. For most of the industry groups, the adjusted census property tax payments were divided by the IRS net physical assets to derive a property tax rate for 1957. The respective industry group property tax rate for 1957 was then applied to the annual IRS net physical asset estimates for the other years included in this study to estimate property tax payments for each industry group.

4. For certain industry groups, the census partial net physical assets exceeded the IRS partial net physical assets.[31] In order to compute a property tax rate that could be used with the

---

[30] The property tax base utilized by the Advisory Commission on Intergovernmental Relations in their report, *Measures of State and Local Fiscal Capacity and Tax Effort* (U.S. Government Printing Office, 1962), pp. 107–12, included net depreciable and depletable assets, land, and all of the inventories. In about one-half of the states, inventories are not included in the property tax base. The population of these states is less than one-half the total for the nation and, therefore, the Advisory Commission on Intergovernmental Relations included all of the inventories in their calculation of the property tax base for their representative tax system. The adjustment to include only one-half of the inventories was suggested by the National Economic Division, Office of Business Economics, U.S. Department of Commerce.

[31] These industry groups were apparel and related products; furniture and fixtures; printing and publishing; fabricated metal products, including ordnance and accessories; and transportation equipment, except motor vehicles and equipment.

IRS net physical asset figures, the *accepted* census property tax estimates were divided by the IRS net physical assets. This procedure tended to compensate somewhat for the exclusive use of IRS data for those industry sectors where unincorporated manufacturing is significant and where estimates of unincorporated net physical assets are not available.

Table 12, column 1, presents the 1957 property tax rate for each of the industry groups in total manufacturing. The weighted average for all the groups was 1.79 percent. The estimates range from a high of 2.89 percent for furniture and fixtures, to a low of 1.04 percent for

TABLE 12. Estimate of Property Tax Rates for Manufacturing Industries, and Ratio of Internal Revenue Service to Bureau of the Census Partial Net Physical Assets, 1957

Industry group	Property tax rate (percent) (1)	Ratio of Internal Revenue Service to Census partial net physical assets (2)
Total manufacturing	1.79	1.30
Food and kindred products	2.00	1.00
Tobacco manufactures	1.16	1.48
Textile mill products	1.04	1.16
Apparel and other finished fabric products	1.89	0.79
Lumber and wood products (except furniture and fixtures)	2.47	1.24
Furniture and fixtures	2.89	0.83
Paper and allied products	1.51	1.09
Printing and publishing	1.91	0.97
Chemicals and allied products	1.46	1.26
Petroleum and coal products	1.70	4.00
Rubber products	2.01	1.26
Leather and leather products	1.93	1.11
Stone, clay, and glass products	1.45	1.15
Primary metal industries	1.55	1.20
Fabricated metal products (including ordnance and accessories)	2.27	0.87
Instruments	1.50	1.25
Machinery (except electrical and transportation)	2.10	1.14
Electrical machinery	1.61	1.09
Motor vehicles and equipment	2.33	1.66
Transportation equipment (except motor vehicles)	2.38	0.81
Miscellaneous manufactures	1.80	1.46

Source: Sources of data and estimation procedures are explained in the section devoted to estimating manufacturing.

textile mill products. The five industry groups in which the census property tax estimates were accepted tend to be at the higher end of the scale of values. These are industry groups that have unincorporated sectors of some importance.

The use of the 1957 property tax rate for all the other years in the 1953–59 period clearly negates the use of the annual computations as a proper measure of the relative burden of property taxes paid by manufacturing. In assuming that the property tax rate for 1957 represented the average for the entire period, we are most likely understating the 1953 to 1959 change in property tax payments made by manufacturing. The increase of 35 percent from 1953 to 1959 that appears in our estimates is only attributable to increases in the book value property tax base, not to changes in property tax rates.

A major deficiency in the estimates for manufacturing is the impossibility of isolating the property taxation of mineral property that may be included in manufacturing. There are no independent estimates of property taxes paid by various types of mineral properties.[32]

Petroleum and coal products, on the census establishment basis, paid $83 million in property taxes in 1957. The property taxes paid by petroleum and coal products in 1957, after comparing IRS and census partial net physical assets, were increased to $332 million or by a factor of 4.0. Aside from substantial mineral properties, petroleum and coal products contain other non-manufacturing properties, such as gasoline and service stations, pipelines, and oil tankers. This is the one manufacturing industry group in which the National Income Division "income originating" exceeds the "value added by manufactures" used by the Bureau of the Census. The census value

[32] The only independent estimate of property taxes paid by mineral properties is for the oil and gas industry for the years 1955, 1956, and 1959. The average annual property taxes paid for those three years was $176 million, and covered only producing properties or equipment, including building, lease or field facilities, and other property used in producing operations. It excluded property taxes paid on underdeveloped properties, office buildings, or other facilities which are used for general and administrative purposes. The average annual 1953–59 direct property taxes estimated in this paper to have been paid by crude petroleum and natural gas ($90 million) and petroleum and coal products ($295 million) were $385 million (column 1 of Table 11). *Joint Association Survey, Estimated Expenditures and Receipts of U.S. Oil and Gas Producing Industry, 1960*, Sec. 2, p. 8 (published jointly by the American Petroleum Institute, Independent Petroleum Association of America, and the Mid-Continent Oil and Gas Association, 1962). Letter dated June 11, 1963, from V. Anne Edlund, Supervisor, Petroleum Research, Economic Research Section of the Committee on Public Affairs of the American Petroleum Institute.

added concept is a broader concept of the net production of goods and services by an industry during a specified period of time.[33] In 1954 and 1958, the census value added was $2,241 million and $2,518 million, respectively. The incomes originating for 1954 and 1958 were $3,694 million and $3,673 million.

None of the other industry groups came at all close to the 4.0 ratio obtained for petroleum and coal products. Column 2 of Table 12 presents these ratios for each of the industry groups in manufacturing.

TOTAL TRADE (ITEM E)

There are no direct estimates of property taxes paid by total trade. An indirect estimate of these taxes was made by applying the property tax rate derived for manufacturing (1.79 percent) to the total net physical assets. The total of $809 million in property taxes paid ($272 million for wholesale trade and $537 million for retail trade) was obtained in this manner.

The corporate net physical assets for trade are available in the IRS, *Statistics of Income, Corporation Income Tax Returns.* Unincorporated net physical assets for trade are not available. The ratio of unincorporated to corporate depreciation published in the national income accounts was used as an approximation of the relationship between the net physical assets of the two sectors.[34]

REAL ESTATE AND HOUSEHOLD EFFECTS (ITEM F)

Real Property. The estimate of the average annual property taxes paid in 1953–59 on the real property of non-farm residential dwellings is based on (a) the estimation procedures suggested by James A.

---

[33] "Income originating ... is the sum of the factor costs incurred by an industry in production" and "excludes, in addition to cost of materials, such other costs as depreciation charges, State and local taxes (other than corporate income taxes), allowance for bad debts, and purchases of services from nonmanufacturing enterprises, such as contract costs involved in maintenance and repair, services of development and research firms, services of engineering and management consultants, advertising, telephone and telegraph expense, insurance, royalties, patent fees, etc." U.S. Bureau of the Census, *U.S. Census of Manufactures: 1958*, Vol. 2, *Industry Statistics, Part I, General Summary and Major Groups 20 to 28* (1961), p. 13.

[34] An alternative calculation of the unincorporated net physical assets of total trade was also made based on the estimation procedure and sources of data used in Table 6. This method utilized the net physical asset information of partners filing balance sheets with their income tax returns for 1959. The estimated average property taxes paid during 1953–59 by total trade using this method was $694 million or $115 million less than the amount included in column 1 of Table 11.

168   Taxation of Income from Capital, by Industry

Maxwell in Appendix C, pages 188–90, of his *Tax Credits and Intergovernmental Fiscal Relations* (Brookings Institution, 1962), and (b) the special tabulation done by the Bureau of the Census from the 1957 Census of Governments.

The Maxwell methodology[35] assumes that property taxes paid by the real property of non-farm residential dwellings can be obtained by multiplying the average state-wide general property tax rate by the total locally assessed valuation of non-farm residential dwellings subject to the general property tax. The calculation of the real property taxes paid by this type of property using the Maxwell methodology was $4,852 million in 1957 and $7,522 million in 1961.

The aim of the special tabulation done by the Bureau of the Census for 1957 was to estimate the real property taxes paid on non-farm residential dwellings with the use of county general property tax rates and assessed valuations by type of property. A sample of 516 of the nation's 3,096 counties and county areas was used. This did not seek to take account of intracounty differences in general property tax rates which are probably not inconsiderable. The real property tax revenues from non-farm residential dwellings obtained for the year from this special tabulation were $5,121 million or 5.5 percent greater than the $4,852 million obtained by using state-wide information.

The ratio of the general property taxes paid in 1957 on the real property of non-farm residential dwellings estimated in the special census tabulation to total property tax revenues for 1957 was 39.8 percent. This percentage was used to derive these general property taxes for the 1953–57 period.

For the year 1961, the estimated non-farm residential dwelling

---

[35] For each state, the total general property tax revenues were divided by the total assessed value subject to tax. This average state property tax rate was multiplied by the gross assessed value of locally assessed taxable real property in the non-farm residential category after adjustment by state for exemptions. For the year 1957, all the relevant information was available in Tables 1 and 2 of U.S. Bureau of the Census, *Census of Governments, 1957*, Vol. 5, *Taxable Property Values in the United States* (1959). In 1961, total property tax revenues were available in U.S. Bureau of the Census, *Governmental Finances in 1961* (1962), Table 14, p. 28. Special property taxes were deducted from total property tax revenues to obtain the total general property tax revenue. It was assumed that the ratio of special property tax revenues to total property tax revenues by state was the same in 1961 as in 1957. Assessed valuations of non-farm residential property were available in Table 2, U.S. Bureau of the Census, *Census of Governments: 1962, Assessed Values for Property Taxation, Preliminary Report No. 5* (1962).

general property tax revenues of $7,522 million were increased by 5.5 percent (the adjustment factor for 1957) to $7,936 million, or 44.1 percent of total property tax revenues in 1961. For the years 1958 and 1959, respectively, it was assumed that the percentage of total property tax revenues accounted for by the real property of non-farm residential dwellings was 40.8 percent and 41.8 percent.

The average 1953–59 property tax revenues on the real property of non-farm residential dwellings was $4,823 million, or 42.9 percent of the total in Table 11.

Personal Property. Dick Netzer of New York University has estimated that the personal property taxes paid on household effects in 1957 were $107 million.[36] The ratio of the 1957 personal property taxes paid by this type of property to total property tax revenues in 1957 was assumed to be applicable to the entire 1953–59 period.

The average annual amount of personal property taxes thus estimated to have been paid on household effects during 1953–59 was $99 million, or 0.9 percent of the total shown in Table 11.

Other. This estimate of property taxes paid, in column 1 of Table 11, is the residual remaining of the census total property tax revenues after (a) various property taxes have been excluded that are not covered in this study (Table 10), and (b) all property taxes paid by the other non-financial industry groups have been deducted.

As mentioned previously, the real estate industry has been redefined to include only non-farm residential dwellings. Property taxes paid by other types of property have been redistributed to other industry groups using the distribution of the rent paid on business property tax deduction available for 1959. The distribution of this residual is shown in column 2 of Table 11.

TOTAL TRANSPORTATION (ITEM G)

Railroads. The Advisory Commission on Intergovernmental Relations estimated that in 1957, railroads paid $348 million in property taxes. This amount of property taxes was 2.7 percent of the total property tax revenues for 1957. This percentage was used to calculate railroad property taxes for the 1953–57 period.

In 1961, the estimate of property taxes paid by railroads had declined to $312 million or only 1.7 percent of property tax revenues

[36] "Property Tax Revenues by Property-Use Classes, 1957," typewritten draft, April 9, 1963.

for that year. This property tax estimate, based on the 1962 Census of Governments, assumed that the general property tax revenues were approximated by multiplying the average state general property tax rate by the state-assessed valuations of railroad real property. Special property taxes on railroads were then added to the general property tax total. In 1958, it was assumed that railroads accounted for 2.4 percent of total property tax revenues; in 1959, 2.1 percent. The average property taxes estimated for railroads in the period 1953–59 were $304 million.

Local and Highway Passenger Transportation. The estimation procedure used was the same as that employed for agricultural services, forestry, and fisheries. The only difference is that the computed property tax rate for electric and gas utilities (1.80 percent) rather than that for manufacturing was applied to net physical assets. Unincorporated net physical assets were 49 percent of the corporate net physical assets for the period.

Water Transportation, Pipeline Transportation, and Services Allied to Transportation. The annual corporate net physical assets for each industry group were multiplied by the annual property tax rate computed for electric and gas utilities (1.80 percent).

Highway Freight Transportation and Warehousing. The estimation procedure is identical with the one used for agricultural services, forestry, and fisheries.

Air Transportation (Common Carriers). The information on property taxes paid by air transportation was obtained from the Civil Aeronautics Board. The data were compiled from the reports filed with the board by common carriers on Schedule P–41 of CAB Form 41. Approximately fifty certificated route air carriers are included in the reporting group.

TOTAL COMMUNICATIONS AND PUBLIC UTILITIES (ITEM H)

Telephone and Telegraph and Electric and Gas Utilities. The total property taxes paid by telephone and telegraph and electric and gas utilities for 1953–59 averaged $1,052 million. Electric and gas utilities paid property taxes of $749 million; telephone and telegraph, $303 million.

The estimate of property taxes paid by electric and gas utilities for 1953 through 1959 was obtained from the Edison Electric Institute and the American Gas Association. Similar information on the telephone and telegraph industry was available only for 1955 through 1959 from the American Telephone and Telegraph Company, United States Independent Telephone Association, and Western Union. For the years 1953 and 1954, it was therefore assumed that the average 1955–59 ratio of property tax payments to corporate net physical assets was applicable.

The ratio of the electric and gas utility property taxes paid to corporate net physical assets for 1953–59 was 1.80 percent; for telephone and telegraph, the ratio was 1.82 percent. For total manufacturing, the ratio of estimated property taxes paid to net physical assets was 1.79 percent.

TOTAL SERVICES (ITEM I)

Hotels and Other Lodging Places. The average 1953–59 property taxes paid by hotels and other lodging places of $122 million (Table 11, column 1) was derived from information obtained from the Bureau of the Census, trade journals, and accounting firms employed by the hotel industry.

The estimation procedure adopted assumed that property taxes are a specified percentage of gross receipts. For the years 1954 and 1958, the Census of Business provided benchmarks of gross receipts. An index of gross receipts was used for the period not covered by the census with the base period of 1958 = 100.

The index of gross receipts for the hotel industry and the ratio of property taxes to gross receipts were obtained from *Trends in the Hotel Business, 1961,* published by Harris, Kerr, Forster and Company. This report was based on a sample of 400 hotels. The *Tourist Court Journal* provided similar information for the motel and tourist court industry.

An alternative calculation of property taxes paid by this service industry was also made based on the stated industry experience that property taxes are normally 2.5 percent of fair value.[37] An approximation of the property taxes paid using this relationship for 1953 through 1958 is shown in Table 13.

If the fair value of hotel, motel, and tourist court property is defined as shown in column 2, in 1947–49 prices, then the results of this estimation procedure and the one based on gross receipts are

---

[37] This opinion was expressed to me in a letter dated January 29, 1963, from J. H. Nolin, a partner in Horwath and Horwath.

TABLE 13. Alternative Estimate of Property Taxes Paid by Hotel, Motel, and Tourist Court Industry, Based on Fair Value of Property, 1953–58
(Millions of dollars)

Year	Value of non-farm non-housekeeping real estate		Estimated property taxes paid at 2.5 percent rate	
	Current prices (1)	1947–49 prices (2)	Current prices (3)	1947–49 prices (4)
1953	6,250	4,929	156	123
1954	6,269	4,905	157	123
1955	6,579	4,924	164	123
1956	7,011	5,040	175	126
1957	7,375	5,183	184	130
1958	7,866	5,391	197	135
Average			172	127

Source: Raymond W. Goldsmith, *The National Wealth of the United States in the Postwar Period* (Princeton University Press for National Bureau of Economic Research, 1962), Table B–13, p. 236.

almost identical. If the fair value of property is to be defined in current prices, then the property taxes shown in column 3 of Table 13 ($172 million) are considerably greater than the $122 million computed by the use of gross receipts.

It should be noted that none of the property tax estimates previously mentioned use an industry classification coincident with the one adopted in the national income accounts, that is, hotels, rooming houses, and other lodging places, Standard Industrial Classification No. 70. This is a broader industrial definition than the one adopted for this service industry. The narrower industry definition was used because of the lack of statistical information.

Personal Services, Business Services, and Recreational Services. The annual net physical assets for each industry group were multiplied by the property tax rate computed for manufacturing.

Annual net physical assets for the corporate sector of each industry group were obtained directly from U.S. Treasury Department, *Statistics of Income, Corporation Income Tax Returns,* various issues.

For the individual unincorporated sector, the ratio of the unincorporated depreciation charge to the corporate depreciation charge (excluding non-profit institutions) was multiplied by the property tax payments computed for the corporate sector.

The distribution of the adjusted total unincorporated depreciation charge in the national income accounts was based on the distribution of depreciation deductions taken for income tax purposes in 1959 as shown in U.S. Treasury Department, *Statistics of Income— 1959–60, U.S. Business Tax Returns*, Tables 5 and 12. The total unincorporated depreciation charge was initially reduced by 23 percent to account for service industries not included in this study.

Miscellaneous Repair Services and Hand Trades. The estimation procedure and sources of data were identical with the previously explained agricultural services, forestry, and fisheries, above. Unincorporated net physical assets were 50 percent of corporate net physical assets for the period.

Cost of Distortions

The preceding parts of this study have provided the factual basis for measuring the cost to the economy of the non-neutral taxation of income from capital by using the Harberger triangle analysis. This cost is determined by the differential impact of the tax system on the use of capital in different industries, and would not exist if all returns to capital were taxed at an equal rate.

Net returns to capital in the economy, after due allowance for differential risk factors and monopoly elements, tend to be equal at the margin. Gross returns are not likely to be equal unless the tax system is neutral and strikes the return to capital equally for all industries. In those industries favored by the tax system, the rate of taxation of income from capital will be lower and the tendency will be to overinvest since the gross margins required to earn the net return will be lower. Capital will be attracted to those industries. The converse will be true for those industries that are at a disadvantage under a non-neutral tax system.

Column 6 of Table 14 shows the average ratio for the period 1953–59 of corporate profits tax liability, plus property taxes paid, to total income from capital for each industry group; the average for all industries is also shown. If each industry group had an average of 37.27 percent for the period 1953–59, the tax system could be considered neutral in its effect on capital use and the cost of the distortions would be zero. This is not the case, as is evident from the variation of the ratios shown in column 6. In those instances in which

TABLE 14. Effect on the Use of Capital of Taxes on Corporate Profits and Property, Non-Financial Industry Group, 1953–59 Average
(Money amounts in millions of dollars)

Industry group	Total income from capital			Taxes on income from capital			Taxes as percentage of income from capital[f] (6)	Calculation of 0.57²g (percent) (7)	Cost of distortion, from taxes on corporate profits and property[h] (8)
	Income from capital[a] (1)	Property taxes paid[b] (2)	Total[c] (3)	Corporate profits tax liability[d] (4)		Total[e] (5)			
Grand total	68,032	11,240	79,272	18,306		29,546	37.27	0.74	587
Total, farms, agricultural services, forestry, and fisheries	6,243	1,238	7,481	64		1,302	17.40	1.97	149
Farms	6,138	1,202	7,340	60		1,262	17.19	2.02	148
Agricultural services, forestry, and fisheries	105	36	141	4		40	28.37	0.40	1
Total mining	1,475	181	1,656	321		502	30.31	0.24	17
Metal mining	289	37	326	117		154	47.24	0.50	2
Bituminous coal mining	99	26	125	32		58	46.40	0.42	1
Crude petroleum and natural gas	876	92	968	105		197	20.35	1.43	14
Non-metallic mining and quarrying; and anthracite mining	211	26	237	67		93	39.24	0.02	j
Contract construction	1,085	110	1,195	325		435	36.40	0.04	j

	26,507	1,904	28,411	11,560	13,464	47.39	0.51	241
Total manufacturing								
Food and kindred products	2,197	191	2,388	982	1,173	49.12	0.70	17
Tobacco manufactures	477	15	492	231	246	50.00	0.81	4
Textile mill products	681	47	728	302	349	47.94	0.57	4
Apparel and other finished fabric products	398	30	428	115	145	33.88	0.06	j
Lumber and wood products (except furniture and fixtures)	662	56	718	150	206	28.69	0.37	3
Furniture and fixtures	263	29	292	113	142	48.63	0.65	2
Paper and allied products	1,162	72	1,234	543	615	49.84	0.79	10
Printing and publishing	1,026	54	1,080	398	452	41.85	0.10	1
Chemicals and products	2,880	142	3,022	1,424	1,566	51.82	1.06	32
Petroleum and coal products	2,717	311	3,028	459	770	25.43	0.70	21
Rubber products	425	34	459	207	241	52.50	1.16	5
Leather and leather products	168	12	180	73	85	47.22	0.50	1
Stone, clay, and glass products	1,103	53	1,156	495	548	47.40	0.51	6
Primary metal industries	2,565	191	2,756	1,191	1,382	50.15	0.83	23
Fabricated metal products (including ordnance and accessories)	1,249	131	1,380	574	705	51.09	0.95	13
Instruments	537	24	561	265	289	51.52	1.02	6
Machinery (except electrical and transportation)	2,406	167	2,573	1,167	1,334	51.85	1.06	27
Electrical machinery	1,702	73	1,775	823	896	50.48	0.87	15
Motor vehicles and equipment	2,598	158	2,756	1,420	1,578	57.26	2.00	55
Other transportation equipment (except motor vehicles)	860	84	944	438	522	55.30	1.63	15
Miscellaneous manufactures	431	31	462	190	221	47.84	0.56	3

Footnotes to table appear on p. 177.

TABLE 14—Continued

Industry group	Total income from capital			Taxes on income from capital			Taxes as percentage of income from capital[f] (6)	Calculation of 0.5T²g (percent) (7)	Cost of distortion, from taxes on corporate profits and property[h] (8)
	Income from capital[a] (1)	Property taxes paid[b] (2)	Total[c] (3)	Corporate profits tax liability[d] (4)	Total[e] (5)				
Total trade	9,897	1,000	10,897	2,493	3,493	32.05	0.14	15
Wholesale trade	3,891	305	4,196	1,070	1,375	32.77	0.10	4
Retail trade and automobile services	6,006	695	6,701	1,423	2,118	31.61	0.16	11
Real estate—non-farm residential dwellings	13,507	4,922	18,429	218	5,140	27.89	0.44	81
Total transportation	2,212	471	2,683	759	1,230	45.84	0.37	14
Railroads	1,207	331	1,538	389	720	46.81	0.46	7
Local and highway passenger transportation	94	15	109	40	55	50.46	0.87	1
Highway freight transportation and warehousing	402	54	456	108	162	35.53	0.02	j
Water transportation	135	26	161	72	98	60.87	2.78	4
Air transportation (common carriers)	138	8	146	52	60	41.10	0.07	j
Pipeline transportation	152	21	173	63	84	48.55	0.64	1
Services allied to transportation	84	16	100	35	51	51.00	0.94	1

176

Total communications and public utilities	5,398	1,091	6,489	2,199	3,290	50.70	0.90	60
Telephone, telegraph, and related services	1,804	308	2,112	816	1,124	53.22	1.27	27
Radio broadcasting and television	176	9	185	87	96	51.89	1.07	2
Utilities: electric and gas	3,343	751	4,094	1,270	2,021	49.36	0.73	30
Local utilities and public services, not elsewhere classified	75	23	98	26	49	50.00	0.81	1
Total services[i]	1,708	323	2,031	367	690	33.97	0.05	11
Hotels and other lodging places	293	132	425	51	183	43.06	0.17	1
Personal services	309	55	364	46	101	27.75	0.45	2
Business services not elsewhere classified	712	37	749	151	188	25.10	0.74	6
Miscellaneous repair services and hand trades	115	40	155	14	54	34.84	0.03	[j]
Motion pictures and other amusements	279	59	338	105	164	48.52	0.63	2

[a] Table 1, column 9.
[b] Table 11, column 3.
[c] Column 1 plus column 2.
[d] Table 9, column 3.
[e] Column 2 plus column 4.
[f] Column 5 divided by column 3.
[g] T^2 is the square of the difference of the ratios of taxes to income from capital for each industry group (column 6) from the grand total average for all the non-financial industry groups. This T^2 is divided by 2 to obtain the $0.5T^2$.
[h] Column 7 multiplied by column 3.
[i] Engineering and other professional services are not included in this study.
[j] Less than 0.5.

the ratio exceeds 37.27 percent, the capital invested in that industry has been kept too low by the non-neutral tax system. For those industry groups in which the ratio is below the average, the amount of invested capital is too high.

The costs of these distortions are presented in column 8 of Table 14. These costs are computed by multiplying the total income from capital, column 3, by $0.5T^2$, column 7. T^2 is the square of the difference between the ratio of taxes to income from capital for each industry and the 37.27 percent average shown in column 6 for all industry groups. This calculation assumes that the elasticity of substitution between labor and capital for any industry and the elasticity of demand for the product of an industry are unity. The costs of the distortions will vary directly with these elasticities.[38]

1953-59 Distributions

The average costs of distortion in capital use, 1953-59, averaged $587 million per year as shown in Table 14, column 8. This estimate can be considered conservative, since with a greater disaggregation of the industry groups the total variations shown in column 6 would increase and, therefore, the total costs would necessarily increase. The major absolute contributors to this $587 million cost of distortion were manufacturing ($241 million), farming ($148 million), non-farm residential dwellings ($81 million), and total communications and public utilities ($60 million). In farms and non-farm residential dwellings these are costs associated with excessive capital investment, as these industry groups are favored by the non-neutral tax system. In manufacturing and total communications and public utilities, the costs are associated with underinvestment of capital.

For each of these major contributors, the welfare cost per dollar of invested capital is measured by the calculation of $0.5T^2$ shown in column 7. If this measure were used to rank the industries, then farms would lead the list with 2.02 percent; followed by 0.93 percent for total communications and public utilities, 0.51 percent for manufacturing, and 0.44 percent for non-farm residential dwellings.

1959 Distributions

Adjusted property tax revenues increased from $9.4 billion in 1953 to $14.0 billion in 1959, the beginning and the end of the time period

[38] See Harberger, "The Corporation Income Tax," pp. 232-33 and 238 for a brief explanation of his analysis of the welfare costs of the non-neutrality of the tax system.

used in this study. It is plausible to assume that the property tax does tend to offset the distorting effect of the corporate profits tax on the corporate sector. It is logical to inquire, therefore, as to costs of distortion for the year 1959.

The estimated costs of the distortions in question amounted to $622 million for 1959, and are presented in Table 15. The difficulties and shortcomings of using the information included in this chapter on an annual basis have been previously mentioned. The 1959 estimate of the costs of distortion should be accepted only as an approximation, indicating that the orders of magnitude for that one year are not appreciably different from the average 1953–59 experience. The offsetting nature of the property tax is still a plausible assumption but its exact quantification requires more accurate information as to the industrial distribution of the property tax payments. It is rather surprising, though, that the 1959 cost is not appreciably lower than the 1953–59 cost; this suggests that even relatively large increases of property tax payments do not greatly alter the magnitude of the estimated distortion costs.

Conclusion

By 1961, adjusted property tax revenues had increased to $18.0 billion, or $3.0 billion over the 1959 figure. Corporate profits before tax and corporate profits tax liabilities in 1961 were approximately $1 billion below the 1959 level. More than likely, the cost of distortion has been decreased by this opposite movement in these taxes on the income from capital. It is unlikely, though, that any substantial portion of the estimated $587 million cost of distortion shown in Table 14 has been eliminated.[39]

The conclusions emerging from this exercise must be qualified in at least two important ways. In the first place, they are based on the assumption of unitary elasticities of substitution between the products of the various industries listed, and between labor and capital in generating the value added of any given industry. They involve inaccuracies, therefore, both because they fail to reflect differ-

---

[39] For the year 1961, an illustrative calculation of these costs of distortion came to $506 million. This estimate was based on (a) the 1959 total income from capital excluding property tax payments; (b) a proportionate increase of 20 percent in property tax payments for each non-financial industry group; and (c) a proportionate decrease of 4 percent in corporate profits tax liabilities for each non-financial industry group.

TABLE 15. Effect on the Use of Capital of Taxes on Corporate Profits and Property, Non-Financial Industry Group, 1959

(Money amounts in millions of dollars)

Industry group	Total income from capital			Taxes on income from capital		Taxes as percentage of income from capital (6)	Calculation of $0.5T^2$ (percent) (7)	Cost of distortion from taxes on corporate profits and property (8)
	Income from capital (1)	Property taxes paid (2)	Total (3)	Corporate profits tax liability (4)	Total (5)			
Grand total	76,991	14,042	91,033	20,444	34,486	37.88	0.68	622
Total, farms, agricultural services, forestry, and fisheries	6,388	1,438	7,826	63	1,501	19.18	1.75	138
Farms	6,248	1,390	7,638	60	1,450	18.98	1.79	137
Agricultural services, forestry, and fisheries	140	48	188	3	51	27.13	0.58	1
Total mining	1,095	203	1,298	239	442	34.05	0.07	26
Metal mining	97	49	146	65	114	78.08	8.08	12
Bituminous coal mining	41	25	66	24	49	74.24	6.61	4
Crude petroleum and natural gas	786	101	887	99	200	22.55	1.18	10
Non-metallic mining and quarrying; and anthracite mining	171	28	199	51	79	39.70	0.02	a
Contract construction	1,129	142	1,271	343	485	38.16	b	a

Total manufacturing	29,635	2,292	31,927	12,577	14,869	46.57	0.38	264
Food and kindred products	2,635	235	2,870	1,169	1,404	48.92	0.61	18
Tobacco manufactures	617	18	635	303	321	50.55	0.80	5
Textile mill products	899	47	946	378	425	44.93	0.25	2
Apparel and other finished fabric products	350	39	389	145	184	47.30	0.44	2
Lumber and wood products (except furniture and fixtures)	798	69	867	172	241	27.80	0.51	4
Furniture and fixtures	278	37	315	123	160	50.79	0.83	3
Paper and allied products	1,271	90	1,361	565	655	48.13	0.52	7
Printing and publishing	1,225	66	1,291	470	536	41.52	0.07	1
Chemicals and products	3,628	169	3,797	1,765	1,934	50.93	0.85	32
Petroleum and coal products	2,746	378	3,124	302	680	21.84	1.29	40
Rubber products	528	45	573	247	292	50.96	0.85	5
Leather and leather products	194	13	207	80	93	44.93	0.25	1
Stone, clay, and glass products	1,306	70	1,376	566	636	46.22	0.35	5
Primary metal industries	2,477	230	2,707	1,090	1,320	48.76	0.59	16
Fabricated metal products (including ordnance and accessories)	1,261	163	1,424	576	739	51.90	0.98	14
Instruments	732	30	762	345	375	49.21	0.64	5
Machinery (except electrical and transportation)	2,629	186	2,815	1,261	1,447	51.40	0.91	26
Electrical machinery	2,030	89	2,119	968	1,057	49.88	0.72	15
Motor vehicles and equipment	2,971	165	3,136	1,509	1,674	53.47	1.21	38
Other transportation equipment (except motor vehicles)	584	117	701	328	445	63.48	3.28	23
Miscellaneous manufactures	476	36	512	215	251	49.02	0.62	3

Footnotes to table appear on p. 183.

TABLE 15—Continued

Industry group	Total income from capital			Taxes on income from capital		Taxes as percentage of income from capital (6)	Calculation of $0.5T^2$ (percent) (7)	Cost of distortion from taxes on corporate profits and property (8)
	Income from capital (1)	Property taxes paid (2)	Total (3)	Corporate profits tax liability (4)	Total (5)			
Total trade	10,746	1,193	11,939	2,896	4,089	34.25	0.07	8
Wholesale trade	4,483	358	4,841	1,253	1,611	33.28	0.11	5
Retail trade and automobile services	6,263	835	7,098	1,643	2,478	34.91	0.04	3
Real estate—non-farm residential dwellings	16,643	6,387	23,030	259	6,646	28.86	0.41	94
Total transportation	2,321	536	2,857	741	1,277	44.70	0.23	13
Railroads	1,076	358	1,434	331	689	48.05	0.52	7
Local and highway passenger transportation	170	15	185	54	69	37.30	b	a
Highway freight transportation and warehousing	554	75	629	141	216	34.34	0.06	a
Water transportation	134	35	169	65	100	59.17	2.27	4
Air transportation (common carriers)	114	12	126	36	48	38.10	b	a
Pipeline transportation	192	23	215	82	105	48.84	0.60	1
Services allied to transportation	81	18	99	32	50	50.51	0.80	1

Total communications and public utilities	7,159	1,428	8,587	2,884	4,312	50.22	0.76	67
Telephone, telegraph, and related services	2,685	428	3,113	1,219	1,647	52.91	1.13	35
Radio broadcasting and television	249	13	262	118	131	50.00	0.73	2
Utilities: electric and gas	4,141	959	5,100	1,515	2,474	48.51	0.56	29
Local utilities and public services, not elsewhere classified	84	28	112	32	60	53.57	1.23	1
Total services included	1,875	423	2,298	442	865	37.64	b	11
Hotels and other lodging places	325	169	494	53	222	44.94	0.25	1
Personal services	318	71	389	56	127	32.65	0.14	1
Business services not elsewhere classified	837	51	888	206	257	28.94	0.40	4
Miscellaneous repair services and hand trades	130	62	192	11	73	38.02	—	—
Motion pictures and other amusements	265	70	335	116	186	55.52	1.55	5

Source: See notes to Table 14.
a Less than 0.5.
b Less than 0.005.

ences in elasticities of substitution between labor and capital in different industries and, probably more important, because the "average" elasticity of substitution may differ from unity. Robert Lucas' study in this volume suggests that the elasticity of substitution between labor and capital in the typical manufacturing industry may be closer to 0.5 than to 1.0. If this is indeed the case, and if the elasticities of substitution in final demand between the products of the industries analyzed also average around 0.5, the effect would be to cut in half the estimates made above of the costs of distortions.

In the second place, it is important to note that the estimates presented here attempt in effect to measure what would be the costs associated with the particular distortions analyzed in this chapter, on the assumption either that no other distortions exist in the economy, or that the adjustments to the welfare cost measures that would be involved in taking account of other distortions would be mutually offsetting. Obviously the first assumption does not hold, and it is highly unlikely that the second does. In particular, the distortions involved in the exemption from personal income tax of the implicit rent on owner-occupied housing operate strongly to reinforce those that have been treated here. And when two sets of distortions are mutually reinforcing, this can have a profound effect on their cost to society. In general, if either of two 10 percent distortions would, if it stood alone, entail a welfare cost of x, both of them standing together and reinforcing each other will have a welfare cost of $4x$.[40] Correspondingly, if the distortions measured in this chapter and those measured by David Laidler in his chapter in this volume would, if each stood alone, carry a welfare cost of over $500 million per year, it is likely that the two sets of distortions taken together will involve welfare costs of over $2 billion per year. There can therefore be no doubt that the pattern of taxation of income from capital in the United States carries with it a high price tag, in terms of the misallocations of resources that it induces.

[40] See Arnold C. Harberger, "Taxation, Resource Allocation, and Welfare," *The Role of Direct and Indirect Taxes in the Federal Revenue System* (Princeton University Press for National Bureau of Economic Research and Brookings Institution, 1964), pp. 33–42.

LUIGI TAMBINI

Financial Policy and the Corporation Income Tax

ECONOMIC FORCES TEND, other things being equal, to equalize the "net" rates of return to capital in alternative investments, while corporate taxes set a wedge between the rate of return required by stockholders and the cost of equity capital to corporations.

In equilibrium the relationship between the cost of equity and the required "net" rate of return depends only on the tax rate. Therefore,

(1) $$P_{ET} = \frac{p_E}{1-t},$$

where t = tax rate on corporate profits, p_E = required "net" rate of return to equity, and P_{ET} = cost of equity to corporations. The corporation income tax increases the equilibrium cost of capital to corporations, and this leads to a distortion in the allocation of resources between the corporate and the non-corporate sectors of the economy; the size of the distortion is, under certain assumptions,[1] proportional to the square of the difference between the equilibrium cost of capital in the two sectors. However, there are basically two

[1] See Arnold C. Harberger, "The Corporation Income Tax: An Empirical Appraisal," in *Tax Revision Compendium*, House Committee on Ways and Means, 86 Cong. 1 sess. (1959), Vol. 1.

alternative forms of financing corporate assets, equity and debt, and the return to debt is not subject to corporate taxes. As long as part of corporate assets are financed by debt and only part of the return to corporate capital is subject to the tax, the tax rate on total income from capital is less than the tax rate on equity income.

The Puzzle of Corporate Financial Structure

It is evident that the more corporations shift from equity to debt financing, the less will be the effective tax rate on corporate income, the lower will be the yield of the tax, and (other things equal) the lower also will be the cost of corporate capital.

The incentive to shift from equity to debt financing has been and continues to be quite substantial. The top rate of the corporation income tax was 52 percent for 1952–63, 50 percent for 1964, 48 percent for 1965–67, and 52.8 percent for 1968, and the yield of the tax has grown to more than $30 billion per year. Manufacturing corporations have paid out in taxes approximately 45 percent of their income from capital. Evidence of the change in taxes from 1927 to 1963 for all manufacturing corporations is provided by Chart 1; line 1 shows the ratio of tax payments to income from capital and line 2, the ratio of tax payments to profits. The distance between lines 1 and 2 appears to be quite small in spite of their increasing level; the interval increases markedly, however, in the 1950's. Line 3 shows the top rate of the corporation income tax; the major discrepancies between this and line 2 occur in 1936–38, because of the undistributed profits tax, and in 1942–45 and 1951–53 because of the excess profits tax. The interruption of lines 1 and 2 in 1932 is due to the fact that corporate profits and corporate income were negative for the whole manufacturing sector for that year. The pinnacles drawn by the two lines in the two adjacent years are similarly due to the fact that the large loss component of corporate profits substantially reduced total profits with respect to taxable profits; correspondingly, the "effective" tax rates, as given by lines 1 and 2, substantially exceeded the nominal tax rate, as given by line 3.

Why corporations do not try to avoid the tax entirely, or at least to avoid more of it, by shifting more to debt financing becomes quite a puzzle if we consider that debt and equity are perfect substitutes in production; corporate income is produced by corporate assets, and

CHART 1. Corporate Tax Payments in Manufacturing as Percentage of Income from Capital and as Percentage of Profits, 1927–63

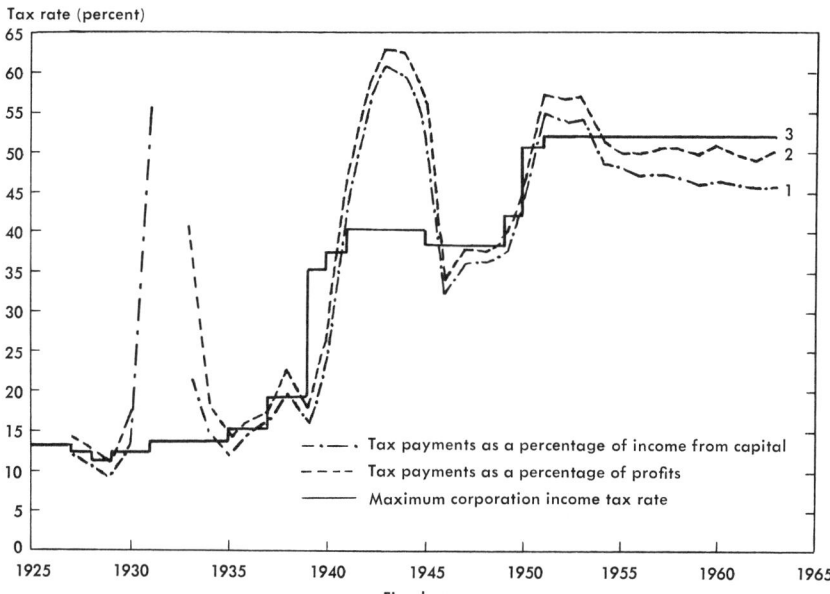

Source: U.S. Treasury Department, Internal Revenue Service, *Statistics of Income*, various issues containing income tax returns data.

the value of the marginal physical product of one dollar's worth of assets is the same, no matter how it is financed. We would accordingly expect large shifts from equity to debt capital and vice versa for small divergences in their respective costs.[2]

In fact, this does not happen. Over the entire period 1927–60, the cost of equity capital has exceeded the cost of debt capital, generally by a non-trivial amount; the difference has tended to increase over time, becoming quite substantial in the last two decades. However, corporations over the same period continued to finance the larger part of their assets through equity.

[2] Franco Modigliani and Merton H. Miller, "The Cost of Capital, Corporation Finance and the Theory of Investment," *American Economic Review*, Vol. 48 (June 1958), pp. 261–97, put forward their basic Proposition I, that the average cost of capital to corporations "in any given class" is a constant, independent of financial structure. If $V = D + E$, where V = market value of the firm, E = market value of equity, p_E = cost of equity, D = market value of debt, p_D = cost of debt, and ρ = cost of capital, then Proposition I can be stated as follows: $(Ep_E + Dp_D)/V = \rho$ = constant.

The following pages refer only to the simplest case of the Modigliani-Miller theory, that is, to that part of the theory which refers to a world without corporate taxes. Their treatment of the corporation income tax affects but does not change the basic characteristics of their theory.

CHART 2. Cost of Debt, Cost of Equity, and Rate of Return to Assets, Corporate Manufacturing, Fiscal Years 1927–63

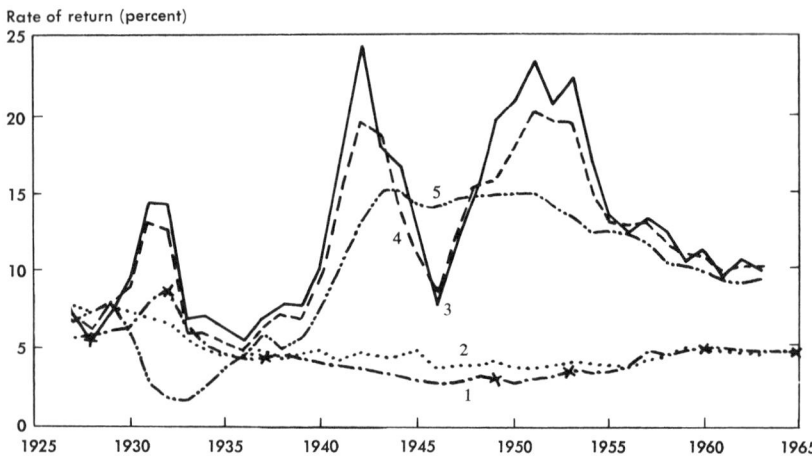

Sources: Line 1, Moody's *Industrial Manual, 1966*; line 2, U.S. Treasury Department, Internal Revenue Service, *Statistics of Income*, various issues; lines 3, 4, and 5, see text.

Key to chart: Line 1 = yield on Baa corporate industrial bonds; line 2 = interest payments as a percentage of interest-paying debt; line 3 = cost of equity—income hypothesis; line 4 = cost of equity—dividend hypothesis; line 5 = pre-tax rate of return to assets; X = yield on the bonds of a sample of industrial corporations.

Debt, Equity, and Corporate Financial Structure

Corporate financial structure may be called a puzzle because the larger part of corporate assets has been and is financed by equity, although the cost of equity substantially exceeds the cost of debt. This is obviously true for most corporations for which the cost of debt and of equity have been measured; however, to draw a valid conclusion about corporate manufacturing as a whole, some estimate of the average cost of debt and of equity for this sector is needed. A possible way of determining the average cost of debt for manufacturing corporations is to take the ratio of interest payments to interest-paying debt;[3] this measure is shown by Chart 2, line 2. A source of bias for this measure, however, can come from the fact that the average amount of debt in a given year may differ from the amount recorded at the end of the year; it is not possible to correct for this kind of bias. Furthermore, even if the bias could be neglected, this measure would at best give the average "actual" cost of debt

[3] U.S. Treasury Department, Internal Revenue Service, *Statistics of Income*, various issues containing corporation income tax returns data (to 1953, Part 2; beginning with 1954, *Corporation Income Tax Returns*).

for corporate manufacturing, but not a measure of the average cost of new debt. In fact, since long-term debt represents a large share of interest-paying debt, one would expect that this measure exceeds the cost of new debt in periods of falling interest rates, and vice versa in periods of rising interest rates. Finally, this measure—given by the ratio of two book values—cannot be compared directly with the cost of equity, which is a market value.

A more useful measure of the cost of debt, for purposes of comparison with the cost of equity, is the yield on long-term industrial bonds. However, nine yields are available,[4] varying according to the bond-grade, and the problem is to determine which can be considered as the "average" cost of debt for the whole sector. To overcome this problem, this study used the data of seven cross-section samples of industrial corporations available for the years 1927, 1932, 1937, 1949, 1953, 1960, and 1965.[5] From each sample the weighted average of bond yields was computed (the weights being the book value of total interest paying debt) for each corporation; the results are shown by the crosses in Chart 2. It is evident that the seven crosses are closely interpolated by line 1, which represents the yield on Baa[6] corporate industrial bonds. The closeness of line 1 to the seven crosses, over a long period of time and under very different economic conditions, suggests that line 1 might be a good estimate of the bond yield as measured by the cross-section samples. There are strong reasons for believing that for every sector or class of corporations the cost of debt depends on financial structure. If, therefore, the financial structure of the corporations composing the sample does not differ substantially from that of the corresponding aggregate, it appears that neither will the cost of debt differ too much, and therefore that the samples are reasonably representative of the aggregate. For example, the ratio of interest paying debt to net worth for the 1960 sample is 0.269, while for the aggregate of manufacturing corporations it is 0.258. We believe, therefore, that the yield on Baa industrial bonds, shown in Chart 2, line 1, can be considered a good estimate of the average cost of new debt to manufacturing corporations.

The cost of equity has been previously defined in terms of the tax

---

[4] See Moody's *Industrial Manual*, various issues.

[5] The data for the first five samples were obtained from Lawrence Fisher, "Risk Premiums on Corporate Bonds" (Ph.D. thesis, University of Chicago, 1956). I collected the 1960 and the 1965 samples.

[6] Moody's *Industrial Manual, 1966*.

rate and of the required rate of return to equity. For any given tax rate, therefore, if the rate of return can be defined and measured, the cost of equity can also be measured. Theoretically, the rate of return to equity can be viewed as the rate at which the expected future income stream is discounted. Given the nature of the return to equity, there are good reasons to believe that actual earnings might be a bad measure of expected earnings, and that the earnings-to-price ratio might be a bad measure of the return to equity. These reasons are (1) the cyclical variability of earnings and (to a lesser extent) of dividends, and (2) earnings retention, which introduces a systematic bias in the difference between actual and expected earnings and between actual and expected dividends. Furthermore, there is the theoretical problem of whether stockholders' expectations refer to earnings or to dividends.

To solve the first problem, exponentially weighted averages were taken. To overcome the second problem, two measures of the cost of equity were constructed, corresponding to an income and to a dividend expectation,[7] or, to an income and to a dividend hypothesis.[8] These two measures can be expressed more precisely by defining

Y = return to equity
Z = dividend payment
b = retention rate
λ_T = rate of return on investment, before taxes
E = market value of equity

and by deriving

$$p_{ET1} = \frac{Y}{E}/(1 - t)$$

$$p_{ET2} = \left[\frac{Z}{E}/(1 - t)\right] + b\lambda_T$$

[7] For a theoretical discussion of this problem, see Merton Miller and Franco Modigliani, "Dividend Policy, Growth, and the Valuation of Shares," *The Journal of Business* (October 1961). Also see Marshall Kolin, "The Relative Price of Corporate Equity" (Ph.D. thesis, University of Chicago, 1963). For the dividend hypothesis see Myron J. Gordon, *The Investment, Financing, and Valuation of the Corporation* (Richard D. Irwin, 1962).

[8] One of the two measures is not considered as "true" and the other as "false"; for the purpose of this study, they are considered as complementary in the sense of setting limits within which the cost of equity can be expected to lie.

In Chart 2, lines 3 and 4 show the two estimates of the cost of equity corresponding, respectively, to p_{ET1} and p_{ET2}; line 5 shows λ_T, the pre-tax rate of return to assets, for corporate manufacturing.[9] The two estimates of the cost of equity, p_{ET1} and p_{ET2}, fluctuate substantially over the period, because of events such as the Great Depression, the 1937–38 recession, World War II, and the uncertainties and adverse expectations of investors in the postwar period, coupled with an exceptional surge of demand and corporate profits. Other changes, such as the heavy and temporary excess profits taxation of wartime and its immediate repeal in 1946 (Chart 1), contributed to the wartime peak in the cost of equity and to the dip of 1946. The maximum discrepancy between the cost of debt and of equity, as given by Chart 2, is over the periods 1942–44 and 1948–53, when the cost of equity exceeds that of debt by at least a factor of six. In the period following 1953, the discrepancy is narrowed by the concomitant sharp fall in the cost of equity and rise in the cost of debt. However, in the 1960's they still were in a ratio of approximately two to one.

Altogether, the puzzle outlined in the previous section is strongly confirmed by Chart 2. Even if the measurements lacked some accuracy, the difference between the cost of equity and the cost of debt—particularly in the post-1940 period—is too large to permit doubt of its existence. Furthermore, comparison of Chart 1 with Chart 2 shows that a large part of the changes and certainly of the trend in the cost of equity is due to corporate taxation. The rate of return to corporate assets, line 5, also substantially exceeds the cost of debt in the post-1940 period.[10]

It might be interesting to see how financial structure changed over the same period. For corporate manufacturing, this is shown in Chart 3, where lines 1, 2, and 3 give the ratio of different definitions of "indebtedness" to net worth. For line 1, the numerator of the ratio is long-term debt; for line 2, it is interest-paying debt; and the

---

[9] In constructing these measures, the effective tax rate was used, i.e., the ratio of tax payments to corporate profits, except for the period 1930–34, for which the top rate of the corporation income tax was used. Exponentially weighted averages were taken for Y, Z, b, λ_T. For a more precise description of the construction of these variables, see Appendix A.

[10] This, of course, is not true for the prewar years, which were dominated by the two depressions; but this is hardly a surprising exception.

CHART 3. Financial Structure, Corporate Manufacturing, 1927–63

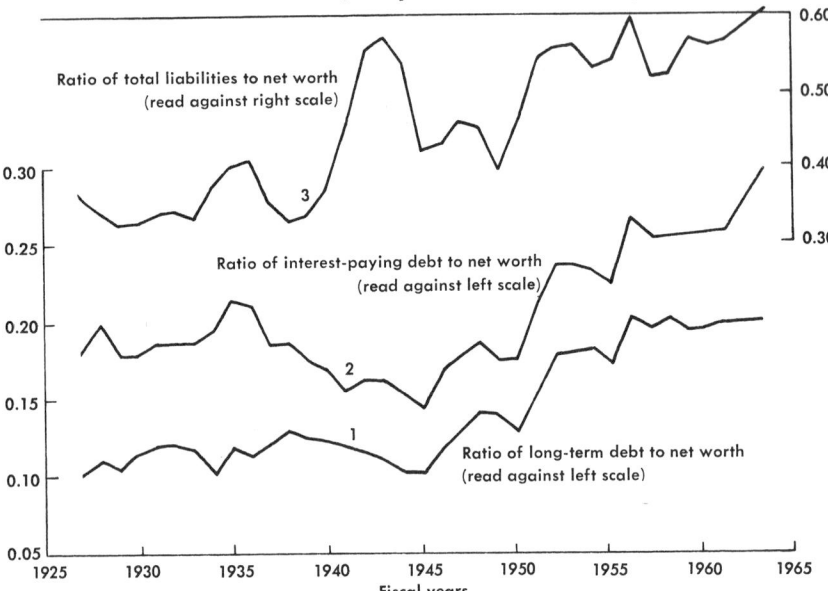

Source: U.S. Treasury Department, Internal Revenue Service, *Statistics of Income*, various issues.

numerator of line 3 is total liabilities, that is, total assets minus net worth.[11] Lines 1 and 2 move asymmetrically during the pre-1940 period, probably because of the adjustments and the considerations prompted by the two depressions, but in the last two decades they are closely correlated. Line 3 (on a different scale in Chart 3) shows behavior opposite to that of lines 1 and 2 in certain periods. This is evident, for example, during World War II, when there was a sharp increase in tax liabilities, from $629 million in 1939 to a peak of $10.4 billion in 1943; this explains the surge in line 3 and (in part at least) the dip in lines 1 and 2, as tax money can in a sense be considered as an interest-free substitute to borrowed money.[12] Over the more normal period of the 1950's the three lines move pretty much together, while in the 1960's line 2 rises much more sharply than line 1. However, according to the more traditional definitions of financial

[11] U.S. Treasury Department, Internal Revenue Service, *Statistics of Income*, various issues containing corporation income tax returns data.

[12] In fact, if one assumes that profits accrue uniformly over time, while taxes are paid at the end of the year, a change in tax liability over the previous year would change liquidity by one-half of the difference in the tax liability between the two years.

structure, as given by lines 1 and 2, the change over the period 1927–63 has not been very large; between 1927 and 1963, line 1 moves from 0.100 to 0.200, a change of 0.100, and line 2 moves from 0.178 to 0.299, a change of 0.121. However, the period 1927–45 was dominated by two major depressions and a world war, and it is difficult to observe a simple relationship between financial structure and the costs of debt and of equity. For this purpose, it is perhaps more meaningful to consider the period following World War II, during which the economic situation has been more reasonably normal, while the cost of equity has substantially exceeded the cost of debt. Between 1945 and 1963, line 1 moves from 0.099 to 0.200, a change of 0.101, and line 2 from 0.142 to 0.299, a change of 0.157. The percentage change, however, is large: 102 percent for line 1 and 110 percent for line 2, corresponding to average annual compound rates of changes of 4.0 and 4.2 percent, respectively.

Evidently, the period 1945–60 is not homogeneous, and one could consider the late 1940's as a period of readjustment for the economy. From the point of view of financial structure, such a distinction could be justified also on the basis of the change in the effective tax rate on corporate profits (see Chart 1) which fell substantially from 1945 to 1950, thus creating a substantial change in the amount of tax money available to corporations, both in absolute terms and as a percentage of interest-paying debt. However, even if one considers only the period 1950–63, during which the effective tax rate on corporate profits did not change much, the average annual percentage change remains quite high, namely, 3.8 percent for line 1 and 5.9 percent for line 2. Furthermore, the highest percentage change per year is in 1950–53 (6.9 percent for line 1 and 8.1 percent for line 2) when the difference between the cost of equity and of debt is at a maximum; the percentage change in financial structure falls in the following years and it seems to taper off at the end of the 1950's. In the early 1960's, line 1 runs slowly, but line 2 resumes a rapid climb. A not implausible hypothesis of this contrasting behavior—a sharp rise in short-term indebtedness but a stable, long-term leverage ratio —might be that manufacturing corporations are close to their optimal financial structure and uncertain as to changes in that structure; thus they may rely on short-term borrowing in order to facilitate a more rapid readjustment of financial structure, should one be required.

194   Financial Policy and the Corporation Income Tax

This hypothesis, however, does not deny the possibility that other forces might affect short-term borrowing by corporations.

Plan of the Work

This brief survey has shown that in the late 1950's and early 1960's, the cost of equity was still approximately twice as high as the cost of debt. The financial structure for corporate manufacturing, though changing through time, has not exhibited a dramatic response to the great rise in tax rates since the 1930's. Total interest-paying debt today is only about 30 percent of net worth. The remainder of this chapter will show that the "puzzle" can be explained within the analytical framework of the neoclassical theory of the firm, in which the conditions for the financial equilibrium of the corporation require the equality not of the average costs, whose movement was analyzed above, but of the marginal costs of debt (MC_D), of equity (MC_E), and of the marginal rate of return to investment.[13] Marginal costs differ from average costs, and are a function of financial structure. Changes in financial structure affect both lender's and borrower's risk,[14] and these changes in turn affect the difference between marginal and average cost.[15]

Some regression results obtained by Lawrence Fisher and Marshall Kolin, who made serious attempts to represent statistically the concepts of lender's and of borrower's risk, will be presented. From these regression equations the change in lender's and borrower's risk will be estimated and then added to average costs to give estimates of the corresponding marginal costs for seven benchmark years. This would suffice in a world without capital gains provisions,

---

[13] Modigliani and Miller ("The Cost of Capital") with their Proposition I, dismiss the problem of corporate financial structure and of the marginal conditions of financial equilibrium.

[14] That is, the riskiness of debt and of equity.

[15] Modigliani and Miller consider explicitly the problem of "lender's" risk in explaining their Proposition II, which gives the cost of equity as a function of financial structure, and of the difference between the cost of capital and the cost of debt. Proposition II is stated as $p_E = \rho + (D/E)(\rho - p_D)$, where the terms have been previously defined. They also explicitly and repeatedly consider the existence of a borrower's risk and its effect on the cost of equity, given the constraint set on p_D and p_E by Proposition I, i.e., a constant average and marginal cost of capital (see Modigliani and Miller, "The Cost of Capital," pp. 274–76).

but since capital gains provisions do exist and affect the cost of equity capital, they are therefore taken explicitly into account and the previous results correspondingly adjusted.

The estimates will show a substantial disequilibrium in the financial structure of corporate manufacturing for the year 1949, while for the year 1965 they show approximate financial equilibrium. Accordingly, this study will investigate the nature of the path by which equilibrium was approached.

Theory of the Firm, Cost Functions, and Risk Premiums

The basic assumption of the theory is that firms aim to maximize a net residual, after having paid all factors of production. This is equivalent to saying that, for given or expected receipts, they attempt to minimize actual or expected costs; correspondingly, it implies that, for given or expected costs, firms tend to maximize receipts. At the margin, residual maximization implies the familiar equality between marginal cost and marginal receipt or revenue. Assets are certainly a factor of production, and we know that (basically) they are financed by equity and by debt. Similarly, we know that the total return to capital net of taxes is allocated between debt-holders and stockholders.

In this area, for given receipts, residual maximization implies that firms attempt to minimize the actual or expected cost of capital; alternatively, for a given cost of capital, they attempt to maximize the expected total return to assets.[16] At the margin, residual maximization implies the equality between the marginal rate of return to assets, λ_T, and the marginal cost of capital. The fact that capital has two components, debt and equity, does not change the problem; it simply implies, as a subsidiary equilibrium condition, that the cost of debt and the cost of equity should equal at the margin the cost of capital, and should therefore be equal. Transitivity implies that, at the margin, the cost of debt and the cost of equity must equal the

---

[16] In the Modigliani and Miller theory, only the second possibility is open to firms, given that the cost of capital is constant. This they put forward in their Proposition III, stating that firms should undertake only those investment projects which yield an expected rate of return greater than ρ, the cost of capital to the firm.

marginal rate of return to assets. In symbols, the condition for the financial equilibrium of corporations is

$$MC_D = \lambda_T = MC_E.$$

The equilibrium condition just derived is in the familiar flow terms, but it can be shown that the maximization of the residual is equivalent to the maximization of the value of the equity of existing shareholders.

The main problems are whether, why, and by how much the marginal cost of debt and equity differ from their average costs. These are different stages of the same question. The basic point is that a change in financial structure affects the riskiness of corporate capital, that is, of debt and of equity, and so it affects their required rates of return and their cost to corporations. In particular, an increase in debt financing, or leverage, increases the riskiness of the firm (and vice versa for a decrease in leverage), and therefore the risk for debt-holders (lender's risk) and the risk for stockholders (borrower's risk). The main reason for the change in lender's and borrower's risk is that, given the probability distribution of expected income from capital, the payment of fixed charges, like interest, leaves the dispersion of the distribution of corporate profits unaffected, but with a smaller mean. The ratio of the standard deviation to the mean of profits—the coefficient of variation—provides us with one measure of risk. On the assumption that stockholders have an aversion to risk and prefer a more certain to a less certain income stream, an increase in debt, by increasing the coefficient of variation of earnings of equity-holders, would cause an increase in borrower's risk.[17] Simi-

---

[17] Here we have a fundamental difference with Modigliani and Miller ("The Cost of Capital," p. 266) who explicitly postulate a net separation between variability and uncertainty of earnings: ". . . uncertainty attaches to the mean value over time of the stream of profits and should not be confused with variability over time of the successive elements of the stream," and again, ". . . the effect of variability per se on the valuation of the stream is at best a second-order one which can safely be neglected for our purposes (and indeed most others too)." If earnings variability can be neglected, so can "financial risk" and therefore financial structure. This is the logic behind Modigliani and Miller's Proposition I; the concept of uncertainty of earnings which refers to non-financial or business risk becomes incorporated in the concept of (risk) "classes of corporations," which is a rather vague and operationally unwieldy concept. However, my major disagreement with Modigliani and Miller refers to the separation between variability and uncertainty of earnings. Each represents a relevant aspect of risk facing the firm and weighing on the investor, and they are interrelated in a multiplicative fashion. What is important for the firm and for the investor at any given moment in time is total risk,

larly, an increase in the coefficient of variation of earnings increases the probability of negative profits, of a suspension in interest payments, and therefore of lender's risk. Of more weight still is the fact that the increase in the coefficient of variation increases the probability of gambler's ruin, i.e., of bankruptcy, on the assumption that bankruptcy is a function of the total "loss" accumulated over one or more years.[18]

A second (possibly alternative) measure of risk for debt-holders and stockholders is the ratio of debt to the market value of equity, D/E. The meaning of the ratio is intuitive for debt-holders, as the market value of equity can be viewed as an estimate of what is left after having paid all other claimants; it is therefore a cushion or a measure of security. Since equity is the present value of expected profits, an increase in the D/E ratio increases the probability of bankruptcy, and hence borrower's risk.

How these factors affect lender's and borrower's risk is statistically analyzed by Fisher and Kolin. However, before turning to these in the next section, it is important to define more precisely the concepts of marginal cost of debt and of equity as a function of average cost and of the change in borrower's and in lender's risk. Accordingly,

MC_D = change in total cost of capital per unit change in the amount of debt

MC_E = change in total cost of capital per unit change in the amount of equity

---

and financial risk can be a large or determining part of the total. Variability of earnings would be perfectly irrelevant only if the time distribution of earnings were known with certainty. Regulated public utilities constitute the only sector of the economy which (although to a limited extent) might fulfill this otherwise utopian assumption. This difference in assumptions goes beyond the formal difference between Modigliani and Miller's "intra-class" theory and the "interclass" theory of this study. To consider hypothetically a corporation shifting from one "class" to another, within each class the Modigliani-Miller theory asserts that firms will have no preferences regarding the debt-equity ratio. It seems a not unfair extension of this assertion to say that there should therefore be no tendency for firms in different classes to have different debt-equity ratios. Yet in fact, there are notable differences in debt-equity ratios among, for example, two-digit industries, and these differences tend to persist over long periods of time. They require an explanation which the Modigliani-Miller theory does not provide.

[18] Modigliani and Miller (*ibid.*, p. 274, note 18) consider these possibilities, but, as of little or no practical consequence.

Let us further define the average costs of debt and of equity as a function of financial structure:

average cost of debt = $p_D = f(D, E)$
average cost of equity = $p_{ET} = g(D, E)$
total cost of debt = Dp_D
total cost of equity = Ep_{ET}

By definition,

$$MC_D = \frac{d}{dD}(Dp_D + Ep_{ET}) = p_D + D\frac{dp_D}{dD} + E\frac{dp_{ET}}{dD}$$

$D\dfrac{dp_D}{dD}$ = premium required for change in lender's risk

$E\dfrac{dp_{ET}}{dD}$ = premium required for change in borrower's risk

Symmetrically the marginal cost of equity can be derived as

$$MC_E = \frac{d}{dE}(Dp_D + Ep_{ET}) = p_{ET} + E\frac{dp_{ET}}{dE} + D\frac{dp_D}{dE},$$

where $D\dfrac{dp_D}{dE}$ = premium required for change in lender's risk

$E\dfrac{dp_{ET}}{dE}$ = premium required for change in borrower's risk

The marginal condition for the financial equilibrium of the corporation can now be rewritten as

$$p_D + D\frac{dp_D}{dD} + E\frac{dp_{ET}}{dD} = MC_D = \lambda_T$$
$$= MC_E = E\frac{dp_{ET}}{dE} + D\frac{dp_D}{dE} + p_{ET}.$$

Since debt expansion generates positive risk premiums, we expect $D\dfrac{dp_D}{dD}$ and $E\dfrac{dp_{ET}}{dD}$ to be positive and MC_D to be greater than p_D. Since equity expansion reduces investors' riskiness, and generates negative risk premiums, we expect $E\dfrac{dp_{ET}}{dE}$ and $D\dfrac{dp_D}{dE}$ to be negative and $MC_E < p_{ET}$.[19]

---

[19] Since equity is inherently riskier than debt, we expect $p_{ET} > p_D$ even (and especially) in the case of high lender's risk. The above inequality follows directly from the equality of MC_D and MC_E required for the financial equilibrium of the firm. Also here, Modigliani and Miller's theory and assumptions differ from those of this study. In fact, when they introduce the assumption that the cost of debt rises with leverage, they

Before turning to the empirical evidence, we will present some of the elements of the work of Fisher and of Kolin.

The Work of Fisher and Kolin

Lawrence Fisher advances the hypothesis that the risk premium[20] on corporate bonds depends on their riskiness and marketability. The hypothesis is tested by the use of multivariate regression analysis on cross-section samples of industrial corporations. The basic regression equation of interest here is of the form

$$\log X_0 = a_1 \log \frac{\Delta y}{y} + a_2 \log X_2 + a_3 \log \frac{E}{D} + a_4 \log D_M,$$

where X_0 = risk premium on corporate bonds

$\frac{\Delta y}{y}$ = earnings variability, expressed as the coefficient of variation of after-tax equity earnings

X_2 = period of solvency

$\frac{E}{D}$ = equity/debt ratio, with equity at market value and debt (all interest-paying debt) at book value

D_M = marketability, defined as market value of bonds outstanding

The dependent variable, X_0, is a measure of lender's risk, or a premium which corporations have to pay above the rate on riskless debt, because of their own riskiness.

By construction, X_0 differs from the cost of corporate debt, p_D, by a constant, r, the rate of interest on riskless debt; in symbols,

$$p_D = r + X_0.$$

Marshall Kolin advances the hypothesis that the market value of equity is a function of expected income and of the riskiness of the

---

draw the conclusion—under the constraint of a constant overall cost of capital—that the cost of equity must be a decreasing function of the debt/equity ratio over any range in which the cost of debt is an increasing function of that ratio and exceeds the cost of capital to the firm.

[20] Defined as the difference between the yields on bonds of a given corporation and the yield on government bonds of corresponding maturity. See Lawrence Fisher, "Determinants of Risk Premiums on Corporate Bonds," *Journal of Political Economy*, Vol. 67 (June 1959), p. 228.

200   Financial Policy and the Corporation Income Tax

firm.[21] Here, also, the hypothesis is tested by the use of multivariate regression analysis on cross-section samples of industrial corporations.

The basic regression equation of interest here is

$$\log E = C_1 \log y + C_2 G + C_3 \log \Delta_D + C_4 \log \frac{D}{E} + C_5 \log \frac{\Delta y}{y},$$

where E = market value of equity

G = a growth variable expressed as the coefficient of the regression of the value of equity over time

Δ_D = earnings variability in the Great Depression

The two risk variables $\frac{\Delta y}{y}$ and $\frac{D}{E}$ are defined as in Fisher's equation.

However, while Fisher's equation is expressed in flow terms, Kolin's is a stock equation; this leads to the problem of moving from the stock equation to a flow equation, that is, a cost function for equity. Given Kolin's definition of y, there is a unique relationship between E and the discount rate or required rate of return, p_E.

In symbols, $E = y/p_E$, that is, given y, p_E and E can be derived one from the other. Here we will derive p_E by taking the logarithm of the above identity, which yields

$$\log E = \log y - \log p_E.$$

Upon substitution in Kolin's stock equation, we have

$$\log E = \log y - \log p_E$$
$$= C_1 \log y + C_2 G + C_3 \log \Delta_D + C_4 \log \frac{D}{E} + C_5 \log \frac{\Delta y}{y}.$$

This transformation of Kolin's equation in flow form is legitimate only if E and p_E are the same function and differ only by a constant; if the variables are correctly defined, this is so, and it implies a coefficient of unity for the income variable in the stock equation, that is, $C_1 = 1$.[22]

On this basis the income variables in the previous expression can be canceled out; the expression then becomes

$$\log p_E = -C_2 G - C_3 \log \Delta_D - C_4 \log \frac{D}{E} - C_5 \log \frac{\Delta y}{y}.$$

[21] Kolin, "Relative Price of Corporate Equity," p. 5.
[22] This result is very closely approximated in Kolin's regression equations, on a "per firm" basis. *Ibid.*, p. 19, Table IV (3).

This equation corresponds to the g function of the previous section. Fisher's equation does not exactly correspond to the f function explaining average cost of debt, but since p_D and X_0 differ only by a constant r, their derivatives are identical; for example, in the case of debt expansion,

$$\frac{dp_D}{dD} = \frac{d(r + X_0)}{dD} = \frac{dX_0}{dD},$$

since the derivative of the constant r is zero.

Now it is a matter of simple differentiation to derive from Fisher's and Kolin's equations the estimated change in lender's risk and in borrower's risk that would stem from expansion of debt or of equity.[23]

Some Empirical Results

The theory will now be tested by deriving some quantitative estimates of MC_D and of MC_E for seven benchmark years, corresponding to the years for which there are regression estimates for the cost function of debt. These regressions span a long period, and the estimates of the regression coefficients are highly stable over time and statistically significant. In using these coefficient estimates, based on large samples of the corporate sector, we assume them to apply to the sector as a whole. Kolin presents seven cross-sectional regression equations for the years 1951–57. The arithmetic average of the coefficients estimated for each variable in these regressions was taken to be an estimate of its "true" coefficient, and was applied to the seven benchmark years. For a measure of λ_T, the marginal rate of return to assets, an exponentially weighted average of the rate of return to assets for corporate manufacturing was used.[24] This rate is presented as a reference point for our estimate of MC_D and MC_E; the relevant value would be the expected marginal rate of return to assets, which is not available.

As alternative measures of the cost of equity, both p_{ET1} and p_{ET2} were used (see Chart 2, lines 3 and 4). In Tables 1, 3, and 4 below, p_{ET1} is the upper figure and p_{ET2} the lower, in any given year. As a measure for the average cost of debt, the yield on Baa corporate industrial bonds was used (see Chart 2, line 1); as a measure of financial

---

[23] See Appendix B for the effect of a change in leverage on the coefficient of variation.
[24] See Chart 2, line 5, and Appendix A.

structure, the ratio of interest-paying debt to the market value of equity for corporate manufacturing during the given year was used.[25]

In brief, the estimates of Fisher and Kolin are taken as valid for the whole of corporate manufacturing. To derive estimates of lender's and of borrower's risk from their regression equations, measures of the cost of debt and of equity—which we considered as representative or average for the whole of corporate manufacturing—have been used.

The resulting estimates are shown in Table 1. These results show that, for every observation, the difference between p_{ET} and p_D (or their ratio) is substantially greater than the difference between MC_E and MC_D (or their ratio). Our condition for financial equilibrium implies equality between MC_E and MC_D; our observations tend to show that corporate manufacturing was reasonably close to financial equilibrium in the three prewar benchmark years, while a substantial amount of disequilibrium exists during the postwar period.

In 1927, while p_{ET1} and p_{ET2} are respectively 25 percent and 24 percent higher than p_D, MC_{E1} and MC_{E2} are, respectively, 10 percent and 11 percent lower than MC_{D1} and MC_{D2};[26] the disequilibrium has reversed itself. In 1932, while both p_{ET1} and p_{ET2} exceed p_D, there is almost perfect equality between MC_{E2} and MC_{D2} and only a small percentage difference between p_{ET1} and p_{ET2}; this is because dividend payments lagged behind profits during the 1934–37 recovery. Although both p_{ET1} and p_{ET2} exceed p_D, respectively, by 63 percent and by 47 percent for 1932, at the margin MC_{E1} only slightly exceeds MC_{D1}, while MC_{E2} is very close to MC_{D2}.

For the three prewar years' observations, our estimates for MC_E and MC_D do not show perfect financial equilibrium, but a reasonably close approximation to it. For those years, then, the "puzzle" of financial structure disappears as a result of shifting the comparison from average to marginal costs. The same thing, however, cannot be said for the four postwar years; here, although the difference between the marginal costs of debt and of equity is much smaller than the difference in average costs, and although the marginal cost disequilibrium is substantially reduced through time, it is still too large, even in 1965, to be considered an equilibrium situation.

In 1949, p_{ET1} and p_{ET2} exceed p_D by factors of 6.4 and of 5.5,

[25] See Appendix A.
[26] MC_{E1} and MC_{D1} correspond to p_{ET1}, as MC_{E2} and MC_{D2} correspond to p_{ET2}.

TABLE 1. Measures of Average and Marginal Cost of Debt and of Equity Financing by Stock Issues, Corporate Manufacturing, Benchmark Years, 1927–65

Year and investment hypothesis	Average cost of equity p_{ET}	Marginal cost of equity MC_E	Marginal rate of return on investment λ_T	Marginal cost of debt MC_D	Average cost of debt p_D
1927					
Income	7.01	6.71	6.80	7.49	5.61
Dividend	6.95	6.65		7.48	
1932					
Income	14.28	13.28	1.58	11.90	8.76
Dividend	12.84	11.79		11.74	
1937					
Income	7.04	6.80	5.88	6.22	4.25
Dividend	6.41	6.19		6.06	
1949					
Income	19.28	18.65	13.72	6.54	3.02
Dividend	16.65	16.10		6.07	
1953					
Income	22.75	21.98	13.53	7.17	3.55
Dividend	19.27	18.61		6.63	
1960					
Income	11.32	10.94	10.00	7.53	5.11
Dividend	10.90	10.53		7.44	
1965					
Income	8.97	8.66	a	6.78	4.92
Dividend	a	a			

Source: See Appendix A.
a Data for 1965 were not available when this series was constructed.

respectively; the corresponding factors relating MC_{E1} and MC_{E2} to MC_D are much smaller, being 2.9 and 2.7, respectively. Similar comments apply to 1953. In 1960, both p_{ET1} and p_{ET2} are more than twice as high as p_D, while at the margin the cost of equity exceeds the cost of debt by 45 percent; in 1965 MC_{E1} exceeds MC_{D1} by about 28 percent. The conclusion which we can draw for these postwar years is that some of the puzzle remains to be explained, even for 1965.

To get some better understanding of corporate financial structure and policy, we must take into account capital gains provisions. These provisions tend to offset the effect of corporate taxes on the cost of equity when part of the earnings are retained, since the increased value of equity due to retention is taxed (1) at a rate lower than that on ordinary income, such as dividends and interest payments, and (2) only on realization,[27] so that the tax payment can be postponed and therefore the "effective" tax rate is reduced below its nominal value. Our estimates of MC_E in Table 1 must therefore be interpreted, for the postwar years, as the marginal cost of equity financing through stock issues.

The effect of capital gains provisions on the marginal cost of equity depends on the relative importance of the marginal tax rate on dividends with respect to the effective marginal tax rate on capital gains. The effect of these provisions on the cost of equity is probably of little importance before the 1930's[28] for several reasons;[29] the principal reasons are the offsetting provisions for dividend taxation, the low rates of the personal income tax, and the provision that the tax rate on the capital gain be related to the holding period.

How capital gains provisions affect the cost of equity financing by earnings retention, and therefore corporate financial policy, can be seen best in our framework of residual maximization or in the equivalent one of maximization of the value of equity. Let us, accordingly, assume that a stockholder has to decide whether the corporation should pay out an extra dollar in dividends or whether it should

[27] See Martin J. Bailey, "Capital Gains and Income Taxation," this volume, pp. 15–26, for a discussion of the effective tax rate on capital gains.

[28] In 1932, the provisions for dividend taxation, partly offsetting the corporation income tax, were abolished. Quantitatively more important changes took place in the early 1940's—the additional rises in the personal income tax rates, the reduction of the holding period to six months, and the 25 percent ceiling for the capital gains tax rate.

[29] Daniel M. Holland, *The Income-Tax Burden on Stockholders* (Princeton University Press for the National Bureau of Economic Research, 1958).

retain it. Let us also assume that he wants to maximize his wealth and that he knows that if a dollar is retained, the value of his share will increase by an amount equal to the present value of the expected income stream generated by the dollar retained, and discounted back at the correct rate, the cost of that share of equity.

Let us now define two marginal tax rates:

t_p = marginal tax rate on dividends

t_g = marginal tax rate on capital gains

If the stockholder opts for the dividend, instead of one dollar, he will receive $1 - t_p$; if he opts for retention he will receive, when he sells, $1 - t_g$ times the increase in value of the share. He will be indifferent between retention and dividend if, net after taxes, he receives the same amount in either case.

His break-even point is therefore given by

(2) $$(1 - t_g)\alpha = 1 - t_p$$

where α is the expected increase in the value of the share. How much the share will increase in value depends on the expected rate of return on the dollar invested, λ, and the discount rate, p_E.[30] For an expected infinite income stream, we have: $\alpha = \lambda/p_E$, and, substituting for α, we have

(3) $$\frac{1 - t_g}{1 - t_p} p_E = \lambda.$$

To determine t_p, a weighted average of the marginal tax rate on dividends was computed for each of four years;[31] the weights are the amounts of dividends received by each income group and the rates are those marginal to the given income group.[32] Similarly, for t_g the year's weighted average of the relevant marginal tax rate was computed using, as for t_p, dividends as weights; within our framework it corresponds to the assumption that the stockholder plans to sell his equity and to cash his income or gain within a year. This assumption gives

---

[30] The corporation income tax does not affect (2), as the tax is applied on the whole of corporate profits, independently of whether they will be retained or distributed.

[31] From U S. Treasury Department, Internal Revenue Service, *Statistics of Income for 1949*, Part 1 (1954); *Statistics of Income for 1953*, Part 1 (1957); *Statistics of Income—1960, Preliminary, Individual Income Tax Returns* (1962); *Statistics of Income—1965, Preliminary, Individual Income Tax Returns* (1967).

[32] The calculations used the tax rate appropriate for a "joint return," with four exemptions and a standard deduction. The optional tax rates were used for the income tax brackets to which they are applicable.

TABLE 2. Marginal Tax Rates on Dividends and Capital Gains, Four Benchmark Years, 1949–65

	Marginal tax rates	
Year	Dividends t_p	Capital gains t_g
1949	0.418	0.165
1953	0.448	0.177
1960	0.438	0.178
1965	0.392	0.160

Source: Derived from data in U.S. Treasury Department, Internal Revenue Service, Statistics of Income for 1949, Part 1 (1954); Statistics of Income for 1953, Part 1 (1957); Statistics of Income—1960, Preliminary, Individual Income Tax Returns (1962); Statistics of Income—1965, Preliminary, Individual Income Tax Returns (1967).

an overestimate of the effective tax rate on capital gains[33] and therefore of the cost of equity obtained through retained earnings. Table 2 shows t_p and t_g for the four benchmark years. These values for t_g and t_p were used to adjust the cost of equity for the four benchmark years according to equation (3), and new measures for borrower's risk were computed. The results are shown in Table 3.

The adjustment for capital gains provisions has substantially reduced the marginal cost of equity financing through retained earnings. In fact, the disequilibrium has disappeared largely by 1960, and completely by 1965. In 1960, the discrepancy between MC_{E1} and MC_{D1} is less than 10 percent; between MC_{E2} and MC_{D2} it is less than 7 percent. In 1965 MC_{D1} slightly exceeds MC_{E1}, a situation which was found before only in 1927. For the aggregate of corporate manufacturing, equity financing by stock issue (Table 1) in the 1960's appears less attractive than financing by debt, while equity financing by retained earnings (Table 3) appears about as attractive as debt financing. For 1949 and 1953, MC_E is still very high relative to MC_D, which is indicative of a strong financial disequilibrium and of an incentive to change financial structure, the problem of an "equilibrium path." However, the rate of return to assets, λ_T, exceeds both estimates of MC_E in 1949, while in 1953 it is slightly higher than MC_{E2} and slightly lower than MC_{E1}. Financing through retained earnings, therefore, is less profitable than financing by debt, but it does not openly contradict the theory of residual maximization as

[33] See Bailey, this volume, pp. 15–26.

TABLE 3. Measures of Average and Marginal Cost of Debt and of Equity Financing by Retained Earnings, Corporate Manufacturing, Four Benchmark Years, 1949–65

Year and investment hypothesis	Average cost of equity p_{ET}	Marginal cost of equity MC_E	Marginal rate of return on investment λ_T	Marginal cost of debt MC_D	Average cost of debt p_D
1949					
Income	13.44	12.99	{13.72	5.50	{3.02
Dividend	11.61	11.21		5.11	
1953					
Income	15.27	14.74	{13.53	6.01	{3.55
Dividend	12.93	12.47		5.64	
1960					
Income	7.74	7.47	{10.00	6.81	{5.11
Dividend	7.46	7.19		6.75	
1965					
Income	6.49	6.25	{a	6.31	{4.92
Dividend	a	a		a	

Source: See Appendix A.
a Data for 1965 were not available when this series was constructed.

equity financing by stock issues would.[34] It is noteworthy that stock issues actually were at an extremely low level during this period.

A comparison of our estimates for MC_E between Tables 1 and 3 indicates that capital gains provisions have created an incentive to change the composition of equity financing. Some idea of the importance of this incentive is given by comparing the composition of equity financing in the predepression period, when there was not a sizable tax incentive to retain earnings rather than to issue stocks, and in the period following World War II, when the magnitude of the incentive (even if conservatively estimated) was quite large. Data for this comparison are available for the aggregate of corporate mining and manufacturing from 1900 on.

[34] Remember that, given the estimate of t_g, the estimates of MC_E in Table 3 represent an upper limit of the marginal cost of equity.

208   Financial Policy and the Corporation Income Tax

For the period 1900–29[35] the ratio of net stock issues to net retained earnings was 0.552, while for the period 1946–60 the ratio was 0.191.[36] However, in the postwar period corporate mining was a net dissaver; for corporate manufacturing alone, the ratio of net stock issues[37] to retained earnings in the period 1946–60 was 0.143. Since corporations have continued to be financed by retained earnings and by stock issues, we can attempt to arrive at a weighted average of the cost of equity.[38]

Table 4 gives the new estimates for the cost of equity, MC_E and MC_D. The results of Table 4 do not differ substantially from those of Table 3 for the years 1949 and 1953, given the fact that for these two years stock issues represented such a small percentage of equity financing. In 1960, the discrepancy between the two estimates of MC_E and MC_D is still small; in 1965, the difference between MC_{E1} and MC_{D1} is so small that we feel justified in considering these data to reflect financial equilibrium. In fact, in the 1960's the large discrepancy of Table 1 between p_{ET} and p_D has been reduced to very modest dimensions; a less conservative estimate of t_g might further reduce or reverse the sign of the discrepancy.

The Equilibrium Path

From Tables 3 and 4 we have seen that corporate manufacturing was in financial disequilibrium in the late 1940's and early 1950's,

---

[35] Daniel Creamer, Sergei P. Dobrovolsky, and Israel Borenstein, *Capital in Manufacturing and Mining, Its Formation and Financing* (Princeton University Press for National Bureau of Economic Research, 1960).

[36] *Ibid.*, for 1946–52 data. For 1953–60, data on stock issues are from U.S. Securities and Exchange Commission, *Statistical Bulletin*, various issues. For retained earnings, the data were taken from U.S. Treasury Department, *Statistics of Income*, various issues containing corporation income tax returns data.

[37] For 1948–60, the data are from U.S. Securities and Exchange Commission, *Statistical Bulletin*, various issues; for 1946–47 they were estimated from Creamer and others, *Capital in Manufacturing and Mining*, by multiplying stock issues for corporate mining and manufacturing by the ratio of the net worth of corporate manufacturing to the sum of the net worth of corporate mining and manufacturing. The data on net worth are from U.S. Treasury Department, *Statistics of Income*, various issues containing corporation income tax returns data.

[38] The two sets of costs of equity used are those given in Tables 1 and 3; the weights are, respectively, the ratio of stock issues and of retained earnings to their sum. The ratios of stock issues to the sum of stock issues and retained earnings were: 0.06 in 1949, 0.06 in 1953, 0.18 in 1960, and 0.14 in 1965.

TABLE 4. Measures of Average and Marginal Cost of Debt and of Equity Financing by Both Stock Issues and Retained Earnings, Corporate Manufacturing, Four Benchmark Years, 1949–65

Year and investment hypothesis	Average cost of equity p_{ET}	Marginal cost of equity MC_E	Marginal rate of return on investment λ_T	Marginal cost of debt MC_D	Average cost of debt p_D
1949					
Income	13.79	13.33	13.72	5.56	3.02
Dividend	11.91	11.50		5.23	
1953					
Income	15.72	15.17	13.53	6.08	3.55
Dividend	13.31	12.84		5.72	
1960					
Income	8.38	8.09	10.00	6.93	5.11
Dividend	8.08	7.80		6.87	
1965					
Income	6.85	6.60	a	6.37	4.92
Dividend	a	a		a	

Source: Derived from Tables 1 and 3.
a Data for 1965 were not available when this series was constructed.

while by 1960 the disequilibrium had nearly disappeared. The percentage change in financial structure over the whole postwar period was quite substantial, and the percentage change per year was highest during the period 1949–53, when the difference between MC_E and MC_D was at a maximum.

These considerations raise the question of whether an "equilibrium path" can be identified—whether the relative proportions of equity and debt financing have been related in a stable fashion to the differences between the marginal rate of return to assets, λ_T, and the marginal costs, respectively, of equity and of debt financing, as the theory in this study postulates. The theory does not directly imply an equilibrium level of financial structure; it merely states that when MC_E and MC_D are equal, there is no incentive to "change" financial structure.

TABLE 5. Ratios of Changes in Debt to Changes in Equity, Corporate Manufacturing, Selected Periods, 1946–63

		Period					
Row	Type of ratio	1946–63	1946–49	1950–53	1954–60	1961–63	1946–60
	Change in long-term debt, ΔL_F, to:						
1.	Change in net worth, ΔN_W	0.250	0.238	0.326	0.229	0.230	0.254
2.	Change in equity, ΔE	0.365	0.238	0.394	0.404	0.474	0.348
	Change in interest-paying debt, ΔL_T, to:						
3.	Change in net worth, ΔN_W	0.377	0.253	0.461	0.305	0.590	0.329
4.	Change in equity, ΔE	0.551	0.254	0.557	0.538	1.217	0.452

Source: Debt, retained earnings, and net worth data from U.S. Treasury Department, Internal Revenue Service, *Statistics of Income, Corporation Income Tax Returns*, various issues; data on stock issues from U.S. Securities and Exchange Commission, *Statistical Bulletin*, various issues.

The analysis of an equilibrium path must obviously be in terms of flows, not of stocks. If

ΔL_F = change in long-term debt[39]
ΔL_T = change in interest-paying debt[40]
ΔE = change in equity (that is, retained earnings[41] plus stock issues[42])
ΔN_W = change in net worth[43]

the figures in Table 5 show the ratio of financial flows over 1946–63 and subperiods thereof.

We have presented two alternative measures for the change in equity, ΔE and ΔN_W. Under certain restrictive assumptions, the two measures ought to be equal; in fact, they are not, except for the subperiod 1946–49. For the subsequent subperiods, ΔN_W exceeds ΔE, and by substantial amounts, as is evident by comparing row 1 with row 2 and row 3 with row 4.

[39] U.S. Treasury Department, *Statistics of Income*, various issues containing corporation income tax returns data.
[40] *Ibid.*
[41] *Ibid.*
[42] U.S. Securities and Exchange Commission, *Statistical Bulletin*, various issues.
[43] U.S. Treasury Department, *Statistics of Income*, various issues containing corporation income tax returns data.

The behavior of row 1 where we use ΔN_W is generally in agreement with the results of Tables 3 and 4. In fact, in row 1 we find that the largest percentage change takes place during the subperiod 1950–53 when the discrepancy between MC_E and MC_D is at a maximum. During 1954–60 and 1961–63, $\Delta L_F/\Delta N_W$ tends slightly to fall toward the level of the ratio of the stocks. As for row 3, $\Delta L_T/\Delta N_W$ falls sharply in 1954–60 as we would expect from Tables 3 and 4, but rises unexpectedly in 1961–63; as we said, however, this might be a short-run phenomenon.

The behavior of rows 2 and 4 of Table 5 is less in agreement with what we would postulate from the results of Tables 3 and 4. The difference between the values presented in rows 1 and 3 and, respectively, in rows 2 and 4, is particularly large after 1954; this could be due, in part, to an understatement of ΔE—or more precisely, of retained earnings which represent by far the larger component of ΔE.[44] Rows 2 and 4, in fact, show continuous growth over the subperiods, with the limited exception of row 4 which shows a slightly larger growth in 1950–53 than in 1954–60.

A stronger statistical test for our hypothesis, that corporations once displaced tend to move toward financial equilibrium, was applied, using regression equations relating yearly changes in debt and equity, respectively, to the difference between λ_T and MC_D and between λ_T and MC_E. Yearly values for MC_E and MC_D were constructed using, as a cost function for debt, Fisher's regression equation with pooled observations.[45] The coefficients for the cost function of equity are the same as those used for Tables 1, 3, and 4. As a measure of p_D the yield on Baa industrial bonds was again used, and for p_{ET} a measure was constructed corresponding to the estimate of p_{ET2} in Table 4. The flows of debt and of equity[46] were deflated by the value of their respective stocks in the previous year, to eliminate the "size" effect. The deflation of the flows by their respective stocks can be interpreted as a measure of the change in financial structure according to the incentive to do so for each of the claims used to finance a given amount of assets. (The data again are for corporate manufacturing.)

[44] For example, see George W. Terborgh, *Sixty Years of Business Capital Formation* (Machinery and Allied Products Institute and Council for Technological Advancement, 1960).

[45] See Appendix C.

[46] As a measure of debt, interest-paying debt was used; the flows of debt and equity are defined as for Table 4.

Let us define:

L_{T-1} = stock of interest-paying debt in the previous period[47]
NW_{T-1} = stock of equity in the previous period[48]
K = capitalization rate, which is $1/p_E$, where p_E is the price/earnings ratio[49]

ΔE[50] and ΔL_T are defined as in Table 5; λ_T, MC_{E2}, and MC_{D2} have already been defined. A three-year moving average was used for ΔE in order to remove, at least in part, the cyclical volatility of corporate profits.

The equation for the equilibrium path of debt is

(4) $$\frac{\Delta L_T}{D_{T-1}} = b_0 + b_1(\lambda_T - MC_{D2}) + b_2 K.$$

The coefficient of the variable $(\lambda_T - MC_{D2})$ is positive, as the theory postulates—financing by debt expansion is a function of the incentive to do so; the sign of K, the capitalization rate, is also correct (Table 6). In fact, in this framework of residual maximization, or in its equivalent of maximization of the market value of equity, an increase in K represents an incentive to borrow more for any given positive difference between λ_T and MC_D.

In the equation for the equilibrium path of equity,

(5) $$\Delta E/NW_{T-1} = c_0 + c_1(\lambda_T - MC_{E2}) + c_2\lambda_T,$$

λ_T was used instead of K, as our second independent variable, because stockholders might view their alternatives not only in terms of debt or equity financing but also in terms of retaining earnings or of receiving dividends. In this case, what is relevant is the expected rate of return on investment, λ_T. Also, in equation (5) the coefficients of $(\lambda_T - MC_{E2})$ and of λ_T are statistically significant and have the signs implied by the theory of residual maximization (Table 7). I am aware of the limitations of the data and of the variety of forces which affect corporate financial decisions also in the short run. To explain these would require a different study, certainly following a different

---

[47] U.S. Treasury Department, *Statistics of Income*, various issues containing corporation income tax returns data.

[48] *Ibid.*

[49] U.S. Securities and Exchange Commission, *Statistical Bulletin*.

[50] ΔE is the measure of change in equity which in Table 5 was less favorable to the hypothesis being tested. A better measure of the change in equity could be constructed by taking the estimate of retained earnings prepared by the U.S. Department of Commerce; however, for reasons of consistency we decided against changing series.

TABLE 6. Equilibrium Path of Debt Using Yearly Changes in Debt, Corporate Manufacturing, 1946–60 and 1946–63

Period and regression statistic	Change in interest paying debt/debt in previous year $\Delta L_T/L_{T-1}$	Difference between marginal rate of return on investment and marginal cost of debt $\lambda_T - MC_{D2}$	Capitalization rate K
1946–60			
Coefficient	−0.2888	0.0357	0.0121
Standard error	0.1123	0.0093	0.0047
t value	−2.5725	3.8224	2.5589
Partial correlation coefficient	—	0.7410	0.5942
R^2	0.5514		
Von Neumann ratio	2.0391		
Durbin-Watson statistic	1.9032		
1946–63			
Coefficient	−0.6504	0.0588	0.0308
Standard error	0.2530	0.0111	0.0189
t value	−2.5705	2.7681	3.1027
Partial correlation coefficient	—	0.6672	0.6243
R^2	0.4485		
Von Neumann ratio	1.8934		
Durbin-Watson statistic	1.7671		

Source: See text, equation (4).

TABLE 7. Equilibrium Path of Equity Using Yearly Changes in Equity, Corporate Manufacturing, 1946–60 and 1946–63

Period and regression statistic	Change in equity/net worth in previous period $\Delta E/NW_{T-1}$	Difference between marginal rate of return to assets and marginal cost of equity $\lambda_T - MC_{E2}$	Rate of return on investment λ_T
1946–60			
Coefficient	−0.0811	0.0026	0.0095
Standard error	0.0209	0.0015	0.0016
t value	−3.8829	1.7588	5.9807
Partial correlation coefficient	—	0.4527	0.8453
R^2	0.7789		
Von Neumann ratio	0.9402		
Durbin-Watson statistic	0.8775		
1946–63			
Coefficient	−0.0833	0.0044	0.0094
Standard error	0.0173	0.0020	0.0013
t value	−4.8268	2.1316	7.4639
Partial correlation coefficient	—	0.5241	0.9071
R^2	0.8258		
Von Neumann ratio	0.8792		
Durbin-Watson statistic	0.8206		

Source: See text, equation (5).

methodological approach. These statistical tests are presented here to point out and to measure the effect of long-run forces on corporate financial structure.

Conclusions

The neoclassical theory of the firm can be used to explain corporate investment and financial policy, if due account is taken of the risk factors. It follows from the theory that corporate financial structure and policy should not be treated with indifference but should be considered a fundamental component of corporate decisions, aimed at maximizing a residual or (in stock terms) the market value of equity. Following this theory, the effect that corporate and individual income taxes have on the cost of equity was analyzed quantitatively; this study then investigated whether, at the margin, corporations can be in financial equilibrium, in an attempt to solve the puzzle created by the comparison of average costs of debt and of equity.

Of the seven benchmark years considered, five (1927, 1932, 1937, 1960, and 1965) showed that corporations were close or very close to financial equilibrium; two (1949 and 1953) showed that the marginal cost of equity financing substantially exceeded the marginal cost of debt financing.

The fact that corporations might not be in financial equilibrium at any moment of time does not require an explanation. It is more interesting, instead, to consider whether corporations, once in disequilibrium, move toward financial equilibrium through a path which can be determined.

The empirical estimates of equilibrium paths show that corporations tend to expand their debt in accordance with the incentive to do so, as indicated by the excess of the rate of return on assets over the marginal cost of debt. Likewise, they show a positive response of equity financing to the excess of the rate of return on assets over the marginal cost of equity. These results imply that, although corporations were out of financial equilibrium in the late 1940's and 1950's, the financial decisions they took during this time brought them closer to equilibrium. By 1960, according to our estimates, the financial structure was close to equilibrium, and by 1965 very close indeed.

APPENDIX A

Definition and Measurement of the Variables

IN THE CONSTRUCTION of the income and dividend expectation measures of the cost of equity, p_{ET1} and of p_{ET2}, I used exponentially weighted averages of return to equity (Y), dividend payment (Z), retention rate (b), and rate of return on investment before taxes (λ_T). For earnings, dividends, and retained earnings, the Standard and Poor's[1] series were spliced to the Cowles Commission series.[2] The two sources were made comparable by taking an arithmetic average for three overlapping years, 1926–29, of earnings, dividends, and retained earnings. The Cowles Commission series were adjusted by multiplying each earlier observation of these three variables by the ratio of the corresponding averages for the two series. The series for λ_T was computed with data from *Statistics of Income* (U.S. Treasury Department, Internal Revenue Service) by taking the ratio of interest payments plus profits before taxes to the book value of assets, for corporate manufacturing, over the period 1926–63. To perform the weighting process the formula

$$(1 - e^{-\beta}) \sum_{i=0}^{T} C_{T-i}\, e^{-\beta i}$$

[1] *Trade and Securities Statistics, Security Price Index Record* (1964); *Trade and Securities Statistics, Current Statistics*, various monthly issues for 1964 and 1965.
[2] Alfred Cowles III, and Associates, *Common-Stock Indexes* (2nd ed.; Bloomington, Ind.: Principia, 1939).

was used;[3] here C_T stands for the observation of the year for which the exponentially weighted average is computed. The value b was computed by taking the ratio of exponentially weighted retained earnings to exponentially weighted earnings.

For these four variables, different values of the exponent β were used, namely, 0.4 for earnings and retained earnings, 0.5 for λ_T, and 0.6 for Z, thus giving increasingly higher weights to recent values of the more stable variables. In performing the weighting process, the number of years used was such that the sum of the weights would differ from unity by less than 0.01. More precisely, for β set to 0.4, 0.5, 0.6, the number of observations required was, respectively, 12, 10, and 8. However, the basic data available from *Statistics of Income* to compute λ_T started in 1926. For the period 1927–34, I had to adapt the weighting process to use all the observations available for any given year, according to the formula

$$\sum_{i=0}^{T} C_{T-i}\, e^{-\beta i} \Big/ \sum_{i=0}^{T} e^{-\beta i},$$

thus setting the sum of the weights exactly equal to 1.

The choice of using the effective tax rate—that is, the ratio of tax payments to profits for t—is also somewhat arbitrary. The correct rate would be the rate which corporations consider in determining their cost of equity and, therefore, their financial policy. In this context, it is possible to maintain that the relevant tax rate is not the effective tax rate, the t used in this study, but the "expected" tax rate. For example, corporations might have given little weight to excess profits taxes and similar items, considering them transitory phenomena and also considering the relevant or expected tax rate to be perhaps the statutory corporation income tax rate, unadjusted for excess profits tax. Which tax rate is closer to the rate used by corporations in determining their financial policy depends on (1) whether there is a cost associated with short-run changes in financial policy and structure, and (2) whether this cost is large or small. This is a different problem in itself. However, the only periods in which a change in our treatment of excess profits taxes would have made a difference are the years 1937 and 1950–53; even here, the difference would have been fairly modest.

To compute the changes in "lender's risk" and in "borrower's risk" from Fisher's cost function of debt and Kolin's cost function of equity an estimate of financial structure was needed; this is defined in the papers of Fisher and Kolin as a ratio of book value of debt to market value of equity (see the section in the text devoted to the work of Fisher and Kolin).

[3] See, for example, Phillip Cagan, "The Monetary Dynamics of Hyperinflation," in Milton Friedman (ed.), *Studies in the Quantity Theory of Money* (University of Chicago Press, 1956).

218   Financial Policy and the Corporation Income Tax

We obtained D/E, where D is interest-paying debt, by multiplying D/NW (computed from *Statistics of Income*) by NW/E (computed with data from Standard and Poor's[4]), where E is the year's average market value and NW is the corresponding book value of equity at the end of the year. Similarly, multiplying E/NW (as obtained from Standard and Poor's) by NW (as obtained from *Statistics of Income*), a market value of equity was determined that was compatible with the measure of debt taken from *Statistics of Income*.

Computing all the values needed for the year 1965 was difficult because at the time of writing, data from *Statistics of Income* were available only up to 1963. It therefore was impossible to compute λ_T, and thus p_{ET2}, for 1965. It was possible, however, to compute p_{ET1} (data on earnings and stock prices were available from Standard and Poor's[5]) if an estimate of t for 1965 were available. For this, the effective tax rate for manufacturing corporations during 1960–63 was divided by the top rate of the corporation income tax for the same period; the resulting number was multiplied by the top rate of the corporation income tax for 1965 to obtain the estimate of t. A similar problem arose in obtaining the proportion of stock issues to stock issues plus retained earnings needed for an estimate of p_{ET1} for Table 4, for 1965. Accordingly, the arithmetic average of this ratio over 1961–63 was computed and used for 1965.[6]

The same method was used to compute $\dfrac{D}{E}$ and $\dfrac{D}{D+E}$ for 1965.

---

[4] *Securities Price Index Record* (1964); and *Current Statistics*, various monthly issues for 1964 and 1965.

[5] *Ibid.*

[6] The U.S. Securities and Exchange Commission's *Statistical Bulletin* was available for 1965, but, in order to get an estimate of retained earnings, we would have had to switch from the source used throughout (U.S. Treasury Department, *Statistics of Income*) to data collected by the U.S. Department of Commerce. The conceptual differences between the two series were sufficiently great to influence us to use the method indicated.

APPENDIX B

The Effect of a Change in Leverage on the Coefficient of Variation of Earnings

IN ORDER TO DERIVE the changes in borrower's and in lender's risk, respectively, from Kolin's and from Fisher's equations, the only mathematical problem is to determine the effect of a change in leverage upon the coefficient of variation of earnings. This can be done by setting the identity $V \equiv D + E$, defining $W \equiv D/V$, and, therefore, $1 - W \equiv E/V$, and remembering that now

$$p_D = f(E, D) = F(W, V)_\theta \text{ and}$$
$$p_E = g(E, D) = G(1 - W, V).$$

We can also express the coefficient of variation as a function of W and V, namely,

$$\frac{\Delta y}{y} = h(W, V).$$

We know that since $\frac{\Delta y}{y}$ is a size-free variable, $\frac{\partial h}{\partial V} = 0$; we can now analyze the effect of leverage. Let us define

$$y = p_E E = V p_E (1 - W)$$

and differentiate the h function

$$\frac{\partial h}{\partial W} = \frac{\partial}{\partial W}\left(\frac{\Delta y}{y}\right) = \frac{\partial}{\partial W}\left(\frac{\Delta y/V}{p_E(1-W)}\right) = \frac{\Delta y}{V}\left(\frac{-(1-W)\frac{\partial p_E}{\partial W} + p_E}{p_E^2(1-W)^2}\right)$$

$$= \frac{\Delta y}{y}\left(\frac{1}{1-W} - \frac{1}{p_E}\frac{\partial p_E}{\partial W}\right).$$

The h function can be differentiated also with respect to D or E, yielding

$$\frac{\partial h}{\partial D} = \frac{\partial h}{\partial W}\frac{\partial W}{\partial D} = \frac{1-W}{V}\frac{\partial h}{\partial W}, \text{ or}$$

$$\frac{\partial h}{\partial E} = \frac{\partial h}{\partial W}\frac{\partial W}{\partial E} = -\frac{W}{V}\frac{\partial h}{\partial W}.$$

Similarly, $\frac{\partial p_E}{\partial W}$ can be expressed as $\frac{\partial p_E}{\partial E}$ and $\frac{\partial p_D}{\partial D}$, that is,

$$\frac{\partial p_E}{\partial W} = \frac{\partial p_E}{\partial E}\frac{\partial E}{\partial W} = \frac{\partial p_E}{\partial E}(-V) \text{ and}$$

$$\frac{\partial p_E}{\partial W} = \frac{\partial p_E}{\partial D}\frac{\partial D}{\partial W} = \frac{\partial p_E}{\partial D}(V).$$

APPENDIX C

Fisher's Cost Functions of Debt and Kolin's Cost Functions of Equity

REGRESSION EQUATIONS developed by Lawrence Fisher[1] were used to determine the change in lender's risk. Fisher's equations for the years 1927, 1932, 1937, 1949, and 1953 were supplemented with equations for 1960 and 1965 that were computed as part of this study. The equations estimate the logarithm of average risk premium on a firm's bonds as a linear function of the logarithms of earnings variability, period of solvency, equity to debt ratio, and value of bonds outstanding. The elasticities, constant terms, standard errors of estimate (in parentheses), and values for R^2 are shown below.

Date	Number of observations	Degrees of freedom	R^2	Constant	Elasticities			
					Earnings variability	Period of solvency	Equity to debt ratio	Bonds outstanding
1927–53	366	361	0.750	0.987	+0.307 (0.032)	−0.253 (0.036)	−0.537 (0.031)	−0.275 (0.021)
1927	71	66	0.756	0.874	+0.233 (0.048)	−0.269 (0.062)	−0.404 (0.039)	−0.169 (0.031)
1932	45	40	0.726	1.014	+0.248 (0.114)	−0.067 (0.114)	−0.531 (0.092)	−0.286 (0.071)
1937	89	84	0.731	0.949	+0.286 (0.051)	−0.254 (0.061)	−0.491 (0.060)	−0.271 (0.038)
1949	73	68	0.786	0.711	+0.228 (0.100)	−0.124 (0.076)	−0.426 (0.084)	−0.329 (0.046)
1953	88	83	0.773	1.012	+0.228 (0.091)	−0.300 (0.089)	−0.474 (0.085)	−0.363 (0.043)
1960	106	101	0.803	1.539	+0.219 (0.048)	−0.232 (0.060)	−0.319 (0.044)	−0.218 (0.035)
1965	115	110	0.747	0.863	+0.287 (0.076)	−0.321 (0.092)	−0.439 (0.053)	−0.245 (0.043)

[1] "Determinants of Risk Premiums on Corporate Bonds," *Journal of Political Economy*, Vol. 67 (June 1959), pp. 217–22.

The results of Fisher's regression equation with pooled observations were used in this study to compute MC_D and MC_E for the equilibrium paths of debt and equity.

Marshall Kolin's regression equations were used to derive the coefficient estimates to determine the change in borrower's risk.[2] Data from cross-section samples of industrial corporations for each year from 1951 to 1957 were used. Kolin's equation was based on the hypothesis that the market value of equity is a function of expected income and of the riskiness of the firm. The results are listed below. The figures in parentheses are t values.

Date	R^2	Income	Growth variable	Earnings variability in the Great Depression	Equity to debt ratio	Coefficient of variation of earnings
1951	0.948	0.980	0.292	−0.293	−0.020	−0.057
		(33.65)	(0.90)	(−4.15)	(−1.01)	(−1.03)
1952	0.950	1.015	0.219	−0.257	−0.032	−0.044
		(35.68)	(0.69)	(−3.71)	(−1.60)	(−0.91)
1953	0.949	1.016	0.263	−0.286	−0.021	−0.146
		(34.33)	(0.79)	(−3.96)	(−0.98)	(−2.68)
1954	0.967	1.028	0.478	−0.174	−0.020	−0.059
		(43.80)	(1.60)	(−2.89)	(−1.09)	(−1.17)
1955	0.964	1.010	0.769	−0.178	−0.014	0.037
		(39.17)	(2.19)	(−2.83)	(−0.69)	(0.63)
1956	0.969	1.023	1.155	−0.171	−0.017	−0.053
		(38.73)	(3.35)	(−2.61)	(−0.85)	(−1.05)
1957	0.968	1.027	0.485	−0.108	−0.009	−0.183
		(33.66)	(1.46)	(−1.45)	(−0.38)	(−3.18)
Average		1.014	—	—	−0.019	−0.072

[2] "The Relative Price of Corporate Equity" (Ph.D. thesis, University of Chicago, 1963).

ROBERT E. LUCAS, JR.

Labor-Capital Substitution in U.S. Manufacturing

IN A NUMBER OF ARTICLES, A. C. Harberger[1] has established that knowledge of elasticities of substitution between labor and capital is essential to any analysis of the taxation-of-income from capital in the United States. This chapter examines the problem of estimating this elasticity for fourteen U.S. manufacturing industries. The new evidence presented here is based on regression analyses of time series for the period 1929 through 1958.

In the last few years, several studies of factor substitution in manufacturing have been completed. Out of these, the most important

Since this paper was written, a number of studies of factor substitution have been published. For references to some of these, see the surveys of M. Nerlove, "Notes on Recent Empirical Studies of the CES and Related Production Functions," Technical Report No. 13 (processed; Stanford University, Institute for Mathematical Studies in the Social Sciences, July 1965); and Zvi Griliches, "Production Functions in Manufacturing: Some Preliminary Results," in Murray Brown (ed.), *The Theory and Empirical Analysis of Production*, Studies in Income and Wealth, Vol. 31 (Columbia University Press for National Bureau of Economic Research, 1967).

[1] See Arnold C. Harberger, "The Corporation Income Tax: An Empirical Appraisal," in *Tax Revision Compendium*, Vol. 1, House Committee on Ways and Means, 86 Cong. 1 sess. (1959), pp. 231–50; "The Incidence of the Corporation Income Tax," *Journal of Political Economy*, Vol. 70 (June 1962), pp. 215–40; and "Efficiency Effects of Taxes on Income from Capital," in Marian Krzyzaniak (ed.), *Effects of Corporation Income Tax* (Wayne State University Press, 1966), pp. 107–17.

of which are discussed below, have come important advances in theory to which this study is deeply indebted. With one exception, these studies have used cross-sectional data only. Roughly speaking, the U.S. cross-sectional studies indicate that elasticities of substitution range around unity; or, in other words, that significant deviations of production functions from the Cobb-Douglas form are rare in manufacturing industries. The conclusion of this study is that, based on time series evidence alone, the elasticity of substitution for *each* industry is significantly less than one, with a "typical" elasticity lying in the range from 0.3 to 0.5.

This finding (time series estimates lying uniformly below cross-section estimates of the same elasticity) is a familiar one in demand studies. A possible solution to this problem, which has been applied with great success to a variety of similar problems, is to relax the assumption that each time series observation lies on the demand curve being estimated, and to postulate instead a process of lagged adjustment. In many previous applications this adjustment-lag hypothesis has been accepted; and, based on it, time series estimates have been obtained which are more nearly consistent with the cross-sectional evidence. In this study, a number of hypotheses of this type were tested, but it was generally found either that the lags in adjustment were not significant, or if they were, that the effect on the elasticity estimates was small.

This secondary conclusion leaves the problem in a highly unsatisfactory state, with (at least) two conflicting sets of estimates of essentially the same parameters. In an attempt to resolve this conflict, possible sources of bias in both cross-sectional and time series estimates were examined. Unfortunately, no single bias, in either type of estimate, appeared capable of resolving the conflict. Nevertheless, I believe it can be established that the cross-sectional estimates are based on a theoretically ambiguous and probably inapplicable model, that they are subject to biases potentially greater than those to which the time series estimates are subject, and finally that they are highly sensitive to changes in specification.

The organization of this chapter is as follows. The theoretical background for the study is collected from various places in the literature and reviewed briefly in the first section. In the next section, evidence from previous studies is reviewed. The third section contains the time series estimates, together with a discussion of bias. Conclusions are reviewed in the final section. The time series data used are described in the appendix.

Theoretical Background

As preparation for the discussion of estimation methods, this section is devoted to the theoretical background of the study. The first part is a review of the basic work of J. R. Hicks[2] and R. G. D. Allen[3] on substitution between factors. The second part sets out the particular form of the three-input production function used in this study. Important recent additions to the theory are reviewed in the third part, and the final part outlines a basic stochastic formulation.

The Hicks-Allen Definition and Results

Consider a single firm, operating under a production function[4]

$$Q = F(K, L),$$

which relates a flow of output, Q, to a labor input, L, and a capital services input, K. If Q is constant, then the elasticity of substitution between labor and capital, σ, is defined by

$$\sigma = \frac{d \log (K/L)}{d \log (F_L/F_K)},$$

where F_L and F_K are the marginal products of labor and capital. If it is assumed that the firm operates under constant returns to scale, an assumption retained throughout this chapter, this constant output condition may be dropped.

If labor and capital are purchased on competitive markets, the ratio of marginal products will equal the ratio of the wage rate, w, to the rental price of capital, r; under these circumstances the elasticity of substitution is

(1) $$\sigma = \frac{d \log (K/L)}{d \log (w/r)}.$$

That is, the elasticity of substitution measures the percentage change in the firm's capital-labor ratio per percentage point change in rela-

[2] J. R. Hicks, *The Theory of Wages* (London: Macmillan, 1932), pp. 241–46.
[3] R. G. D. Allen, *Mathematical Analysis for Economists* (London: Macmillan, 1938), pp. 340–45, 369–74, 503–09.
[4] F is assumed to be defined and positive for all positive K and L; it is assumed to be continuous, with continuous first and second partial derivatives, F_L, F_K, F_{LL}, F_{LK}, and F_{KK}; and it is assumed that: $F_L > 0$, $F_K > 0$, and $F_{LK} > 0$.

tive factor prices. As defined here, it may take any positive value. If factor price changes have no effect on methods of production,[5] the elasticity is defined as zero. This is, of course, the case of fixed proportions, by which is meant not that K/L does not change, but only that the movements of this ratio are not systematically related to price changes. At the other extreme, one can imagine a firm so sensitive to factor price changes that small swings in the price ratio lead to drastic shifts in factor proportions. As one approaches the case of perfect substitution between factors, σ approaches infinity. A familiar intermediate case is given by the Cobb-Douglas production function:

$$Q = \gamma K^\delta L^{(1-\delta)}.$$

The elasticity of substitution for this function is unity.

On the assumptions that the firm is minimizing costs at each output level, and that factor markets are competitive, the "constant output" factor demand elasticities may be obtained in terms of σ and the expressions

$$S_L = \frac{F_L L}{F}, \text{ and } S_K = \frac{F_K K}{F},$$

as follows:

$$\frac{\partial \log(L)}{\partial \log(w)} = -\frac{\partial \log(L)}{\partial \log(r)} = -S_K \sigma$$

$$\frac{\partial \log(K)}{\partial \log(r)} = -\frac{\partial \log(K)}{\partial \log(w)} = -S_L \sigma$$

It also follows, from the assumption of constant returns to scale, that long-run marginal cost for the firm is constant with respect to changes in output. Therefore, if the product market is also perfectly competitive, equality of price and marginal cost at one output implies equality at all output levels. Thus, as is well known, adding the assumption of profit maximization to this model is *not* sufficient to yield unique equilibrium output or inputs for the firm. As Allen has shown, however, this indeterminacy does not carry over to the competitive *industry* model based on these assumptions. Suppose each firm in a competititive industry has the same production function and faces the same product and factor prices. Then the above defini-

---

[5] Formally, this case is excluded by the definition of F.

tion and results apply to the industry as well, and the cost minimization assumption again yields the marginal productivity conditions,

$$w = \lambda F_L \quad \text{and} \quad r = \lambda F_K,$$

where λ is marginal cost. If p is product price, and $f(p)$ is the demand curve facing the industry, there is a third equilibrium condition:

$$f(p) = F(K, L) = Q.$$

Finally, note that if $p > \lambda$, all firms will be able to increase profits by increasing output, while the reverse holds for $p < \lambda$. This represents the fourth equilibrium condition, $p = \lambda$. From this model, one can derive the industry labor demand elasticities with respect to w and r,

$$\frac{\partial \log (L)}{\partial \log (w)} = -S_K \sigma + S_L \eta$$

$$\frac{\partial \log (L)}{\partial \log (r)} = S_K (\sigma + \eta)$$

where

$$\eta = \frac{\partial \log (f)}{\partial \log (p)}$$

is the elasticity of product demand. Similar formulas hold for capital demand. Note that for these industry formulas, the terms S_L and S_K can be identified with the shares of labor and capital in the total receipts of the industry. Most applications of elasticities of substitution rest on these familiar Allen formulas.

The indeterminacy of individual firm output in the Allen model is frequently held to disqualify it for use in the analysis of a competitive industry, and it might be worthwhile to deal with this objection before proceeding. The objection that the usual assumptions of the theory of the firm do not yield as much mileage in the constant costs case as in the case of increasing costs is of course mathematically valid. But this lack of uniqueness does not imply either instability of industry output in the usual dynamic sense, or instability of competition in the sense of a tendency for a single firm to take over the industry. This point, and in particular the fundamental difference between the constant and decreasing costs cases, has been developed fully by Paul A. Samuelson.[6]

[6] Paul A. Samuelson, *Foundations of Economic Analysis* (Harvard University Press, 1947), pp. 78–80.

Extension to Three Inputs

To apply this theory to actual industries, it is necessary to add at least one more input: materials purchased from outside the industry. While Allen has generalized the theory of the preceding section to any number of inputs, with appropriate extension of the "smoothness" conditions on the production function, the form in which data are available makes it convenient to assume that output bears a fixed proportion to materials input. That is, suppose that

$$Q = G(L, K, M) = \min [F(K, L), \alpha^{-1} M],$$

where M is materials, α is a non-zero constant, and F is as in the two-input case. Then if each firm is operating with maximum technical efficiency, both

$$Q = F(K, L)$$

and

$$Q = \alpha^{-1} M$$

will hold for the industry.

This modification of the production function necessitates a revision of the Allen model and conclusions. Again, the conditions are

$$w = \lambda F_L \text{ and } r = \lambda F_K,$$

but λ is no longer equal to marginal cost. Instead,

$$\frac{\partial (Cost)}{\partial Q} = \lambda + \alpha p_m = p,$$

where p_m is the price of materials. Thus the effect of introducing a third input in this way is exactly the same as the effect on the original two-input problem of introducing a tax of (αp_m) per unit of output.

Later on, a measure of "net marginal cost," λ, will be needed. A measure could of course be obtained from knowledge of p, p_m, and the constant α; but one can also be derived from value added, V, defined by

$$V = pQ - p_m M.$$

Since $M = \alpha Q$,

$$V = Q(p - \alpha p_m)$$
$$= Q\lambda,$$
$$\lambda = V/Q.$$

Once these issues are clear, it will be convenient to return to the language of the two-input model. Where no confusion will arise, V

has been used interchangeably with pQ, and hence p with λ. The literature provides ample precedent for this usage.

Recent Theoretical Developments

So far, the argument has proceeded entirely in marginal terms. Both for estimation and for numerical application it is necessary to deal with finite changes, and hence convenient to assume the constancy of σ. It has been shown that if the production function, F, is homogeneous of degree one and has a constant elasticity of substitution, it must have the form

$$F(K, L) = \gamma[\delta K^{-\rho} + (1 - \delta)L^{-\rho}]^{-1/\rho},$$

where

$$\sigma = \frac{1}{1+\rho}.[7]$$

This function has been named the CES (constant elasticity of substitution) function by its discoverers. The parameters γ, δ, and ρ are termed the efficiency, distribution, and substitution parameters.[8] As ρ approaches zero (σ approaches 1) the CES function approaches the Cobb-Douglas

$$F(K, L) = \gamma K^{\delta} L^{1-\delta}.$$

The CES function is thus ideal for estimating σ, or for testing the hypothesis $\sigma = 1$ within the more general hypothesis that σ may take any positive value.

Another useful property of the CES function lies in the form taken by its first partial derivatives (marginal productivities). For example, if F has the CES form, the condition $w = pF_L$ can be written

$$Q/L = \gamma^{1-\sigma}(1 - \delta)^{-\sigma}(w/p)^{\sigma},$$

or, taking logs,

(2) $\qquad \log(Q/L) = \log[\gamma^{(1-\sigma)}(1 - \delta)^{-\sigma}] + \sigma \log(w/p).$

Thus if one has a CES production function, he can determine the elasticity of substitution, σ, by calculating the slope parameter in a

---

[7] See K. J. Arrow, H. B. Chenery, B. S. Minhas, and R. M. Solow, "Capital-Labor Substitution and Economic Efficiency," *Review of Economics and Statistics*, Vol. 43 (August 1961), pp. 225–50.

[8] It is easy to show that the restrictions placed on F in note 4 imply: $0 < \delta < 1$, $\rho > -1$, $\gamma > 0$.

log-linear marginal productivity condition. This condition, equation (2), is the regression equation used in all recent work on substitution, including the present study.

Statistical Formulation

The use of equation (2) as the basis for estimating σ has two major advantages over methods derived directly from equation (1), which yields a log-linear relationship between K/L and w/r. First, it should be noted that equation (1) is a long-run equilibrium condition, referring to a change between two positions in which *both* capital and labor inputs are at their desired levels, given factor prices. We are of course interested in σ for a long-run problem, but for estimation a relationship which can be expected to hold (except for a serially independent error term) for each observation is required. Annual data will be used, and, as is well known, firms do not adjust their stocks of capital to equilibrium levels on a year-to-year basis. Equation (2), on the other hand, requires for its validity *no* assumptions about capital adjustments. All it requires is that labor be a variable input. In fact, as will be pointed out below, it will be possible to *test* the hypothesis that labor is variable on an annual basis, but even without this "escape clause" it is evident that equation (2) is far more likely to hold continuously through time than is equation (1).

A second practical advantage of equation (2) over equation (1) lies in the variables the former employs. Neither capital services nor the rental price of these services are directly observable market variables. This need cause no conceptual difficulties, as Haavelmo has shown,[9] and even the practical difficulties may be met, as Jorgenson has done.[10] Nevertheless, construction of these series, and specification of the errors to which they are subject, are matters of some controversy. In addition, the basic series needed for this task are not available for all of the period 1929–58, for all of the industries studied. For these reasons, the estimation in this study is based on equation (2).

Estimation of marginal productivity conditions has long been a problem of interest to econometricians, and a justifiable tendency

---

[9] Trygve Haavelmo, *A Study in the Theory of Investment* (University of Chicago Press, 1960), pp. 162–65.

[10] Dale W. Jorgenson, "Capital Theory and Investment Behavior," *American Economic Review*, Vol. 53 (May 1963), pp. 247–59.

to mistrust estimates obtained by application of ordinary least squares to equations such as (2) is by now widespread among economists. It is not difficult to see the content of this mistrust, if one tries to formulate an experiment out of which observations may be supposed to have been generated. First, suppose that the ratio (w/p) appears in equation (2) in lagged form, so that firms in the industry are conceived as observing this price ratio in *this* period, and selecting input and output quantities for the *next* period on this basis. In this case, the "left-hand variable" in equation (2) is clearly *reacting to* changes in the "right-hand variable." If (w/p) is not lagged, this sequence is not so simple. Firms presumably still react to changes in (w/p), but at the same time, the input and output levels they select on this basis will evidently influence the value taken by output price, p, in this period. Thus if firms "by chance" turn out an output per unit of labor input which is "too large" on the basis of the level of (w/p) and the true σ, output price will fall along the industry demand curve, and (w/p) will thus rise. In other words, a movement of the two variables in the same direction has hypothetically been generated. This has nothing to do with factor substitution, but is rather a reflection of random technological factors and a downward sloping industry demand curve.[11] A similar, though I think substantively less interesting, argument can be developed on the labor market side.

These difficulties, which I believe to be very real ones, gain in importance with the observation that they constitute the only obvious and potentially important source of bias which should affect time series estimates of equation (2) more seriously than cross-sectional estimates. Equation (2) will be estimated using both current and lagged w/p as the independent variable. Since "the" correct form is unknown, this procedure evidently does not meet the problem squarely. In fact, this cannot be done using single equation methods only. In the discussion of bias, however, I argue that the resulting estimates are not seriously biased.

No provision has as yet been made for shifts over time in the production function. Provision may be made for smooth, neutral,

[11] This verbal argument suggests that the "simultaneous equations bias" in estimates of σ obtained from equation (2) will be upward. In fact, the sign of the bias will depend on the true σ, on the distribution of the error terms in *all* equations of a stochastic version of the Allen model, and on the particular form taken by the capital adjustment equations for the industry. An analysis of this problem is available in my Ph.D. thesis (University of Chicago, 1963), App. Chaps. 2 and 5.

technological change[12] by supposing that the production surface shifts outward by λ percent per year, so that the production function is written

(3) $$Q_t = \gamma[\delta K_t^{-\rho} + (1-\delta)L_t^{-\rho}]^{-1/\rho} e^{\lambda t}.$$

The statistical hypothesis to be used in estimating σ may now be stated formally. Let w_t^* and p_t^* denote the wage and price that firms consider relevant for selecting inputs and outputs in period t. Suppose that

$$w_t^* = w^*(w_t, w_{t-1}, \ldots) \text{ and}$$
$$p_t^* = p^*(p_t, p_{t-1}, \ldots).$$

Based on equation (3), the stochastic version of equation (2) may be written as

(4) $\quad \log(Q_t/L_t) = A + \sigma \log(w_t^*/p_t^*) + (1-\sigma)\lambda t + \eta_t,$

where

$$A = \log[\gamma^{(1-\sigma)}(1-\delta)^{-\sigma}]$$

and the η_t are independent and identically distributed random variables, with mean zero and variance τ^2. The properties of estimates obtained from least squares fitting of equation (4) will depend on whether or not w_t^* and p_t^* depend on current prices. If they do not involve current prices, estimates from equation (4) will be consistent estimates of the true σ and $(1-\sigma)\lambda$. If they do, these estimates will be subject to an unknown "simultaneous equations bias."

Review of Empirical Work

Production function studies have always formed a major part of the applied econometric literature. Until recently, these studies could be classified into two groups: the estimation of Cobb-Douglas production functions, begun by Douglas and his associates in the 1930's; and the input-output work begun by Leontief at about the same time. Both these approaches have since been generalized, the most important development on the neoclassical side being the discovery of the CES function discussed in the preceding section. Although virtually all of this work deals with issues that are relevant to the central problem of this study, this review will treat only those studies

---

[12] The assumption of *neutral* change is actually more restrictive than necessary. See below, pp. 261–62.

which attempt to estimate elasticities of substitution under the assumption that the production function takes the CES form. In the first part of this section, results of three cross-sectional studies are presented. Possible biases in these estimates are then discussed. This theoretical argument is supplemented by some additional tests in the next following section. The fourth part deals with existing time series evidence on factor substitution.

Cross-Sectional Estimates of Elasticities of Substitution in Manufacturing

The studies of Arrow, Chenery, Minhas, and Solow,[13] of Solow,[14] and of Minasian[15] are considered here. Each of these papers attempts to estimate cross-sectionally the marginal productivity condition of equation (2), based on the following model. Suppose there are observations on a single industry in each of N regions, and suppose also that output price, p, is constant over these regions. Then equation (2) becomes

(5) $\quad \log (V_i/L_i) = \log [\gamma^{1-\sigma} (1 - \delta)^{-\sigma} p^{1-\sigma}] + \sigma \log (w_i) + u_i,$

where $i = 1, \ldots, N$, and $V_i = pQ_i =$ value added in region i. It is assumed that $w_1, \ldots, w_N$ are observed parameters, and that $u_1, \ldots, u_N$ are independent and identically distributed random variables, with mean zero and variance τ^2. If these conditions are satisfied, and if all variables are correctly measured, application of least squares to equation (5) yields best linear unbiased estimates of the elasticity of substitution, σ. It should be noted that equation (5) is an incomplete statistical characterization of an industry in a region, and that the embedding of equation (5) in a complete model will therefore yield additional testable implications. Some of these are developed below.

The estimates by Arrow, Chenery, Minhas, and Solow are shown in Table 1. They are based on samples of varying number of countries, for varying years in the mid-1950's. The definitions of the variables are taken from the United Nations International Standard Industrial Classification, and are comparable to those used in the U.S. Census

[13] In "Capital-Labor Substitution."
[14] Robert M. Solow, "Capital, Labor, and Income in Manufacturing," *The Behavior of Income Shares* (Princeton University Press for National Bureau of Economic Research, 1964), pp. 101–42.
[15] Jora R. Minasian, "Elasticities of Substitution and Constant-Output Demand Curves for Labor," *Journal of Political Economy*, Vol. 69 (June 1961), pp. 261–70.

TABLE 1. Elasticities of Substitution Between Labor and Capital by Arrow, Chenery, Minhas, and Solow, Varying Countries and Industries, Mid-1950's

International standard industrial classification number	Industry	Number of countries	Elasticity σ	Standard error	Coefficient of determination R^2
202	Dairy products	16	0.721	0.073	0.921
203	Fruit and vegetable canning	14	0.855	0.075	0.910
205	Grain and mill products	16	0.909	0.096	0.855
206	Bakery products	16	0.900	0.065	0.927
207	Sugar	13	0.781	0.115	0.790
220	Tobacco	15	0.753	0.151	0.629
231	Textiles: spinning and weaving	18	0.809	0.068	0.892
232	Knitting mills	15	0.785	0.064	0.915
250	Lumber and wood	18	0.860	0.066	0.910
260	Furniture	16	0.894	0.042	0.952
271	Pulp and paper	16	0.965	0.101	0.858
280	Printing and publishing	16	0.868	0.056	0.940
291	Leather finishing	14	0.857	0.062	0.921
311	Basic chemicals	16	0.831	0.070	0.898
312	Fats and oils	14	0.839	0.090	0.869
319	Miscellaneous chemicals	16	0.895	0.059	0.938
331	Clay products	13	0.919	0.098	0.878
332	Glass	13	0.999	0.084	0.921
333	Ceramics	12	0.901	0.044	0.974
334	Cement	12	0.920	0.149	0.770
341	Iron and steel	13	0.811	0.051	0.936
342	Non-ferrous metals	10	1.011	0.120	0.886
350	Metal products	13	0.902	0.088	0.897
370	Electrical machinery	14	0.870	0.118	0.804

Source: See text note 7.

of Manufactures. The labor input, L_i, is number of employees, and the wage is obtained by dividing L_i into the corresponding wage-bill figure. Value data have been converted to U.S. dollar terms, but are modified in no other way.

Table 2 contains the estimates obtained by Minasian and by Solow. Minasian uses a sample from the U.S. Census of Manufactures. The Solow sample consists of observations for 1956 from the annual Survey of Manufactures for each of the nine census regions, excluding those regions for which the value added of the industry in question falls below a cut-off point. The labor variable is the number

TABLE 2. Elasticities of Substitution Between Labor and Capital by Minasian, 1957, and Solow, 1956, Selected U.S. Industries

Standard industrial classification number	Industry	Number of states	Minasian Estimates			Number of census regions	Solow Estimates		
			Elasticity σ	Standard error	Coefficient of determination R^2		Elasticity σ	Standard error	Coefficient of determination R^2
20	Food	31	0.59	0.17	0.29	9	0.69	0.22	0.58
21	Tobacco	8	3.46	0.52	0.88	6	1.96	0.30	0.92
22	Textiles	17	1.57	0.35	0.58	8	1.27	0.15	0.93
23	Apparel	19	1.62	0.20	0.80	9	1.01	0.13	0.89
24	Lumber and wood	19	0.93	0.11	0.82	9	0.99	0.09	0.94
25	Furniture and fixtures	18	1.12	0.24	0.58	8	1.12	0.10	0.95
26	Pulp and paper	24	1.60	0.35	0.49	9	1.77	1.01	0.31
27	Printing and publishing	25	0.89	0.18	0.53	9	1.02	0.21	0.78
28	Chemicals	24	1.12	0.38	0.28	9	0.14	0.95	0.00
29	Petroleum and coal	8	−0.54	1.06	0.04	9	1.45	0.71	0.37
30	Rubber	10	0.83	0.29	0.50	9	1.48	0.88	0.29
31	Leather	13	0.95	0.29	0.50	9	0.89	0.27	0.62
32	Stone, clay and glass	21	0.59	0.25	0.22	9	0.32	0.46	0.06
33	Primary metals	22	0.92	0.24	0.42	9	1.87	1.25	0.24
34	Fabricated metals	22	0.78	0.24	0.34	8	0.80	0.30	0.55
35	Non-electrical machinery	19	0.31	0.21	0.12	9	0.63	0.45	0.22
36	Electrical machinery	13	1.26	0.33	0.57	9	0.37	0.54	0.06
37	Transportation equipment	18	2.04	0.49	0.52	9	0.06	0.82	0.00

Source: See text notes 14 and 15 and text, pp. 234 and 236.

of employees (total) and the wage was obtained as in Table 1. The Minasian sample consists of states rather than census regions, and is subject to a similar cut-off restriction. Minasian uses man-hours of production workers as his labor variable. He experiments with two definitions of w_i. The one on which results in Table 2 are based was obtained by dividing L_i into the production worker wage bill. Minasian obtains estimates for several years, but the estimates shown in Table 2 are for 1957.

These tables show three sets of estimates with (in many cases) essentially the same parameters. Since the primary goal of this chapter is to obtain the "best" time series estimates of these same parameters, it would be helpful if it could first be determined which of these sets is the "best" set of cross-sectional estimates, in order to facilitate comparison of the two types of evidence. I believe there can be little question that the estimates of Minasian are superior to the other two sets, particularly with respect to estimates of parameters in a U.S. production function. The Solow estimates for the United States rest on essentially the same data as Minasian's, and Minasian's have the overwhelming advantage of having standard errors small enough to discriminate between hypotheses of interest. The all-inclusive labor definition used by Solow is, I think, preferable for the present purposes,[16] but this choice is not of major quantitative importance.

Considerations of statistical significance in turn favor the estimates of Table 1 over those of Minasian in Table 2, not because the former is based on a larger sample but because of the enormous range of the independent variable in the international sample. For this comparison, however, the question of the relative applicability of the model to the two samples is the crucial one.

Bias in Cross-Sectional Estimates

Three possibly important sources of bias in the above estimates, all of which will be seen to fit into a single statistical framework, will be discussed here. First, note that the constant term of equa-

---

[16] For all practical purposes, equation (5) must be derived from a two-input production function (although McKinnon, cited below, derives it from a particular type of n-input model) so that if non-production workers are excluded from the labor variable, they must be "taken care of" in a manner similar to the way materials are handled. That is, it must be assumed that non-production workers are used in fixed proportion to production workers, output, or physical capital, or that they are perfectly substitutable for physical capital.

tion (5) contains the term $(1 - \sigma) \log (\gamma)$, so that an estimate of equation (5) as it stands assumes that the "efficiency parameter," γ, is a constant across observations. If this assumption is false, equation (5) should be replaced by

(6) $\quad \log (V_i/L_i) = \log [(1 - \delta)^{-\sigma} p^{1-\sigma}] + \sigma \log (w_i)$
$\qquad\qquad\qquad\qquad\qquad + (1 - \sigma) \log (\gamma_i) + u_i.$

Second, recall that in passing from equation (2) to equation (5), output price, p_i, was assumed to be constant in cross-sectional analysis. If this does not hold, equation (5) must be replaced by

(7) $\quad \log (V_i/L_i) = \log [\gamma^{1-\sigma} (1 - \delta)^{-\sigma}] + \sigma \log (w_i)$
$\qquad\qquad\qquad\qquad\qquad + (1 - \sigma) \log (p_i) + u_i.$

Finally, observe that whether the labor input is measured in man-hours or number of employees, estimation of equation (5) assumes that the quality of a unit of labor does not vary. Alternatively, suppose that the "true" labor input in area i is L_i^*, and that the observed data are for

$$\log (L_i) = \log (L_i^*) - v_i,$$

where v_i is an unknown parameter, depending on i. Since w_i is defined as the wage bill (assumed to be correctly measured) divided by measured L_i,[17] then

$$\log (w_i) = \log (w_i^*) + v_i,$$

where w_i^* is the true wage rate. Equation (5) should therefore read

(8) $\quad \log (V_i/L_i) = \log [\gamma^{1-\sigma} (1 - \delta)^{-\sigma} p^{1-\sigma}] + \sigma \log (w_i)$
$\qquad\qquad\qquad\qquad\qquad + (1 - \sigma) v_i + u_i.$

Each of these three sources of bias can thus be reduced to the hypothesis that a variable ($\log (\gamma_i)$, $\log (p_i)$, or v_i) has been incorrectly omitted from the right side of equation (5). If the estimate of σ obtained from fitting equation (5) is denoted by σ_1, and the estimate which would have been obtained by fitting the correctly specified equation is denoted by σ_2, then as a computational identity,

$$\sigma_1 - \sigma_2 = (1 - \sigma_2) b_{xw},$$

where b_{xw} is the simple regression coefficient of the left out variable

---

[17] In some of his regressions, Minasian uses a wage variable not actually computed as wage bill divided by labor input, in the hope that measurement error of this type will be avoided. It is clear, however, that as long as the error under consideration arises from genuine variation in labor quality, any wage measure not explicitly corrected for quality will be defective.

(say x_i) on the log of the wage rate, w_i. Regarding both x_i and w_i as parameters, expectations may be taken to obtain

$$E(\sigma_1) = \sigma + (1 - \sigma)b_{xw}. \tag{9}$$

Estimates of σ obtained from equation (5) will therefore be biased toward unity if the "left out variable" is positively correlated (in the particular sample) with the wage rate, and biased away from unity if this correlation is negative.

For the case of variation in the neutral efficiency parameter, equation (6), there is no obvious a priori argument on the sign of the term b_{xw} which is at the same time consistent with the model used. For the U.S. regressions, it seems reasonable to suppose that variation in γ is unimportant. For the international sample, however, Arrow, Chenery, Minhas, and Solow offer evidence that γ does vary across countries, and that it is positively correlated with wages.[18] This fact, as the authors recognize, implies a bias toward a value of one in the estimates.

To analyze deviations from the assumption of constant price, where equation (7) is the correct specification, the model needs to be elaborated. If the entire nation (or world!) is not a single, perfect market for all manufactured goods, with no transportation costs, the way in which the separate markets are in fact related must be specified. This is of course a difficult problem in full generality, but some information may be obtained from an examination of a case at the opposite extreme from the "single market model." Suppose that each region constitutes a market separate from all the others, and suppose in addition that capital rental prices, r_i, are uncorrelated with wage rates. Then, from the Allen model,

$$E(b_{xw}) = E\left[\frac{\partial \log (p_i)}{\partial \log (w_i)}\right] = \bar{S}_L,$$

where $\bar{S}_L$ is an average share of labor for the industry. Then as a large sample approximation to the bias,

$$\sigma_1 = \sigma + \bar{S}_L(1 - \sigma).$$

Since labor's share for most industries varies between 0.5 and 0.8, variation in p_i may induce a substantial bias toward 1.0. As in the first case, this source of bias might be expected to be far more serious in the international sample than in the U.S. sample.

[18] Arrow and others, "Capital-Labor Substitution," Table 3, p. 235, and associated text.

For the case of quality variation in the labor and wage variables, if S_{vw} denotes the sample moment of the log of the measured wage and the "error" v_i, and so forth, then

$$b_{xw} = \frac{S_{vw}}{S_w^2} = \frac{S_{vw}^* + S_v^2}{S_w^2}.$$

If the errors in each sample are assumed to be uncorrelated with the true wage, w^*, the case can be reduced to

$$b_{xw} = S_v^2/S_w^2,$$

which, as a ratio of sample variances, is positive. Thus error in the labor variable, satisfying the above assumptions, provides a third possible bias toward unity. One might suppose that this bias, as well, is more serious for the international estimates, since presumably labor quality varies more widely over this sample. However, the relevant quantity is the *fraction* of total observed wage variation accounted for by variation in quality. It is difficult to say anything about this ratio, whether each sample is considered separately or the two are compared. It does seem safe, however, to guess that among the biases discussed, quality variation is probably more important in the U.S. samples, relative to the other two sources of bias, than it is in the international sample.

To summarize the preceding paragraphs, it may be concluded that all estimates in Tables 1 and 2 suffer from biases which derive from several sources. Both casual observation and supplementary evidence presented by Arrow, Chenery, Minhas, and Solow indicate that these biases are far more serious in the estimates shown in Table 1 than in those shown in Table 2. That these biases do not tell the whole story, however, is evident from a comparison of the two tables. In fact, it is clear that correction for the hypothetical biases discussed above will further separate the two sets of estimates. Without supporting the claim with formal argument, I would suggest, however, that for most of the industries in the international sample, there is little justification for supposing the cross-sectional model to be even approximately correct. In particular, for many industries in the sample, the product markets for the various countries will not be even loosely connected. When added to the preceding analysis, this criticism—which would of course be empty if no other cross-sectional estimates existed—seems to me sufficient reason for discarding the estimates in Table 1 in favor of the Minasian estimates shown in Table 2.

I mentioned in passing, above, the possibility of deriving implications from a complete cross-sectional model containing equation (5) as one of its equations. The appropriate specification of such a model is not obvious, however. Since the demand curve facing each region is assumed to be horizontal, the Hicks-Allen theory does not determine regional output. This fact gives no justification whatever for the assumption that Q_i is exogenous, since it is simply an expression of our ignorance about the statistical properties of Q_i. Nevertheless, if this assumption is made, the addition of a production function completes a model whose endogenous variables are L_i and K_i, and whose exogenous variables are Q_i and w_i. (Product price, p, is not a variable at all here.) Equation (5) is one of the two reduced form equations of this model. If, as would seem appropriate, the marginal productivity of capital condition is added as a third equation, then the rental price of capital is defined to be *endogenous* to the model. This fact is not recognized at all by Minasian, who believes the *constancy* of r_i to be a necessary assumption in his model, and its implications are not well developed by Arrow, Chenery, Minhas, and Solow.

Evidently, under competition, r_i will not be determined in any economic sense by the actions of a single industry in the *i*th region. What then is the economic meaning of the endogeneity of r_i? A horizontal demand curve has been postulated for each region, so that the cost curves (also horizontal) for all regions with non-zero output must coincide with one another. Since wages are observed to vary across regions, the fact that an industry exists in more than one region implies that capital prices must vary in a "compensating" manner so as to leave marginal and average costs the same in these regions. There are no economic forces tending to make r_i compensate in this way, but unless r_i does so by chance, a non-zero output will be observed in one region only. The implications of what may be called the "full equilibrium" cross-sectional model cannot be developed precisely without more theorizing of an adjustment or frictional type. Nevertheless it seems fair to conclude that if this model holds for an industry, one would not expect to observe more than, say, a half dozen states producing in a given year. Yet the number of observations used by Minasian ranges from eight in tobacco and in petroleum to twenty-five in printing and publishing and thirty-one in food and kindred products. To conclude this line of argument, it has been pointed out that there are strong reasons for suspecting that industry composition varies quite significantly among states, and, to make matters worse, this problem will be more serious the more closely the critical assumption of constant price applies to an industry.

Supplementary Cross-Sectional Tests

In the preceding part of this section, a rather general "left out variable" model was proposed which permitted the derivation of signs for certain types of biases in cross-sectional estimates. In general, however, little was said about the quantitative importance of these biases. Similarly, it was argued that variation in industry composition among states was a possibly important source of bias, but no statement was made about the size or direction of this bias. Thoroughgoing testing of these hypotheses is beyond the scope of this study, and in some cases cannot be carried out, given existing data; but for purposes of both illustration and support, two "spot checks" of these arguments are discussed below.

It has been seen that equation (5) can usefully be generalized to

(10) $\qquad \log(V_i/L_i) = \alpha + \sigma \log(w_i) + \beta_i + u_i,$

where w_i and u_i are distributed as in the section above, and where $\beta_1, \ldots, \beta_N$ are unknown parameters. Since equation (10) has a constant term, α, β_N is set equal to zero. Clearly, equation (10) cannot be estimated from a single cross-sectional sample, but suppose there are T observations on the same sample of N, each at a different point in time. Suppose in addition that the "state constants" or "errors," β_i, do not vary over time. Then there are NT observations, where for the observation of the ith state in year t,

(11) $\qquad \log(Q_{it}/L_{it}) = \alpha + \sigma \log(w_{it}/p_t) + \sum_{j=1}^{N-1} \beta_j x^j_{it} + u_{it}.$

It is assumed that the u_{it} ($i = 1, \ldots, N$; $t = 1, \ldots, T$) are independent and identically distributed, with mean zero and variance τ^2. The x^j_{it}, $j = 1, \ldots, N-1$, are $N-1$ "dummy variables":

$$x^j_{it} = \begin{matrix} 1 \text{ for } i = j \\ 0 \text{ otherwise.} \end{matrix}$$

Note that in considering observations at two or more points in time, deflation by p_t is necessary. The assumption that p_t does not vary cross-sectionally is retained.[19] Neglecting for the moment complica-

---

[19] Actually, with the introduction of the β_i, this assumption can be relaxed to permit p_t to vary cross-sectionally, as long as relative regional prices do not change over time. The assumption that the demand curve facing each region be horizontal must be retained.

tions introduced by the inclusion of p_t, it can be seen that equation (11) is a standard analysis-of-covariance model.[20]

A difficulty with this model is that, as noted previously, p_t is properly considered an endogenous variable (is not independent of u_{it}) so that the usual finite sample theory does not apply. It can be shown, however, using a log-linear approximation to the supply curves for the individual states, that under certain conditions estimates of σ obtained from equation (11) are consistent, in the sense that for fixed T

$$\plim_{N \to \infty} \hat{\sigma} = \sigma\text{[21]}$$

This model has been used to test the hypothesis that $\beta_i = 0$, which underlies the Minasian regressions. The chemical and allied products industry (SIC 28), for which Minasian obtained an elasticity of roughly unity in all his tests, is the first examined. The data used are from the Census of Manufactures for the years 1947, 1954, and 1958. Minasian's sample consisted of twenty-four states. Here a sample of twenty-five has been used, yielding seventy-five observations in all. Table 3 contains results for the following regression equations:

(12) $\log (Q_{it}/L_{it}) = \alpha + \sigma \log (w_{it}/p_t) + u_{it}$
(13) $\log (Q_{it}/L_{it}) = \alpha + \sigma \log (w_{it}/p_t) +$ "time dummies" $+ u_t$
(14) $\log (Q_{it}/L_{it}) = \alpha + \sigma \log (w_{it}/p_t) +$ "time dummies"
$\qquad\qquad\qquad\qquad\qquad\qquad\qquad\qquad +$ "state dummies" $+ u_{it}$

Equation (12) was estimated for each year separately, while equations (13) and (14) were estimated for the pooled sample.

The F-statistic for testing the hypothesis that $\beta_1 = \ldots = \beta_{N-1} = 0$ is

$$F = 6.945,$$

which may be compared to

$$F_{.01;\ 24,\ 49} = 2.21.$$

This F-test is of course only approximate in this application.

While this test establishes conclusively the existence of non-zero "state effects" for this particular industry, its implications for the elasticity of substitution estimates are not so clear. In the first place, as is always true when dummy variables are used, one cannot be

[20] See, for example, Henry Scheffé, *The Analysis of Variance* (Wiley, 1959), Chap. 6.
[21] See my Ph.D. thesis (University of Chicago, 1963), App., Chap. 3.

TABLE 3. Elasticities of Substitution Between Labor and Capital, Using Cross-Sectional Tests and Time Series Data, Chemical and Allied Products Industry, Twenty-five States, 1947, 1954, and 1958

Equation	Year	Elasticity σ	Standard error	Coefficient of determination R^2
(12)	1947	1.146	0.313	0.368
(12)	1954	1.204	0.276	0.453
(12)	1958	0.994	0.324	0.290
(13)	1947, 1954, 1958 (pooled)	1.128	0.173	0.767
(14)	1947, 1954, 1958 (pooled)	1.351	0.325	0.947

Source: U.S. *Census of Manufactures*, 1947, 1954, 1958, and sources given in the Appendix to this chapter.

sure what economic significance to attach to the state effects. Second, while the effect of including state dummies on the elasticity estimate worked in the predicted direction (away from unity), the "bias" thus discovered is not significant. In other words, while the state effects "left out" of equation (12) were significant, they were not highly correlated with the wage rate.

Evidence of variation among states in industry composition has not yet been examined. An obvious source of information on this subject would be elasticity estimates for the three- or four-digit components of a two-digit industry appearing in Table 2. If industry composition is not highly variable, the two-digit estimate should fall somewhere in the middle of the component estimates. Minasian has conducted several such tests, and reports that the general order of magnitude of the three-digit estimates is the same as that of the two-digit estimates. Reviewing these results, two-digit industry by two-digit industry, one finds that the aggregate estimates are in general close to the component estimates. However, for one of the highest Minasian elasticities, obtained for transportation equipment in 1957, the following results were obtained:

SIC Number	Industry	σ
37	Transportation equipment, total	2.04
371	Motor vehicles and equipment	1.47
372	Aircraft and parts	−0.08
373	Ship and boat building and repairing	0.69

Another industry for which Minasian finds high elasticities is tobacco (SIC 21). This industry exists in few states, and for none of its three-digit components do enough observations exist for a test of the above type. From examination of the census industry maps, however, it appears that in three states, Virginia, North Carolina, and Kentucky, the tobacco industry is largely cigarette manufacturing, while in the remaining states it contains virtually no cigarette production. Since cigarette manufacturing is much more capital intensive than the other components, there is reason to suspect that the estimates for this industry are biased. To test this hypothesis, equations (13) and (14) were estimated for tobacco, for the years 1947, 1954, and 1958. In addition, a new variable was added to these equations: z_{it} = value added, cigarettes only, divided by total value added for tobacco. Since value added for cigarettes is given only for the above three states, z_{it} was defined to be zero for the other states. A total of eleven states was used, but since for some years figures for some states are omitted by the census to protect individual firms, the pooled sample size was only twenty-eight. (See Table 4.)

Table 4 shows two striking results. First, as conjectured, the inclusion of the "industry composition variable," z_{it}, does lower the elasticity estimate significantly—compare the two versions of equation (14). Second, inclusion of the state dummies in this instance also lowers the elasticity estimate—compare equations (13) and (14), with or without z_{it}. Finally, note that when the state dummies and z_{it} are used together, they tend to reinforce each other.

TABLE 4. Cross-Sectional Tests and Time Series of Elasticities of Substitution Between Labor and Capital, Tobacco Industry, Eleven States, 1947, 1954, and 1958 Pooled

Equation	Value added variable: cigarettes/total tobacco z_{it}	Elasticity σ	Standard error	Coefficient of z_{it}	Standard error of coefficient of z_{it}	Coefficient of determination R^2
(13)	Excluded	3.508	0.443	—	—	0.725
(14)	Excluded	2.289	0.420	—	—	0.978
(13)	Included	2.673	0.470	0.207	0.068	0.804
(14)	Included	1.409	0.225	0.903	0.223	0.987

Source: U.S. *Census of Manufactures*, 1947, 1954, 1958, and sources given in the Appendix to this chapter.

The estimate for tobacco of 1.409 is still well above unity, and further still above the time series estimates presented on p. 250. Nevertheless, the fact that use of these crude methods reduces the estimate from 3.5 to 1.4 is extremely encouraging. Recall that the analysis of bias above indicated that equations such as (14) should yield estimates farther from 1 than equations such as (13), which do not allow for variation across states in efficiency, labor quality, or output price. This conclusion received some confirmation from the experiment with chemicals in Table 3. The experiment with tobacco essentially destroys it. At the close of the discussion of bias, it appeared that no cross-sectional bias discussed could contribute to the reconciliation of time series and cross-sectional evidence. Reconciliation has not been achieved here, but it has been seen that the biases discussed can work in either direction, and that their effects can be large.

Time Series Estimates of Elasticities of Substitution

Among existing studies of factor substitution, the one most directly comparable to the present chapter is the study of postwar time series by McKinnon.[22] McKinnon estimates:

(15) $\log(Q_t/L_t) = \pi_0 + \pi_1 \log(w_t/p_t) + \pi_2 t + \pi_3 \log(Q_{t-1}/L_{t-1}) + u_t$.

The data used are comparable to, though not identical with, the series discussed in the following section. Equation (15) is related to equation (4) by an adjustment hypothesis of the Koyck[23] type so that $\pi_1/(1 - \pi_3)$ provides an estimate of σ. The results are shown in Table 5.

The general picture afforded by Table 5 (elasticity estimates below unity, and often below one-half) is very similar to that which emerges from the discussion of time series estimates, below. In a sense, then, this study can be viewed as a confirmation of McKinnon's results, based on a larger sample (twenty-eight to thirty observations as opposed to eleven). As McKinnon notes, however, the inclusion of

[22] Ronald I. McKinnon, "Wages, Capital Costs, and Employment in Manufacturing: a Model Applied to 1947–58 U.S. Data," *Econometrica*, Vol. 30 (July 1962), pp. 501–21.

[23] L. M. Koyck, *Distributed Lags and Investment Analysis* (Amsterdam, North Holland-Publishing Co., 1954), Chap. 2.

TABLE 5. Elasticities of Substitution Between Labor and Capital by McKinnon, Using Time Series Data, Eighteen U.S. Industries, 1947–58[a]

Industry	Regression coefficient π_1	π_2	π_3	Elasticity σ	Coefficient of determination R^2
Food	0.216 (0.221)	0.378 (0.378)	0.419 (0.326)	0.373	0.977
Tobacco	0.603 (0.317)	−0.240 (0.556)	0.345 (0.297)	0.921	0.902
Textiles	0.112 (0.092)	0.860 (0.568)	0.309 (0.323)	0.162	0.988
Apparel	0.607 (0.150)	0.024 (0.203)	0.125 (0.215)	0.694	0.927
Lumber and wood	0.613 (0.262)	−0.016 (0.909)	0.236 (0.322)	0.802	0.962
Furniture and fixtures	0.720 (0.161)	−0.158 (0.313)	0.296 (0.178)	1.021	0.959
Paper	0.077 (0.357)	0.907 (1.161)	0.178 (0.578)	0.094	0.911
Printing	0.639 (0.364)	−0.051 (0.294)	0.244 (0.284)	0.844	0.922
Chemicals	−0.617 (0.599)	2.602 (0.886)	0.444 (0.310)	−1.109	0.948
Rubber	0.222 (0.046)	0.422 (0.098)	0.372 (0.091)	0.354	0.994
Leather	0.168 (0.112)	0.470 (0.351)	0.330 (0.294)	0.251	0.958
Stone, clay, and glass	−0.423 (0.304)	0.798 (0.382)	0.623 (0.349)	−1.124	0.943
Primary metals	0.040 (0.483)	0.838 (0.665)	−0.233 (0.503)	0.033	0.526
Fabricated metals	0.231 (0.050)	0.104 (0.092)	0.296 (0.173)	0.328	0.904
Non-electrical machinery	0.384 (0.245)	−0.103 (0.260)	0.491 (0.245)	0.754	0.764
Electrical machinery	0.406 (0.185)	0.627 (0.741)	0.060 (0.398)	0.432	0.924
Transportation equipment	0.157 (0.319)	0.954 (0.292)	0.137 (0.360)	0.182	0.800
Instruments	0.519 (0.099)	1.439 (0.283)	−0.371 (0.158)	0.379	0.989

Source: Ronald I. McKinnon, "Wages, Capital Costs, and Employment in Manufacturing: A Model Applied to 1947–58 U.S. Data," *Econometrica*, Vol. 30 (July 1962), p. 518.
[a] Numbers in parentheses are standard errors of the coefficients.

the lagged dependent variable, log (Q_{t-1}/L_{t-1}), on the right side of equation (15) implies that estimates of π_1, π_2, and π_3 will be biased for small samples, and in addition, if serial correlation is present in the u_t, these estimates will not even be consistent. Also, as McKinnon does not appear to recognize, product price is also an endogenous variable, so that even in the absence of serial correlation, least squares estimation of equation (15) will not yield consistent estimates. Fortunately, there are many possible lag hypotheses besides those which underly equation (15) and, as will be seen below, several of these perform more satisfactorily than does equation (15).

Time Series Estimates

This section presents the evidence, based on time series data, of substitution in manufacturing. Although most of the evidence here is based on estimation of equation (4), it may be of interest to preface this discussion with an informal look at the trends, from 1929 to 1957, in factor quantities and prices. It was pointed out in the section on theoretical background that if an industry operates under constant returns to scale, if factor markets are competitive, if the elasticity of substitution (σ) is a constant, and if technological change is neutral, then between any two equilibrium points,

$$\sigma = \frac{\Delta \log (K/L)}{\Delta \log (w/r)}.$$

The first two columns of Table 6 present the numerator and denominator, respectively, of this fraction, in which Δ denotes the change from 1929 to 1957. Logs are to the base ten so that, for example, a doubling of K/L yields 0.301; a 50 percent rise, 0.176; a halving, -0.301; and a decline by one-third, -0.176. The labor quantity and price figures are derived by the method shown in the appendix. The capital quantities are end-of-period stocks taken from Creamer's studies.[24] They include both fixed and working capital. The capital price, r, is a rental price, gross of both taxes and depreciation, ob-

[24] The 1929 figures are from Daniel B. Creamer, Sergei P. Dobrovolsky, and Israel Borenstein, *Capital in Manufacturing and Mining: Its Formation and Financing* (Princeton University Press for the National Bureau of Economic Research, 1960), Table A–8. The 1957 figures are from Daniel Creamer, *Capital Expansion and Capacity in Postwar Manufacturing* (New York: National Industrial Conference Board, 1961), Tables G–1 and G–2.

248 Labor-Capital Substitution in Manufacturing

TABLE 6. Trends in Factor Quantities and Prices, Fourteen U.S. Industries, 1929–57

Industry	Capital-labor ratios $\Delta \log (K/L)$ (1)	Wages-capital cost ratios $\Delta \log (w/r)$ (2)	Changes in relative factor shares[a] $\Delta \log \left(\dfrac{S_L}{S_K}\right)$ (3)	Elasticity of substitution[b] σ (4)	Deviation of 10 percent in elasticity[c] σ min (5)	σ max (6)
Food	0.072	0.185	0.113	0.39	0.14	0.79
Tobacco	0.477	0.286	−0.191	1.67	1.33	2.11
Textiles	0.168	0.381	0.213	0.44	0.30	0.62
Wood	0.000	−0.036	−0.036	0.00	−0.53	8.47
Paper	0.028	0.048	0.020	0.58	−0.15	10.37
Printing	−0.062	0.050	0.112	−1.24	−2.36	−1.13
Chemicals	0.123	0.191	0.068	0.64	0.35	1.10
Petroleum	0.238	0.650	0.412	0.37	0.28	0.46
Rubber	0.070	0.080	0.010	0.88	0.24	2.92
Leather	−0.038	0.250	0.288	−0.15	−0.27	0.01
Stone, clay, and glass	−0.009	−0.114	−0.105	0.08	−0.21	0.69
Metals	0.048	0.190	0.142	0.25	0.03	0.60
Machinery	0.074	0.152	0.078	0.49	0.17	1.04
Automobiles	0.214	0.048	−0.166	4.46	1.93	39.26

Source: See text note 24 and Appendix to this chapter.
[a] Column 2 minus column 1.
[b] Column 1 divided by column 2.
[c] Assuming the measured ratios deviate by 10 percent below (min) or 10 percent above (max) their equilibrium values.

tained by dividing K into the gross return to capital (gross value added minus compensation of employees). The third column of Table 6 shows the change in relative factor shares, or

$$\Delta \log (S_L/S_K).$$

This column is simply the difference between columns 2 and 1.

The division of column 1 by column 2 produces the estimates of σ shown in the fourth column. This is equivalent to obtaining the slope of a line in the plane using the coordinates of two points lying *exactly* on the line. Since 1929 and 1957 are both cycle peaks, one may hope that if they do not lie exactly on the line, they will deviate from it in a similar way so that the estimates of σ are not widely incorrect. A measure of the relative reliability of the numbers in column 4 is obtained by supposing that the measured ratios deviate from their equilibrium values by less than 10 percent. This assumption yields bounds on σ which are presented in columns 5 and 6.

The information contained in this table is not very reliable, as anyone familiar with problems of comparing factor quantities at widely separated points in time will realize. Nevertheless, it lends support to a few generalizations. From the first two columns, it can be seen that capital labor ratios have, for the most part, risen over the period from 1929 to 1957 and that wages have risen more rapidly than have capital costs. From column 3, it is clear that relative shares have by no means remained constant over this period, and that in ten of fourteen industries, labor's share has risen. Column 4 shows that the estimated elasticities are generally between zero and one, or that a given percentage change in w/r has, for ten of fourteen industries, given rise to a *smaller* percentage change in K/L, in the same direction. For two industries, tobacco and automobiles, the percentage change is greater than one. These observations must be qualified by noting that for five industries—wood, paper, printing, rubber, and automobiles—the change in w/r has been so small that the trends yield essentially no information.

The remainder of this section is concerned with the estimation of equation (4), repeated here for reference:

(16) $\qquad \log(Q_t/L_t) = A + \sigma \log(w_t^*/p_t^*) + (1 + \sigma)\lambda t + \eta_t.$

Recall that w_t^* and p_t^* are "anticipated" prices, assumed to depend in an unknown way on prices in periods $t, t-1, t-2, \ldots$. The data used are the time series (1929–57) for individual industries described in the preceding section.

Two Simple Versions of Equation (16)

In the section on theory, above, it was noted that the statistical properties of least squares estimates of σ obtained from equation (16) depend critically on whether or not firms take current wages and prices into account in making input and output decisions. It was also observed that it is not possible to answer this question using single equation methods. Accordingly, we continue to "hedge" on this issue by estimating the simplest regression equation corresponding to each of these two hypotheses. If firms *do* utilize the current wage-price ratio, the simplest assumption is that $(w_t^*/p_t^*) = (w_t/p_t)$, and equation (16) becomes

(17) $\qquad\qquad y_t = A + \sigma x_t + (1 - \sigma)\lambda t + \eta_t,$

TABLE 7. Elasticities of Substitution Using Wages and Prices, Current and Past, Fourteen U.S. Industries, 1931–58[a]

	Coefficients based on					
	Current wage-price ratios[b]			Past wage-price ratios[c]		
Industry	Elasticity x_t	Trend t	Coefficient of determination R^2	Elasticity x_{t-1}	Trend t	Coefficient of determination R^2
Food	0.397 (0.056)	0.101 (0.001)	0.971	0.235 (0.085)	0.013 (0.002)	0.934
Tobacco	0.152 (0.050)	0.031 (0.003)	0.956	0.089 (0.055)	0.033 (0.003)	0.945
Textiles	0.131 (0.063)	0.017 (0.001)	0.957	0.070 (0.061)	0.018 (0.001)	0.952
Wood	0.480 (0.068)	0.009 (0.001)	0.800	0.418 (0.093)	0.010 (0.002)	0.673
Paper	0.505 (0.098)	0.008 (0.001)	0.793	0.599 (0.076)	0.008 (0.001)	0.876
Printing	0.488 (0.069)	0.008 (0.001)	0.921	0.477 (0.065)	0.008 (0.001)	0.924
Chemicals	0.678 (0.089)	0.012 (0.003)	0.975	0.368 (0.150)	0.022 (0.005)	0.934
Petroleum	0.375 (0.068)	0.011 (0.002)	0.852	0.154 (0.076)	0.014 (0.002)	0.719
Rubber	0.323 (0.062)	0.018 (0.002)	0.927	0.286 (0.064)	0.018 (0.002)	0.915
Leather	0.407 (0.095)	0.007 (0.001)	0.797	0.320 (0.088)	0.007 (0.001)	0.769
Stone, clay, and glass	−0.205 (0.107)	0.029 (0.002)	0.956	−0.273 (0.101)	0.030 (0.002)	0.961
Metals	0.641 (0.193)	0.008 (0.002)	0.600	0.422 (0.215)	0.010 (0.003)	0.501
Machinery	0.476 (0.152)	0.013 (0.003)	0.780	0.175 (0.173)	0.017 (0.004)	0.706
Automobiles	0.730 (0.094)	0.018 (0.004)	0.796	0.486 (0.144)	0.019 (0.006)	0.521

Source: Based on data from U.S. *Census of Manufactures*. Also see the Appendix to this chapter.
[a] Numbers in parentheses are the standard errors of the coefficients.
[b] Equation (17).
[c] Equation (18).

where $y_t = \log(Q_t/L_t)$ and $x_t = \log(w_t/p_t)$. Similarly, if firms utilize only past prices, it can be assumed that $x_t^* = x_{t-1}$, and thus

(18) $$y_t = A + \sigma x_{t-1} + (1-\sigma)\lambda t + \eta_t.$$

In both equation (17) and equation (18), η_t is assumed to have the properties discussed in the part of the section on theory, above, which deals with statistical formulation.

Results of fitting these equations are shown in Table 7. In the first three columns are reported the coefficients of x_t and t in equation (17), and the associated multiple correlation coefficient (uncorrected for degrees of freedom). Standard errors appear in parentheses, below the corresponding estimated coefficients. In the second three columns, results of fitting equation (18) are shown. In each case, the coefficient of x_t (or x_{t-1}) is the estimate of the elasticity of substitution, σ, for the industry.

Some of the results in Table 7 are supplanted below by results from superior regression equations, but on the whole, the picture given in this table is only slightly revised when more sophisticated techniques are used. Up to this point, the differences between equations (17) and (18) have been emphasized, and for some industries (notably chemicals, metals, machinery, and automobiles), the differences in estimated elasticities appear to be considerable. The striking feature of these regressions, however, is the difference between *either* equation (17) or equation (18) and the cross-sectional estimates made by Minasian and shown in Table 2. For all but one or possibly two industries, the time series estimate is less than the corresponding cross-sectional estimate.[25] Whereas unity appears to be a central value in the U.S. cross-sectional tests, the time series estimates are centered in the range from 0.3 to 0.5. The rest of this section is devoted to a search for possible downward bias in these time series estimates, of sufficient magnitude to reconcile the difference between the two sets of estimates.

Tests of Lagged Adjustment Hypotheses

As noted at the beginning of this chapter, the frequency with which hypotheses of lagged adjustment have been used to reconcile divergent time series and cross-sectional estimates makes the testing

---

[25] In many cases, the corresponding cross-sectional estimate must be a weighted average of two Minasian estimates.

of such hypotheses a natural sequel to the estimation of time series results. A word about why such hypotheses might be expected to achieve this reconciliation is perhaps in order. Suppose the firms in an industry are reluctant to revise their methods of production on the basis of recent and possibly transitory changes in factor and product prices, preferring to postpone some of the adjustment in factor quantities until these changes persist over several months or years. In this case, the relevant price variables for the marginal productivity condition in equation (16)—that is, w_t^* and p_t^*—will not be any single, actual values (such as w_t or w_{t-1}) but rather a *weighted average* of actual values over several past periods. By hypothesis, these series of weighted averages will be "smoother" than the corresponding series of actual values. What appears in equations such as (17) to be a "small" reaction of quantities to changes in the relatively volatile actual price series, may in fact be a "large" reaction to changes in the smoother and more relevant series of weighted averages. Since relative prices across states do not vary widely over short periods of time, this downward bias should not affect the cross-sectional estimates.

To examine this question, a more general regression equation must be postulated, which permits both the estimated elasticity and the above mentioned weights to be determined by the data. In doing so, it is assumed that w_t^* and p_t^* do *not* depend on the current values, w_t and p_t, so that the desired regression equation is a generalization of equation (18) rather than of equation (17). This decision is not substantively critical, and it will help to avoid the unnecessary duplication which is required by a symmetrical treatment of these two assumptions. To simplify the writing, the constant A and the trend term, $(1 - \sigma)\lambda t$, are suppressed, and[26]

$$P_t = \log(p_t) \quad \text{and} \quad W_t = \log(w_t).$$

Then, for example, equation (16) becomes

(19) $$y_t = \sigma x_t^* + \eta_t.$$

An adjustment hypothesis which is more than adequate for present purposes is the assumption that W_t^* and P_t^* are each weighted

---

[26] In practice, whenever P_t or W_t is not used in ratio form, it has been deflated by the implicit deflator for GNP. In economic terms, this means that one assumes that equation (20) describes the way in which expectations about relative prices are formed, while changes in the general price level are perfectly anticipated.

averages, with weights summing to one, of actual values over the previous three periods:

(20)
$$P_t^* = (1 - a_1 - a_2)P_{t-1} + a_1 P_{t-2} + a_2 P_{t-3},$$
$$W_t^* = (1 - b_1 - b_2)W_{t-1} + b_1 W_{t-2} + b_2 W_{t-3}.$$

Note that it is not initially assumed that the weights for wage and price are the same (that $a_i = b_i$). An alternative form of equation (20) is

(21)
$$P_t^* = P_{t-1} - (a_1 + a_2)\Delta P_{t-1} - a_2 \Delta P_{t-2},$$
$$W_t^* = W_{t-1} - (b_1 + b_2)\Delta W_{t-1} - b_2 \Delta W_{t-2}.$$

The combination of equations (19) and (21) produces the desired "general" regression equation:

(22) $$y_t = \sigma x_{t-1} - \sigma(b_1 + b_2)\Delta W_{t-1} - \sigma b_2 \Delta W_{t-2} + \sigma(a_1 + a_2)\Delta P_{t-1} + \sigma a_2 \Delta P_{t-2} + \eta_t.$$

In what follows, it is assumed that equation (22) is the relevant equation. This assumption is highly plausible, for equation (22) is sufficiently "flexible" to ensure that no important bias is induced in the estimated substitution elasticities through the imposition of unwarranted restrictions on the form of the functions W^* and P^*.

If equation (22) is acceptable, then three successively more restrictive hypotheses can be tested. First, suppose that W_t^* and P_t^* are determined in the same way, so that $a_1 = b_1$, and $a_2 = b_2$. Then equation (22) becomes

(23) $$y_t = \sigma x_{t-1} - \sigma(a_1 + a_2)\Delta x_{t-1} \sigma a_2 \Delta x_{t-2} + \eta_t.$$

Further simplification is obtained if $a_2 = 0$,

(24) $$y_t = \sigma x_{t-1} - \sigma a_1 \Delta x_{t-1} + \eta_t,$$

and finally, if $a_1 = 0$, equation (18) recurs,

(25) $$y_t = \sigma x_{t-1} + \eta_t.$$

For testing equation (23) within equation (22)—that is, for testing $a_1 = b_1$ and $a_2 = b_2$ an approximate F-test is used, based on the statistic

$$F = \left[\frac{T-7}{2}\right] \times \left[\frac{\text{Residual } SS \text{ under equation (23)} - RSS \text{ under equation (22)}}{RSS \text{ under equation (22)}}\right].$$

TABLE 8. Test of Use of Lagged and Other Wage and Price Restrictions in Elasticity of Substitution Regressions, Fourteen U.S. Industries, 1932–58[a]

Industry	Statistic	
	F	t
Food	0.594	−0.602
Tobacco	1.618	−0.388
Textiles	0.336	1.628
Wood	2.480	−2.583
Paper	1.140	0.242
Printing	0.765	0.174
Chemicals	0.682	1.284
Petroleum	0.191	−1.297
Rubber	0.871	−0.384
Leather	0.705	−0.931
Stone, clay, and glass	0.031	0.738
Metals	0.705	−0.769
Machinery	28.635	1.564
Automobiles	7.023	1.149

Source: Based on data from U.S. *Census of Manufactures*. See also the Appendix to this chapter.
[a] Equations (22) and (23).

Since the introduction of lagged variables reduces the sample size to twenty-seven ($t = 32, \ldots, 58$), $T = 27$. Critical values are

$$F_{0.05;\ 2,\ 20} = 3.49, \text{ and}$$
$$F_{0.01;\ 2,\ 20} = 5.85.$$

Results of this test, for all fourteen industries, are shown in column 1 of Table 8. In the second column of this table are the *t*-statistics for testing equation (24) within equation (23). This test is simply a test of the significance of the coefficient of Δx_{t-2} in equation (23). A two-tail critical value is

$$t_{0.05;\ 22} = 2.086.$$

The first column of Table 8 indicates that for all but two, or possibly three, industries, equation (23) is acceptable. The results of estimating equation (22) for the three exceptional industries are shown in Table 9.

The results shown in Table 9 for the wood products industry display exactly the sort of behavior one might expect. The implied forms of W^* and P^* are

$$P_t^* = 0.172 P_{t-1} + 0.351 P_{t-2} + 0.477 P_{t-3},$$
$$W_t^* = 0.998 W_{t-1} + 0.354 W_{t-2} - 0.356 W_{t-3}.$$

TABLE 9. Test of Use of Lagged and Other Wage and Price Restrictions in Elasticity of Substitution Regressions, Three U.S. Industries, 1932–58[a]

Industry	Lagged wage-price ratios x_{t-1}	Elasticities using					Trend t	Coefficient of determination R^2
		Lagged wages		Lagged prices				
		ΔW_{t-1}	ΔW_{t-2}	ΔP_{t-1}	ΔP_{t-2}			
Wood	0.758 (0.098)	0.002 (0.392)	0.270 (0.368)	0.628 (0.131)	0.362 (0.115)		0.012 (0.001)	0.853
Machinery	−0.295 (0.117)	−0.057 (0.309)	−1.010 (0.296)	−0.891 (0.133)	−0.617 (0.150)		0.023 (0.002)	0.939
Automobiles	0.040 (0.152)	−1.102 (0.634)	−1.669 (0.617)	−0.611 (0.165)	−0.355 (0.179)		0.022 (0.005)	0.764

Source: Based on data in U.S. Bureau of the Census, *U.S. Census of Manufactures*, various issues. See also the Appendix to this chapter. Numbers in parentheses are the standard errors of the coefficients.
[a] Equation (22).

Given the standard errors for this regression, a plausible (though certainly not the only) interpretation might be that firms in this industry base their decisions for this period's inputs on last period's wage, plus an equally weighted average of product price for the last three periods. For the machinery industry, the negative estimate of the elasticity, σ, implies rejection of the model represented by equation (22), together, of course, with all more restrictive versions of equation (22). The odd pattern of weights estimated for automobiles leads to a suspicion that results for this industry may also be meaningless. This suspicion is confirmed below.

For the remaining eleven industries, interest may be restricted to equations (23), (24), and (25). Table 10 presents estimates of the latter two equations for all industries, together with estimates of equation (23) for those industries (textiles, wood, chemicals, petroleum, machinery, and automobiles) to which it may be relevant. Again, the coefficient of x_{t-1} in each case is the estimated elasticity of substitution.

For equations (24) and (25), the stone, clay, and glass industry shows negative elasticity estimates, implying rejection of the model for this industry. Of the remaining ten (that is, all except wood; stone, clay, and glass; machinery; and automobiles), seven industries (food, tobacco, textiles, printing, petroleum, rubber, and metals) show an insignificant coefficient for Δx_{t-1} in equation (24), as well as no significant improvement for still more complicated equations. For these seven, therefore, it may be concluded that equation (25) or equation (18) is the best of the four proposed equations. The chemicals and allied products industry shows a significantly positive coefficient for Δx_{t-1} in equation (24), although no higher lag terms are significant. Positive Δx_{t-1} coefficients are also obtained in this regression for machinery and automobiles. A positive coefficient here is easily interpreted as a tendency on the part of firms in the industry to extrapolate the *change in* the price ratio as opposed to the level. It does not imply instability of industry equilibrium. As Table 10 shows, a positive coefficient for Δx_{t-1} in equation (24) implies a lower elasticity estimate from equation (24) than from equation (25).

Only four industries (wood, paper, leather, and metals) bear significantly negative coefficients for Δx_{t-1} in equation (24). Of these, wood products also exhibits a significant Δx_{t-2} coefficient in equation (23). For these industries, the lagged adjustment hypothesis

TABLE 10. Test of Elasticities of Substitution Using Wage-Price Adjustment Patterns, Fourteen U.S. Industries, 1931–58[a]

		Elasticities using				Coefficient of determination R^2
Industry	Equation	Past wage-price ratios x_{t-1}	Change in past wage-price ratios Δx_{t-1}	Lagged wage-price ratios Δx_{t-2}	Trend t	
Food	(25)	0.235			0.013	0.934
		(0.085)			(0.002)	
	(24)	0.203	0.084		0.013	0.935
		(0.097)	(0.114)		(0.002)	
Tobacco	(25)	0.089			0.033	0.945
		(0.055)			(0.003)	
	(24)	0.068	0.047		0.034	0.946
		(0.064)	(0.069)		(0.003)	
Textiles	(25)	0.070			0.018	0.952
		(0.061)			(0.001)	
	(24)	0.073	−0.007		0.017	0.952
		(0.068)	(0.070)		(0.001)	
	(23)	−0.057	0.047	0.104	0.019	0.958
		(0.076)	(0.066)	(0.064)	(0.001)	
Wood	(25)	0.418			0.010	0.673
		(0.093)			(0.002)	
	(24)	0.543	−0.315		0.011	0.751
		(0.094)	(0.115)		(0.002)	
	(23)	0.657	−0.473	−0.271	0.012	0.817
		(0.093)	(0.118)	(0.105)	(0.001)	
Paper	(25)	0.599			0.008	0.876
		(0.076)			(0.001)	
	(24)	0.668	−0.286		0.007	0.910
		(0.070)	(0.094)		(0.001)	
Printing	(25)	0.477			0.008	0.924
		(0.065)			(0.001)	
	(24)	0.459	0.106		0.009	0.927
		(0.068)	(0.105)		(0.001)	
Chemicals	(25)	0.368			0.022	0.934
		(0.150)			(0.005)	
	(24)	0.190	0.521		0.028	0.952
		(0.142)	(0.170)		(0.005)	
	(23)	0.083	0.515	0.244	0.031	0.952
		(0.175)	(0.176)	(0.190)	(0.006)	
Petroleum	(25)	0.154			0.014	0.719
		(0.076)			(0.002)	
	(24)	0.143	0.084		0.014	0.727
		(0.078)	(0.097)		(0.003)	
	(23)	0.166	0.107	−0.138	0.013	0.696
		(0.108)	(0.099)	(0.106)	(0.003)	

Table continued on p. 258.

TABLE 10—Continued

Industry	Equation	Elasticities using Past wage-price ratios x_{t-1}	Change in past wage-price ratios Δx_{t-1}	Lagged wage-price ratios Δx_{t-2}	Trend t	Coefficient of determination R^2
Rubber	(25)	0.286 (0.064)			0.018 (0.002)	0.915
	(24)	0.311 (0.069)	−0.079 (0.082)		0.018 (0.002)	0.918
Leather	(25)	0.320 (0.088)			0.007 (0.001)	0.769
	(24)	0.479 (0.080)	−0.299 (0.074)		0.005 (0.001)	0.862
Stone, clay, and glass	(25)	−0.273 (0.101)			0.030 (0.002)	0.961
	(24)	−0.424 (0.130)	0.166 (0.095)		0.033 (0.003)	0.965
Metals	(25)	0.422 (0.215)			0.010 (0.003)	0.501
	(24)	0.563 (0.258)	−0.234 (0.238)		0.009 (0.003)	0.520
Machinery	(25)	0.175 (0.173)			0.017 (0.004)	0.706
	(24)	0.037 (0.171)	0.500 (0.219)		0.019 (0.003)	0.758
	(23)	−0.185 (0.218)	0.454 (0.222)	0.426 (0.272)	0.022 (0.004)	0.763
Automobiles	(25)	0.486 (0.144)			0.019 (0.006)	0.521
	(24)	0.367 (0.147)	0.381 (0.186)		0.020 (0.005)	0.592
	(23)	0.271 (0.173)	0.397 (0.189)	0.232 (0.202)	0.021 (0.006)	0.598

Source: Based on data from U.S. Bureau of the Census, *U.S. Census of Manufactures*. See also the Appendix to this chapter.

[a] 1932–58 for equation (23), which is included only for industries with significant, or nearly significant, coefficients for Δx_{t-2}. Numbers in parentheses are the standard errors of the coefficients.

works in the expected direction, and the elasticity estimates are revised from 0.418, 0.599, and 0.322 in equation (25) to 0.657, 0.668, and 0.479 in either equation (24) or equation (23).

With due regard for the differences between individual industries, it may be concluded from the preceding discussion that the adjustment hypotheses tested make essentially no contribution to the reconciling of time series and cross-sectional evidence of substitution. Since the regression equation used is simply a marginal productivity condition for labor, this finding is just another way of saying that labor is a variable input. For this reason, perhaps, such a finding should not come as a great surprise.

In addition to the regressions reported in Tables 7 through 10, a number of additional tests have been performed. Since these, in general, do not alter the picture given above, their results are not reported here in detail,[27] but a brief description of some of them may be of interest. All of the regressions of Table 10 were rerun using x_t in place of x_{t-1}, Δx_t in place of Δx_{t-1}, and Δx_{t-1} in place of Δx_{t-2}. These tests do not affect the conclusions reached about adjustment for any of the industries studied. Equation (17) (reported in Table 7) was rerun for all industries, omitting the years 1942 through 1945. For thirteen industries, the elasticity estimates were substantially unaffected, but for automobiles the following result was obtained,

$$y_t = A_0 - 0.113x_t + 0.010t,$$

which may be compared to

$$y_t = A_0 + 0.730x_t + 0.018t,$$

with the war years included. This comparison confirms the suspicion that results for this industry are not meaningful.

The adjustment or expectations hypotheses used—equation (20) or (21)—all relate "expected price," x_t^*, to actual prices in the past *three* periods only. This assumption excluded from consideration one of the most popular expectations hypotheses, in which this period's expected price (ratio) is assumed to be an average of last period's expected and actual prices:

(26)
$$x_t^* = (1 - \beta)x_{t-1} + \beta x_{t-1}^*$$
$$= (1 - \beta) \sum_{i=1}^{\infty} \beta^{i-1} x_{t-1},$$

---

[27] They may be found in full in my Ph.D. thesis, Chap. 5.

where $0 < \beta < 1$. Two common alternatives exist for estimating equation (19) on the assumption that equation (26) holds. The method used by McKinnon[28] was to solve

$$y_t = \sigma x_t^* + \eta_t$$
$$y_{t-1} = \sigma x_{t-1}^* + \eta_{t-1}$$
$$x_t^* = (1 - \beta)x_{t-1} + \beta x_{t-1}^*,$$

to obtain

(27) $$y_t = \sigma(1 - \beta)x_{t-1} + \beta y_{t-1} + \eta_t - \eta_{t-1}.$$

Estimation of equation (27) by least squares produces an estimate of σ from the coefficients of x_{t-1} and y_{t-1}. Note that if the η_t are serially independent, as assumed earlier, the errors of equation (27) will not have this property. Equation (27) has been estimated for all fourteen industries. On the whole, the results are similar to previous results in this chapter, and to McKinnon's, but they are more erratic (there are larger standard errors,[29] and four industries bear negative elasticity estimates) than estimates obtained from other equations.

An alternative method of estimating equation (19), on the assumption that equation (26) holds, is to select a trial value for β and an initial value for the x_t^* series, and then to compute the x_t^* series from the x_t series. Equation (19) is then estimated by least squares. Since the true β is unknown, one tries several values, selecting as the true equation the one yielding the highest R^2. This method has been used for the five industries (wood, paper, rubber, leather, and metals) which, judging from Table 10, appeared most likely to exhibit a β different from zero. Although in some respects this method is superior to the other, these regressions behaved in a highly unsystematic manner, yielding essentially no new information. To summarize all results based on equation (26), one may note that the only advantage of equation (26) over equation (21) is that the former permits x_t to depend on values of x_t prior to x_{t-3}. For values of β close to one (slow adjustment) this advantage may be considerable, but for a β near zero, one expects equation (21) to perform more adequately.

[28] In "Wages, Capital Costs, and Employment in Manufacturing," Sec. 3, Pt. D.
[29] Equation (27) does not, of course, yield a standard error on the estimate of σ, but even the standard error of $\sigma(1 - \beta)$ is larger than that of σ from other formulations.

Bias in Time Series Estimates

A number of biases in the cross-sectional estimates were analyzed in the general discussion of bias, above. It is natural to begin the discussion of time series bias by examining the effect on the time series estimates of the bias sources addressed in the earlier discussion. Of these, the most interesting questions concern unmeasured variation in input quality and non-neutral technological change. To discuss these, it is useful to relax the assumption of neutral, exponential, production function shifts and to consider two examples.

First, let L_t^* be labor input in terms of some "quality constant" measure, and let w_t^* be the true wage rate. Suppose that the measured variables are related to the true ones by

(28)
$$L_t = L_t^* e^{\mu t},$$
$$w_t = w_t^* e^{-\mu t}.$$

(Once the relation between L_t and L_t^* is specified, that between w_t and w_t^* follows from the assumption that the wage bill is correctly measured, or $w_t L_t = w_t^* L_t^*$.) The true regression line, equation (17), is

(29) $\quad \log(Q_t/L_t^*) = A + \sigma \log(w_t^*/p_t) + (1-\sigma)\lambda t + \eta_t.$

Combining equations (28) and (29) yields the regression line in terms of the measured variables:

(30) $\quad \log(Q_t/L_t) = A + \sigma \log(w_t/p_t) + (1-\sigma)(\lambda+\mu)t + \eta_t.$

Thus changes in labor quality of a smooth, exponential type will not lead to bias in the time series estimates. Deviations of the path of quality change from the exponential path will induce a bias toward one in the estimates, exactly as in the cross-sectional case.

As an even simpler example, non-neutral change can be introduced by the assumption[30]

$$(1-\delta) = (1-\delta_0)e^{\mu t}.$$

Then the coefficient of trend in equation (17) becomes

$$(1-\sigma)\lambda - \sigma\mu.$$

Neither of these examples represents a particularly attractive formalization of the idea of non-neutral change, but unless such change can

---

[30] Since δ is restricted to the interval $(0, 1)$ this hypothesis evidently cannot hold for an unbounded interval of time. Recall that δ is one of the parameters of the CES production function, $F(K, L) = \gamma[\delta K^{-\rho} + (1-\delta)L^{-\rho}]^{-1/\rho}$.

TABLE 11. Runs Test for Serial Correlation, on Regression Equations (24) and (25), 13 U.S. Industries, 1931–58

	Equation (25)			Equation (24)		
Industry	Number of runs X	Number of positive residuals N^+	Normalized number of runs X	Number of runs X	Number of positive residuals N^+	Normalized number of runs X
Food	9	12	2.25[a]	13	12	0.67
Tobacco	8	15	2.69[b]	8	15	2.69[b]
Textiles	16	15	−0.41	16	15	−0.41
Wood	9	15	2.30[a]	13	15	0.75
Paper	10	15	1.91[a]	8	17	2.57[b]
Printing	9	12	2.25[a]	11	13	1.52
Chemicals	9	16	2.25[a]	15	14	0.00
Petroleum	8	14	2.69[b]	8	12	2.64[b]
Rubber	9	15	2.30[a]	9	15	2.30[a]
Leather	8	16	2.64[b]	10	17	1.77[a]
Stone, clay, and glass	7	13	3.07[b]	11	13	1.52
Metals	11	14	1.54	11	14	1.54
Machinery	9	12	2.25[a]	13	13	0.75

Source: Based on data from U.S. Bureau of the Census, *U.S. Census of Manufactures*, various issues. See also the Appendix to this chapter.
[a] Positive serial correlation at 0.05 level.
[b] Positive serial correlation at 0.01 level.

be identified with specific economic forces, they are about as good as any other. In fact, the hypothesis of technological change is far more general than is usually possible in production function studies. As the price of this generality, the components of the trend coefficient cannot be identified. For present purposes, however, this cost is negligible.

A second problem which deserves notice in any time series analysis is that of serially correlated residuals. The problem has two aspects. First, in any regression, the presence of serial correlation implies that the least squares regression coefficients are not efficient, and that their estimated variances are biased. Second, if, as in almost all regressions reported in this section, lagged endogenous variables appear on the right side of the regression equation, the estimated coefficients will not be consistent. Table 11 shows the results of tests for non-independence of residuals in equations (24) and (25), reported in Table 10. The test statistic is the number of runs in the twenty-eight computed residuals. If X is the number of runs, N^+ is the number of positive residuals, and N^- the number of negative ones, then X is asymptotically normal, with mean and variance given by[31]

$$E(X) = \frac{2N^+N^-}{N^+ + N^-} + 1,$$

$$\text{Var}(X) = \frac{2N^+N^-(2N^+N^- - N^+ - N^-)}{(N^+ + N^-)^2(N^+ + N^- - 1)}.$$

For each equation, the first column shows values for X, the second for N^+, and the third the normalized value for X, or

$$X = \frac{X - E(X)}{\text{Var}(X)}.$$

One-tail critical values are 2.32 (0.01 level) and 1.64 (0.05 level). Table 11 indicates, as one might have expected, that serial correlation is a problem in both equations (25) and (24). It appears that the problem is less serious for equation (24), which includes the lagged difference, Δx_{t-1}, as an additional independent variable.

It has been observed that serial correlation will lead to non-consistent estimates of σ from equations such as (22) through (25). It was noted earlier that estimates from equation (17) will be consistent under *no* conditions, since output price p_t is endogenous to the industry model. A third problem of this general type arises in equation (17) if the wage rate is correlated with the error term in the regression, either because of an upward sloping labor supply curve to the industry, or because of an upward sloping aggregate labor supply curve together with non-independence across industries of error terms in labor demand curves. These three sources of bias can be analyzed in a similar way,[32] but unfortunately, even using what appear to be highly restrictive sets of assumptions (about the other equations in the model), one finds it impossible to determine even the sign of the asymptotic bias. All one can conclude from such an

---

[31] See A. Wald and J. Wolfowitz, "On a Test Whether Two Samples Are from the Same Population," *Annals of Mathematical Statistics*, Vol. 11 (1940), pp. 147–62.

[32] See my Ph.D. thesis, Chap. 5, App. In Chap. 6, "two-stage least squares" estimates of equation (17) are given for the rubber products industry. The result of primary interest is

$$y_t = A_0 + 0.338x_t + 0.019t,$$
$$\quad\quad\quad\;\; (0.088) \quad\;\; (0.001)$$

which may be compared to the direct least squares estimate for the same sample,

$$y_t = A_0 + 0.371x_t + 0.018t.$$
$$\quad\quad\quad\;\; (0.057) \quad\;\; (0.001)$$

analysis is that if production function shifts, unaccounted for by trend, are the major contributors to the error term in the marginal productivity equation, all three biases will tend to be upward. If, on the other hand, this error largely consists of "mistakes" on the part of firms (that is, of failures to equate marginal physical product with the wage-price ratio), the bias will tend to be downward. Since some attempts have been made here to control for the latter source of error, there is perhaps some weak basis for favoring the suspicion of an upward bias. At any rate, I have found no grounds for believing that any of these biases is a promising route to reconciliation of the two time series with the cross-sectional results.

The possibility of deviations from competition in the various product markets should perhaps be mentioned as a possible source of bias. First, note that if the elasticity of product demand is a constant, the condition

$$F_L = w/p$$

may be replaced by

$$F_L = \frac{W}{p(1 + 1/\eta)}.$$

Thus only the constant term in the regressions is affected. If the elasticity, η, is not constant, the effect of monopoly is not clear. It is no doubt unnecessary to remark that one should avoid the common error of thinking of the chemical and allied products industry as "Du Pont and a couple of other firms," and so forth. Each of these "two-digit" industries consists of dozens, and more often hundreds, of firms. While this fact does not rule out the possibility of significant monopoly influence, it makes it impossible to support by observation of a few noted firms.

Finally, we come to the problem of changes in industry composition. It was argued above that there are theoretical reasons for suspecting this to be a problem in the cross-sectional tests. There are no such arguments on the time series side, but there is no doubt that industry composition has in many cases changed radically over time. The changes in composition, together with classification changes (the two are, of course, related), in my opinion constitute the probable source of trouble in the "unruly" industries: stone, clay, and glass; machinery; automobiles; and possibly chemicals. Controlling for these shifts in composition would probably lead to revision of many or all of the estimates presented in this section, but there is no reason to believe that these should operate systematically in one direction or another.

Conclusions

The main results of this study can be summarized in two sentences. First, time series estimates of elasticities of substitution between labor and capital in U.S. manufacturing are (with a single exception) well below cross-sectional estimates. Second, differences cannot be accounted for by hypotheses of lagged adjustment.

The results supporting these conclusions are summarized in Table 12, below. In the first column appear the elasticity estimates obtained from equation (17), which related the current ratio of output to

TABLE 12. Summary of Elasticities of Substitution Between Labor and Capital, U.S. Manufacturing Industries, 1931–58

Industry	Author's time series elasticities: Equation					Minasian's cross-sectional elasticities[a]
	(17)	(18)	(24)	(23)	(22)	
Food	0.397	0.235	0.203			0.59
Tobacco	0.152	0.089	0.068			3.46
Textiles	0.131	0.070	0.073			1.60[b]
Wood	0.480	0.418	0.543	0.657	0.758	1.00[c]
Paper	0.505	0.599	0.668			1.60
Printing	0.488	0.477	0.459			0.89
Chemicals	0.678	0.368	0.190	0.083		1.12
Petroleum	0.375	0.154	0.143	0.166		−0.54
Rubber	0.323	0.286	0.311			0.83
Leather	0.407	0.320	0.479			0.95
Stone, clay, and glass	−0.205	−0.273	−0.424			0.59
Metals	0.641	0.422	0.563			0.86[d]
Machinery	0.476	0.175	0.037	−0.185	−0.295	0.67[e]
Automobiles	0.730	0.486	0.367	0.271	0.040	2.04[f]

Source: Tables 2, 7, 9, 10.
[a] Based on data for 1957.
[b] A weighted average of Minasian estimates for Standard Industrial Classifications 22 and 23, using man-hours of production workers, 1957 (Annual Survey of Manufactures) as weights. Estimate is: (0.47)(SIC 22) + (0.53)(SIC 23).
[c] Aggregate: (0.63)(SIC24) + (0.37)(SIC25).
[d] Aggregate: (0.54)(SIC 33) + (0.46)(SIC 34).
[e] Aggregate: (0.62)(SIC 35) + (0.38)(SIC 36).
[f] Estimate is for Transportation Equipment (SIC 37).

labor input, y_t, to the current ratio of wages to output price, x_t (both ratios in logs), and trend, t. Estimates from equation (18), relating y_t to x_{t-1} and t, are shown in the second column. The next three columns present estimates from successively more general equations. Equation (24) relates y_t to x_{t-1}, Δx_{t-1}, and t; equation (23) adds Δx_{t-2} as an additional variable; and equation (22) regresses y_t on x_{t-1}, $\Delta \log (w_{t-1})$, $\Delta \log (w_{t-2})$, $\Delta \log (p_{t-1})$, $\Delta \log (p_{t-2})$, and time. Results for equations (23) and (22) are included only if these equations represent significant improvements over equation (24). Finally, in the last column, Minasian's cross-sectional results are repeated from Table 2. For certain industries (textiles, wood, metals, and machinery), the estimates in Table 12 are weighted averages of the original Table 2 estimates.

Table 12 also facilitates a review of the results for individual industries. For three industries (stone, clay, and glass; machinery; and automobiles), the time series model must be rejected as inadequate, either because of negative elasticity estimates (for stone, clay, and glass; and for machinery) or because of erratic behavior of estimates from different equations (for automobiles). On the latter ground, the results for chemicals might well be discarded also. For the remaining ten industries, Table 12 shows that the model performed well, yielding estimates consistent with the theoretical restrictions on σ, and exhibiting a sensible pattern over different regression equations. In some of these industries (wood, paper, leather, and metals), hypotheses of lagged adjustment led, where accepted, to higher elasticity estimates than were obtained from the simpler models represented by equations (17) and (18). For the rest, the effect of the lag hypotheses on the estimates was slight. In *no* case did the assumption of lagged adjustment lead to a reconciliation of time series and cross-sectional evidence.

What one would like to be able to do, at this point, is to proceed to the assertion that the time series estimates are, on the whole, more accurate than the cross-sectional estimates. The evidence collected in this study will not, however, support so strong a conclusion. The analysis and supplementary tests discussed in the review of empirical work emphasized the theoretical ambiguity of the cross-sectional model, and demonstrated the sensitivity of the estimates to certain types of specification changes, but did not succeed in reconciling the two types of evidence. Similarly the last section includes a discussion of several biases which may possibly affect the time series estimates. While no evidence was found to indicate that any of these biases are important, none of them was empirically demonstrated to be insignificant.

The problem of substitution between factors in manufacturing remains, therefore, unsolved. Until such a solution is produced, however, I believe one can reasonably argue that for time series applications of substitution elasticities, the time series estimates should be preferred. Given the present state of knowledge, I do not believe it is defensible to predict that future changes in relative factor prices will have effects substantially greater than those which have been observed in the past.

APPENDIX

Time Series Data

THIS APPENDIX DESCRIBES in detail the data series used in the time series analysis and gives the sources of the data. Abbreviations which are used in subsequent paragraphs appear in parentheses following each reference.

Data Sources

Board of Governors of the Federal Reserve System, *Federal Reserve Bulletin* (U.S. Government Printing Office, monthly series). (*FRB*)

Board of Governors of the Federal Reserve System, *Industrial Production: 1959 Revision* (U.S. Government Printing Office, 1959). (*Ind. Prod.*)

U.S. Department of Commerce, Office of Business Economics, *Business Statistics, 1959 Edition* (1959). (*BS*)

U.S. Department of Commerce, Office of Business Economics, *National Income: 1954 Edition, A Supplement to the Survey of Current Business* (1954). (*NI*)

U.S. Department of Commerce, Office of Business Economics, *Survey of Current Business* (monthly series). (*SCB*)

U.S. Department of Commerce, Office of Business Economics, *U.S. Income and Output* (1958). (*IO*)

U.S. Department of Labor, Bureau of Labor Statistics, *Handbook of Labor Statistics, 1947 Edition* (1947). (*BLS Hbk 1947*)

U.S. Department of Labor, Bureau of Labor Statistics, *Monthly Labor Review* (monthly series). (*MLR*)

U.S. Department of Labor, Bureau of Labor Statistics, *Techniques of Preparing Major BLS Statistical Series*, Bulletin 1168 (1954). (*Bull. 1168*)

U.S. Treasury Department, Internal Revenue Service (formerly Bureau of Internal Revenue), *Statistics of Income* (annual series). (*SI*)

Industries Included in the Study

Fourteen manufacturing industries are treated in this study. Generally, these are two-digit industries, as defined in the U.S. Standard Industrial Classification, but some are aggregates of two such industries. In the tabulation, below, of these industries, a numbering system for reference in this appendix has been adopted.

Number	Name	SIC number	SIC name
1.	Food and kindred products	20	same
2.	Tobacco	21	same
3.	Textiles and products	22 + 23	Textiles, and apparel
4.	Wood products	24 + 25	Lumber, and furniture and fixtures
5.	Paper and allied products	26	same
6.	Printing and publishing	27	same
7.	Chemicals and allied products	28	same
8.	Petroleum and coal products	29	same
9.	Rubber products	30	same
10.	Leather products	31	same
11.	Stone, clay, and glass products	32	same
12.	Metal products	33 + 34	Primary, and fabricated metal products (formerly ferrous and non-ferrous metals)
13.	Machinery	35 + 36	Electrical, and non-electrical machinery
14.	Motor vehicles	371	same

This industry classification is the most detailed for which continuous time series data for the required variables are available. I have not attempted to justify it on economic grounds. Industries which represent residual classes have been omitted from the study, since they are particularly sensitive to classification changes.

The basic definition of an industry was taken from U.S. Department of Commerce sources, since these provided most of the series used. Prior to 1942 industry definitions were based on the 1942 SIC, with the 1945 SIC used in subsequent years. For five industries (numbers 4, 7, 8, 12, and 13) overlapping figures are published for 1948. The post-1948 Department of Commerce series for these industries, which I denote $X_t(45 \text{ SIC})$, have been put on a 1942 SIC basis by application of the formula

$$X_t(42 \text{ SIC}) = X_t(45 \text{ SIC}) \frac{NI_{48}(42 \text{ SIC})}{NI_{48}(45 \text{ SIC})},$$

where X_t(42 SIC) is the new, corrected series, and NI_{48}(42 SIC) and NI_{48}(45 SIC) are the overlapping 1948 figures for national income originating in the industry.[1] This adjustment was the only one made, on any data used, to correct for changes in classification. The two major reclassifications in the period 1929–58 occurred in 1945 and 1957. The greatest impact of the first change was felt in the metals industry; here the effect is "avoided" by aggregation. Other large shifts occurred between metals and machinery, and these have not been corrected for. Most of the series described below do not use the 1957 SIC; where they do, it is noted. The source series used, and their relation to their theoretical counterparts, are described below.

Labor Input and Wages

SOURCE SERIES

N_t = "number of full-time equivalent employees"
    = average number of employees per year
    1929–45   *NI*, Table 25
    1946–55   *IO*, Table VI–13
    1956–58   *SCB* (7–61), Table 50

This series is preferred to "persons engaged in production" (*IO*, VI–16) since it is consistent with the wage-bill series used (see below). Disregarding consistency, however, persons engaged in production, which include proprietors and unpaid family workers, are a better measure of labor input than is number of employees. For eleven of the fourteen industries studied, the ratio of persons engaged to N_t did not exceed 1.03 for any of the years 1929, 1937, 1948, or 1957. The ratios for the three exceptions are as follows:

Industry	Ratio in			
	1929	1937	1948	1957
1	1.036	1.025	1.020	1.017
4	1.020	1.014	1.029	1.047
6	1.024	1.025	1.032	1.026

No correction has been made for this discrepancy.

[1] A more natural adjustment procedure might have been

$$X_t(42 \text{ SIC}) = X_t(45 \text{ SIC}) \frac{X_{48}(42 \text{ SIC})}{X_{48}(45 \text{ SIC})}.$$

Under the assumption that each firm in the industry has an identical production function, however, a single ratio for 1948 should be used to adjust all OBE series. National income originating was arbitrarily selected for this purpose. The choice is of no quantitative significance.

$w_t L_t$ = "compensation of employees"
- 1929–45   *NI*, Table 14
- 1946–55   *IO*, Table VI–1
- 1956–58   *SCB* (7–61), Table 48

A_t = average hours worked per week
- 1939–58   BLS *Hbk 1947* and issues of *MLR*, Table C–1
- 1932–38   (Industry 14 only) same source

For the years 1929, 1931, 1933, 1935, and 1937, and 1929 and 1931 (industry 14), A_t was obtained through the courtesy of John Kendrick and his assistant, Maude Pech, in connection with their study of productivity in the United States.[2] They are based primarily on the Census of Manufactures, with National Industrial Conference Board data used to fill in some of the gaps. I have been warned that these data are not considered by these authors to be of high quality.

For most industries, then, A_t for the years 1930, 1932, 1934, 1936, and 1938 is available in no published source. Figures for these years have been interpolated as follows. For the years t = 1929, 1931, 1933, 1935, 1937, 1939, 1947, . . . , 1958, two regressions have been run for each industry:

$$\log (A_t) = b_0 + b_1 \log (G_t) + b_2 \log (G_{t+1}) + b_3 t,$$
$$\log (A_t) = b_0 + b_1 \log (G_t) + b_2 \log (\bar{A}_t) + b_3 t,$$

where G_t = GNP in 1954 dollars, and $\bar{A}_t$ is the hours series for all manufacturing which is comparable to A_t. For each industry, the regression with the higher multiple R^2 was used to interpolate A_t.

Conceptually, A_t is average hours of hired nonsupervisory or production workers (see *Bull. 1168*). The ideal series would show hours actually worked by all employees. The relation between the actual series and the ideal one is not known.

FINAL SERIES

$$L_t = N_t A_t = \text{man-hours per year (divided by 52)}$$

This labor series is a product of annual averages as opposed to the more desirable average of products:

$$w_t = (w_t L_t)/L_t = (w_t L_t)/(N_t A_t)$$
$$= \text{average hourly wage (times 52)}.$$

Note that on this definition of w_t, a given percentage measurement error in L_t induces an error of opposite sign and equal magnitude in w_t. For the implications of this fact, see the review of empirical work in the main body of this chapter.

---

[2] John W. Kendrick, *Productivity Trends in the United States* (Princeton University Press for the National Bureau of Economic Research, 1961).

Output and Output Price

SOURCE SERIES

V_{Nt} = "national income originating"
 = net value-added

1929–55	*IO*, Table I-10
1956–58	*SCB* (7-61), Table 8

V_{Nt} is computed (by the OBE) as: value of output minus materials costs, business transfer payments, and indirect business taxes.

D_t = stated depreciation

1929–33	*SI*, Table 15
1934	*SI*, Part 2, Table 4
1935–53	*SI*, Part 2, Table 3, Part I
1954–58	*SI*, Table 3

Statistics of Income covers corporate firms only, so that some adjustment of the data as given is required. The basis of this adjustment was an average of the 1948 and 1957 ratios of total sales for an industry (*BS*, 1959) to corporate sales (*IO*, Table VI-17 and *SCB* (7-61), Table 62). If this ratio was less than 1.05, no adjustment was made. In this class fall industries 2, 5, 7, 8, 9, 12, 13, and 14. For the following industries, D_t is obtained by multiplying the *SI* figures by the given factor:

Industry	Factor
1	1.08
3	1.06
4	1.25
6	1.06
10	1.06
11	1.06

Difficulty also arises because *SI* data become more highly aggregative as one goes back in time. Necessary depreciation (D) adjustments, with industry numbers in parentheses, were as follows:

1929–30	D(1) = 0.96 D(1 + 2)
	D(2) = 0.04 D(1 + 2)
1929–35	D(7) = 0.31 D(7 + 8)
	D(8) = 0.69 D(7 + 8)
1936–37	D(12) = 0.58 D(12 + 13)
	D(13) = 0.35 D(12 + 13 + *)
For 1929, 1935	D(12) = 0.50 D(12 + 13 + 14 + *)
	D(13) = 0.31 D(12 + 13 + 14 + *)
	D(14) = 0.14 D(12 + 13 + 14 + *)

In the series above, (*) denotes transportation equipment other than motor vehicles. In each case, the disaggregation weights selected were based on the composition of the industry in the earliest disaggregated year. For example, in 1931 total stated depreciation for industries 1 and 2, taken together, was 96 percent of the depreciation from industry 1 and 4 percent from industry 2.

Q_t = Federal Reserve index of industrial production
 = output

1929–38	*FRB* (8–40)
1939–41	*FRB* (10–43)
1942–46	*FRB* (various current issues)
1947–58	*Ind. Prod.*

The 1947–58 observations for Q_t are based on the 1957 *SIC*. Normal procedures for linking the index for these years to previous years preclude discontinuity as a result of reclassification.

The Federal Reserve index for a two-digit industry is a weighted sum of indexes of total physical output of subindustries, where the fractions of total value added of the industry contributed by each subindustry are used as weights. For present purposes, neither the base series nor the weights used are correct; and in any case, the two are not consistent with each other. What is needed is a measure of total output of all subindustries, *minus* sales from one firm to another within the industry. If one wishes to use weighted indexes, therefore, the base series should be indexes of "sales to the outside" and the weights should be fractions of total "sales to the outside."

A second problem with the index is that series on man-hours are sometimes used to interpolate between observations on the base series. This would, of course, if prevalent, be fatal in a study of factor substitution. Fortunately, this practice is in general restricted to the building of monthly output series from annual data.

To conform with other series, some of these indexes had to be aggregated. The weights used were as follows:

$Q(3) = (0.53)$ (textiles) $+ (0.47)$ (apparel)
[Weights are unweighted average of 1929 and 1957 V_{Nt} weights.]

$Q(4) = (0.57)$ (lumber) $+ (0.43)$ (furniture)
[1948 output weights are taken from Creamer.[3]]

$Q(12) = (0.30)$ (non-ferrous metals) $+ (0.70)$ (iron and steel)
[Unweighted average of 1929 and 1937 output weights are from Creamer.]

$Q(12) = (0.60)$ (primary metals) $+ (0.40)$(fabricated metals)
[For the latter part of the period, weights are 1953 V_{Nt} weights.]

$Q(13) = (0.38)$ (electrical machinery) $+ (0.62)$ (non-electrical machinery)
[1948 output weights are from Creamer.]

---

[3] Creamer and others, *Capital in Manufacturing and Mining.*

These weights were taken from Creamer where possible and, otherwise, from "national income originating." If industry composition remained fairly stable, a single central year was used for the weights. Otherwise, two end-point years were averaged.

FINAL SERIES

Q_t = output, as above

$p_t = V_t/Q_t$, where V_t is gross value added, defined as $V_t = V_{Nt} + D_t$

The justification for these definitions of Q_t and p_t is discussed in the section on theory in the main text. The note on measurement errors in L_t and w_t applies equally well to Q_t and p_t as defined here.

Auxiliary Time Series

G_t = gross national product in 1954 dollars
- 1929–55   *IO*, Table I–2
- 1956–58   *SCB* (7–61), Table 5

P_{Gt} = implicit deflator for GNP above
- 1929–55   *IO*, Table VII–2
- 1956–58   *SCB* (7–61), Table 6

It is clear that some of the series described above are quite crude. I have not dealt in detail with the faults in the data, or in the adjustments performed, except in those cases where correction could be made or where inference about the induced bias could be drawn. The labor input and wage series seem to me to be the strongest; the output and output price series are probably less reliable.

COLIN WRIGHT

Saving and the Rate of Interest

IF SAVING IS RESPONSIVE to changes in the rate of interest, then corporate and personal income taxes create a welfare loss to society by lowering the rate of return available on savings. One measure of this welfare loss for any current year is $½ \Delta S \dfrac{t}{(1-t)}$ where ΔS is the change in saving due to the substitution effect associated with the change in the rate of return induced by imposing the tax rate, t.[1]

This chapter reports on one attempt to measure that parameter necessary for estimating ΔS, namely, the compensated interest elasticity of saving. By way of introduction, I first review the simple aspects of the received theory concerning the relationship between consumption (saving) and the rate of interest. (Appendix A provides the derivation of the income and substitution effect of a change in the rate of interest upon current consumption.) I then proceed to generalize this theory in a form susceptible to empirical verification and report on some tests of the resulting model.

[1] See Arnold C. Harberger, "The Measurement of Waste," *American Economic Review*, Vol. 54 (May 1964), p. 74.

Theory of the Relationship Between Consumption and the Rate of Interest

The received theory explaining the relationship between consumption and the rate of interest may be reviewed by using a simple two-period model in which an individual is assumed to have a utility function of the form

(1) $$U = U(C_1, C_2),$$

where C_1 denotes current consumption and C_2 future consumption. For an individual having no wealth and planning to hold no wealth at the end of the second period, the appropriate budget constraint is

(2) $$Y_1 + \frac{Y_2}{(1+r)} - C_1 - \frac{C_2}{(1+r)} = 0,$$

where Y_1 and Y_2 denote labor income in the first and second periods and r is the rate of interest appropriate for discounting expected future income. Rational individuals are then assumed to maximize (1) subject to the constraints of (2), which is equivalent to finding the critical values for the Lagrangean expression

(3) $$U^* = U(C_1, C_2) + \lambda \left[Y_1 + \frac{Y_2}{(1+r)} - C_1 - \frac{C_2}{(1+r)} \right],$$

where λ is the undetermined Lagrangean multiplier.

Differentiating equation (3) with respect to C_1, C_2, and λ, and denoting $\partial U/\partial C_1$ as U_1, we obtain the necessary conditions for a constrained maximum,

(4a) $$U_1 - \lambda = 0,$$

(4b) $$U_2 - \frac{\lambda}{(1+r)} = 0,$$

(4c) $$C_1 + \frac{C_2}{(1+r)} = Y_1 + \frac{Y_2}{(1+r)},$$

which, upon eliminating λ, are equivalently expressed as

(5a) $$\frac{U_1}{U_2} = (1+r),$$

(5b) $$C_1 + \frac{C_2}{(1+r)} = Y_1 + \frac{Y_2}{(1+r)},$$

where U_1/U_2 is the marginal rate of substitution between present and future consumption.

CHART 1. Relation Between Consumption and Rate of Interest

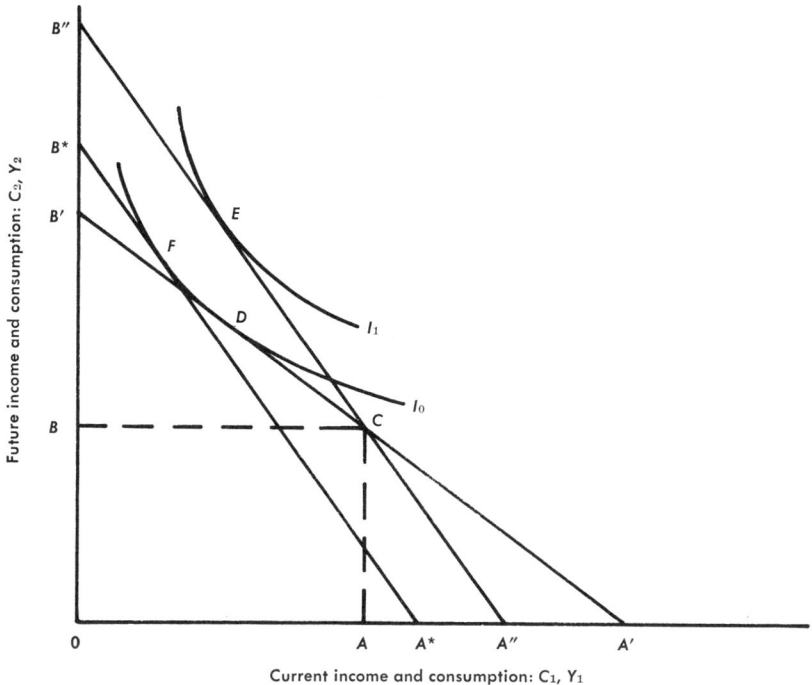

These results are presented geometrically in Chart 1 where current and future consumption are measured along the abscissa and ordinate respectively. Current income is also measured along the abscissa and is denoted as OA while future income is measured along the ordinate as OB. The maximum amount of consumption attainable in the current period is denoted as OA' and maximum future consumption is OB'.[2] The line $A'B'$ is the budget constraint equivalent to equation (2), having a negative slope of $(1 + r)$, and passing through point C.

The utility function in equation (1) is represented by the indifference curve I_0, the slope of which is the marginal rate of substitution between present and future consumption. The point D is

---

[2] If it is assumed that the borrowing and lending rates are identical and that individuals may borrow on the basis of expected future income, then $A' = Y + Y_2/(1 + r)$ and $B' = Y_2 + Y(1 + r)$. Substituting for this assumption a more realistic one only complicates the analysis without altering the basic conclusions. See Don Patinkin, *Money, Interest, and Prices*, 2nd ed. (Harper and Row, 1965), pp. 440–73.

the highest level of utility attainable with the given budget constraint and is a point of tangency between the indifference curve I_0 and the budget constraint $A'B'$, thereby fulfilling the conditions stated in equation (5a).

If an increase in the rate of interest in Chart 1 is posited, the result is a new budget constraint, obtained by rotating $A'B'$ clockwise through C. The new budget constraint is denoted as $A''B''$ and the new point of equilibrium as E. The movement from D to E is the result of an income and substitution effect the identification of which is facilitated by constructing a budget constraint parallel to $A''B''$ and tangent to I_0. The individual is thus allowed to obtain the same level of utility he enjoyed at D but is confronted with a rate of interest identical to the one existing at E. Along the third budget constraint, denoted A^*B^*, the highest level of utility is denoted by the position F. The substitution effect of the increase in the rate of interest is then identified as the movement from D to F and the income effect from F to E.

Implicit in this exposition is the assumption that the substitution effect with respect to current consumption is negative; that is, that as the rate of interest increases, income being held constant, current consumption decreases. The income effect is assumed to be positive, consumption being a superior good. In this simple model the size of the income effect is positively related to the amount of saving. This can be demonstrated by performing the preceding exercise with the initial equilibrium at alternative points along $A'B'$. In the limit there exists no income effect if D is equal to C, where all current income is consumed, and a maximum positive effect if D is equal to B', where all current income is saved.[3] The size of the substitution effect depends upon the magnitude of the marginal rate of substitution between present and future consumption.[4]

The mathematical expression describing the movement from D to E is obtained by partially differentiating equations (a), (b), and (c) with respect to the rate of interest and solving the resulting equations

---

[3] Throughout the analysis saving is assumed to be greater than or equal to zero. If saving is negative then some of the results are changed. For a discussion of the effects of changes in the rate of interest when individuals are net borrowers see D. V. T. Bear, "The Relationship of Saving to the Rate of Interest, Real Income, and Expected Future Prices," *Review of Economics and Statistics*, Vol. 43 (February 1961), pp. 27–35.

[4] For a discussion of the effects different assumptions about the substitutability of present for future consumption imply, see Richard A. Musgrave, *The Theory of Public Finance* (McGraw-Hill, 1959), pp. 264–68.

for the partial derivative of current consumption. Doing so, we obtain

$$\text{(6)} \qquad \frac{\partial C_1}{\partial r} = \left(\frac{\partial C_1}{\partial r}\right)_{U=\text{constant}} + \frac{S}{(1+r)} M,$$

where S is saving and M the marginal propensity to consume out of income.[5] The first term in the right-hand side of equation (6) is the substitution effect, which shall be denoted as $\partial^s C_1/\partial r$, and the second term is the income effect.

Here we are particularly concerned with estimating $\partial^s C_1/\partial r$. The related elasticity, or compensated interest elasticity of consumption, is $(\partial^s C_1/\partial r)(r/C_1)$, denoted as η^s_{cr}. Since $\partial^s C_1/\partial r = -\partial^s S/\partial r$, the compensated interest elasticity of saving may be expressed as $\eta^s_{sr} = (-\eta^s_{cr})(C/S)$, thus permitting estimates of consumption-interest relationships to be expressed as saving-interest relationships.

General Relationship Between Consumption and Rate of Interest

The results of the preceding section must be generalized and placed in a form susceptible to empirical analysis. The first assumption here is that individuals make their economic decisions in a sequential rather than simultaneous manner. Initially the individual is assumed to choose between work and leisure. Subsequent to this decision the consumption-saving choice is made (the intertemporal problem) after which decisions are made regarding the composition of consumption (the intratemporal problem) and the composition of saving (the asset portfolio problem). To investigate the intertemporal problem, discrete time periods are posited and it is assumed that economic decisions are planned on the first day of each period for all subsequent periods in the planning horizon.

If an individual has a planning horizon N periods in length for which he plans the level of his consumption and the value of his desired net worth at the end of his planning horizon, his utility function may be expressed as

$$\text{(7)} \qquad U(C_1, \ldots, C_i, \ldots, C_N, W_N),$$

[5] It can be shown that M is the marginal propensity to consume current income and $M/(1+r)$ the marginal propensity to consume future income. Consequently, the income effect can be thought of as being related to the *MPC* from either current or future income. See James M. Henderson and Richard E. Quandt, *Microeconomic Theory; A Mathematical Approach* (McGraw-Hill, 1958), pp. 229–34.

where C_i denotes planned real consumption in period i and W_N the value of his desired real net worth at the end of period N. Denoting expected real labor income in the ith period as Y_i^e and net worth at the beginning of the planning period as W_0, and, for economy of notation, defining C_N to include W_N, the level of planned net worth at the end of the planning horizon, or the budget constraint for such an individual, can be written as

(8) $$W_0 + \sum_{i=1}^{N} \frac{(Y_i^e - C_i)}{(1+r)^i} = 0.$$

Defining a rational consumer as one who acts as though he maximized equation (7) with W_N amalgamated into C_N, subject to equation (8), we execute this constrained maximization problem to obtain the necessary conditions for a maximum. These conditions may then be differentiated totally and solved for the differential of present consumption, which is

(9) $$dC_1 = V_{N+1,\,1} \left[dW_0 + \sum_{i=1}^{N} \frac{dY_i^e}{(1+r)^i} + \left(\sum_{i=1}^{N} \frac{i(C_i - Y_i^e)}{(1+r)^{i+1}} \right) dr \right]$$
$$- \sum_{i=1}^{N} \frac{i\lambda V_{i1}}{(1+r)^{i+1}} dr,$$

where V_{ij} denotes the ratio of the ijth cofactor to the determinant of the bordered Hessian arising from the second order conditions of the maximization process. The above result is derived explicitly in Appendix A.

It is also shown in Appendix A that the expression

$$\sum_{i=1}^{N} \frac{i(C_i - Y_i^e)}{(1+r)^{i+1}}$$

is equal to

$$\sum_{j=0}^{N-1} \frac{W_j}{(1+r)^{j+1}}.$$

Making the appropriate substitution in equation (9), we can consider it as a differential equation having locally constant coefficients, the solution of which is

(10) $$C_1 = K + V_{N+1,\,1}(PW_0) + \frac{\partial^s C_1}{\partial r}(r).$$

Here K is the constant of integration, $\partial^s C_1/\partial r$, the substitution effect of a change in the rate of interest, defined as

$$-\sum_{i=1}^{N} \frac{i\lambda V_{i1}}{(1+r)^{i+1}}$$

and

(11) $$PW_0 = W_0 + \sum_{i=1}^{N} \frac{Y_i^e}{(1+r)^i} + \sum_{j=0}^{N-1} \frac{W_j}{(1+r)^{j+1}} r.$$

PW_0 contains current net worth, (W_0), the present value of expected labor income,

$$\left(\sum_{i=1}^{N} \frac{Y_i^e}{(1+r)^i}\right),$$

and the present value of property or interest income,

$$\left(\sum_{j=0}^{N-1} \frac{W_j}{(1+r)^{j+1}} r\right),$$

and is defined as the present worth of the consumer in period zero.

Normally, the present worth of an individual is defined as his existing net assets plus the present value of his future income from labor. This definition is expanded here to include the present value of his future interest income, a step necessary in order to capture the income effects of changes in the interest rate within the portmanteau variable PW_0. In effect, PW_0 can grow either through an increase in the consumer's current portfolio, or through an increase in his expected future labor income, or through a rise in the rate of return that he will get on his existing and planned savings.

Note that the assumption of constant coefficients in equation (9) requires that the discount rate in $\partial^s C_1/\partial r$ and PW_0 be constant.[6] If this rate is taken to be $\bar{r}$, the mean rate over the sample period used to test the model, an approximation to equation (9), derived with an eye toward testing the model, may be expressed as

(12) $$(C_1 - \bar{C}) = \frac{\partial^s C_1}{\partial r}(r - \bar{r}) + V_{N+1,\,0}\left[(W_{-1} - \overline{W})\right.$$
$$\left. + \sum_{i=0}^{N} \frac{(Y_i^e - \overline{Y_i^e})}{(1+\bar{r})^i} + \sum_{j=0}^{N} \frac{W_j}{(1+\bar{r})^i}(r - \bar{r})\right],$$

[6] The necessity of requiring a constant discount rate in PW_0 follows from the fact that the *MPC* out of income in the ith period is $V_{0,\,N+1}/(1+r)^i$.

where the barred terms are means over the sample period for the respective variables. Since the barred terms are constants, equation (12) reduces to

(13) $$C = \alpha_0 + \alpha_1 PW_0 + \alpha_2 r,$$

in which standard notation has been substituted for the coefficients in equation (12), and in which α_0 is a constant.

An understanding of the last term in PW_0 is important for an appreciation of the analysis to follow and therefore requires special comment. W_j denotes net worth held at the end of period j. The path of W_j through time is determined by the initial level of net worth and the optimal consumption plan of the individual. The product of W_j and the rate of return on saving is the interest income which will be forthcoming in the period $j + 1$. Consequently, the last term in PW_0 denotes the present value of all future interest income and represents the income effect of a change in the rate of interest.

Having expressed present consumption as a function of an interest variable and present worth, where the coefficient of the interest variable is interpreted as the substitution effect only, the unobservable present worth needs to be related to observable variables. One way of doing this is to use estimates of net worth and total income which have been used in previously fitted consumption functions. Since the income variable must be a surrogate for current and expected future total income, we invoke a variant of Friedman's permanent income hypothesis and use an exponentially weighted moving average of current and past total income which shall be referred to as "normal" income and defined as

(14) $$Y_t^* = B \sum_{i=0}^{\infty} (1 - B + \alpha)^i Y_{t-i},$$

where Y_t^* is "normal income," Y_t is total income in period t, B the coefficient of adjustment in an adaptive expectations model, and α a growth factor to account for the trend in measured or observed income.[7] Alternatively, equation (14) may be expressed as

(15) $$Y_t^* = BY_t + (1 - B + \alpha) Y_{t-1}^*,$$

[7] For a detailed exposition of the adaptive expectations model, see Marc Nerlove, *The Dynamics of Supply: Estimation of Farmers' Response to Price* (Johns Hopkins Press, 1958), Chap. 8.

which reveals more readily the necessity of making certain computational decisions the nature of which is discussed below.

If the available estimates of current net worth are denoted by W, Y^* and W can be substituted for PW_0 and the consumption function is expressed as

(16) $\qquad C = b_0 + b_1 Y^* + b_2 W + b_3 r + u,$

where u denotes the error term.

Because current estimates of net worth have been used for W_0 in PW_0, Y^* is implicitly being used as a surrogate for both

$$\sum_{i=0}^{N} \frac{Y_i^e}{(1+r)^i} \quad \text{and} \quad \sum_{j=0}^{N-1} \frac{W_j r}{(1+r)^{j+1}}.$$

However, as indicated previously, the latter is the present value of future property income, and since current estimates of net worth do not include property income available in the initial period, the present value of current and future property income may be expressed as

$$\sum_{i=1}^{N} \frac{Y_i^p}{(1+r)^i},$$

where Y_i^p denotes property or interest income available in the ith period.

PW_0 may therefore be equivalently expressed as

(17) $\qquad PW_0 = W + \sum_{i=1}^{N} \frac{Y_i^T}{(1+r)^i},$

where

$$Y_i^T = Y_i^e + Y_i^p.$$

The use of expected total income is an attempt not only to have the income variable "pick up" the effect of future income but also the income effect of a change in the rate of interest. Since the observed income variable used in generating expected income contains income from wealth, the construction of such an income variable from the adaptive expectations model is assumed to reflect the individual's expectations of future interest income given his planned consumption and expected interest rates. Insofar as expected income fails to do this the interest coefficient fails to provide an unbiased estimate of the substitution effect.

The bias (if any exists) in the resulting estimate of the substitution effect of changes in interest rates on consumption is likely to be in a positive direction, owing to the failure of the expected income variable to capture fully the income effects of changes in r.

It is now necessary to make two final assumptions. First, although a consumption function has been derived for the individual, it is assumed to be applicable to aggregate per capita consumption functions also. This requires that several problems be ignored, but there is precedent for doing so. Second, it has been noted that individuals plan their consumption levels on the basis of the level of the net of tax variables. This implies that the income variables defined above be interpreted as disposable income and the interest variable as a net rate of return. Data are readily available on disposable income but not on the interest variable. The existence of a progressive tax structure over the period examined in the regressions requires the construction of an average marginal tax rate for the economy by which to adjust the published gross interest rates. Adjustments of the theory to take these considerations into account are slight, amounting to little more than a change in notation. It will be assumed therefore that the above notation refers to net of tax concepts wherever applicable.

Measuring the Response of Consumption to Changes in the Rate of Interest

It appears that only two attempts to measure the responsiveness of either consumption or saving to changes in the rate of interest have found their way into the literature. Such meager empirical evidence, in light of the considerable theoretical interest in the subject, may reflect the pessimism of Keynes, who, although giving impetus to the estimation of consumption functions, regarded the interest rate as an unimportant variable. Alternatively, the lack of evidence may suggest that attempts to ascertain the effects of the interest rate upon consumption have proved either unsuccessful or inconclusive and therefore were not published. Whatever the cause, little empirical knowledge exists concerning the relationship between consumption and the rate of interest.[8]

E. A. Radice, in 1939, using British data for the period 1922–34,

---

[8] See Thomas Mayer, "Multiplier and Velocity Analysis: An Evaluation," *Journal of Political Economy*, Vol. 72 (December 1964), p. 567.

estimated the responsiveness of savings—in the form of post office savings certificates, bank deposits, and insurance—to changes in the rate of interest on consols and fixed interest securities.[9] He found that such savings, both separately and in the aggregate, were negatively associated with changes in the rate of interest. Such results, however, are not inconsistent with a positive substitution effect between saving and the rate of interest because the interest coefficient did not necessarily isolate the substitution effect. In addition, since Radice did not use total saving, the results he obtained may have reflected the substitution between forms of saving which occur when the interest rate of one form changed relative to that of another. In other words, it is quite likely that Radice was picking up considerable cross effects and not adequately measuring the responsiveness of aggregate saving to changes in an appropriate interest variable.

Zellner, Huang, and Chau, in a recent study of the short-run consumption function, introduced the open market money rate on four- to six-month commercial paper as the interest variable relating quarterly consumption to lagged consumption, total disposable income, and liquid assets.[10] In such a model they obtained insignificant positive coefficients. Their explanation for such a result was that the interest rate measures both an opportunity cost of holding money and a rate of return for the other assets included in the liquid asset variable. In addition to this explanation, their use of the money rate on commercial paper can be questioned on the ground that it is hardly the appropriate interest variable to use for assessing the responsiveness of household saving to changes in the rate of interest, unless such a rate is highly correlated with the more appropriate ones such as yields on stocks and bonds. The use of quarterly rather than annual data may also explain their insignificant results since it is quite reasonable to suppose that consumption reacts to changes in the interest rate with a lag in excess of three months.

In summary, no evidence exists which supports the hypothesis that the substitution effect upon consumption of changes in the rate of interest is negative.

---

[9] Edward A. Radice, *Savings in Great Britain, 1922–1935: An Analysis of the Causes of Variations in Savings* (London: Oxford University Press, 1939).

[10] A. Zellner, D. S. Huang, and L. C. Chau, "Further Analysis of the Short-Run Consumption Function with Emphasis on the Role of Liquid Assets," *Econometrica*, Vol. 33 (July 1965), pp. 571–81.

Empirical Evidence

The income and consumption data used in this study can be conveniently labeled according to the sources from which they were obtained. Thus the "Goldsmith data" will refer to R. W. Goldsmith's *A Study of Saving in the United States*,[11] and the "MBA data" to the time series used in both "The 'Life Cycle' Hypothesis of Saving" by Modigliani and Ando[12] and "Lags in Fiscal Policy" by Ando and Brown.[13]

Since detailed accounts of the derivation of the series are readily available from the sources themselves, only the notation and exact location of the data will be established in this section.

In addition to the income and consumption figures, data on wealth were also used. The MBA data contained a net worth series which was used in a subset of those regressions based on the MBA data. In addition to this series, other wealth series were used which were kindly supplied by Allan Meltzer and correspond to the wealth concepts used by him in his recent studies of the demand for money.[14]

Several interest rates were used; their sources are listed below. Of greatest importance are the series of net and average interest rates used in this study. It was noted above that the net rather than the gross interest rate is the relevant variable consumers take into consideration when formulating their present and future consumption plans. Consequently, since all available data on the various interest rates are gross of personal income taxes, some adjustments must be made to obtain the more appropriate net rates. In addition, since many different interest rates reflect the rate of return on the various assets in which saving may be invested, the selection of a single interest rate for inclusion in the consumption function requires that such a rate be defensible either as "representative," meaning that it is

---

[11] Raymond W. Goldsmith, *A Study of Saving in the United States* (Princeton University Press, Vols. 1 and 2, 1955; Vol. 3, 1956).

[12] Albert Ando and Franco Modigliani, "The 'Life Cycle' Hypothesis of Saving: Aggregate Implications and Tests," *American Economic Review*, Vol. 53 (March 1963), pp. 55–84.

[13] Albert Ando and E. Cary Brown, "Lags in Fiscal Policy," in *Stabilization Policies*, Prepared for the Commission on Money and Credit (Prentice-Hall, 1963), pp. 97–163.

[14] Allan H. Meltzer, "The Demand for Money: The Evidence from the Time Series," *Journal of Political Economy*, Vol. 71 (June 1963), pp. 219–46.

highly correlated with all or most of the other rates, or as a relevant average rate.

In light of the existence of a progressive income tax, the use of a net rate of return requires the construction of an average marginal tax rate. This follows from the fact that individuals regard the relevant net rate for themselves to be

(18) $$r_n = r_g(1 - t_m),$$

where r_n and r_g are net and gross rates respectively and t_m is the marginal tax rate relevant to the individual's income bracket. The variation of t_m over income thus necessitates the use of an averaging mechanism to generate a tax rate applicable to the household sector.

Though property income arises from numerous sources, this study will assume that only two categories need be considered for purposes of constructing an average tax rate, t^*. These categories are dividend and interest income. All other sources of property income are assumed to be positively related to either of these.

Definitions and notations are established, as follows:

D = total dividend income
B = total interest income
d_i = amount of dividend income in the ith class
b_i = amount of interest income in the ith class
$V_i = \dfrac{d_i}{D}$ = proportion of total dividend income contained in the ith income class
$W_i = \dfrac{b_i}{B}$ = proportion of total interest income contained in the ith income class
t_i = marginal tax rate in the ith income class

With these definitions the average marginal tax rate applicable to dividend income is

(19) $$t_s^* = \sum_{i=1}^{N} V_i t_i$$

and for interest income is

(20) $$t_b^* = \sum_{i=1}^{N} W_i t_i,$$

where the t^*'s have been subscripted as (s) and (b) respectively on the assumption that, in general, dividend income is related to yields on stocks and interest income is related to yields on bonds.[15] This last association then leads to the following definitions:

YS = gross-of-tax yield on common stocks
$NYS = YS(1 - t_s^*)$ = net-of-tax yield on common stocks
YB = gross-of-tax yield on (corporate AAA) bonds
$NYB = YB(1 - t_b^*)$ = net-of-tax yield on bonds

Constructing an average rate of return from the preceding rates is accomplished in the following manner:

$$AYSB = \frac{D \cdot YS}{D + B} + \frac{B \cdot YB}{D + B}$$
= average yield on stocks and bonds;

$$ANYSB = \frac{D \cdot NYS}{D + B} + \frac{B \cdot NYB}{D + B}$$
= average net yield on stocks and bonds.

If YB is defined as the yield to maturity, both the expected rate of change in the general price level and the expected rate of capital gains or losses are contained in the gross rate and, hence, in the net rate. This is not true for YS, however. To account for the capital gain or loss element, some explicit adjustment needs to be made. On the assumption that this is reflected in the price of stocks, the following adjustment to stock yields may be made. With the following definitions,

$P^s(t)$ = index of prices on common stock
$P(t)$ = consumer price index
$CG(t)$ = real rate of capital gains and losses (as the result of divergent price changes and the effect of undistributed profits)
$$= \frac{P^s(t)}{P^s(t-1)} \frac{P(t-1)}{P(t)} - 1,$$

the total gross yield on common stocks is

$$TYS = YS + CG.$$

The total net yield on stocks is

$$TNYS = NYS + CG,$$

where it is assumed that the effective rate of tax on CG is zero.

---

[15] These tax rates are listed in App. B, p. 300.

Using TYS and $TNYS$ in the averaging of rates gives

$$ATYSB = \frac{D \cdot TYS}{D + B} + \frac{B \cdot YB}{D + B}$$
$$= \text{average total yield on stocks and bonds, and}$$
$$ATNYSB = \frac{D \cdot TNYS}{D + B} + \frac{B \cdot NYB}{D + B}$$
$$= \text{average total net yield on stocks and bonds.}$$

In addition to the notation for the interest rates established above, which are identical for both sets of data, it is necessary to establish the notation for the other variables, as follows:

Goldsmith Data, 1897–1949

Y_T = total real per capita disposable income = total disposable income from Goldsmith[16] divided by the consumer price index (P) and population (N)

C = real per capita consumption = $Y_T - S$ where S is personal saving from Goldsmith[17] deflated by P and N

$W(g)$ = real per capita national wealth = national wealth from Goldsmith[18] deflated by P and N

$W(m) = W(g) - [(\text{net government assets} + \text{government debt} + \text{non-metallic money})/(PN)]$.[19]

MBA Data, 1929–58

Y_L = real per capita labor income after tax
Y_P = real per capita property income after tax
$Y_T = Y_L + Y_P$ = real per capita total disposable income
W = real per capita net worth = nominal net worth/PN, where nominal net worth is defined as in Goldsmith.[20]

---

[16] The observations on total disposable income were obtained from Goldsmith, *A Study of Saving*, Vol. 3, Table N–1, column 9. The observations on P and N were obtained from U.S. Bureau of Census, *Historical Statistics of the United States, Colonial Times to 1957* (1960), Series E, column 113 and Series A, column 2, respectively.

[17] Goldsmith, *A Study of Saving*, Vol. 1, Table T–6, column 1.

[18] *Ibid.*, Vol. 3, Table W–1, column 1.

[19] These data were supplied by Allan Meltzer. A more detailed description may be found in his previously cited articles.

[20] Goldsmith, *A Study of Saving*, Vol. 3, Tables W–12 through W–16.

The source of gross-of-tax interest rate was the *Historical Statistics of the United States*,[21] where

YS = Yields on common stocks, Moody's (Table X339), and Cowles Commission (Table X335)

YB = Moody's yields on high grade bonds (Table X333)

A Test of the Model

The theoretical model developed above indicates that consumption is related to the present worth of the consumer and the rate of return available on the unconsumed portion of his income. Since present worth was an unobservable variable, a requirement for relating this concept to observable magnitudes was that the consumption function could be written as

(21) $$C = A_0 + A_1 Y^* + A_2 W + A_3 r + u.$$

Estimating equation (21) requires that a method be devised for constructing Y^*, that the appropriate wealth concept be used, and that either a representative interest rate or a weighted average of several rates be chosen.

Using an adaptive expectations model to derive the concept of expected income, the income variable, Y^*, was constructed using equation (15). In the Goldsmith data the first observation on Y^*_{t-1} was taken to be equal to the observed Y_t for 1897. Starting with this as a base, subsequent data for Y^*_t were generated using equation (15). For the empirical work reported below, the initial year was 1905. Thus, the initial value of Y^*_t actually used in the regression was an estimate based on eight previous years of observed values of Y_t. In the case of the MBA data, the available series was judged to be too short to warrant the loss of a number of observations. Hence, the initial value of Y^*_{t-1} was taken to be the first value of Y_t in the MBA series.[22]

[21] From U.S. Bureau of the Census, Tables X339, X335, and X333. (For the Goldsmith data, Tables X339 and X335 were spliced.)

[22] A stepwise regression program was used to estimate Y^*. This program calculated alternative Y^*'s by setting α to a predetermined level and allowing B to vary over the range 0.05 to 1.0 in multiples of 0.05. After "forcing" the program to accept the wealth and interest variables, it was then "allowed" to choose that Y^* which maximized R^2. For a detailed exposition of this program see Hodson Thornber, "Manual for a Stepwise Regression Program," Report 6603 (University of Chicago, Center for Mathematical Studies in Business and Economics, March 8, 1966).

It is also necessary to choose among alternative methods for handling the war years in constructing Y^*, for these observations are not included in any of the regressions. The method easiest to compute, that of treating the war years as any other year, was chosen after it was observed that alternative methods produced only slightly different results.

The wealth variable used in the Goldsmith data is an adjusted national wealth concept while in the MBA data the wealth variable is an estimate of the net worth of the household sector. Net worth and national wealth are defined as follows:

Net worth = cumulated saving plus net capital changes plus net realized and unrealized capital gains or losses

National wealth = current value of domestic reproducible tangible assets plus domestic non-reproducible tangible assets plus net foreign assets

= cumulated saving plus net realized and unrealized gains or losses on reproducible and non-reproducible assets

National wealth can be viewed as the consolidated net worth for the entire nation, the ultimate holders being households, private non-profit institutions, and government. The adjusted wealth concept used in the Goldsmith regressions deletes government assets, leaving, in addition to the household sector's holdings, those of the non-profit institutions. The size of the latter is expected to be a relatively small fraction of the remaining total. Estimates for national wealth exist for the entire period covered by the Goldsmith sample while estimates of net worth exist only for benchmark years and therefore require interpolation, which was done for the MBA sample. Although differences exist between the adjusted national wealth and net worth series, they are not large; for the time period common to both samples the correlation between the two was 0.95.

In this study, the series on bond yields is taken to be representative of yields on fixed income obligations generally, while the series on stock yields is taken to be representative of the return on equities. The two series show substantial independent variation. The interest variable, YB, is considered preferable to YS because (1) when YB

and *YS* were introduced as alternative interest variables in equations otherwise the same, *YB* consistently proved to have higher explanatory power, and (2) dividend yields on stocks are poor indicators of the earnings which investors expect from their securities, both because investors also value the retained earnings of corporations and because dividend yields vary inversely with expected changes in earnings.

Among the adjusted interest variables *NYB* is considered the best. This position is taken because (1) combining unadjusted bond and stock yields causes the resulting average rate to have the inferior characteristics of stock yields alluded to in the previous paragraph, and (2) attempts to use an estimate of the total return to stocks, both singly and incorporated into an average rate, were unsuccessful. However, caution is needed in using *NYB*, not only because the calculations of the average marginal tax rate were necessarily rough in nature, but also because increasing tax rates over time impose a downward trend upon the net rate, making such a variable (and all other variables adjusted similarly) likely suspects for picking up spurious correlations.

Table 1 contains the results of using *YB* and *NYB* in both the Goldsmith and MBA samples. Both interest variables enter with significantly negative coefficients and provide estimates of the slope of the consumption function with respect to the interest rate which are similar in magnitude for each rate. The estimates of the interest elasticity of consumption, obtained by multiplying the slope of the consumption function with respect to the rate of interest by the value of r/C for 1949, are also similar in magnitude.

The low values observed for the marginal propensities to consume out of expected income stem from the fact that wealth is also present in the regressions reported in Table 1. These marginal propensities can be converted into magnitudes that are comparable to those derived from other studies in which no wealth variable appeared, by assuming a given relationship of wealth to income. If the average values of W/Y^* over the period of observation are used for this purpose, the "comparable" marginal propensity to consume out of income is $A_1 + A_2(W/Y)$. The figures thus computed for the four regressions of Table 1 all lie between 0.60 and 0.75, an order of magnitude which is not surprising in comparison with other estimates of marginal propensities to consume.

TABLE 1. Effect of Interest Rates on Consumption: Regression Results Using Gross and Net-of-Tax Bond Rates with Goldsmith Data, 1905–49 and Modigliani, Brown, and Ando Data, 1929–58 [a]

Source of data	Constant	Expected income	Coefficient of adjustment B	Wealth	Interest rate	Coefficient of determination R^2	Durbin-Watson statistic D.W.	Income elasticity [b] η_{cy}	Wealth elasticity [b] η_{cw}	Interest elasticity [b] η_{cr}
Goldsmith										
Gross bond rates	332.53 (4.84)	0.3835 (5.36)	0.85	0.0469 (3.82)	−1761.1 (−2.22)	0.96206	1.57	0.44	0.35	−.026
Net bond rates	393.02 (5.15)	0.4210 (5.82)	0.80	0.0323 (2.25)	−2372.0 (−2.15)	0.96369	1.64	0.48	0.22	−.026
Modigliani, Brown, and Ando										
Gross bond rates	168.20 (7.90)	0.4799 (15.90)	0.65	0.0650 (9.46)	−1795.4 (−3.41)	0.99868	1.41	0.54	0.35	−.032
Net bond rates	192.24 (8.43)	0.4425 (14.62)	0.65	0.0670 (11.36)	−2210.4 (−4.51)	0.99902	1.60	0.50	0.36	−.022

Source: Derived from equation (21). See footnotes 11–21 for source of basic data upon which regressions are based.
[a] Numbers in parentheses are t values.
[b] The elasticity estimates were computed using the 1949 values of the relevant variables.

The figures displayed in Table 1 show little indication of serial correlation; the Durbin-Watson statistic in no case shows significant serial correlation, and only in one case is the test inconclusive at the 2.5 percent level of significance. Moreover, even though the simple correlations between the regressors are relatively large, all of the estimated coefficients in Table 1 are significant. Hence, there is no need for concern with problems of multicollinearity.

Using the maximum likelihood ratio test, the null hypothesis that B equals 1 was rejected if

$$N \log \frac{1 - R^2(1)}{1 - R^2(B)} \geq \chi_p^2 (1),$$

where $R^2(1)$ is the coefficient of multiple determination obtained when current, rather than expected, income is used with the wealth and interest variables. At a value of 0.05 for p, both of the MBA regressions reject the null hypothesis while none of the Goldsmith regressions do.

Evidence in support of a significant substitution effect is weaker when the interest variable incorporates the yield on common stocks.[23] When $ANYSB$ is used in the Goldsmith sample a significant though smaller coefficient is obtained, the resulting estimate of the interest elasticity being -0.02. In the MBA sample the coefficient of $ANYSB$ is negative but insignificantly so. The Goldsmith result reflects the negative coefficient obtained when NYS is used, while the MBA result is the consequence of a positive, though insignificant, coefficient for NYS. Similar coefficients are obtained when the gross stock yields are used.

When stock yields are adjusted to incorporate the rate of return in the form of capital gains or losses, they always produce coefficients similar in magnitude to those obtained when CG is used alone. An example of this is the insignificant value of -37.79 obtained for CG in the Goldsmith sample, compared with values of -40.89, -40.78, and -55.77 obtained when TYS, $TNYS$, and $ATNYSB$ are used respectively. These results are explained by the fact that the variance of CG is so large as to dominate any composite rate which incorporates it.

The performance of stock yields, whether adjusted or unadjusted,

[23] Yields on preferred stocks provide results quite similar to those obtained from common stock yields.

may be attributable to the deficiencies discussed previously. Inclusion of the rate of capital gains or losses represented an attempt, which proved unsuccessful, to rectify some of these deficiencies. An adaptive expectations model applied to stock yields also failed to produce any significant improvements. The poor performance of stock yields is not entirely unexpected, for it is reasonable to assume that the method investors use to calculate the return to such assets is more complicated than the one assumed in this study.

Conclusion

The results obtained from using gross and net of tax corporate bond yields in a consumption function containing income and wealth offer convincing evidence that consumption is responsive to changes in the rate of interest. If the interest elasticity of saving is related to the interest elasticity of consumption as shown in the first section of this chapter, estimates of η_{sr}^s range from 0.18 to 0.27 when they are computed from the elasticity estimates in Table 1 and the average value for C/S. Such elasticity estimates are much larger than those assumed to exist by many economists who feel that saving is unresponsive to changes in the rate of interest.[24] Evidence for such a conclusion is often sought in the constancy of the savings-income ratio during periods when the interest rate has fluctuated considerably. It must be recognized, however, that income effects were present when interest rates were changing and that the constancy of the savings-income ratio may have been the consequence of an offsetting substitution effect. The evidence in Table 1 indicates that a substantial substitution effect did in fact exist.

[24] See Daniel B. Suits, "The Determinants of Consumer Expenditure: A Review of Present Knowledge," in Daniel B. Suits and others, *Impacts of Monetary Policy*, Prepared for the Commission on Money and Credit (Prentice-Hall, 1963), pp. 1–57.

APPENDIX A

Derivation of the Income and Substitution Effect of a Change in the Rate of Interest upon Current Consumption

CRITICAL VALUES MUST BE DETERMINED for the Lagrangean expression

(A1) $\quad U^* = U(C_1, C_2, \ldots, C_N) + \lambda \left[W_0 + \sum_{i=1}^{N} \frac{(Y_i^e - C_i)}{(1 + r)^i} \right],$

where C_N is taken to include the consumer's desired net worth at the end of the planning horizon. The necessary conditions for the constrained maximum of the utility function are then

(A2a) $\quad U_i - \dfrac{\lambda}{(1 + r)^i} = 0 \quad i = 1, 2, \ldots, N,$

(A2b) $\quad W_0 + \sum_{i=1}^{N} \dfrac{(Y_i^e - C_i)}{(1 + r)^i} = 0,$

where $U_i = \partial U / \partial C_i$.

If (A2) is totally differentiated, the result is

(A3a) $\quad \sum_{j=1}^{N} \left(U_{ij} dC_j - \dfrac{d\lambda}{(1 + r)^i} \right) = \dfrac{-i \lambda dr}{(1 + r)^{i+1}} \quad i = 1, 2, \ldots, N,$

(A3b) $\quad \sum_{j=1}^{N} \dfrac{dC_j}{(1 + r)^j} = dW_0 + \sum_{i=1}^{N} \dfrac{dY_i^e}{(1 + r)^i} + \sum_{i=1}^{N} \dfrac{i(C_i - Y_i^e)}{(1 + r)^{i+1}} dr,$

where $\quad U_{ij} = \dfrac{\partial^2 U}{\partial C_i \partial C_j}.$

If the above system of $N + 1$ equations is solved for dC_1, the result is

$$(A4) \quad dC_1 = -\sum_{i=1}^{N} \frac{i\lambda dr}{(1+r)^{i+1}} \cdot V_{i1} + V_{N+1,\,1}\left[dW_0 + \sum_{i=1}^{N} \frac{dY_i^e}{(1+r)^i}\right.$$
$$\left. + \sum_{i=1}^{N} \frac{i(C_i - Y_i^e)}{(1+r)^{i+1}} dr\right].$$

Here V_{ij} denotes the ratio of the cofactor of the $i^e j$th element in the matrix to the determinant of that matrix.

$$\begin{array}{cccc} U_{11} & U_{12} & U_{1N} & \dfrac{-1}{1+r} \\ U_{21} & U_{22} & U_{2N} & \dfrac{-1}{(1+r)^2} \\ \cdot & \cdot & \cdot & \cdot \\ \cdot & \cdot & \cdot & \cdot \\ \cdot & \cdot & \cdot & \cdot \\ U_{N1} & U_{N2} & U_{NN} & \dfrac{-1}{(1+r)^N} \\ \dfrac{1}{1+r} & \dfrac{1}{(1+r)^2} & \dfrac{1}{(1+r)^N} & U \end{array}$$

The partial derivative of C_1 with respect to r is therefore

$$(A5) \quad \frac{\partial C_1}{\partial r} = -\sum_{i=1}^{N} \frac{i\lambda V_{i1}}{(1+r)^{i+1}} + V_{N+1,\,1} \sum_{i=1}^{N} \frac{i(C_i - Y_i^e)}{(1+r)^{i+1}}.$$

The first of these two terms incorporates the substitution effect of a change in r, and the second embodies the income effect.

The income-effect term can be expressed in a more convenient and intuitively appealing form. Consider the expression

$$\sum_{i=1}^{N} \frac{i(C_i - Y_i^e)}{(1+r)^{i+1}}$$

and expand it as follows:

$$(A6) \quad \sum_{i=1}^{N} \frac{i(C_i - Y_i^e)}{(1+r)^{i+1}} = \sum_{i=1}^{N} \frac{(C_i - Y_i^e)}{(1+r)^{i+1}} + \sum_{i=2}^{N} \frac{(C_i - Y_i^e)}{(1+r)^{i+1}} + \sum_{i=3}^{N} \frac{(C_i - Y_i^e)}{(1+r)^{i+1}}$$
$$+ \cdots + \sum_{i=N-1}^{N} \frac{(C_i - Y_i^e)}{(1+r)^{i+1}} + \frac{C_N - Y_N^e}{(1+r)^{N+1}}.$$

Each of the terms in the expansion (A6) can be identified with the wealth of the consumer as of a particular point in time, adjusted by a discount factor. From the basic budget constraint, it is known that

$$W_0 = \sum_{i=1}^{N} \frac{(C_i - Y_i^e)}{(1+r)^i};$$

therefore the first term in the expansion is equal to $W_0/(1+r)$.

Similarly, if the budget constraint facing the consumer at the end of the first period is written as

$$W_1 = \sum_{i=2}^{N} \frac{(C_i - Y_i^e)}{(1+r)^{i-1}},$$

the second term in the expansion is seen to be equal to $W_1/(1+r)^2$. All the other terms can be transformed in an analogous fashion. The last term, for example, can be expressed in terms of the budget constraint facing the consumer at the end of period $N - 1$. This constraint is

$$W_{N-1} = \frac{(C_N - Y_N^e)}{(1+r)},$$

and the last term of the expansion is therefore equal to $W_{N-1}/(1+r)^N$. The result is therefore that

$$\sum_{i=1}^{N} \frac{i(C_i - Y_i^e)}{(1+r)^{i+1}}$$

can be expressed equivalently as

$$\sum_{j=0}^{N-1} \frac{W_j}{(1+r)^{j+1}}.$$

Thus (A5) may be rewritten as

(A7) $$\frac{\partial C_1}{\partial r} = -\sum_{i=1}^{N} \frac{i\lambda V_{i1}}{(1+r)^{i+1}} + V_{N+1,\,1} \sum_{j=0}^{N} \frac{W_j}{(1+r)^{j+1}}.$$

This transformation permits an intuitively clear interpretation of the income effect of a change in the interest rate upon consumption. The expression $V_{N+1,\,1}$ is a coefficient measuring the effect on consumption during period 1 of changes in wealth brought into period 1, and also of changes in the present value of future labor income. Equation (A7) permits one to see that $V_{N+1,\,1}$ also measures the effect on consumption of changes in the present value of future property income. Property income accruing in period 1 will be rW_0; if r changes, the change in this income will be $W_0 dr$; if this is discounted back to the end of period zero, the result is $W_0 dr/(1+r)$. Property income anticipated to accrue in period N will be rW_{N-1}, and its change, as r changes, will be $W_{N-1} dr$. The present value of this change in property income, again discounted to the end of period zero, is $W_{N-1}dr/(1+r)^N$. The income effect of a change in the interest rate therefore measures the impact on consumption of the changes in property income that the interest rate change would bring about if the consumer maintained his previously planned pattern of wealth-holding through time.

APPENDIX B

Average Marginal Tax Rates, 1913–58

TABLE B-1. Average Marginal Dividend and Interest Income Tax Rates, 1913–58

Year	Dividend Income t_s^*	Interest income t_b^*	Year	Dividend income t_s^*	Interest income t_b^*
1913	0.0165	0.0179	1936	0.2986	0.1760
1914	0.0165	0.0179	1937	0.2856	0.1725
1915	0.0165	0.0179	1938	0.2380	0.1443
1916	0.0230	0.0317	1939	0.2552	0.1527
1917	0.1402	0.1147	1940	0.2870	0.1679
1918	0.2271	0.2143	1941	0.3638	0.2471
1919	0.2145	0.1819	1942	0.4508	0.3472
1920	0.1958	0.1423	1943	0.4639	0.3663
1921	0.1752	0.1116	1944	0.5888	0.4359
1922	0.1672	0.1165	1945	0.5401	0.4464
1923	0.2230	0.1016	1946	0.5348	0.4339
1924	0.1390	0.0743	1947	0.5512	0.4308
1925	0.0739	0.0749	1948	0.5139	0.3711
1926	0.1013	0.0792	1949	0.4934	0.3487
1927	0.1029	0.1417	1950	0.5278	0.3740
1928	0.1112	0.0919	1951	0.5259	0.3495
1929	0.1532	0.0969	1952	0.4829	0.3155
1930	0.1368	0.0793	1953	0.5245	0.3710
1931	0.1311	0.0719	1954	0.5127	0.3473
1932	0.2709	0.1440	1955	0.5325	0.3532
1933	0.2771	0.1424	1956	0.5294	0.3566
1934	0.2880	0.1551	1957	0.5202	0.3364
1935	0.2985	0.1630	1958	0.5317	0.3334

Source: Derived from equations (19) and (20), using dividend and interest income and tax rates from U.S Treasury Department, Internal Revenue Service, *Statistics of Income*, annual issues containing 1913–58 data on individual income tax returns. Beginning with 1948, it was assumed that married couples filed joint returns.

MARVIN KOSTERS

Effects of an Income Tax on Labor Supply

THE EFFECT OF AN INCOME TAX on the incentive to supply labor services has elicited considerable academic and public discussion. Theoretical expositions of the problem in the economic literature typically focus on an individual's choice between work and leisure, and usually assume that an individual bears the tax himself and regards it as equivalent to a reduction in his real wage. The problem is then reduced to the effect of a change in wage rate on leisure demanded and hence on labor supplied.

A change in the wage rate carries with it an income and a substitution effect. The income effect on the quantity of leisure demanded which results from an increase in the wage rate is positive if leisure is not an inferior good. The substitution effect of a wage increase on leisure demanded is negative since the opportunity cost of a unit of leisure time (its price in terms of market goods foregone) has increased. The two effects thus bear opposite signs, the income effect

This chapter is an outgrowth of "Income and Substitution Effects in a Family Labor Supply Model" (P-3339, The RAND Corporation, December 1966), which was originally prepared as the author's doctoral dissertation (University of Chicago, June 1966).

on labor supplied being negative and the substitution effect positive.[1]

To determine the effect of an income tax on aggregate labor supply, it is necessary to consider not only the change in relative prices that an income tax implies, but also the overall impact on income as perceived by the taxed workers. For example, if incremental expenditures from tax receipts on services provided by the government have a value to society equal to the incremental value of purchases that individuals would otherwise make for themselves, then, as a first approximation, an incremental change in the tax rate will carry only a substitution effect. The change in labor supply as a result of such a tax rate change will depend on an income-compensated wage rate effect. On the other hand, if tax receipts are spent in such a way that workers perceive no effect on their income from these expenditures, the gross or total effect of a wage rate change represents the response of labor supply to such a tax rate change.

As an alternative to a change in only the income tax, which results in changes in tax revenues, the substitution of an income tax for other taxes can be considered as a way of avoiding changes in tax receipts. The distribution of income can be held constant by considering alternative tax packages which bear similar incidence by income class. The effect of a change in the income tax itself under these circumstances will depend on compensated wage rate effects, but it is important to recognize that the alternative taxes which are reduced when income taxes are raised may also have independent effects on labor supply.

A different aspect of the effect of an income tax is its effect on welfare. An income tax implies a shift in the relative prices confronting a worker; that is, the price of a unit of market goods is made artificially high relative to a unit of non-marketed time or leisure. If a unit of leisure is defined as the amount of time in which a worker can earn a dollar, the marginal cost of producing a dollar's worth of market goods in the economy is a unit of leisure. However, the worker can obtain only $(1 - t)$ dollar's worth of market goods in return for a unit of leisure if t is the marginal income tax rate. This distortion between marginal rates of substitution in production

---

[1] The treatment of the problem in Richard A. Musgrave, *The Theory of Public Finance* (McGraw-Hill, 1959), Chap. 11, reflects well the current state of thinking in this field, and provides numerous references.

and consumption implies a lower level of satisfaction for the worker than he could achieve if the tax revenue were raised in a manner which left the price ratio undisturbed. This difference in the level of satisfaction achieved is the welfare cost of such a tax.[2]

Since it is not feasible to tax leisure, a pattern of taxation that leaves all relative prices undistorted is not a practical alternative. Thus the existence of relative price distortions may be regarded as a necessary consequence of the resource requirements of governmental bodies, but the cost to society of these distortions will depend on the pattern in which taxes are imposed.

If an income tax is imposed in order to finance government-provided goods and services which are direct substitutes for those being purchased privately, real incomes will be unchanged by the tax. Whether the income distribution is altered will depend on what goods are provided and to whom they are made available, as well as on the form of the tax. The welfare cost associated with the imposition of the tax will depend on the reaction of the labor supply to this change in relative prices, and that reaction will be the compensated wage rate effect.

In the case where an income tax is substituted for a neutral tax yielding the same revenue, consumers are left with the same quantity of resources and hence the same real income. The welfare cost of such a change in the income tax again depends on the compensated wage rate effect. Where an income tax is substituted for a set of excises or other non-neutral taxes, the measurement of welfare cost depends upon the entire pattern of taxes involved, but once again the compensated elasticity of supply of labor plays an important role in the analysis.

A taxpayer may of course experience a loss of welfare from taxation in addition to what I have called the welfare cost of the tax. If tax revenues are wasted or exacted as tribute, that loss in welfare is measured by the amount of tax revenue given up. However, this loss corresponds to an income effect on the taxpayer and does not depend on the magnitude of substitution relations among commodities.

A number of studies have presented empirical evidence of the

---

[2] For a detailed exposition of welfare cost analysis, see Arnold C. Harberger, "Taxation, Resource Allocation, and Welfare," *The Role of Direct and Indirect Taxes in the Federal Revenue System*, A Conference Report of the National Bureau of Economic Research and Brookings Institution (Princeton University Press, 1964), pp. 25–70.

relationship between labor supplied and the wage rate.[3] This evidence in general supports the notion of a backward-bending labor supply function, the income effect outweighing the substitution effect, for male primary workers. For another important segment of the labor force, married women, the substitution effect appears to outweigh the income effect.[4] Since these studies were designed to estimate the total effect of wage rates on labor supply or to examine other aspects of labor force behavior, no attempt was made in most of them to estimate the two effects separately.[5]

A family labor supply model is developed in the following section of this chapter as a means of analyzing effects of wage rate changes on labor supply. Expressions are derived for compensated wage rate effects in terms of coefficients estimated in alternative regression models. In the next succeeding section some empirical evidence is presented on the magnitude of wage rate effects for three components of labor supply. The effect of wage rates on hours of work per week and per year of older males (ages fifty through sixty-four) is examined using regression analysis. The expressions for compensated wage rate effects derived below allow a reinterpretation of regression results presented in other studies which deal with labor force participation of males and of married women, the two other components of labor supply considered in this chapter. The results are summarized in a final section.

[3] See Paul H. Douglas, *The Theory of Wages* (Macmillan, 1934), pp. 295–314; Clarence D. Long, *The Labor Force Under Changing Income and Employment* (Princeton University Press, 1958); Ethel B. Jones, "New Estimates of Hours of Work per Week and Hourly Earnings, 1900–1957," *Review of Economics and Statistics*, Vol. 45 (November 1963), pp. 374–85; and T. A. Finegan, "Hours of Work in the United States: A Cross-Sectional Analysis," *Journal of Political Economy*, Vol. 70 (October 1962), pp. 452–70.

[4] See Jacob Mincer, "Labor Force Participation of Married Women: A Study of Labor Supply," in *Aspects of Labor Economics*, A Conference of the Universities-National Bureau Committee for Economic Research (Princeton University Press for National Bureau of Economic Research, 1962), pp. 63–105; Glen G. Cain, *Married Women in the Labor Force: An Economic Analysis* (University of Chicago Press, 1966); and William G. Bowen and T. A. Finegan, "Labor Force Participation and Unemployment," in Arthur M. Ross (ed.), *Employment Policy and the Labor Market* (University of California Press, 1965), pp. 115–61.

[5] Mincer and Cain discuss the estimation of a substitution effect in their studies cited in note 4.

The Labor Supply Model

Analyzing the supply of labor in terms of the demand for leisure brings consumption theory to bear on the problem of labor supply. The family will constitute the unit of analysis here since it is regarded, appropriately, as the decision-making unit in studies of consumption behavior. Total family income is assumed to be pooled. The family's consumption of leisure is positively related to family income if leisure is not an inferior good. The distribution of leisure, non-market work, and market work among family members will depend on the labor market opportunities and other characteristics of individual members. Labor supplied to the market and response to economic variables will differ among family members because of the role of the wife in child rearing, for example, and her comparative advantage in producing home goods. Similarly, young members of the family can be expected to devote a large share of their time to investment activity in the form of schooling. Since earning powers of individual family members and marginal productivities in alternative activities differ among family members, this set of relative prices should affect the pattern of activities to which family members allocate their time. Total family income from market work is regarded as the outcome of a maximizing process which takes into account total resources available to the family, the productivity of its members in market and non-market activities, and the tastes of the family.[6]

If the analysis is restricted to husband-wife families where opportunities for work by other family members are negligible, the key economic variables are the wage rates of the husband and wife and income from non-employment sources. To obtain an estimate of the substitution effect of a wage rate change, a component attributable to the income effect must be subtracted from the total effect of the change in the wage rate. With no other changes taking place (that is, with no change in the spouse's wage rate or in non-employment income), a change in the wage rate, dw, for a worker supplying L units of labor causes a change in income of $dy = Ldw$. The total effect of a wage rate change is the partial derivative $\partial L/\partial w$, and the component which is due to the associated change in income is

---

[6] This framework is essentially that employed in Mincer, "Labor Force Participation," pp. 65–68.

$(\partial L/\partial y)(\partial y/\partial w)$. The derivative $\partial L/\partial y$ represents the effect of a change in income with no change in wage rates, such as the receipt of an annuity, and L can be substituted for the derivative $\partial y/\partial w$. Hence, an expression for the substitution effect or compensated wage rate effect is

$$(1) \qquad S = \frac{\partial L}{\partial w} - L\frac{\partial L}{\partial y},$$

or, in elasticity form,

$$(2) \qquad \epsilon = \frac{\partial L}{\partial w}\frac{w}{L} - \left(\frac{wL}{y}\right)\left(\frac{\partial L}{\partial y}\cdot\frac{y}{L}\right).$$

The labor supply elasticities in these expressions for the compensated wage rate effect are simply the reaction coefficients of labor supplied by the worker, reflecting his response to changes in his wage rate, holding the wage rate of his spouse and non-employment income constant, and to changes in income, holding both wage rates constant. Estimates of these coefficients can be obtained by separately regressing measures of labor supplied by the husband and wife both on wage rates and on non-employment income. The coefficients of wage changes estimated in such regressions are estimates of the total effects of wage rate changes, but they can be adapted via equations (1) and (2) to provide estimates of compensated wage rate effects.

In such a regression model (hereafter, method A) the effect of income on labor supplied is estimated from the effect on labor supplied of changes in non-employment income, one measure of which is money income that accrues to the family from sources other than labor earnings. There are several reasons, however, for questioning the reliability of an income effect estimated from this type of variable. Since only income received in cash is used to measure non-employment income, income in the form of a stream of services from the family's equity in housing and other durables is neglected. Cash receipts from non-employment sources may also include transfer payments such as unemployment compensation or disability insurance benefits, elements of family income which reflect, as well as help to determine, the worker's labor supply experience. Along with these conceptual problems, measurements of the variable may also be significantly in error because this type of income is frequently under- and mis-reported. Moreover, because non-employment income is usually a small fraction of total family income, inaccuracies tend to be magnified when the estimated effect of non-employment income is used to compensate for the larger differences in income associated with wage differences.

An alternative to use of non-employment income to estimate an income effect is use of a measure which includes all of family income except that earned by the member whose labor supply is being studied (method B). The "income" variable in this approach is likely to be more accurately measured and usually represents a significantly larger fraction of family income. If this method is employed, the income variable which appears in the husband's labor supply equation will be different from that which appears in the wife's. These new income variables appear in place of non-employment income, with both wage rates remaining as variables in each equation. The coefficients estimated in the two equations of this model will differ from those in the other model because the income variable is no longer exogenous. Hence, the expression for the compensated wage rate effect will also differ from that obtained in the model which includes only non-employment income.

The regression model for method A, where non-employment income is used as the income variable, can be succinctly written

$$(3) \qquad L_i = a_i(w_1, w_2, Y),$$

where Y is non-employment income and the subscripts are $i = 1$ for the husband and $i = 2$ for the wife. Holding non-employment income constant, the change in real income associated with a rise of dw in the husband's wage rate will be simply $L_1 dw_1$. The income effect of this upon the husband's own labor supply will therefore be $a_{1y} L_1 dw_1$ where $a_{1y} = \partial L / \partial y$ from a relation of the form of equation (3). Hence S_{11}, representing the substitution effect of the rise in the husband's wage rate, can be written

$$(4) \qquad S_{11} = a_{11} - L_1 a_{1y},$$

where $a_{11} = \partial L_1 / \partial w_1$, and correspondingly the substitution-response of the wife's labor effort to the change in the husband's wage rate can be written: $S_{21} = a_{21} - L_1 a_{2y}$, where $a_{21} = \partial L_2 / \partial w_1$, $a_{2y} = \partial L_2 / \partial y$, again from a relation of the form of equation (3).

Method B expresses the labor supply of husband or wife as a function of both wage rates and a more global income concept—non-labor income of the family plus labor income of the spouse. Under method B, the basic labor supply equations are

$$(5) \qquad L_1 = b_1(w_1, w_2, Z),$$
$$(6) \qquad L_2 = b_2(w_1, w_2, V),$$

where $Z = w_2L_2 + Y$ and $V = w_1L_1 + Y$. The partial derivatives of the labor supply functions expressed in terms of these variables will differ from those of equation (3). Therefore, to obtain expressions for compensated wage rate effects in terms of the coefficients estimated in regressions using method B, how they differ must be determined.

Consider the husband's labor supply equation. A rise of dw in the husband's wage, holding Z constant, will now produce a dual income effect. The real income of the family will in this case rise by $L_1 dw_1 - w_2 S_{21} dw_1$, the second effect representing the value of the increase in leisure taken by the wife in response to the rise in the husband's wage, the presumptive sign of S_{21} being negative. The added leisure of the wife is a genuine increase in real income in this case, for if Z is to remain constant the loss of earnings of the wife must be hypothetically compensated from some other source (for example, an annuity). Thus, for method B,

(7) $$S_{11} = b_{11} - b_{1Z}(L_1 - w_2 S_{21}).$$

Using the relationship $S_{12} = S_{21}$, which is a general property of substitution terms involving cross effects, equation (7) can be written

(8) $$S_{11} = b_{11} - b_{1Z}(L_1 - w_2 S_{12}),$$

which in turn can be converted into elasticity form

(9) $$\epsilon_{11} = B_{11} - \frac{E_1}{Z} B_{1Z}(1 - \epsilon_{12}),$$

where the capital B's are the elasticity counterparts of the lower case b's and $E_i = w_i L_i$.

The coefficients estimated in the regression model suggested by equation (5) are estimates of b_{11}, b_{12}, and b_{1Z} (or their elasticity counterparts if the equation is estimated in logarithmic form); but the regression does not provide an estimate of ϵ_{12}. Since

$$\epsilon_{12} = \frac{E_2}{E_1} \epsilon_{21}$$

and the ratio E_2/E_1 is usually small, the assumption that $\epsilon_{12} = 0$ may not lead to serious bias in an estimate of ϵ_{11}.

However, it is possible to derive an expression for ϵ_{12} in a fashion similar to that used in equations (7) through (9) to obtain ϵ_{11}. When the effects of a rise in the wife's wage rate on the husband's labor supply are measured through equation (5), the implicit rise in real income of the family will be $-w_2 S_{22} dw_2$, reflecting the decreased leisure of the wife. No term in $L_2 dw_2$ appears here, because in a function of the form of equation (5), Z is implicitly held constant as the effects of a rise in w_2 are explored. Hence, corresponding to equation (7) we have

(10) $$S_{12} = b_{12} + b_{1Z} w_2 S_{22},$$

and corresponding to equation (9) we obtain

(11) $$\epsilon_{12} = B_{12} + \frac{E_2}{Z} B_{1Z} \epsilon_{22}.$$

Similar reasoning applied to the wife's labor supply function yields the following equations:

(12) $$S_{22} = b_{22} - b_{2V}(L_2 - w_1 S_{21})$$

(13) $$\epsilon_{22} = B_{22} - \frac{E_2}{V} B_{2V}(1 - \epsilon_{21})$$

(14) $$\epsilon_{21} = B_{21} + \frac{E_1}{V} B_{2V} \epsilon_{11}$$

An estimate of the compensated elasticity for the wife can therefore be obtained by applying method B and using the coefficients estimated in the regression suggested by equation (6) if a plausible value can be assigned to the compensated elasticity, ϵ_{11}.[7]

The Empirical Evidence

The labor supply parameters are based on cross-sectional regression analyses of U.S. Bureau of the Census data. The market context in which the measures of labor supply and wage rates were generated is viewed as one in which the observed measures of labor supply reflect the amount of market work that workers chose to supply, given their market earning capacity, family income, and

---

[7] Given the above expressions for ϵ_{11}, ϵ_{12}, ϵ_{22}, and ϵ_{21}, it is easy to solve for ϵ_{11} or ϵ_{22} in terms of the coefficients from both the husband's and wife's regressions. This is not done in this chapter, however, because reliable estimates of all of the appropriate coefficients are not available, and the estimate of one of the compensated own-wage-rate elasticities is not sensitive to the size assumed for the other so long as B_{1Z} and B_{2V} are small. Estimating the compensated elasticity by using the coefficients from only one of the regressions offers the advantage that the evidence provided by each of the regressions can be evaluated separately with little loss in the accuracy of the estimate.

other characteristics. Self-employed persons have a great deal of freedom to vary their hours of work. Although those not self-employed are more likely to be constrained by institutional forces, a significant degree of choice is often available to them while working for a single employer. In addition, multiple job holding, "moonlighting," and part-time work supplement these opportunities to vary labor supplied. The decision to seek employment is even more clearly at the individual's discretion. For these reasons, workers can typically choose employment situations consistent with their tastes. Wage rate and income coefficients are therefore treated here as estimates of labor supply parameters.

Hours of Work for Males

Selected results from regressions in which hours of work per week and per year were defined as dependent variables are reported in this section. The data were taken from the one-in-a-thousand sample of the 1960 census.[8] The segment of the labor force analyzed consisted of male household heads fifty through sixty-four years old for whom labor supply and wage rate variables could be defined.

This age group was chosen for two reasons. First, variation in reported hours of work is somewhat greater for this group than for younger workers. Second, income of the family other than earnings of the husband is likely to be a more important component of total family income than it is for younger families.

There may be more opportunity for varying the quantity of labor supplied for males in this age group, since persons approaching retirement age are more likely than younger persons to have accumulated sufficient savings to free family income from as great a dependence on current market work as was required in earlier years. The expense commitments of males in this group are also likely to be smaller and less fixed since most former dependents are now self-supporting and installment contracts for a stock of consumer durables are more likely to be paid up or nearly so.

It is crucial in the estimation of an income effect for the husband that family income other than earnings of the head be a significant component of total family income for at least some families, since

[8] U.S. Bureau of the Census, Population Division, "U.S. Censuses of Population and Housing: 1960, 1/1,000 and 1/10,000, Two National Samples of the Population of the United States" (magnetic computer tape).

independent variation in family income can occur only to the extent that there is some component not derived from the husband's earnings.

The regressions reported were selected from a much larger set of experiments in which the data were organized in different ways and alternative functional forms and definitions of variables were employed. Wage rate and income coefficients, the corresponding elasticities, and compensated wage rate elasticity estimates are reported in Table 1. The compensated elasticity estimates from the first eight regressions were obtained via equation (9) using method B with the compensated cross elasticity, ϵ_{12}, assumed to be zero, and estimates from regressions nine through twelve were obtained via equation (4) using method A.

The wage rate elasticity estimates are consistently negative and significant. They are also consistent with previous evidence of the effect of the wage rate on labor supply, and roughly consistent in size across samples and for either arithmetic or logarithmic forms.[9] In order to obtain positive estimates of the compensated wage rate elasticity, ϵ_{11}—given this evidence of the size of the income effect through the husband's wage—income coefficients are required that are negative and sufficiently large to imply an income effect at least comparable in size to the total wage rate effect. However, income coefficients of sufficient magnitude with the appropriate sign were not in general obtained.

The income coefficients estimated in the larger set of regressions from which those reported in Table 1 were selected were almost always small, usually not statistically significant, and often positive and insignificant. These results are puzzling in view of the consistently negative and significant coefficients obtained for the wage rate. This failure to obtain sufficiently large negative estimates of the income effect leads to compensated elasticity estimates that are not uniformly positive, as one would expect them to be.

Only four of the twelve compensated elasticity estimates reported in Table 1 are positive, and only one of these is based on an income coefficient significant at the 5 percent level. Although the compensated wage rate elasticities reported for the first eight equations are esti-

[9] The total elasticity estimates tend to cluster in the range -0.07 to -0.09 with relatively few estimates obtained in a variety of estimating procedures outside the range -0.06 to -0.10.

TABLE 1. Effects of Wage Rate and Income on Hours of Work of Husbands Aged 50–64, Selected Regression Results, 1960

Equation number and form[a]		Dependent variable, hours of work[b]	Independent variables					Additional control variables[f]	Compensated wage rate elasticity, ϵ_{11}	Coefficient of determination R^2
			Husband's wage[c]		Income[e]					
			Coefficient[d]	Elasticity	Coefficient[d]	Elasticity				
1. (9)	A	H	−1.040 (12.63)	−0.073	−0.0001 (0.46)	−0.014		0	−0.018	0.48
2. (9)	A	HW	−51.900 (11.80)	−0.075	−0.012 (1.21)	−0.009		0	−0.040	0.46
3. (9)	A	H	−1.150 (8.16)	−0.082	−0.004 (1.20)	−0.015		1	−0.024	0.48
4. (9)	A	HW	−54.600 (7.27)	−0.081	−0.023 (1.25)	−0.017		1	−0.015	0.46
5. (9)	A	H	−1.110 (9.70)	−0.079	0.0 (0.0)	0.0		14	−0.079	0.77
6. (9)	A	HW	−59.300 (7.58)	−0.088	−0.018 (0.97)	−0.014		14	−0.033	0.66
7. (9)	L	H	−0.062 (21.60)	−0.062	−0.0024 (2.34)	−0.002		15	−0.018	0.17
8. (9)	L	HW	−0.094 (21.27)	−0.094	−0.0073 (4.93)	−0.007		15	+0.041	0.10
9. (4)	L	H	−0.065 (9.05)	−0.065	−0.016 (1.77)	−0.016		0	+0.109	0.53
10. (4)	L	HW	−0.062 (6.42)	−0.062	−0.023 (1.84)	−0.023		0	+0.189	0.38
11. (4)	L	H	−0.043 (4.73)	−0.043	−0.010 (0.91)	−0.010		9	+0.066	0.69
12. (4)	L	HW	−0.056 (4.23)	−0.056	−0.004 (0.22)	−0.004		9	−0.012	0.53

Source: U.S. Bureau of the Census, Population Division, "U.S. Censuses of Population and Housing: 1960, 1/1,000 and 1/10,000, Two National Samples of the Population of the United States" (magnetic computer tape).

Equations 1 through 6: 1960 census aggregations for families with income other than husband's earnings and for families with none of such other income pooled with observations weighted by the square root of the number of families in the cell; 200 observations.

Equations 7 and 8: Disaggregated 1960 census data; 8,467 observations.

Equations 9 through 12: The aggregation containing only families with some income other than the husband's earnings. The observations are weighted by the square root of the number of families in the cell; 100 observations.

Aggregation was performed by stratifying by five-cent intervals of the husband's wage rate between 50 cents and 4 dollars per hour, with progressively wider intervals used beyond these limits. The aggregated data cover 6,739 husband-wife families with no family members (except the husband and perhaps his spouse) of age 20 or over in the labor force. The disaggregated data cover all families with a male head of age 50 through 64.

[a] See p. 311 for a description of the equations. The forms denoted by A have all the variables in arithmetic form and those denoted by L have the dependent variable and the wage rate and income variables in logarithmic form. The numbers in parentheses indicate the equations in the text used to obtain compensated elasticity estimates.

[b] The dependent variable, H, is reported hours of work for the week preceding the U.S. Bureau of the Census count in 1960. HW is the hours of work estimate, H, times weeks of work reported for the year preceding the census year and is thus an estimate of hours worked per year.

[c] The wage rate variable is an average wage rate computed by dividing earnings of the husband in 1959 by number of hours worked in that year (HW).

[d] Numbers in parentheses are t values.

[e] The income variable in equations 1 through 8 is Z, income other than the husband's earnings. For equations 9 through 12 it is Y, nonemployment income or income from nonemployment sources as reported in the census data.

[f] Additional variables included were selected from a set of variables including race, region, size of place of residence, and number of dependents.

mated using method B on the assumption that $\epsilon_{12} = 0$, the estimates are not substantially altered by introducing plausible alternative assumptions about ϵ_{12}. The positive estimates are small in terms of economic significance, and since they are so few, the statistical evidence they offer of a positive substitution effect is not persuasive in terms of the overall regression results.[10] Thus the estimates obtained from the regression analysis suggest that the compensated wage rate elasticity for hours of work for males is close to zero.

There are several factors which may have contributed to my obtaining estimated income effects which are usually small when negative, and sometimes even slightly positive. Serious measurement error in the income variable, especially non-employment income, is one possibility. Measurement error could be a consequence of under- or mis-reporting or possibly a result of census-editing procedures. Some negative estimates of ϵ_{11} might be expected if its true value were near zero. But measurement error in the income variable, which tends to bias its coefficient toward zero, would produce a negative bias in estimates of ϵ_{11}.

Another problem is that the variable for non-employment income —income from non-employment sources as reported in the census— is conceptually not entirely appropriate, for three reasons. First, it represents only a part of non-employment income, since income in the form of services of durable goods and housing is omitted from the census concept. Second, some of the income reported in this category represents payments which are contingent on not being at work, such as workmen's compensation, temporary disability payments, or unemployment compensation. This type of income should be negatively correlated with labor supplied in a different way and for different reasons than income from an annuity, but the census data on non-employment income do not permit identification of its source. A third defect of the non-employment income variable is that it measures income received by the family rather than income which actually accrued to the family, including changes in its wealth position. Some of the differences in reported non-employment income may therefore result from differences in the composition of assets held by different

---

[10] The positive compensated elasticity estimates reported in Table 1 provide weak evidence. The estimate in regression 8 may have been influenced by the use of geometric means in adjusting for the income effect. When regressions 9 through 12 were estimated in arithmetic form, the income coefficients were near zero.

families rather than from differences in income streams which could be realized on a sustainable basis.

A third area of concern in the estimating procedure is the problem of controlling for the wife's wage rate. The expressions in equations (8) and (9) involve partial derivatives. However, in the regressions reported, the wife's wage rate was not included as an independent variable. Only a crude estimate of her wage rate based on the family's place of residence and her years of schooling was available. It was not included in the regressions reported because (1) including it usually did not substantially affect the size of other wage and income coefficients, (2) including a selection of control variables reduced its partial correlation to an insignificant level, (3) the other control variables included probably hold constant the wife's earning capacity as well as the crude estimate available, and (4) there is reason to expect the coefficient of the wife's wage rate to be small. This last point may be elucidated by referring to equation (11). One component of B_{12}, ϵ_{12}, is expected to be small because E_2/E_1 is small. Although ϵ_{22} may be of significant size, the other component is likely to be small since $E_2/Z < 1$ and B_{1Z} is likely to be small. Moreover, one would expect the two components to have opposite signs. Thus wage and income coefficients are treated as estimates of the appropriate partial derivatives, as if the wife's wage rate were held constant.

Two additional factors may tend to produce income-effect estimates smaller than the long-run income effect of wage rate changes or the income effect of a broad, general change in wage rates, such as would occur for the net wage rate if the tax rate were changed. Labor supplied may be adjusted to *permanent* levels of income. *Current* measures of income may therefore lead to an underestimate of the income effect for equations like the first six reported in Table 1, which are based on data aggregated in such a way that families were placed in separate aggregations according to the *current* presence or absence of income other than the husband's earnings.

Some workers may possess skills or have union affiliations which severely limit the extent to which they can deviate from normal hours of work for their group. Their only alternative to accepting these hours may be a different (and perhaps lower paying) job. Normal working hours will be determined by the wage rate and average income and tastes of those in the group. Workers constrained in this way may thus work somewhat different hours than they would like.

A more fundamental question than those discussed above is whether the simple model employed is adequate for estimating the substitution effect. Perhaps a more complicated model, such as that outlined by Becker,[11] which recognizes consumption aspects of work as well as expenditure components in the enjoyment of leisure, would perform better in an investigation of labor supply parameters for the husband.

In spite of shortcomings of the data and reservations about the adequacy of the regression models, the results obtained provide some evidence of the size of the compensated wage rate elasticity of hours of work for males. The sample was selected from a group whose age would insure them a somewhat larger share of income from sources other than their own employment than the overall population would receive. Workers in this age group might also be expected to react more readily than younger workers to economic variables by moving toward shorter hours, part-time work, or partial retirement. However, the data consistently showed negative wage rate coefficients, while the income coefficients estimated were small and often not statistically significant. In summary, this evidence suggests that the compensated elasticity, ϵ_{11}, is probably close to zero for the *hours* component of male labor supply.

Labor Force Participation Rates for Males

The Bowen and Finegan study of labor force participation reports regression results obtained in an equation explaining variation across metropolitan areas in labor force participation rates for males from twenty-five to fifty-four years old. This age group represents a substantial fraction of the male labor force, and wage rate coefficients are reported for data from the censuses of 1940, 1950, and 1960. Since the earnings variables for 1950 and 1960 which serve as proxies for wage rates are comparable, these coefficients along with those on non-employment income, are shown together with summary statistics, in Table 2.

The earnings coefficients are positive and significant for both 1950 and 1960 and are of roughly comparable magnitudes. A measure of unemployment is also included in the regressions as an independent variable. Differences in unemployment rates may have affected the

[11] Gary S. Becker, "A Theory of the Allocation of Time," *Economic Journal*, Vol. 75 (September 1965), pp. 493–517.

TABLE 2. Wage Rate and Income Coefficients for Labor Force Participation Rates of Males Aged 25–54, 1960 and 1950[a]

Dependent variable[b]	Coefficients on		Number of additional variables[e]	Coefficient of determination R^2
	Earnings[c]	"Other" income[d]		
Male labor force participation rate, 1960 (mean, 96.4 percent)	+0.11 (5.11)	−0.38 (3.78)	4	0.54
Male labor force participation rate, 1950 (mean, 94.1 percent)	+0.20 (3.27)	−0.69 (4.29)	4	0.51

Source: William G. Bowen and T. A. Finegan, "Labor Force Participation and Unemployment," in Arthur M. Ross (ed.), *Employment Policy and the Labor Market*, Table 4–2, p. 127.

[a] Figures in parentheses below coefficients are values of *t*; all of the *t* values are significant at the 1 percent level.
[b] Labor force participation rate of males twenty-five to fifty-four in census weeks of 1960 and 1950. The 1960 regression is based on aggregate data for the 100 largest Standard Metropolitan Statistical Areas and the 1950 regression on the 78 largest Standard Metropolitan Areas.
[c] Median income in the preceding year of all males who worked 50 to 52 weeks.
[d] 1960: mean income from non-employment sources in 1959 per recipient of any kind of income; 1950: median income in 1949 of all persons fourteen years of age and over with income from non-employment sources only.
[e] The additional variables included in each regression were a measure of unemployment for the labor force, a measure of schooling completed, a measure of percentage nonwhite, and a dummy variable for the South.

earnings measures used as wage rate variables. However, if the earnings coefficients are accepted as estimates of the effects of the wage rate, these coefficients provide evidence that for this dimension of labor supply and age group, the substitution effect outweighs the income effect.[12] Non-employment income is controlled in these regressions; if the results are analyzed as if the wife's wage rate were also controlled, the wage rate coefficients will underestimate the substitution effect unless the income effect is zero for this component of labor supply.

These regressions also include a variable for non-employment income. Its coefficient could be used via equation (4) to estimate the compensated elasticity if the earnings coefficient is regarded as an estimate of the partial derivative with respect to the wage rate, and if the partial derivative with respect to the wife's wage rate is near zero. However, the measure of non-employment income used covers a broader population group than that covered by the depen-

[12] Bowen and Finegan argue that since labor force participation is largely an all-or-nothing decision, the income effect is less likely to predominate for this dimension of labor supply than for hours of work. Bowen and Finegan, in Ross (ed.), *Employment Policy*, p. 120.

dent variable. The influence of transfer payments on labor supply is likely to be greater when labor force participation, rather than hours of work, is the measure of labor supply, and a large proportion of the negative correlation between labor force participation and non-employment income may be a result of this influence. Thus it appears that although the wage rate elasticity, +0.06, may underestimate the compensated elasticity for this component of labor supply, an estimate based on the income coefficient may seriously overestimate the compensated elasticity.[13]

Labor Force Participation of Married Women

Married women have become a substantial fraction of the labor force. Over 30 percent of married women were in the labor force in 1960 according to census statistics. The order of magnitude of the substitution effect is a question of special interest for this segment of the labor force because working wives often represent a supplementary source of income. Their labor force behavior is therefore likely to be more responsive to wage rate changes, and to tax measures affecting the take-home pay corresponding to a given wage, than is the behavior of their husbands.

Labor force participation rates for married women have been examined by regression analyses in studies by Mincer, Cain, and Bowen and Finegan. The results they report for variables representing the wife's wage rate and the husband's income include coefficients from regressions using metropolitan area statistics, with the labor force participation rate of married women as the dependent variable. Coefficients and summary information from their regressions are shown in Table 3 along with estimates of the compensated elasticity.

One set of estimates of the compensated elasticity reported in Table 3 is obtained using method B under the assumption that ϵ_{21} in equation (13) is equal to zero. For the other set obtained using method B, ϵ_{21} is estimated via equation (14). Although the assumption that ϵ_{12} is zero in the discussion of male labor supply may not result in serious bias, it seems less plausible to assume that ϵ_{21} is near zero because

$$\epsilon_{21} = \frac{E_1}{E_2} \epsilon_{12}.$$

---

[13] The estimate of the compensated elasticity obtained via equation (4) using the coefficient of non-employment income is +0.26.

TABLE 3. Wage Rate and Income Coefficients and Compensated Elasticities for Labor Force Participation Rates of Married Women with Husbands Present, Selected Areas, 1950 and 1960[a]

Source of data, sample, and year	Coefficients for independent variables			Compensated Elasticity, ϵ_{22}		Number of additional variables[g]	Coefficient of determination R^2
	Husband's Income[b]	Wife's Wage[c]	Other Income[d]	$\epsilon_{21} = 0$[e]	$\epsilon_{21} \neq 0$[f]		
Mincer Regression:							
1. 57 northern SMA's, 1950	−0.53	1.52		1.62	1.68	0	0.51
Elasticities at means	−0.83	1.50					
Cain Regressions:							
2. 100 SMSA's, 1960	−0.52	0.38		0.48	0.52	4	0.43
Standard error	(0.18)	(0.17)					
3. 77 SMA's, 1950	−0.59	1.15		1.24	1.33	3	0.62
Standard error	(0.30)	(0.22)					
Bowen and Finegan Regressions:							
4. 100 SMSA's, 1960	−0.25	0.37	−1.27	0.46	0.50	7	0.71
t values	(2.66)	(3.04)	(4.45)				
Elasticities	−0.42	0.38					
5. 78 SMA's, 1950	−0.52	1.05	−1.09	1.01	1.07	7	0.76
t values	(2.81)	(4.71)	(3.02)				
Elasticities	−0.62	0.92					

Source: Equation 1: Jacob Mincer, "Labor Force Participation of Married Women: A Study of Labor Supply," in *Aspects of Labor Economics*, A Conference of the Universities-National Bureau Committee for Economic Research, Table 1, p. 72. Equations 2, 3: Glen G. Cain, *Married Women in the Labor Force*, Table 15, p. 59, and Table 11, p. 48. Equations 4, 5: William G. Bowen and T. A. Finegan, "Labor Force Participation and Unemployment," *Employment Policy and the Labor Market*, Table 4–4, pp. 136–37. Compensated elasticities were compiled by the author.

[a] Equations 1, 4, and 5 were estimated in arithmetic form; equations 2 and 3 were estimated in logarithmic form. The dependent variable is the labor force participation rate for married women or its logarithm. The equations are based on 1950 and 1960 census data.
[b] Median income in the preceding year of all men married with spouse present.
[c] Median income in the preceding year of all females who worked 50–52 weeks that year.
[d] "Other" income: 1960, mean other income reported in census statistics for 1959 for recipients of any kind of income; 1950, median income in 1949 of all persons aged 14 and over with income from non-employment sources only.
[e] Assumes that ϵ_{21} in equation (13) is equal to zero. See text for discussion.
[f] Assumes that ϵ_{21} in equation (14) is not equal to zero. See text for discussion.
[g] Additional control variables included in the regressions were similar in all cases except for equations 4 and 5 in which supply and demand variables were also included.

Since variation in the husband's income is largely attributable to variation in his wage rate, its coefficient is used as an estimate of B_{21} in equation (14). For all of the compensated elasticity estimates reported in Table 3, the coefficient of the wife's wage rate was taken as an estimate of that partial derivative and the coefficient of the husband's income as an estimate of B_{2V}.[14]

A more serious problem in estimating the compensated elasticity for married women than the question of the magnitude of ϵ_{21} may be the problem of controlling the husband's wage rate. It was argued in the discussion of the husband's labor supply equation for hours of work that since the wife's wage rate coefficient, an estimate of B_{12}, was likely to be small, the coefficients obtained in the regression would not be seriously biased as estimates of the other partial derivatives. However, the coefficient for husband's income in the wife's labor supply equation may not be a good estimate of the partial derivative, B_{2V}, since the husband's wage is not controlled and its coefficient is not expected to be negligible. Indeed, equation (14) suggests that the partial derivative, B_{21}, is approximately equal to ϵ_{21} if ϵ_{11} is near zero. Collinearity between the husband's wage and his income would probably preclude estimating their coefficients separately even if a variable for the husband's wage rate were available. A bias in estimates of the wife's compensated wage elasticity may therefore be introduced through bias in estimates of B_{22} and B_{2V} as well as through inaccurate estimates of the compensated cross effect, ϵ_{21}, when method B is used.

In addition to the wage rate and income variables in all of the equations in Table 3, a non-employment income variable is included in the Bowen and Finegan equations. For the latter neither method A nor method B is strictly appropriate. However, if the husband's income variable is regarded as an estimate of his wage rate in equation 4 of Table 3, an estimate of the compensated elasticity can be obtained by applying method A. The resulting estimate is $+0.82$, which is somewhat larger than the other estimates reported for 1960.

The main objective of the Bowen and Finegan study was to estimate the effect of unemployment on labor supply. However, both Mincer and Cain discuss the estimation of a substitution effect in their studies of labor force behavior of married women. The estimate

[14] The estimate used for ϵ_{11} is 0.06 (see the section on male labor force participation rates).

Mincer suggests is obtained by simply subtracting the coefficient of husband's income from the coefficient of the wife's wage rate.[15]

That approach fails to recognize the fact that the income effect of a change in the market wage rate depends on the quantity of labor supplied, as is evident from the definition of the compensated wage rate effect. Moreover, the method assumes that earnings and therefore labor supply of a spouse, in this case the husband, is given independently of the other's wage rate. The model outlined in this chapter indicates the parameters required to estimate a compensated wage rate effect when labor supplied by the husband and wife depend on both wage rates and non-employment income. It also shows how the coefficients they report can be used to obtain estimates of the compensated elasticity, provided these coefficients can be interpreted as estimates of the appropriate partial derivatives.

The evidence for the labor force participation component of labor supply for married women suggests that the compensated wage rate effect may be of significant magnitude, though substantially smaller than was inferred by Mincer and Cain from their respective studies.[16] However, the elasticity estimates reported in Table 3 are subject to considerable uncertainty because of the problems encountered in passing from the reported regression coefficients to estimates of the compensated wage rate effect.

Summary and Conclusions

The regression results for data on hours of work per week and per year for older males in the labor force consistently show a net negative relationship between hours of work and the wage rate. Total wage rate elasticities estimated for this age group were usually in the range from -0.07 to -0.09. This evidence is consistent with that presented in other cross-sectional studies of hours of work, although the estimates are somewhat smaller than those obtained in analyses of time series data. These results provide additional empirical support for a backward bending labor supply curve, with the income

[15] Mincer, "Labor Force Participation," pp. 69–70.

[16] For the elasticity formulation of the method suggested by Mincer, if the coefficients for husband's income and the wife's wage rate are accepted as estimates of B_{2V} and B_{22} and their signs are negative and positive, respectively, their method will lead to an overestimate of the substitution effect if $(E_2/V)(1 - \epsilon_{21}) < 1$, an inequality almost certain to be fulfilled.

effect outweighing the substitution effect for this dimension of labor supply.

However, the coefficients estimated for the purpose of isolating the income effect in the same set of regressions tended to be both economically and statistically insignificant, and in many cases, of positive sign. Moreover, even if one rejects those regressions which yield positive estimates of the income coefficients, one still obtains estimates of the compensated elasticities which are often negative, and which, even when positive, are usually less than $+0.1$. I conclude from this evidence that the substitution elasticity for the hours of work component of labor supply for males is unlikely to be large and is probably near zero.

For the total effect of wage rates on labor force participation rates of males from twenty-five to fifty-four, an elasticity estimate of $+0.06$ was obtained. The compensated wage rate effect is presumably somewhat larger, although I suspect that it is lower than the estimate of $+0.26$ which was obtained by using the non-employment income coefficient (probably a biased measure of the income effect) to adjust the $+0.06$ estimate to obtain a compensated elasticity.

The evidence for labor force participation rates of married women suggests that this compensated wage rate elasticity may be as large as unity or somewhat larger, as estimated from the 1950 data, or as small as $+0.5$, as estimated from the 1960 data. If the coefficient for the wife's wage rate is regarded as an estimate of the total wage rate effect, elasticity estimates range from $+0.4$ to $+1.5$.

The substitution effect, as it applies to labor force participation rates, appears to be larger for married women than for men. It also appears to be larger for labor force participation rates than for hours of work for males. However, if the relative sizes of income and substitution effects differ for different dimensions of labor supplied by a class of similar workers, as suggested by the signs of the wage rate coefficients for males, a more comprehensive measure of labor supplied by married women might yield a lower estimate of their substitution elasticity than those obtained from the labor force participation rate regressions.

Within the parameters discussed above, the effect of the income tax on labor supplied depends on the nature of the tax change considered. If the income tax is increased to finance a pattern of expenditures such that real income is unchanged, or if it is substituted for existing taxes of equal yield which have no impact on labor supply, the change in labor supply will be that induced by the compensated wage rate effect. The reaction of labor supplied by male primary workers to such a tax rate change is likely to be very small, especially for the hours of work component. However, the evidence suggests that for married women an increase in the tax rate which results in a given percentage decrease in the net wage rate might be accompanied by as much as an equal percentage decline in the labor force participation rate.

On the other hand, if the income tax is increased and workers bear the full impact of its income effect, the evidence is fairly clear that the quantity of labor supplied by male primary workers will be increased. However, the increase in measured national income that this implies should not be viewed as a net gain to society. It is offset by a decrease in leisure roughly equal in value to the additional market goods produced. Moreover, if the substitution effect is not zero the relative price distortion will result in some welfare cost. For married women, on the other hand, it appears that such a tax rate change will result in a decline in labor force participation since for them the substitution effect outweighs the income effect. For this component of labor supply, the welfare cost associated with the income tax is likely to be significant, since the estimates of the compensated elasticity of labor supply for married women lie in the range from 0.5 to 1.6.

A change in the income tax rate is likely to have a smaller effect on labor supplied by a family than is suggested by estimates derived from wage rate changes. A single tax rate applied to a family when a joint return is filed, for example, provides no incentive for substitution between family members since their net relative wages are unchanged. The substitution reaction of labor supply to such a tax rate change in a family context will therefore be somewhat smaller than the effect estimated from wage rate changes. Hence welfare costs and changes in labor supply induced by the substitution effect will be smaller than is suggested by the compensated own-wage-rate elasticity estimates.

This discussion of the effects of an income tax on labor supply and welfare has been presented in the context of highly simplified models abstracted from problems such as shifts in the distribution of income and from other complications introduced by progressivity.

The discussion was designed to identify the kinds of labor supply parameters on which changes in labor supply depend when alternative tax changes are considered, and to assemble some evidence on the welfare cost of an income tax. However, the evidence for compensated wage rate effects was obtained from analysis of only some readily measurable dimensions of labor supply and of only a few components of the labor force. Although the effect on the allocation of time of a relative price distortion at the labor-leisure margin appears to be very small, except as it affects the labor force behavior of married women, an income tax can also affect consumption-savings decisions as well as the allocation of labor among different types of employment.

Index

Abandonment; *see* Loss on abandonment
Accruals, corporate shares: of capital gains, 13, 14, 16, 17; effective tax rate and, 24; ratio of realizations to, 3, 17, 19–26; real rate of, 23, 45
Acquisition costs, 99, 100
Adjustment-lag hypothesis: evaluation of, 259–60; purpose of, 224, 251; testing of, 252–58
Advisory Commission on Intergovernmental Relations, 164n, 169
Agria, Susan R., 3, 5, 77
Agriculture: income from capital in, 136–39; property tax on, 159
Agriculture, Department of, 136, 159
Allen, R. G. D., 225, 226, 227, 228, 231n, 240
Allocation of resources; *see* Resources allocation
Andersen, Arthur, 84n
Anderson v. *Helvering*, 310 U.S. 404 (1940), 81–82
Ando, Albert, 8, 286
Announcement effect: of capital gains tax, 13–15, 26, 38; of corporate income tax, 30–33; explained, 12–13
Arrow, K. J., 229n, 233, 238n, 239, 240
Audit Control Study of the Internal Revenue Service, 140

Bailey, Martin J., 3, 4, 11, 124n, 204n, 206n
Basevi, Giorgio, 3n
Bear, D. V. T., 278n
Becker, Gary S., 316
Bell, Philip W., 131n
Berglas, Eitan, 3n
Bird, Ronald, 159n

Black Mountain Corporation case (21 T.C. 246 [1954]), 86
Bonds: interest income from, 287–88, 290; measure of debt financing by, 189, 201
Borenstein, Israel, 208n, 247n
Bowen, William G., 304n, 316, 317n, 318, 320
Boyne, David H., 139n
Bregger, John E., 147n
Brown, E. Cary, 8, 286
Brown, Murray, 223n
Burstein, M. L., 42n
Business investment; *see* Investment

Cagan, Phillip, 217n
Cain, Glen G., 9, 10, 304n, 318, 320, 321
California Portland Cement Co. v. *Riddell* (S.D. Cal. 1958), 86
Capital: debt, compared with equity capital, 2, 6, 188–89, 191–93; discount factor and rate of return on, 96; elasticity of substitution between labor and, 7–8, 179, 184; expenditures of, for oil and gas, 89–90; *see also* Debt financing; Equity financing; Income from capital
Capital gains: accruals of, 3, 13, 14, 16, 17; average tax rate with exclusion of, 35–36; in depression, 16, 44; effect of, on cost of equity financing, 195, 204–06; and holding period, 3, 19–20, 28–29; as percentage of gross sales of shares, 22; as predictable income, 14, 25, 40; preferred tax treatment of, 15; ratio of, to dividends, 36, 37; in real estate, 40, 133–34; realization ratio and, 3, 17, 19, 20; realized, 40–41, 130, 131, 132
Capital gains tax: on accruals of corporate shares, 14–17, 38; announcement effect

325

of, 13–14; avoidance of, through evasion, 16; avoidance of, through gifts, 16; compared with percentage depletion, 105; deferral effect and, 16, 22, 24; effect on income distribution of, 12, 33–38; effective, 3, 24–25, 27, 46; inheritance and, 16, 20, 25, 48; for mineral industries, 78, 104–07; rate of, 27–28, 28n; realization ratio and, 17, 19–20, 24–26; and retained earnings, 14–15, 41; *see also* Effective capital gains tax rate
Census, Bureau of the, 102, 154, 163, 164, 166, 168
Census tracts, use of data from, 52, 66, 67, 68, 71, 72
CES; *see* Constant elasticity of substitution function
Chau, L. C., 285
Chemical and allied products industry, 242
Chenery, H. B., 229n, 233, 239, 240
Chicago, use of data from census tracts in, 68, 71, 72, 75, 76n
Chow, Gregory, 42n
Christ, Carl F., 66n
Coal: capital gains treatment of, 106, 107, 119–20; incentive to invest in, 98; and lease costs, 110; severance tax on, 104
Cobb-Douglas production function, 224, 226, 232
Commerce, Department of, 130, 140; *see also* National Income Division
Commissioner v. *Southwest Exploration Co.*, 340 U.S. 308 (1956), 83
Communication industries, 170
Constant elasticity of substitution function (CES), 229–30
Construction industries, 163–67
Consumption: compensated interest elasticity of, 279; derivation of data used for, 290–94; marginal rate of substitution between current and future, 276–78; response of, to interest rate, 284–86; substitution and income effect on, 278, 281–84, 296; utility function of, 8, 276–78
Corporate income tax; *see* Income tax, corporate
Corporate shares: accrual of real value of, 14, 45; price level and, 43–44; value of, and retained earnings, 43
Corporations: advantageous tax treatment for, 30–32; and income tax (*see* Income tax, corporate); profits of, before taxes, 125–31; retained earnings versus investment by, 15
Cost depletion, 84, 88

Cost of distortion, 173; major contributors to, 178; property tax and, 178–79
Costs: of debt versus equity financing, 6, 191–93; of equity financing, 195, 204–06; development, 78, 90, 94–95; expensing (*see* Expensing privilege); exploration, 78, 91–92, 94–95; as function of debt and equity, 197, 211, 217, 221–22; of housing, 57, 58, 60; marginal versus average, 194, 196–98; residual maximization and, 195–96; to welfare of housing subsidy, 55–64; write-off of, 96, 98
Couzens Committee, 80
Cowles, Alfred, III, 43, 216n
Craemer, Daniel, 208n, 247n
Cragg, John G., 3n
Cross-sectional studies: of factor substitution in manufacturing, 224, 233–41; of income elasticity of demand for housing, 4–5, 65–76

Debt financing, 2; cost of, compared with equity financing, 6, 7, 188–89, 191–93; incentive to shift to, 186; marginal versus average cost of, 194, 196–98; measurement of, by long-term bonds, 189
Deferral effect: on effective capital gains tax rate, 24; importance of, 16–20; in mineral industries, 95, 96; realization ratio and, 17, 20, 21, 22, 38; rollover of shares and, 17, 23
Delay rentals, 108, 109
Demand for housing, 4–5, 65–76
Denison, Edward F., 141n, 142
Depletion allowance: broadening of, 92; cost versus percentage, 88, 130n; defense of, 101; by discounting profits, 81; discovery as basis for, 80–81; historical development of, 79–92; limitations in, 89, 91; "reasonable," 79, 83; *see also* Cost depletion; Percentage depletion
Depreciation: errors in allowance for, 42–43; housing, 57; in mineral industries, 77, 95; tax, 130
Development, of mineral industries: costs of machine versus natural resource in, 94–95; effective cost of, 94; expenditures for, 90–92; incentives for, 99–100; percentage depletion favorable to, 99
Discount factors, in mineral industries, 96, 118, 119
Dividends: excluded from net profit, 130; income from, 287, 300; as measure of cost of equity, 205–06, 216–17; ratio of, to earnings (the payout ratio), 27–29, 35–36; personal income tax on, 1; ratio

Index

of long-term capital gains to, 36, 37; versus retained earnings, 205
Dobrovolsky, Sergei P., 208n, 247n
Douglas, Paul H., 304n
Dragon Cement Co. v. U.S., 244 Fed 2d 513 (1957), 86
Dreze, Jacques, 68n

Earnings, retained: capital gains tax and, 14–15, 41; compared with corporate accruals, 14–15, 45; compared with stock issues, 206–08; depreciation allowance and, 41–43; versus dividends, 205; equity cost of financing and, 204–05; real rate of, 23
"Economic interest," 83
Economies of scale, 32
Edwards, Edgar O., 131n
Effective capital gains tax rate, 3; defined, 24–25; effect of home ownership on, 51; versus expected tax rate, 217; holding period and, 47; realization ratio and, 27, 46–48; resulting from change from equity to debt financing, 186, 204
Elasticity of substitution: in chemical and allied products industry, 242; studies of, 7–8, 224, 233–36; in tobacco industry, 244–45; in transporation industry, 243; *see also* Factor substitution
Employment, income from capital and, 142–43, 143n
Equilibrium: financial, 7, 202; in rate of return, 30–33, 38
Equilibrium path, 206, 208–15
Equity financing, 2, 6; compared with debt financing, 7, 188–89, 191–93; earnings retention and cost of, 204–05; effect of capital gains on, 195, 204–06; effect of income taxes on, 26–29; incentive to shift from, 186; marginal versus average costs of, 196–98; measurement of cost of, 190; negative return to, 147; payout ratio and, 27–28
Evasion, of capital gains tax, 16; realization ratio and, 20
Expensing privilege, 2, 77, 78; as incentive to overproduction, 98; items subject to, 90; for mining industries, 91–92; possible reform in, 112–13
Exploration, in minerals industry, 5; costs of machine versus natural resource in, 94–95; effective cost of, 94; expenditures for, 90

Factor substitution: adjustment-lag hypothesis and, 224, 251–60; comparison of cross-section and time series studies of, 265–67; cross-section studies of, 224, 233–36; in manufacturing industries, 223–67; time series studies of, 224, 245–51; *see also* Elasticity of substitution
Farioletti, Marius, 140n
Finegan, T. A., 304n, 316, 317n, 318, 320
Fisher, Lawrence, 6, 189, 194, 197, 199, 201, 211, 217, 219, 221, 222
Friedman, Milton, 66n, 147n, 217n

Gas industry: capital expenditures in, 89–90; capital gains treatment of, 106; gross income from property in, 84–85; and severance tax, 104
Gifts: avoiding capital gains tax with, 16; realization ratio and, 20, 25
GNP; *see* Gross national product
Goldsmith, Raymond W., 8, 16, 19n, 286n, 289n; *see also* Goldsmith data
Goldsmith data, 286, 289, 290, 291, 294
Gordon, Myron J., 190n
Gore amendment, to the *Internal Revenue Code* (1960), 87
Gort, Michael, 131n
Grayson, Charles Jackson, Jr., 108n
Great Depression, capital gains in, 16, 44
Greenidge, S. M., 80
Griliches, Zvi, 42n, 223n
Gross income from property, 77, 84–87
Gross national product (GNP), 15
Gross rent, 69, 70
Grunfeld, Yehuda, 42n

Haavelmo, Trygve, 230, 230n
Harberger, Arnold C., 1, 3n, 35, 35n, 42n, 51n, 92, 92n, 105n, 115n, 123, 124, 142n, 143, 146, 173, 178n, 184n, 185n, 223, 275n, 303n
Helvering v. Elbe Oil Land Development Co., 303 U.S. 372 (1938), 85
Helvering v. Mountain Producers Corp., 303 U.S. 376 (1938), 85
Helvering v. Twin Bell Oil Syndicate, 293 U.S. 312 (1934), 85
Henderson, James M., 279n
Hicks, J. R., 225, 240
Holding period: effective capital gains tax rate and, 47; incentives to lengthen, 28–29; realization ratio and, 19–20, 25
Holland, Daniel M., 204n
Hours of work for males, effect of wage rates on, 310–16, 321, 322
Housing, owner-occupied: income elasticity of demand for, 4–5, 50, 51, 52, 54, 65–73; marginal costs of, 57, 58, 61;

price elasticity of demand for, 50, 51, 52, 58, 73–76; rate of return on capital in, 57; tax subsidy of, 52–64; welfare loss from subsidizing, 51, 60–63, 184

Housing, rental: depreciation costs of, 57; income elasticity of demand for, 65–73; price elasticity of demand for, 51, 73–76

Huang, D. S., 285

Incentives to hold assets, 30–37; *see also* Announcement effect

Income: adjusted gross, 34–35; gross, 84–87; dividend, 287, 300; from future interest, 281–82; from interest, 282, 287, 300; marginal utility of, 55–56; as measure of cost of equity, 216–17; nonemployment, 306–07, 314, 317; permanent, 66; proprietary, 32; reductions in, before tax, 35; rental, 150; of self-employed, 144–46

Income distribution, effect of capital gains tax on, 12, 33–35

Income from capital: in agriculture, 136–39; based on net physical assets, 147–48; components included in concept of, 125; from corporate profits before taxes, 125–30; in farm real estate, 137; fluctuations in, 30–33; in housing, 57; labor and property share of, 141–42; measurement of, 124; negative, 143, 147; for non-farm unincorporated enterprise, 38, 139–40, 152–53; non-neutral taxation of, 173, 178; and return to labor, 136–37, 141, 142–46; in service industries, 148–49; tax on, in manufacturing, 186–87

Income tax, corporate, 1; advantages of, 30–32; announcement effects of, 12–13; discriminatory effects of, 2; effect of, on changes in investment, 110; effect of, on corporate equity, 26–29; effect of, on resource allocation, 33, 185; liabilities of, 153–54

Income tax, individual, 1; announcement effects of, 12–13; effect of, on corporate equity, 26–29; effect of, on labor supply, 302–03, 322–24; exclusion of accruals for durable goods from, 50; exemption of imputed rent from, 4, 52–54; progressivity of, 33–37, 52, 54; on windfall income, 13

Income Tax Act of *1913*, 85

Interest: income from, 282, 287, 300; net monetary, 134–35

Interest-paying debt, 188, 189, 194

Interest rate, 188–89; effect on savings of, 8, 9, 279–84, 296; negative responsiveness of forms of saving to, 285; net versus gross, 286–87; open-market money, 285; relationship between consumption and, 279–84, 296; utility function and, 276, 277, 279; welfare loss from lowering, 275; and yield on bonds, 288–92, 294; and yield on common stocks, 288–92, 294

Internal Revenue Code, 104, 106, 133

Internal Revenue Service (IRS), 130, 132, 164, 165

Investment: changes in tax law and, 4, 110–14; credit on, 2; incentives for, in mineral industries, 78, 93, 98

Iron: incentives to invest in, 98; and severance tax, 104

Johnson, D. Gale, 137, 137*n*, 141*n*, 142
Jones, Ethel B., 304*n*
Jorgenson, Dale W., 230, 230*n*

Kendrick, John, 271
Keynes, John M., 284
Kolin, Marshall, 6, 190*n*, 194, 199, 201, 217, 219, 221, 222
Kosters, Marvin, 7, 9, 301
Koyck, L. M., 245
Kravis, Irving B., 141, 142
Krzyzaniak, Marian, 3*n*, 223*n*

Labor: elasticity of substitution between capital and, 7–8, 179, 184; as input, 270; participation rate for males and supply of, 316, 322; participation rate for married women and supply of, 318–21; and share of income from capital, 136, 137, 141, 142–46

Labor supply: demand for leisure and, 301, 305; effect of income tax on, 9, 10, 302–03, 322–24; effect of non-employment income on, 306–07, 314, 317; elasticity of, 9–10, 306; measure of husband's, 307–08; measure of wife's, 309; relation between wage rate and, 304, 309–10, 318–21; self-employment and, 310

Laidler, David, 3, 4, 50, 184
Lease costs, 98, 107–10
Lebergott, Stanley, 141*n*, 142
Leisure, labor supply and, 301, 305
Leontieff, Wassily W., 232
Livestock, capital gains tax on sale of, 14, 40
Long, Clarence D., 43*n*, 304*n*

Index

Los Angeles, use of data from census tracts in, 68, 69n
Loss on abandonment, 95, 96
Lucas, Robert E., Jr., 7, 8, 223

Machines, tax treatment of, 118–19
McKinnon, Ronald I., 236n, 245
Manufacturing: average cost of debt in, 188–89; property tax paid by, 163; studies of factor substitution in, 223–67; tax on income from capital in, 186–87
Marginal propensity to consume (MPC), 279, 281n, 292
Marginal utility, of income, 55–56
Married women, taxation and supply of, 10, 309
Marshallian consumer surplus, 51
Maxwell, James A., 167–68
Mayer, Thomas, 284n
MBA (Modigliani, Brown, and Ando) data, 286, 289, 290, 294
Meltzer, Allan H., 286, 289n
Mieszkowski, Peter, 3n
Miller, Kenneth G., 83n, 85n, 88n
Miller, Merton H., 187n, 190n, 194n, 195n, 196n, 197n, 198n
Minasian, Jora R., 233n, 234, 236, 237n, 240, 242, 251
Mincer, Jacob, 9, 10, 304n, 305, 318, 320, 321
Minerals industries: capital gains tax treatment in, 2, 5, 14, 40, 77, 133; discount factor for, 96, 118, 119; incentives to invest in, 78, 93, 98, 110–14; methods for deducting expenses in, 91; property taxes in, 163, 166n
Minhas, B. S., 229n, 233, 239, 240
Modigliani, Franco, 8, 187, 190n, 194n, 195n, 196n, 197n, 198n, 286
MPC; *see* Marginal propensity to consume
Musgrave, Richard A., 33, 34, 35n, 37, 278n, 302n
Muth, Richard F., 51, 51n, 52, 58, 66, 75

National Income Division, Department of Commerce, 132, 133, 135, 152, 166
National wealth, defined, 291
Natural resources: capital gains treatment of the sale of, 118–19; income from, versus income from machines, 94–95, 105; percentage depletion treatment of, 118
Nerlove, Marc, 223n, 282n
Net monetary interest: by non-farm sector, 134–35; from real estate, 135, 152

Net national product (NNP), 1
Net rent, from farm real estate, 137, 149–50
Net worth: consumption function and, 282–83; defined, 291; planned, 279; present, 281
Netzer, Dick, 169
New York Stock Exchange (NYSE), 16, 22
NNP; *see* Net national product
Nolin, J. H., 171n
NYSE; *see* New York Stock Exchange

Oil industry: capital expenditures in, 89–90; capital gains treatment of, 105, 106; gross income from property in, 84–85; incentives to invest in, 98; lease costs in, 107, 108–09; percentage depletion for, 83, 85; and severance tax, 104
Owner-occupied dwellings; *see* Housing, owner-occupied

Palmer v. *Bender*, 287 U.S. 551 (1933), 83
Parsons v. *Smith*, 359 U.S. 215 (1959), 83
Patinkin, Don, 277n
Payout ratio: effect on corporate equity of, 27–28; incentives to lower, 28–29; and progressivity of income tax, 35–36
Percentage depletion, 2, 5, 81–83; arguments against, 84, 114; arguments for, 114–15; compared with capital gains tax, 105; and concept of "economic interest," 83; cost depletion and, 88; as incentive to overproduction, 98, 100; lease costs and, 107–10; "mining vs. manufacturing" test for, 86; for new capital equipment, 118; proposed elimination of, 113–14; proposed reduction in, 110, 112; Supreme Court clarification of, 81–82
Petroleum; *see* Oil industry
Philadelphia, use of data from census tracts in, 68
Pigou, Arthur C., 12n
Portfolio: effect of presumptive accruals on, 48–49; turnover of shares in, 17, 19, 21, 22, 22n, 23
Prices: and value of corporate shares, 43–44; indexes of consumer and wholesale, 43–44
Production function: capital-labor, 225–28; CES (constant elasticity of substitution), 229–30; Cobb-Douglas, 224, 226, 232; evaluation of, 230–32; neutral technological change and, 231–32, 232n; non-neutral technological change and, 261; three-input, 228–29

Profits, corporate: before taxes, 125–31; net realized capital gains excluded from, 132
Property, in mineral industries, defined, 88
Property tax, 1; in communications and public utilities industries, 170–71; in construction industries, 163–67; cost of distortion and, 178–79; defined, 154, 157; discrimination in, 2; on farms and farm services, 159, 162; in manufacturing sector, 163; in minerals industries, 101, 163; in real estate, 167–69; in service industries, 171–73; in trade industries, 167; in transportation industry, 169–70; varied tax base for, 157–59
Proprietary income, tax disadvantage of, 32
Public utilities, property taxes paid by, 170–71

Quandt, Richard E., 279n

Radice, Edward A., 284, 285
Real estate, 6; capital gains on sale of, 40, 133–34; corporate profits tax on, 154; farm, 136, 137; net monetary interest from, 135, 152; net rents from, 137, 149–51; property tax paid by, 167–69; rental income of persons as largest portion of value in, 151
Realization ratio: deferral effect and, 23–24; effective capital gains tax rate and, 24–26; holding period and, 19–21; incentive to minimize, 37; interest rate and, 22; measures of, 17; progressivity of personal income tax and, 35–36, 37
Rees, Albert, 43n
Reid, Margaret, 51, 66
Rent, gross, 69, 70
Residual maximization, 195–96, 206
Resources allocation: cost of inefficient, 4; effect of corporate income tax on, 33, 39, 185; housing and, 57; welfare economics and, 55
Revenue Act of *1932*, 86
Revenue Act of *1943*, 86
Revenue Act of *1950*, 86
Revenue Act of *1951*, 82, 91
Risk: effect of expanding debt or equity financing on, 201–08; lender's and borrower's, 196–201, 217; marketability of stock and, 199–200; premium, 199
Rollover, of shares, 17, 23
Rosenberg, Leonard G., 5, 6, 58n, 63, 123
Ross, Arthur M., 304n, 317n
Royalty earnings, 152
Samuelson, Paul A., 227

San Francisco, use of data from census tracts in, 68, 69n, 75, 76n
Savings: effect of interest rate on, 8, 9, 279–84, 296; negative response to interest rate of, 285; *see also* Consumption
Scofield, William H., 136
SEC; *see* Securities and Exchange Commission
Securities and Exchange Commission, 16n, 17, 26
Self-employed, 310; income of, 144–46
Seltzer, Lawrence H., 16n, 19n
Senate Select Committee on the Investigation of the Bureau of Internal Revenue; *see* Couzens Committee
Service industries: property taxes paid by, 171–73; return to capital in, 148–49
Severance tax, 101–04
Sheffé, Henry, 242n
Sherfy, Lawrence P., 86n
Solow, R. M., 229n, 233, 234, 236, 239
Standard and Poor's index of corporate share prices, 16, 17, 44
Steiner, Peter O., 5, 92, 96, 98n
Stocks: dividend income and, 287–88, 290, 294–95; incentive to issue, 207–08
Subsidy, housing, 52; consumer reaction to, 65–68; effects of, 54; imputed rate for, 59–61; social stability and, 53; welfare cost of, 55–63; welfare cost of, compared with other welfare expenditures, 63–64
Suits, Daniel B., 295n

Tambini, Luigi, 6, 7, 185
Tax: corporate profits, 26–33, 153–54, 185; depreciation, 130; labor supply and, 302–03, 322–24; non-neutral, 173, 178; personal income, 26–29, 33–37, 50, 52–53; severance, 101–04; welfare cost from changes in, 303, 323; *see also* Capital gains tax; Income tax
Taxable income, from property, 88–92; defined, 88
Taylor's expansion, 46
Terborgh, George, 19n, 41, 43, 211n
Thornber, Hodson, 290n
Three-input production function, 228–29
Timber, capital gains treatment of, 14, 40, 133
Time series studies: evaluation of, 261–64; for factor substitution, 224, 245–51; industries included in, 269; source of data for, 268
Tobacco industry, elasticity of substitution in, 244–45

Trade industries, property tax paid by, 167
Transportation industry: elasticity of substitution in, 243; property taxes paid by, 169–70
Treasury Department, 5, 16, 93, 96, 98n, 99, 102, 121, 162
Turnover of portfolio, 17, 19, 21, 22, 23

United Nations International Standard Industrial Classification, 233
U.S. v. Cannelton Sewer Pipe Co., 268 Fed 2d 334 (1959), 86, 87
U.S. v. Cherokee Brick and Tile Co., 218 Fed 2d 424 (1955), 86

Wage income, defined, 142n
Wage rate: elasticity of, 310–16, 321; husband's, 311–12; relation between labor supply and, 304, 309–10, 315, 318–21; response of age groups to, 9, 10; substitution effect of change in, 301, 305–09, 322; unemployment rate and, 316–17
Wald, A., 263n
Welfare cost: from change in tax, 303, 323; of tax subsidy, 55–63
Welfare economics, 55
Windfall income, tax treatment of, 13
Winnick, Louis, 134n
Wolfowitz, J., 263n
World War II, tax liabilities during, 192
Wright, Colin, 7, 8, 9, 275
Write-off, of costs, 96, 98

Zellner, A., 285